PAN-TURKISM: FROM IRREDENTISM TO COOPERATION

Pan-Turkism

From Irredentism to Cooperation

JACOB M. LANDAU

INDIANA UNIVERSITY PRESS
BLOOMINGTON AND INDIANAPOLIS

This second revised and updated edition first published in 1995
in the United Kingdom by C. Hurst & Co. (Publishers) Ltd.,
38 King Street, Covent Garden, London WC2E 8JZ
and in North America by Indiana University Press,
601 N. Morton Street, Bloomington, Indiana 47404

Manufactured in Hong Kong

Library of Congress Cataloging-in-Publication Data

Landau, Jacob M.
    Pan-Turkism : from irredentism to cooperation / by Jacob M.
Landau — 2d rev. and updated ed.
                p.   cm.
    Revised and updated ed. of the author's: Pan-Turkism in Turkey.
1981.
    Includes bibliographical references and index.
    ISBN 0–253–32869–1 (alk. paper) : $ 35.00
    ISBN 0–253–20960–9 (pbk. : alk. paper) : $ 14.95
    1. Pan-Turanianism. 2. Irredentism—Turkey. 3. Turkey—Relations
—Asia, Central. 4. Asia, Central—Relations—Turkey.
I. Landau, Jacob M. Pan-Turkism in Turkey. II. Title.
DS17.L32 1995
320.5′4′09561—dc20   94–42974
                                                  CIP

1 2 3 4 5 00 99 98 97 96 95

ACKNOWLEDGEMENTS

In preparing this study, I was privileged to benefit from advice and criticism of scholars and librarians in Turkey, the Commonwealth of Independent States (formerly the Soviet Union), Europe and the United States. In addition, members of various Pan-Turkist groups have been unstinting in providing useful information for the research which resulted in both the earlier version of this book and the new one. The publishers — C. Hurst & Co. in London and the Indiana University Press in Bloomington — have spared no effort in preparing for publication the revised and enlarged edition presented here. I owe them all a debt of gratitude. I alone am responsible for everything written here.

January 1995   J.M.L.

ACKNOWLEDGMENTS

CONTENTS

ILLUSTRATION

SPELLING AND PRONUNCIATION

A brief note on spelling and pronunciation is necessary. Ottoman script has been rendered into modern Turkish, in accordance with current Turkish scholarly practice. Modern Turkish is a phonetic language. The following may assist the anglophone reader: *a* is pronounced *a* as in mama; c like *j* in *jar*; ç like *ch* in *church*; g hard, as in *good*; ğ is a glottal stop, barely audible; i like *ee* in *seed*; ı (dotless) like *u* in *podium*; ö and ü as in German; ş like *sh* in *shop*.

ABBREVIATIONS

BSECR	Black Sea Economic Cooperation Region
CIS	Commonwealth of Independent States
CO	Colonial Office series (in PRO)
EC	European Community
ECO	Economic Cooperation Organisation
EI[1]	*The Encyclopaedia of Islam*, 1st edn (Leiden)
EI[2]	*The Encyclopaedia of Islam*, 2nd edn (Leiden)
FO	Foreign Office series (in PRO)
MEA	*Middle Eastern Affairs (New York)*
OM	*Oriente Moderno* (Rome)
PRO	Public Record Office (London)
RFE/RL	Radio Free Europe/Radio Liberty
RMM	*Revue du Monde Musulman* (Paris)
TK	*Türk Kültürü* (Ankara)
TL	Türk Lirası (Turkish pounds)

INTRODUCTION

Irredentism, a phenomenon of long standing in the Near and Middle East, is defined as an ideological or organisational expression of passionate interest in the welfare of an ethnic minority living outside the boundaries of the state peopled by that same group. Moderate irredentism expresses a desire to defend the kindred group from discrimination or assimilation, while a more extreme manifestation aims at annexing the territories which the group inhabits. Although not a universal phenomenon, irredentism appears to be more prevalent than is generally assumed. Professor Myron Weiner has analysed the subject briefly with particular reference to the Balkans,[1] although much of what he says applies equally to the late Ottoman Empire and the Republic of Turkey, where the main source of irredentism was for many years the ideology of Pan-Turkism. In its heyday, the guiding objective of this movement is to strive for some sort of union — cultural or physical, or both — among all peoples of proven or alleged Turkic origins, whether living both within and without the frontiers of the Ottoman Empire (subsequently of the Republic of Turkey).

There is a distinction[2] between Pan-Turkism, the aims of which are defined above, and Turanism (sometimes called Pan-Turanism), which had as its chief objective rapprochement and ultimately union among all peoples whose origins are purported to extend back to Turan, an undefined Shangri-La-like area in the steppes of Central Asia. In a Turkish document of 1832 regarding the Khanate of Khokand, Turan was variously identified with Turkestan, Tatarstan, Uzbekistan and Moghulistan, according to its ruling inhabitants at different times. Its limits were given there as China in the east, Tibet, India and Iran in the south, the desert of Dasht-i Kipchak and the Caspian Sea in the west and, again, the desert of Dasht-i Kipchak in the north.[3] Turanism has consequently been a far broader concept than Pan-Turkism, embracing such peoples as the Hungarians,[4] Finns and Estonians. Turanism[5] enjoyed a wave of popularity, as a response to the Slav menace, in Hungary, where a journal entitled *Turan* appeared regularly from 1913 till 1970. The idea also appealed to many Pan-Turkists in Turkey, who adopted the term Turan into their own writings, to signify Turkish Homeland,[6] in a very broad sense,

1

not necessarily accepting, however, their own affinity with non-Turkic peoples.

The man most responsible for first popularising the concepts of Turan and Pan-Turkism was apparently the Jewish-Hungarian traveller and orientalist Arminius (Hermann) Vambery.[7] Besides introducing the readers of his numerous books and articles to Central Asian languages and folklore in general, Vambery devoted an entire chapter of his book *Sketches of Central Asia*, first published in 1868,[8] to the Turanians. He contended that all Turkic groups belonged to one race, subdivided according to physical traits and customs. In another book, *Travels in Central Asia*, published three years earlier,[9] he drew up a grand design for a Pan-Turk empire, as follows:

In its character of Turkish dynasty, the house of Osman might, out of the different kindred elements with which it is connected by the bond of a common language, religion and history, have founded an empire extending from the shore of the Adriatic far into China, an empire mightier than that which the great Romanoff[10] was obliged to employ not only force, but cunning, to put together, out of the most discordant and heterogeneous materials. Anatolians, Azerbaydjanes, Turkomans, Özbegs, Kirghis, and Tartars are the respective members out of which a mighty Turkish Colossus might have arisen, certainly better capable of measuring itself with its great northern competitor than Turkey such as we see it in the present day.

Although in later years Vambery retracted and labelled Pan-Turkism a chimera,[11] the vision of a Pan-Turk empire had been offered to whomever might wish to adopt it. Vambery's close relations with several of the Young Turk leaders[12] may have been instrumental in their adoption of the principles of Pan-Turkism.

Pan-Turkism, although one of the most important and interesting ideologies among Near and Middle Eastern peoples, has never been examined in its entirety in the context of Turkey. Various aspects of Pan-Turkism, particularly its early history among the Turkic groups in Southern Russia and Central Asia, have been described in several useful monographs[13] — although much of the literature on Pan-Turkism has been tendentious and indeed more in the nature of source materials than of definitive studies. Moreover, Pan-Turk ideology and organisation in Turkey proper has hardly been researched at all. Two works which have chronicled the history of Pan-Turkism do touch on Turkey as well. They are Yusuf Akçura's 'Türkçülük', at the end of *Türk Yılı*, an annual he edited in 1928,[14] and Hüseyin Namık Orkun's *Türkçülüğün tarihi*, which was published sixteen years later and drew heavily upon Akçura's account.[15] Later, Professor Bayur has devoted to it a perceptive chapter in his massive historical work.[16] This neglect is all the more remarkable in that the movement has been

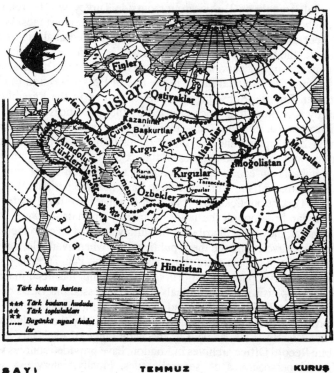

HER IRKIN ÜSTÜNDE TÜRK IRKI!

BOZKURT

SAYI
11

TEMMUZ
1941

KURUŞ
20

The cover of *Bozkurt*, a Pan-Turk journal published between 1939 and 1942, showing the claimed extent of the Turkic ethnic homeland. The meaning of the slogan at the top is 'The Turkish race above all others', and the *bozkurt*, i.e. the steppe wolf, is symbolised below the title.

developing in Turkey since the early twentieth century; in fact, Turkey has been the focus of its activity since the First World War. Moreover, Pan-Turkism grew in importance during the 1960s and 1970s, and in those years gradually acquired a significant place in politics in Turkey.

We therefore focus our attention on Pan-Turkism in Turkey, analysing its nature and course (although not in all its details, evidently), as well as its role in forming the new type of nationalism which was to become prevalent in Turkey. In addition, however, the national struggle of Turkic groups outside Turkey will be relevant throughout, particularly in the light of its Pan-Turk overtones. While the scope of this study does not allow for detailed analysis of this struggle, the impact of its vicissitudes will be indicated nonetheless. The awakening of national consciousness among the Turkic groups is shown to be a crucial factor in the rise of Pan-Turkism in the late Ottoman Empire. Subsequently, public opinion in the Republic of Turkey was more than once aroused by the grievances (real or imaginary) of Turkic groups abroad. Finally, the break-up of the Soviet Union once again renewed direct contacts between the Turks of Turkey and the Turkic peoples in the ex-Soviet republics, but with an emphasis on economic and cultural cooperation rather than on political irredentism, which seems to have become peripheral.

Pan-Turkist publications, issued in Europe, have been useful for our research; although the latter — mainly journals — were often ephemeral, they were distributed in Turkey and had an echo then and there. We have examined these publications, when available, but our chief source materials were those issued by the Pan-Turkists themselves (or their opponents) in Turkey. An attempt has been made to lay due emphasis upon periodicals which expressed the views of the various Pan-Turkist groups and reflected their organisation. The records of the German Foreign Ministry, especially those relating to the two World Wars, as well as the wide range of materials in the Public Record Office archives in London, have provided sources with different perspectives on several issues. Finally, interviews with several Pan-Turkist leaders and spokesmen in Turkey have served to clarify a number of doubtful points.

This study strives to provide more than a mere account and analysis of Pan-Turkism in Turkey and elsewhere against the background of awakening nationalism among Turkic groups; also, it is not intended solely as a review of Pan-Turkism's role in Turkish nationalism or politics. Pan-Turkism was a characteristically irredentist ideology and movement, its broad-based objectives being typical of the genre. We attempt to compare some of the basic characteristics of Pan-Turkism with those of similar movements elsewhere and offer some observations on both their common and disparate features.

In conclusion, Pan-Turkism is a subject charged with deep-rooted sentiments and opinions among those involved. As a foreign observer, I hope to avoid value judgements and strive for a dispassionate presentation. However, as one is always dependent upon one's sources, certain pitfalls may not have been successfully avoided. My aim throughout has been neither to praise nor to condemn, but to study objectively a controversial phenomenon. This applies, also, to the recent changes in the progress of Pan-Turkism, discussed in the final chapter newly written for this edition.

NOTES

1. 'The Macedonian syndrome: an historical model of international relations and political development', *World Politics* (Princeton), xxiii (4): July 1971, pp. 665–83.
2. One of the first to point this out was A.J. Toynbee, in his *Report on the Pan-Turanian movement*, 1917, pp. 3–4. See also L. Stoddard, *The new world of Islam*, 1921, pp. 161 ff.
3. Cf. J.L. Bacqué-Grammont, *'Turan*: une description du Khanat de Khokand vers 1832 d'après un document ottoman', *Cahiers du Monde Russe et Soviétique* (Paris), *XIII* (2): 1972, esp. pp. 194–9.
4. For Hungarian Turanism cf. 'Turkey, Russia and Islam', *The Round Table* (London), Dec. 1917, pp. 101 ff. For the term and its use, see V. Minorsky, 'Tūrān', *EI¹*, s.v. As early as 1839, Hungarian scholars were using 'Turan' to describe the Turkish lands of Central and Southeast Asia. Cf. Bernard Lewis, *The emergence of modern Turkey*, p. 341. In subsequent years, linguists spoke increasingly of 'Turanian languages'. Cf. Naval Staff — Intelligence Department, *A manual on the Turanians and Pan-Turanianism*, 1918, p. 14. A while later, in 1873, Fr. von Hellwald, a German geographer, was already writing about 'the Nations of Turan' as a matter of course, in his book, translated into English a year later as *The Russians in Central Asia*, London, King, 1874, pp. 96 ff; see also ibid., pp. 1–2, 42.
5. See, for Turanism, ibid. and Karl Wipert, 'Der Turanismus', *Der Neue Orient* (Berlin), vi (4): Dec. 1922, pp. 202–10.
6. Cf. Geoffrey Wheeler, *The Peoples of Soviet Central Asia*, 1966, p. 65.
7. In addition to his numerous publications, there are also two large volumes of Vambery's manuscript correspondence between 1889 and 1911 with the Foreign Office in London. These may be consulted in the Public Record Office (PRO) in London, Foreign Office series (FO) 800/32 and 800/33. A recent monograph on him has appeared by Lory Alder and Richard Dalby, *The dervish of Windsor Castle: the life of Arminius Vambery*, 1979.

8.   Ch. 16, pp. 282–312.
9.   Pp. 485–6.
10. Peter the Great.
11. *Western culture in Eastern lands*, 1906, p. 348.
12. X, 'Le Panislamisme et le Panturquisme', *Revue du Monde Musulman (RMM)* (Paris), XXII: Mar. 1913, p. 196.
13. Of which I have found one of the best-informed to be C.W. Hostler's, *Turkism and the Soviets: the Turks of the World and their objectives*.
14. This was reprinted, in Latin characters, as Dr Yusuf Akçura, *Türkçülük: 'Türkçülüğün tarihi gelişimi'*, Istanbul, 1978. Edited by Sâkin Öner.
15. Hüseyin Namık Orkun, *Türkçülüğün tarihi*, 1944. A discussion of Pan-Turkism in Turkey and abroad is provided on pp. 50–101.
16. Yusuf Hikmet Bayur, *Türk inkilâbı tarihi*, vol. II, part 4, pp. 398–436.

1

THE OUTSIDE TURKS: THE RISE AND FALL OF PAN-TURKISM ABROAD

The *Dış Türkler*, or 'Outside Turks', is a term frequently employed by Pan-Turkists in Turkey in recent years; it covers a wide range of groups comprising people of Turkic origins. At least some of them have been in close contact with the Turks for many centuries.[1] During the late nineteenth and early twentieth centuries, most such groups living outside the borders of the Ottoman Empire resided in Czarist Russia. Imbued with a new brand of nationalism, a handful of intellectuals among these Turkic groups in Russia planted and nurtured the seeds of Pan-Turk ideology. This chapter briefly describes and examines the development of Pan-Turkism in Russia and the Soviet Union, a topic which has been considered, to some extent, by other works as well (not all of which have been equally objective and scholarly).[2]

The most prominent Turkic groups during that period[3] were the Volga Tatars, Crimea Tatars, Kazakhs, Turkmens, Uzbeks, Kirghiz and Azeris, although there were Turkic elements among the Tajiks as well. Virtually all were Muslims. While precise demographic figures are not available, and estimates vary considerably, the Russian census of 1897 indicated their total number as 13,600,000 out of a total population of 125,600,000,[4] i.e. almost 11 per cent. In their own areas, of course, these groups predominated, although, as a rule, they shared them with others, especially Russian settlers. Russian rule in Central Asia, imposed only during the nineteenth century,[5] was essentially bearable thanks to the remoteness of the central government and the insufficiency and inefficiency of local control. As the economic situation in these areas did not change for the worse during the late nineteenth century, local grievances were generally not of an economic nature. At that time, however, two main trends in the relations of the Russian authorities with Turkic groups (and several others) became increasingly evident: Christianisation and Russification. Many of these Turkic people reacted by standing more strongly

7

by their faith and national origins; Islam and Turkism, both separately and jointly, were their rallying points. As the Turkic groups were rather isolated from others, their search for potential allies lay naturally within the parameters of Pan-Islam, Pan-Turkism, or both. Pan-Islam was especially available and convenient, because of the relative proximity of the Ottoman Empire, whose Sultan Abdul Hamid II was partial to Pan-Islam and had been attempting to foster it since the late nineteenth century. Pan-Turkism, however, was more of an innovation, not easily grasped by the uneducated. It was largely conditioned by the development of nationalism in Southeastern Europe in the late nineteenth century; in this particular case it was further encouraged by the Russo-Turkish War of 1877–8, with the attendant suffering of the defeated Turks at the hands of Russian and Bulgarian troops.[6]

The concept of a common origin for all Turkic groups (bolstered by racial 'proofs' which look odd nowadays[7]), leading to the possibility — and desirability — of a future union, was largely a response to Pan-Slavism and its pressures[8] (such as Russification). This was especially relevant in the light of the increase in Pan-Slavist activities in the late nineteenth and early twentieth centuries, as demonstrated for example in the policies of Izvolskiy. Pan-Slavism was directed primarily against the Germans, especially because, even after 1871, there were still several strong undercurrents of public opinion in the new German state, declaring that German unity was not yet complete.[9] However, a secondary target of attack for Pan-Slavist propaganda was the Ottoman Empire, as expressed, for example, in an aggressive book by I. de Malkhazouny, *Le Panslavisme et la question d'Orient*,[10] which claimed that 'Turkey will disappear from the political scene of Europe . . . The Southern Slav race will acquire the heritage of the Oriental Empire . . . The Southern Slavs will sit upon the Throne of the Levant . . . '[11]

Thus, although the concept of Pan-Turkism was original, many of the tactics — and even some of its terms — were largely borrowed from Pan-Slavism. It is therefore highly understandable why those who took the lead in initiating and propagating Pan-Turkism were Tatars, i.e. the very group which had been longest under Russian rule. Furthermore, the Tatars were most heavily subjected to the pressures accompanying Christianisation and Russification.[12] The Crimea Tatars in particular lived in relative proximity to the Turkish population of the Ottoman Empire, thus providing greater opportunities for the latter to influence them. Moreover, they were surrounded by non-Tatars and their only hope of survival as an entity was rapprochement with other Turkic groups. A large and active bourgeoisie had been developing among the Tatars since the end of the seventeenth century,[13] capable of leading the nationalist awakening from the late nineteenth century on. Pan-Turkism provided a convenient ideological basis for this bourgeoisie's commercial rivalry with the Russians, as Bennigsen and Quelquejay have pointed out.[14] In addition, Tatar intellectuals were the first to grasp that, since Turkic groups were not contiguous geographically, some other element should be selected and developed to bring them closer to one another. The linguistic element was obviously the first choice, as languages were similar, although not identical, among these groups, and intellectuals could communicate in a sort of 'High Turkish'. The main difficulty in this respect was that vernaculars often varied markedly, and literacy rates were very low. Not unexpectedly, increasing literacy and the creation of a common language for cultural rapprochement became the order of the day as a first step towards union. In consequence, education, language reform, and journalistic propaganda were focal activities of Tatar nationalist intellectuals.[15] The prevalent printing presses in Southern Russia and Central Asia during the second half of the nineteenth century[16] assisted in the dissemination of ideas amongst Tatars and others, thus encouraging publication of periodicals and other works.[17]

One man whose life work exemplified such activities was İsmail Gasprinsky (or Gasparinsky), better known in Turkey as Gaspıralı (1851–1914). Born in Gaspara, in the Crimea, he was highly active in all three above-mentioned domains — education, language-reform, and journalism. Gasprinsky, a schoolmaster and one-time mayor of the Tatar town of Bahçesaray, had studied in Russia, Turkey and France. He fought simultaneously against two powerful adversaries: the Russian government and the Muslim *mullahs*. With both he had to tread cautiously, as the Russian authorities disapproved of any Tatar renaissance; while Islam was strongly entrenched among the masses and served as a powerful bond between them. Noting that Tatar intellectuals were fluent in Russian or French, rather than in their own language, and that a major portion of the five-or six-year Tatar school curriculum concentrated on Arabic and the Koran, Gasprinsky devised 'a new [that is, modern] system' (*usul-i cedid*), first experimenting with it in 1884 at a Bahçesaray school. Reforming both the curriculum and the methods, he introduced the Turkish language together with Arabic. The system was subsequently adopted by other schools in Tatar centres and elsewhere. Graduates of schools which employed the new system proved to be better equipped for advanced studies (including university) than did those who had studied at institutions which did not opt for reform.[18]

An achievement of Gasprinsky which had no less impact was his journalistic activity. The spread of printing presses among the Tatars and other Turkic groups had already brought about a substantial increase in the publication of books and circulation of periodicals,[19] most of which had little, if anything, to do with politics. However, the very availability of newsprint, together with the increase in literacy, afforded an opportunity for preaching of nationalist ideas, both local and Pan-Turk in nature. In this context, a special role was played by Gasprinsky's journal, started on 10 April 1883, and named *Tercüman* (Interpreter). This was the most important, although not the only journal published by the Turkic groups in Russia.[20] Its first issue promised to acquaint readers with the knowledge required for national needs. It indeed accomplished all this — and more, fostering interest in educational reform, social affairs, and modern science. Careful not to antagonise the *mullahs* (and even attempting to win them over), it advocated secular nationalism with very definite Pan-Turk nuances. Pan-Turk sentiment was expressed cautiously, due to official press censorship, focusing chiefly upon the oft-repeated phrase: 'unity in language, thought and action' (*Dilde, fikirde, işte birlik*).

Briefly stated, Gasprinsky's basic approach in advocating Pan-Turkism was to work for a union of all the Turkic groups in Russia, under the spiritual guidance of Turkey, based upon a culture rejuvenated by a common language — a modified version of Crimean Tatar. The emphasis on language was not accidental; Gasprinsky's *usul-i cedid* curriculum reform[21] and journal *Tercüman* both advocated a common language as a top-priority means of rapprochement (implying subsequent union) among all Turkic peoples. As dialect differences consisted chiefly of vocabulary variations, a special effort was made to 'purify' the language of foreign words, such as those of Russian, Arabic, or Persian origins — which presumably were employed in only a part of the Turkic languages — and substitute for them others of Turkish or Turkic origin as used in the Ottoman Empire, also the object of linguistic reform. A parallel effort (apparently less successful) was directed at minimising phonological diversity. The result was a language somewhere between Ottoman Turkish and Tatar, reasonably comprehensible to both groups and to others as well.[22] This hybrid, called 'the Common Language' (*Lisan-ı umumî*), was one of the factors contributing to the success of *Tercüman*, which reached not only Southern Russia, but also Central Asia and Eastern Turkestan, with a circulation of about 5,000 in the 1880s,[23] and 6,000 some twenty years later,[24] an impressive figure for that time. This emboldened its contributors as well as those of similar publications in Tatar and other Turkic areas to speak more openly about the objectives of Pan-Turkism. *Tercüman* advocated with increasing frankness a union of all 'Turkish peoples' in Russia. A report of the Russian secret police, the *Okhrana*, shows that they had then correctly surmised that the Islamic propaganda of this and other journals was being used as a cover for Pan-Turkism.[25] Indeed, the theme of Pan-Turkism, along with that of language reform, was taken up, after 1905, by other Tatar journals, several Azeri ones (to be discussed later) or, in the years immediately preceding the First World War, by such Uzbek periodicals as *Turan* and *Bukhoro-i Şarif*, both of which were closed down in 1913 (the former after forty-nine issues, the latter after 153).[26]

Nationalist sentiment, with Pan-Turk overtones, thus found support among several of the Turkic groups in Russia, varying in both content and form in different areas. For example, Gasprinsky's strongly secularist stand was opposed by those who considered Islam a meaningful common bond, while his Pan-Turk propaganda was rejected by the 'Young Tatars' wishing to liberate the Tatars via a revolution against Czarist autocracy. Anyway, the awakening of nationalist sentiment, with its concomitant variations, was propelled into the arena of practical politics by the 1904–5 Russo-Japanese war (in which the former's weakness was revealed, in its defeat by an Asiatic state) and then by the proclamation of the constitution, the convocation of the 1905 *Duma* and the events which followed it. Earlier, Gasprinsky had promoted the creation of philanthropic societies as an organisational framework. Ostensible democratisation and liberalisation in 1905 prompted several Turkic intellectuals to more concerted action. From that time on, political aspirations became more pronounced,[27] as expressed in a series of public meetings among leaders of the various groups, wherein intellectuals generally had the major say. The first such Congress met at Nidzhni-Novgorod, between 15 and 28 August 1905, and was attended by approximately 150 delegates, mostly from the middle or upper bourgeoisie. Gasprinsky was one of the chairmen and Tatars predominated, although Azeris and other Turkic groups from Turkestan, Siberia and Inner Russia were very much in evidence. The Congress was presented as a Muslim gathering;[28] the first of its resolutions demanded union (*Ittifak*) of all Russia's Muslims, which would strive to obtain reforms similar to those demanded by the young liberal bourgeoisie in Russia. The Congress also decided to set up a permanent organisation of all Muslims in Russia, dividing them into sixteen districts, each with an elected local assembly (*meclis*) of its own, while the union's Central Assembly was to meet in Baku. In practice, although several local meetings were held, only the Kazan Assembly functioned regularly.

A second Congress, with Gasprinsky presiding, met in St. Peters-

burg, between 13 and 23 January 1906, with the participation of some
100 Tatar, Kirghiz, Crimean and Caucasian delegates. The Congress
resolved to establish the 'Union of the Muslims of Russia' (*Russiya
Müsülmanlarının İttifakı*), which appeared from the outset to be chiefly an association of Tatar and Azeri nationalists, rather than a true
representation of the Empire's Muslims. Much of this Congress's
time was taken up in arguing over which common attitude members
should adopt in the *Duma*.

The third Congress met, near Nidzhni-Novgorod, between 16 and
20 August 1906, with Kazan Tatars predominating once again: the
presiding committee's fourteen members comprised ten Volga Tatars,
one Crimean Tatar (Gasprinsky), one Azeri, one Kazakh and one
Turkestani (who was also a Tatar in fact). Turkestanis had shown
considerable interest in Pan-Turkism during those years,[29] although
they hardly participated actively in these Congresses. The third Congress decided to transform the *İttifak* into a political party, with the
programme adopted at the Second Congress as its platform.[30]

The party, whose full name was 'the Union of Muslims' (*İttifak-
ul-Muslimin*), had to act with caution. It sponsored the formation of
literary, educational and philanthropic societies, such as the Society
for Assisting the Cultural Development of Muslims, established in
the Khanskaya Stavka of Astrakhan, whose main declared aim was
to unite all Muslims in Russia under the banner of a common language. Most of these societies were organised along similar lines and
cooperated in their political moves, expressed in such journals as
Vakit (Time) of Orenburg and *Sada* (Voice) of Baku.[31]

The Tatars had been very active in the three Congresses, the Union
of Muslims and the *Duma*. Their failure to recruit wide support for
their Pan-Turkist organisational plans among other Turkic groups in
Russia was probably due no less to objective factors (such as the vast
distances separating these groups), than to their inability to set up an
effective political organisation.[32] This was only partly offset by the
zeal which inspired Tatar spokesmen, as such enthusiasm raised
doubts among others regarding the feasibility of an equal partnership
in the future. Even though the resolutions of all three Congresses
dealt with 'Muslims', the misgivings aroused were not dispelled.
Consequently, during the decade before the defeat of the Russian
Empire and the overthrow of the Czar, nationalist propaganda among
Turkic groups was promulgated mostly through the press and other
publications. The number of periodicals issued rose impressively:
some 250 were published by Turkic groups between 1905 and 1917.[33]
Many of the journals published in Russian Central Asia during the

period immediately preceding the First World War[34] were short-lived. Nevertheless, they served to heighten interest in politics.

Difficulties in engaging in active politics were further compounded by the tightening of government control. At first, press censorship was none too effective, principally because Russian censors were rarely fluent in the Turkic languages. Over the years, however, government supervision became increasingly thorough, and nationalist editors and journalists had to emigrate, along with their periodicals. Some were prudent enough to leave of their own free will; others were exiled. Several settled in the Ottoman Empire, or at least maintained close relations with similarly-inclined circles there, thus making a substantial contribution to the development of Pan-Turkism in Turkey itself.[35]

Notwithstanding these obstacles, nationalist activities with a Pan-Turk flavour continued in the Russian Empire, even though no single Turkic group was sufficiently strong or acceptable to the others to serve as the decisive leading force. For some time the Tatars continued to be the most articulate speakers and writers. However, since the *Duma* era — which had heralded closer ties, although not more meaningful cooperation — additional voices favouring nationalism were heard among some other Turkic groups as well. The Kazakhs were not too active in this respect; from 1850 on, Russian authorities had been careful to ban Tatar teachers from Kazakh schools, precisely because they feared the nationalist impact.[36] Other groups, in Azerbayjan and Turkestan, were more vocal; some expressed Pan-Turk sentiments; others called for narrower, local types of patriotism, or, conversely, for a wider nationalism rooted in Islam; still others were partial to new ideas and ideologies prevalent in Russia during the years preceding the 1917 Revolution.

Hence, it is to the Tatars in the Russian Empire that one turns, once again, for the clearest formulations of Pan-Turk nationalism and its attendant debates, which raised arguments often to be repeated in Turkey itself in both the near and distant future. Thus the Caucasus Tatar Ali Hüseyinzade (1864–1941), writing in his journal *Füyûzât* (Abundance, or Enlightenment) in 1907, defined the objectives of Turkish nationalism as 'Turkism, Islamism and Europeanism'. His approach reflected three stages in the crystallisation of nationalism among his own people, with Turkism considered as the last and most significant.[37] Others, such as the above-mentioned Yusuf Akçura (or Akçuraoğlu), a Tatar and Gasprinsky's relative who, from October 1906, edited another journal, *Kazan Muhbiri* (The Correspondent of Kazan) was even more explicit in the matter. We shall have more to say about him later.[38] In the present context, it suffices to state that Akçura was not only deeply involved in Pan-Turk politics in Russia in 1905–8 — he had been very active in all three Congresses — but was also most probably the most influential ideologue of Pan-Turkism in the Russian Empire. As early as April-May 1904, his article 'Üç terz-i siyaset' (Three systems of government), anonymously printed in the Cairo journal *Türk* (he surely could not have published it in Russia), stated Pan-Turkism's *raison d'être*.[39] Akçura had considered Ottomanism, and rejected it because it minimised the rights of the Turks; Pan-Islamism was criticised for antagonising non-Muslim groups in the Ottoman Empire; and Turkism was lauded as offering the only real opportunity for union. Akçura and his supporters argued for a national union of all Turkic groups as 'a closed circle', with Turkey at its centre. For the first time, nationalism was proposed as a coherent alternative to Ottomanism and Pan-Islamism, to which it was implicitly preferred due to its feasibility and its usefulness for the Empire's survival. This article also served as a concise presentation of the essence of Pan-Turkism, with the emphasis transferred from the cultural level, so ably fostered by Gasprinsky and his collaborators, to the political one.[40] The debates about Pan-Turkism continued in the Cairene *Türk* for a while.[41]

It has already been indicated that during the early twentieth century, the Azeris were highly active in terms of their Pan-Turk nationalist awakening, second only to the Tatars. It is difficult to determine whether such activity was influenced by proximity to Turkey of the Crimea and of Azerbayjan, respectively, or to the stimuli of intellectual life (Kazan University had been established in 1804, while Baku was an important meeting ground for intellectuals from various communities).[42] In any event, the nineteenth century witnessed a cultural awakening among the Azeris, which first found political expression in the periodical *Ekinci* (Harvester),[43] first published in Baku in 1875. Founded by Hasan Serdabi, this was the first national newspaper of any Turkic group in Russia. *Ekinci* was closed down by the authorities in its second year, as it was considered too politically-oriented. It was followed by others, notably *Hayat* and *İrşad*, all nationalist with a Pan-Turk tendency.[44] Official control of all political expression served only to alienate the Azeris; after the 1905 Revolution, they were among the most outspoken anti-Russian groups and proceeded to establish schools, found newspapers (mostly in Turkish),[45] and set up political parties. Their nationalist pronouncements showed a growing trend towards secession from the Russian Empire and drawing closer to the Ottoman Empire.[46]

The First World War appeared to some activists among the Turkic groups in the Russian Empire as the watershed of their nationalist hopes. Significantly, the Russians and the Ottomans were fighting in opposite camps. In 1916, several leaders of Turkic groups in Russia, such as the Tatars Kazi Abdür-Reşid İbrahim,[47] Ali Hüseyinzade, and Yusuf Akçura, together with the Azeri Ahmet Ağaoğlu, met in Lausanne with the League of the Allogenes of Russia and presented a petition to United States President Wilson regarding religious, cultural and socioeconomic oppression in Russia.[48] The first serious revolt in Central Asia against the Czarist government occurred during the same year as a series of risings among the Kirghiz and others.[49] These have been variously interpreted by Soviet and other analysts;[50] nevertheless, virtually all experts tend to agree that Pan-Turk sentiment was one of the basic motivating factors in this revolt. In a parallel — although not necessarily coordinated — manner, agitation began among the Crimean Tatars against arbitrary Russian rule, demanding the re-establishment of the Khanate of the Crimea under the protection of the Ottoman Sultanate.[51]

Much more ferment was to follow both during and after the eventful year 1917. The February Revolution and the overthrow of the Czarist regime rendered mere opposition to the central government redundant; instead, numerous options of a more concrete nature were now available to the politically-minded among the Turkic groups in the Empire. Pan-Turkism was often only of secondary importance within the gamut of solutions discussed at that time, such as 'complete independence', 'cultural autonomy' within a federal state, or 'territorial autonomy' within a centralised state, for example. Between 15 and 17 March 1917, soon after the February Revolution, *Duma* Delegates of Turkic and several other groups established a Provisional Central Bureau of Russian Muslims in St. Petersburg, charged with convening a general congress of the Muslims in Russia.[52] An All-Russian Muslim Congress did meet in Moscow between 1 and 11 May 1917, reportedly attended by about 800 delegates. This Congress was an impressive indication of an attempt at Muslim solidarity, and representatives of Turkic groups predominated. While the Congress had no little trouble in attempting to reconcile divergent views on social reform or religion (the status of women, for instance), there was apparently a wide measure of support for the formation of national entities, in which primary schooling would be in the local language and the continuing education take place in the 'Pan-Turk' language of Gasprinsky's *Tercüman*. However, since concrete political resolutions had to be passed, the Congress was sharply divided and had to compromise on the establishment of a National Council to formulate future policies, presumably to strike a balance between

the majority — which favoured a federalist pattern of national territorial units — and proponents of other solutions. The compromise
reflected the misunderstandings at this Congress and the growth of
local patriotism — under the guise of support for a federalist solution
— in Azerbayjan, as well as among the Kirghiz and Bashkirs. The
National Council, dominated by the Tatars, soon lost all real significance.

Missed opportunities rarely, if ever, recur. Thus, the failure of the
All-Russian Muslim Congress to agree upon a comprehensive and
common plan of action, Pan-Turkist or otherwise, spelled indefinite
postponement for practical materialisation of Pan-Turk ideology.
Subsequent conventions, such as those held in Kazan during July the
same year, involved representatives of certain Turkic groups only.
These representatives were largely concerned with other matters, such
as the future of their local autonomy and relations with the central
government. There were cleavages between the religious and
secularist proponents, as well as between the bourgeois and other
classes. Such divergences were characteristic not only of those meetings, but of coming events as well. Geographic distance,[53] variations
in ideology and clashes of interest — resulting in inability to
cooperate meaningfully — brought about not only the breakdown of
the Pan-Turk vision, for all practical purposes, but also the shelving
of all plans for local nationhood.

Turkic groups in the defunct Russian Empire exhibited varied
responses to the challenge of communism. The initial reaction was
apparently joy and relief at the defeat of Czardom and all it represented. In several Turkic-inhabited areas there was pride in what was
considered as victory for the Ottoman Empire and hope for independence and Pan-Turk union — e.g. between Turkestan and the
Tatars of Kazan.[54] Insofar as there was some opposition to the new
regime, it obtained no assistance — except from the Ottoman armies
in Azerbayjan — and eventually fell apart, as all Turkic-inhabited
territories were eventually incorporated into the Soviet Union, in this
case within the former frontiers of the Russian Empire. While this
study does not intend to describe these events in detail,[55] suffice it to
say that the Soviets obviously could not allow the continued existence
of an ideology that preferred an ethnic-linguistic internationalism over
their own class internationalism, particularly as Pan-Turkism had a
separatist character too. Immediately after the Revolution, the Tatars
and the Bashkirs indeed initiated a separatist-inspired struggle for
self-rule.[56] Soon the whole area was in revolt.[57] In Transcaucasia, the
struggle for independence was the order of the day,[58] led by the
Azeris,[59] and assisted for a time by the intervention of the Ottoman

Empire's military forces.[60] In Central Asia, the Kazakhs also sought a solution on the same lines. In Turkestan, Bukhara and Khiva, revolts were initiated against the local aristocracy no less than against the Russian rulers. Only rarely did activists aim consciously at fostering Pan-Turkism, as in the case of Mustafa Chokayev (Çokay), a young nationalist leader (1890–1941) who had set up an independent government in Khokand in 1917, subsequently wiped out in February 1918.[61] Although his movement was hardly the great Pan-Turk nationalist movement described by some writers, it did possess the requisite components: the Khokand Autonomous Government in fact comprised delegates of most major tribal units in that area of Turkes-tan.[62] In several instances, to be considered later,[63] there is evidence of official Ottoman involvement both during the war and immediately afterwards, in anti-Russian (then, anti-Soviet) activities of the Turkic groups.

Opposition to the forces of the Soviet Union was most probably doomed to failure in any case, not only because of the Red Army's superiority, but also because of political factors. Each Turkic group was in a different situation, and the views of their leaders diverged as to the preferable courses of action. Political parties had come into existence among the Turkic groups only shortly before the Com-munist Revolution, and their leaders and other activists were no match for the more astute Soviet cadres headed by Lenin's revolutionaries. The Soviets successfully pitted the groups against one another and formed separate, nominally autonomous districts, stressing the smaller, rather than the broader, ethno-cultural subdivisions among Turkic groups.[64] This raised greater obstacles in the path of both Pan-Turkism and Pan-Islamism — both of which the Soviets dreaded for a long while,[65] for several good reasons. Pan-Turkism, sometimes coloured by strong Islamic sentiments, was, in the early 1920s, 1) at the root of the Basmachi revolt;[66] 2) in the Sultangalievism among the Tatars, first expressed within the Communist Party, then outside it, with the declared intention of establishing an independent Republic of Turan uniting all Turks in the Soviet Union within a powerful separate state,[67] 75 per cent of whose people were to be Turks and 80 per cent Muslims;[68] 3) in the clandestine *Irk* (Race) Party set up by Turan Riskulov, promoting Turkestan as an independent unit and a centre for a 'Turanian state';[69] 4) in the April 1922 meeting of the Congress of the Muslim Anti-Bolshevik organisations, the most im-portant of whose resolutions called for establishing a provisional government, entitled the Government of the Independent Turk Republic of Turkestan;[70] and 5) in the considerable resistance to the officially-imposed modifications of the Kazakh and other alphabets, intended to emphasise the differences among the Turkic languages.[71] Uzbek writers, for instance, protested that these modifications were aimed at hampering Pan-Turk unity;[72] others viewed alphabet reform, particularly the transfer to Cyrillic characters in 1936, as one stage in the drive for Russification.[73]

Soviet propaganda against Pan-Turkism and Pan-Islamism continued, however, without any let-up, through official channels, which published and distributed pamphlets and articles continuously.[74] Official Soviet periodicals, supplanting earlier ones, appeared in various languages.[75] Further, in 1921, the tenth Congress of the Communist Party of the Soviet Union condemned both Pan-Turkism and Pan-Islamism as deviations tending towards 'bourgeois democratic nationalism'.[76] As these sentiments appeared, nevertheless, to continue to manifest themselves among the Turkic groups,[77] a pamphlet, published in 1925,[78] trenchantly described the 'evil character' of these two movements, accusing them of separatism motivated by feudal reactionaries, committed to local nationalisms and supported by the worst elements in society. Side by side with this propaganda, Pan-Turkism was combatted by studies published, over the years, in scholarly and quasi-scholarly works — in both articles[79] and books. An example of the latter is a volume in Georgian by Otar Gigineish-vili, entitled *Turkizmi da osmaletis sagares politika* (Pan-Turkism and the foreign policy of the Ottoman Empire). Published in Tiflis in 1963, this work argued forcibly that Pan-Turkism, hostile in 1918 to the Georgians, Armenians and Azeris, was far from being a phenomenon of the past; on the contrary, it was maintained, it continued to be exploited by the capitalist states for their own ends.

Possibly the best indication of sustained official propaganda is provided by the three editions of the *Great Soviet Encyclopaedia*, which defined Turan as a geographical term, without additional comment. The first edition[80] did state that Turanian peoples (*Turanskiye narodi*) are those who inhabit the Turan mountain-ranges and form a common linguistic group. The second and third editions omit this observation, however. On the other hand, 'Pan-Turkism, not mentioned at all in the first edition, was given some consideration in the second and third. In the second,[81] an unsigned article of less than half a column in length designated Pan-Turkism as 'the chauvinistic doctrine of the Turkish reactionary bourgeois circles, whose aim is to extend the rule of Turkey to encompass all people speaking Turkic languages'. The article went on to say that, since the Young Turks, those 'falsifiers of history' had striven to prove the unity of these peoples and their common racial affiliation. The third edition[82] devoted an entire column to 'Pan-Turkism', essentially repeating the above with some further elaboration.

Along with their official propaganda, the Soviet authorities took practical steps for instituting firm-handed rule in all Muslim and Turkic areas.[83] The boundaries set up for the new territorial units[84] were yet another means of discouraging Pan-Turkism, Pan-Islamism and even Pan-Iranism. The introduction of the Russian language into the schools,[85] the influx of Russians into areas largely populated by Turkic and Muslim groups, and the appointment of Russians to key positions were intended to weaken nationalist and Pan-Turk sentiments even further.[86] Despite all this — or perhaps because of it — at the Baku Congress of Turcologists, convened in 1926, the Turkic scholars from the Volga region (presumably Tatars) demanded establishment of a 'Turkish language Federation', openly proclaiming: 'We Turks cannot isolate ourselves from one another.'[87] Significantly, this declaration was made in the presence of participating scholars from Turkey. Similar pronouncements were not stated openly again for some time, however, probably as a result of stronger measures by the authorities taken since 1927. A systematic campaign in the press and other publications[88] against 'nationalist deviations' was accompanied by official purges of those considered to be the politically unreliable intelligentsia of the Turkic groups.[89] These activities extended even as far as the Soviet Far East, where a Yakut writer, Altan Sarın, had been agitating for Pan-Turkism.[90] Strictures were continuously applied during the 1930s; most of the Muslim intelligentsia — which had rallied to the new regime after the Revolution — were physically liquidated under suspicion of having maintained an attachment to Pan-Islam or Pan-Turkism.[91] Even Stalin himself appeared to have been rather wary of Pan-Turkism.[92] The regime's efforts did not quite produce the expected results in Azerbayjan and elsewhere;[93] and in the case of the Tatars even less so.[94] The process reached a climax with the wholesale deportation of Tatars from the Crimea in May 1944.[95]

A distinction should be made between Soviet official attitudes to the Muslims as a whole and to the Turkic peoples who comprised a major component among them. The main problem concerning the former seemed one of re-education,[96] while a containment had to be found for the latter — what Pierre Rondot once called, in this very context, *nationalisme dirigé*.[97] As a result, broadly speaking, since the mid-1920s (and more so since the late 1920s), there has been no meaningful organised Pan-Turkist activity within the Soviet Union; of course, this has been patently impractical in the new conditions.

However, Pan-Turk sentiments persisted, finding expression in the
preservation of the Turkic languages[98] and in literary works. Learned
studies written by scholars belonging to the Turkic groups, as well
as poems and stories contributed by their intellectuals, emphasised
the great achievements in their historical and literary past, thus affording Turkic groups a feeling of superiority over their immediate
neighbours of Iranian descent, such as the Tajiks, as well as over the
'Big Brothers', the Russians.[99] Attempts were made at showing how
Turkic groups had influenced Iranian and Russian civilisations, indicating a marked Pan-Turk attitude.

Characteristic of this approach were various literary works by
Uzbek writers, widely received among the Uzbeks, but a source of
annoyance to the Soviet authorities,[100] which were striving for the
Sovietisation of Uzbekistan.[101] The same applied to the Tatars as well;
although they had lost their role as quintessential *Kulturträger* for
the other Turkic groups, they continued nonetheless to foster
nationalist sentiments in their writings, strongly imbued with Pan-
Turkism — again, to the great displeasure of the Soviet authorities.[102]
The latter were highly incensed, in particular, by nationalist expression among the Turkic groups.[103] At times, these activities were
carried out under the guise of Islam,[104] practice of which was allowed
in the Soviet Union,[105] but at other times they were coated with
Marxist verbiage or even Marxist theory[106] — leading the authorities
to fear the peril of 'Turanian Communism'.[107] Consequently, Russification in word and deed continued and was even intensified.[108] A
late instance of the former is found in a book, first written in Kazakh
and then translated into Russian in 1972 and published in Alma Ata
as *Padyeniye Bol'shogo Tyurkyestana* (The defeat of *The Great
Turkestan*). Defined by its author Syerin Shakibayev as 'a chronicle-
story', it recounts how proponents of the 'Great Turkestan' concept
aided the Nazis against the Soviet Union during the Second World
War.[109] The unabated official propaganda against Pan-Turkism would
suggest the continuing existence of Pan-Turk sentiment in the Soviet
Union and, after its break-up, in the ex-Soviet Muslim republics.
Evidently, these sentiments were weakened to some extent, after the
death of their early protagonists, by the competition of other levels
of identification — local, religious, ideological (Communism), all-
national (Soviet patriotism) — all opposed to the supra-national one
of Pan-Turkism.

The campaign for Russification and Sovietisation notwithstanding,
the Turkic groups in the Soviet Union remained apart and increased
numerically. According to the Soviet Census of 1979 (rounded up to
thousands), there were 43,772,000 Muslims in the Soviet Union, of

whom Turkic groups made up 37,203,000. In descending order of size, these were the Uzbeks, Kazakhs, Tatars, Azeris, Turkmens, Kirghiz, Bashkirs, and seven other, smaller groups of less than one third of a million each. If one adds to these the people living in other parts of the Diaspora, such as Afghanistan, Iran, Irak, Syria, Romania, Bulgaria, Greece and Cyprus, their overall numbers at least equalled the 44,236,000 living in the Republic of Turkey in mid-1979.[110] Consequently, one may understand the concern, past and present, felt by some of the inhabitants of Turkey for their large Diaspora of Outside Turks.

NOTES

1. Cf. E.H. Parker, *A thousand years of the Tatars*, 2nd edn, repr. 1969, passim.
2. Among these, special mention ought to be made of Zarevand (pseudonym of Zaven and Vartouhie Nalbandian), *United and independent Turania: Aims and designs of the Turks* (English translation by V.N. Dadrian); A. Arsharuni and Kh. Gabidullin, *Ochyerki Panislamizma i Pantyurkizma v Rossii*; C.W. Hostler, *Turkism and the Soviets*; S.A. Zenkovsky, *Pan-Turkism and Islam in Russia*. See also the following footnotes.
3. For an expert discussion of these groups in the 1880s, see H. Vámbéry, *Das Türkenvolk*, first publ. in 1885, repr. in 1970.
4. The census, published in St. Petersburg in 1905, p. 286, is quoted by Eugen Oberhummer, *Die Türken und das osmanische Reich*, p. 17.
5. On the imposition of Russian rule on this area, the most thoroughly researched work in Russian is N.A. Khalfin, *Prisoyedinyeniye Sryedniyey Azii k Rossii (60–90 godi xix v.)*, Moscow, 1965. In English, a useful volume, mainly on the military and political problems involved, is D.C. Boulger, *Central Asian questions*, 1885. A lively description is provided by F.H. Skrine and E.D. Ross, *The heart of Asia*, 1899, part 2. In German, a very detailed book is Reiner Olzscha and Georg Cleinow, *Turkestan: die politisch-historischen und wirtschaftlichen Probleme Zentralasiens*, 1942.
6. For which see the anonymous *The extermination of the Turkish people by Russia and the true policy for England*, 1878 (a copy may be consulted in the British Library, London).
7. These looked odd, even then, to some observers. On the baselessness of the argument of race among Turks, see M.A. Czaplicka, *The Turks of Central Asia in history and at the present day*, 1918, repr. 1973, pp. 14–16.
8. Cf. Hans Kohn, *Pan-Slavism: its history and its ideology*, 1953, esp. pp. 201 ff. For sources of Pan-Slavism and its main course in the nineteenth century, as seen by a Turkish historian, cf. Akdes Nimet

Kurat, 'Panslavizm', *Ankara Üniversitesi Dil ve Tarih-Coǧrafya Fakültesi Dergisi*, XI (2–4): June–Sep.–Dec. 1953, pp. 241–78.

9. See, e.g., M.S. Wertheimer, *The Pan-German league 1890–1914*, 1924.
10. Paris, Féchoz, 1898.
11. Ibid., p. 86. Translation mine.
12. For Tatar-Russian relations and the Tatar cultural and nationalist revival, see S.A. Zenkovsky, 'A century of Tatar revival', *The American Slavic and East European Review*, XII: Oct. 1953, pp. 303–18; id., *'Kulturkampf* in pre-revolutionary Central Asia', ibid., XIV: Feb. 1955, pp. 15–41.
13. On which see Alexandre Bennigsen and Chantal Quelquejay, *Les mouvements nationaux chez les Musulmans de Russie: le «Sultangalievisme» au Tatarstan*, pp. 28 ff.
14. Ibid., p. 40.
15. The man who first called attention in Europe to the nationalist awakening of the Tatars and to its cultural and political significance was the above-mentioned Vambery. See his 'The awakening of the Tartars', *The Nineteenth Century*, LVII: Feb. 1905, pp. 217–27; 'Constitutional Tartars', ibid., LIX: June 1906, pp. 906–13; 'Die Kulturbestrebungen der Tataren', *Deutsche Rundschau*, XXXIII (10): July 1907, pp. 72–91.
16. Edward Allworth, *Central Asian publishing and the rise of nationalism*, 1965.
17. For which see X, 'Le Panislamisme et le Panturquisme', *RMM*, XXII: 1913, pp. 179–220.
18. Not unexpectedly, Soviet historiography has taken a different view of *cedidism*. See, e.g., 'Jadidism — a current Soviet assessment', *Central Asian Review* (London), XII (1): 1964, pp. 30–9.
19. For the periodicals, the most valuable study is Alexandre Bennigsen and Chantal Lemercier-Quelquejay, *La presse et le mouvement national chez les Musulmans de Russie avant 1920*, 1964.
20. For some of the others cf. *RMM*, XII: 1913, p. 197.
21. For which see the contemporary appraisals of Sophy Bobrovnikoff, 'Moslems in Russia', *The Moslem World* (London), I (1): Jan. 1911, esp. pp. 15 ff; and of K.K. Pahlen, *Mission to Turkestan*, 1964, pp. 44 ff (Pahlen's memoirs refer to 1908–9).
22. A study of this language has been prepared by Gustav Burbice, 'Die Sprache Ismāīl Bey Gaspyralys', unpublished Ph.D. thesis, Hamburg University, 1950; cf. *EI²*, II, p. 366.
23. Vincent Monteil, *Les Musulmans soviétiques*, 1957, p. 22.
24. Acc. to Vambery, in *The Nineteenth Century*, LVII: Feb. 1905, p. 219.
25. H.C. d'Encausse, *Réforme et révolution chez les Musulmans de l'Empire russe*, 1966, pp. 103–4.
26. For Gasprinsky's lifework and impact on Pan-Turkism see, in addition to Vambery's above articles, the following: G.V. Mende, *Der nationale Kampf der Russlandtürken: ein Beitrag zur nationalen Frage in der*

Sowjetunion, 1936, pp. 44 ff. Cafer Seydahmet Kırımer, *Gaspıralı İsmail Bey*, 1934. Ayhan Göksan, 'Gaspıralı İsmail Bey', *Türk Kültürü (TK)* (Ankara), 23: Sep. 1964, pp. 23–30. Nâdir Devlet, *İsmail Bey (Gaspıralı)*, 1988. İlber Ortaylı, 'Reports and considerations of İsmail Bey Gasprinskii in *Tercüman* on Central Asia', *Cahiers du Monde Russe et Soviétique*, XXXII (1): 1991, pp. 43–6. For his *Tercüman*, see Altan Deliorman, 'İsmail Gaspıralı ve Tercüman gazetesi', ibid., 69: July 1968, pp. 653–8. For his views, cf. Mehmet Kaplan, 'Gaspıralı İsmail'in Avrupa medeniyeti, sosyalizm ve İslâmiyet hakkındaki eseri', ibid., 180: Oct. 1977, pp. 716 ff; Ahmet Caferoğlu, *İsmail Gaspıralı. Ölümünün 50. yıldönümü münasebetile bir etüd*, 1964. See also F.W. Fernau, *Moslems on the march: people and politics in the world of Islam*, transl. by E.W. Dicks, 1954, pp. 245–8; d'Encausse, *Réforme*, pp. 103–11; S. Zyenkovskiy, 'Rossiya i Tyurki', *The New Review — Noviy Dzurnal* (N.Y.), XLVI: 1956, pp. 185 ff; Bennigsen and Quelquejay, *Les mouvements*, p. 39, n. 1, list additional references.
27. For these political aspirations, in the years 1905–16, see *RMM*, LVI: Dec. 1923, pp. 136–48.
28. A.W. Fisher, 'Social and legal aspects of Russian-Muslim relations in the nineteenth century: the case of the Crimean Tatars', in Abraham Ascher *et al.* (eds), *The mutual effects of the Islamic and Judeo-Christian worlds: the East European pattern*, 1979, esp. pp. 85–90.
29. Details in Ahmed Zeki Velidi Togan, *Hâtıralar*, 1969. A.V. Pyaskovskiy, *Ryevolutsiya 1905–1907 godov v Tyurkyestanye*, Moscow, Soviet Academy of Sciences Press, 1958, esp. pp. 98–102, 543 ff.
30. On these three Congresses see, *inter alia*: *RMM*, 1: Dec. 1906, pp. 145–68, and LVI: Dec. 1923, pp. 136 ff; Mende, pp. 92 ff; d'Encausse, *Réforme*, pp. 119–21; R.A. Pierce, *Russian Central Asia 1867–1917: a study in colonial rule*, pp. 255–8; Bennigsen and Quelquejay, *Les mouvements*, pp. 57–61.
31. Details in J. Reby, 'Un cri d'alarme russe', *RMM*, X: Jan. 1910, pp. 106–7.
32. As remarked perspicaciously by A.J. Toynbee in a 16-page type-written memorandum on 'The nationality problem in the Caucasus', now in PRO, FO 371/3016, file 194969, no. 194969. It is dated 9 October 1917.
33. Mende, p. 93.
34. Details in Pierce, pp. 258–61.
35. See below, ch. 2.
36. Cf. H.C. d'Encausse, 'The stirring of national feeling', in Edward Allworth (ed.), *Central Asia: a century of Russian rule*, 1967, pp. 174–5.
37. See Mende, pp. 71 ff.
38. See below, ch. 2, where we shall list sources about him and his lifework.
39. This has been reissued since, in the form of a booklet, by the Turkish Historical Society (*Türk Tarih Kurumu*) and other presses.

40. See David Thomas, 'Yusuf Akçura and the intellectual origins of "Üç tarz-i siyaset" ', *Journal of Turkish Studies*, II: 1978, pp. 127–40. Cf. Akçura's own evaluation of it, in his *Türkçülük*, Sakin Öner (ed.), 1978, pp. 169 ff.
41. An incomplete set of *Türk* may be consulted in Atatürk Kitaplığı, Istanbul.
42. Cf. Mary Holdsworth, *Turkestan in the nineteenth century*, 1959, pp. 33–4. On the intellectual movements in nineteenth-century Azerbayjan see, *inter alia*, Hüseyin Baykara, *Azerbaycan'da yenileşme hareketleri*. XIX. *yüzyıl*, Ankara, Türk Kültürünü Araştırma Enstitüsü, 1966.
43. On this journal see Akçura, *Türkçülük*, pp. 87–9; Sakin Öner, *Ülkücü hareketinin meseleleri*, p. 37.
44. Hilal Munschi, *Die Republik Aserbeidschan: eine geschichtliche und politische Skizze*, 1930, pp. 15–16.
45. For *Ekinci* and other periodicals, published in Turkish in Azerbayjan, cf. E.R. (= Ettore Rossi), 'La stampa turca dell'Azerbaigian Caucasico', *Oriente Moderno (OM)* (Rome), VI (4): Apr. 1926, pp. 237–9; and A. Caferoğlu, *Azerbaycan*, pp. 28 ff.
46. M.E. Resul-Zade, *Das Problem Aserbeidschan*, 1938, pp. 26–8.
47. For his article, signed Scheich Abdurreschid Ibrahim, 'Vom Sein und Werden der tatarischen Nation', see *Der Neue Orient*, I (1): 7 April 1917, pp. 10–12.
48. Text and interpretation in *RMM*, LVI: Dec. 1923, pp. 146–8.
49. For the risings of the Kirghiz and the Tungans, in Russian Turkestan, in late 1916, see FO 371/2914, file 6130, no. 6130, Alston's no. 355, to Grey of Fallodon, dated Peking, 7 Dec. 1916.
50. One of the earlier evaluations was by G.I. Broydo, *Vosstaniye Kirgizov v 1916 g.*, 1928. Broydo had been delegated by the Soviet authorities to investigate the 1916 events. A somewhat later, and larger, Russian work is a collection of articles edited by P. Galuzo and F. Bodzhko, *Vosstaniye 1916 v Sryednyey Azii*, 1932. The most recent Soviet study in the matter seems to be Z.D. Kastyel'skaya, *Iz istorii Tyurkyestanskogo kraya (1865–1917)*, 1980, pp. 89–99. For a Western interpretation, see E.D. Sokol, *The revolt of 1916 in Russian Central Asia*, Baltimore, Johns Hopkins Press, 1954. See also Pierce, ch. 18.
51. Acc. to the evidence of Inorodetz (pseudonym), *La Russie et les peuples allogènes*, 2nd edn (1st edn appeared in 1917), p. 209.
52. On these and subsequent developments, see Mende, pp. 121 ff; Bennigsen and Quelquejay, *Les mouvements*, pp. 64 ff; Richard Pipes, *The formation of the Soviet Union: communism and nationalism 1917–1923*, 2nd edn, 1964, pp. 76 ff.
53. Particularly in huge Turkestan, where a meaningful awakening, cultural and national, was thus greatly hampered in the nineteenth century. See Edward Allworth, 'The "Nationality" idea in Czarist Central

Russia', in Erich Goldhagen (ed.), *Ethnic minorities in the Soviet Union*, 1968, pp. 229–50.

54. As observed in Turkestan by a British emissary in 1917–18 — see George Macartney, 'Bolshevism as I saw it in Tashkent in 1918', *Journal of the Central Asian Society*, VII: 1920, esp. p. 42.

55. For a general survey, see Mende, pp. 139 ff. A readable account of this period, as well as of pre-Soviet and Soviet rule of this area is provided by Geoffrey Wheeler, *The modern history of Soviet Central Asia*, 1964.

56. For the struggle of the Crimea Tatars for independence in 1917–18, see Edige Kirimal, *Der nationale Kampf der Krimtürken*, pp. 33–277; for later years, cf. pp. 278 ff. E.A. Allworth (ed.), *Tatars of the Crimea*, 1988.

57. See A. Gugushvili, 'The struggle of the Caucasian peoples for independence', *The Eastern Quarterly* (London), IV (4): Oct. 1951, pp. 33–41.

58. Cf. P.J.A.G. La Chesnais, *Les peuples de la Transcaucasie pendant la guerre et devant la paix*, 1921.

59. Resul-Zade, pp. 28–31. Munschi, p. 22.

60. This will be dealt with more specifically below, in ch. 2.

61. See Mustafa Chokaev's (*sic*!) own evidence, in his 'The Basmaji movement in Turkestan', *The Asiatic Review* (London), XXIV: Apr. 1928, pp. 273–88; and his (Mustafa Chokayev) 'Turkestan and the Soviet regime', *Journal of the Royal Central Asian Society*, XVIII (3): 1931, pp. 403–20; his (M.A. Tchokaieff) 'Fifteen years of Bolshevik rule in Turkestan', ibid., XX (3): 1933, pp. 351–9; and his (Moustapha Chokaieff) *Chez les Soviets en Asie Centrale*, 1928, enlarged as Mustafa-Ogli, *Turkyestan pod vlast'yu Sovyetov*, 1935. See also A. Oktay, *Türkistan millî hareketi ve Mustafa Çokay*, 1950; M. Delil, *Türkistan Türklerinin büyük milliyetçi ve yurtseverlerinden Mustafa Çokay albümü*, Istanbul, n.d. [1942]; and Holdsworth, pp. 66–7. Personal testimonies of the war in Turkestan, 1918–20, are available in L.V.S. Blacker, 'Wars and travels in Turkestan, 1918–1919–1920', *Journal of the Central Asian Society*, IX (2): 1922, pp. 4–20; and in W. Malleson, 'The British military mission to Turkestan', ibid., pp. 96–110.

62. Park, pp. 161–3; Wheeler, *Peoples*, p. 53; Baymirza Hayit, *Some problems of modern Turkistan history*, 1963.

63. See below, ch. 2 of our study.

64. G.J. Massell, *The surrogate proletariat: Moslem women and revolutionary strategists in Soviet Central Asia, 1919–1929*, 1974, pp. 32–4.

65. Lowell Tillett, *The great friendship: Soviet historians on the non-Russian nationalities*, 1969, pp. 176, 185, 187, 205, 253, 400.

66. For which cf. Chokaev in *The Asiatic Review*, XXIV: Apr. 1928, pp. 273–8. Joseph Castagné, *Les Basmatchis: le mouvement national des indigènes d'Asie Centrale depuis la révolution d'Octobre 1917 jusqu'au Octobre 1924*, 1925. See also A.G. Park, *Bolshevism in*

Turkestan, 1917–1927, 1957, pp. 161–3. For an official view cf. Yu.A. Polyakov and A.I. Chugunov, *Konyets Basmachyestva*, 1976.

67. Bennigsen and Quelquejay, *Les mouvements*, part 2.
68. A.A. Bennigsen and S.E. Wimbush, *Muslim national communism in the Soviet Union*, pp. 66–7.
69. See Baymirza Hayit, *Sowjetrussische Orientpolitik am Beispiel Turkestans*, pp. 123 ff. For the anti-Soviet movement in Turkestan, cf. J. Castagné, in *RMM*, L: June 1922, pp. 28–73.
70. An English translation of the resolutions is enclosed in FO 371/8075, N 8141/6/97, in a secret intelligence report no. CX 2787, dated 28 Aug. 1922.
71. E.E. Bacon, *Central Asia under Russian rule: a study in cultural change*, 1966, pp. 144–5. Cf. Mende, pp. 172 ff. A Turkish translation of this work appeared as *Esir Ortaasya*, N.p. [Istanbul], Tercüman, n.d. [1979–80].
72. Edward Allworth, *Uzbek literary politics*, 1964, pp. 169, 182.
73. See Stefan Wurm, *Turkic peoples of the USSR*, esp. pp. 45–51.
74. Some of these, for the years 1918–20, may be consulted in the India Office (London), L/P&S/10/741, file 1735/1918.
75. See, e.g., R.M. Nurullina, *Stanovlyeniye partiyno-sovyetskoy pyechati na Tatarskom yazikye*, 1978.
76. Details in Hostler, *Turkism*, p. 118; cf. ibid., pp. 119–20.
77. Details in Castagné, *Les Basmatchis*, pp. 61 ff.
78. Entitled *Natsional'noye razmyedzhyevaniye Sryednyey Azii*, 1925.
79. Examples are articles by A.Kh. Babakhodzhayev, 'Pantyurkizm — orudiye idyeologichyeskov divyersii impyerializma', *Trudi Instituta Vostokovyedyeniya Akademii Nauk Uzbyekskoy SSR*, II: 1954, pp. 25 ff; and Yu.V. Marunov, 'Pantyurkizm i Panislamizm Mladoturok', *Kratkiye Soobshchyeniya Instituta Narodov Azii* (Moscow), XLV: 1961, pp. 38–56.
80. LV: 1947, col. 181.
81. XXXII: 1955, p. 13.
82. XIX: 1975, p. 153.
83. Cf. for Turkestan and Bukhara, India Office, L/P&S/10/722, file 4377/1917, parts 2 and 3, Major F.M. Bailey's, 'Report on the Kashgar mission, 1918–1920'. About Bailey himself, see A. Swinson, *Beyond the frontiers: the biography of Colonel F.M. Bailey, explorer and special agent*, 1971. For Soviet views of these measures, cf. F.K. Kasimov, *Pyeryekhod narodov Sryednyey Azii sotsializmu, minuya kapitalizm*, 1979.
84. On which see 'The partition of Central Asia', *Central Asian Review*, VIII (4): 1960, pp. 341–51. For these and other measures of Sovietisation, up to 1922, see Joseph Castagné, 'Les organisations soviétiques de la Russie musulmane', *RMM*, LI: Oct. 1922, pp. 1–24; and Limitaris (pseudonym?), 'Turkestan since the revolution', *The Asiatic Review*, XIX (4): Oct. 1923, pp. 601–19. For later years, see Pipes, chs 4 and 5.

85. Cf. 'The teaching of Russian in Central Asian schools', *Central Asian Review*, v (1): 1957, pp. 37–41.
86. Details in Robert Conquest, *The last empire*, 1962, esp. ch. 3, and Garip Sultan, 'Demographic and cultural trends among Turkic peoples of the Soviet Union', in Goldhagen (ed.), *Ethnic minorities*, pp. 251–73.
87. Fernau, p. 253.
88. For one instance, out of many, see the early Soviet analysis of Turkmen relations with the Russians and the Soviets in Ye. L. Shteynbyerg, *Ochyerki istorii Turkmyenii*, 1934.
89. Hayit, passim. See also the selected readings in Rudolf Schlesinger, *The nationalities problem and Soviet administration*, 1956.
90. Cf. Walter Kolarz, *The peoples of the Soviet Far East*, pp. 106 ff.
91. Alexandre Bennigsen, 'The Muslims of European Russia and the Caucasus', in W.S. Vucinich (ed.), *Russia and Asia: essays on the influence of Russia on the Asian peoples*, 1972, p. 158.
92. Walter Kolarz, *Russia and her colonies*, p. 32.
93. See Hüseyin Baykara, *Azerbaycan istiklâl mücadelesi tarihi*, passim.
94. Cf. T. Dawletschin, *Cultural life in the Tatar Autonomous Republic* (in Russian, with English title), 1953 (= Mimeographed series, no. 49).
95. Details in Ann Sheehy, *The Crimean Tatars, Volga Germans and Meskhetians: Soviet treatment of some national minorities*, 1973, pp. 9–10; Kirimal, pp. 323 ff; Robert Conquest, *The nation killers: the Soviet deportation of nationalities*, 2nd edn, 1970; Alan Fisher, *The Crimean Tatars*, ch. 14; A.M. Nekrich, *The punished peoples: the deportation and fate of Soviet minorities at the end of the Second World War*, 1978.
96. See Hans Bräker, *Kommunismus und Weltreligionen Asiens: Zur Religions- und Asienpolitik der Sowjetunion. i, 1, Kommunismus und Islam*, 1969.
97. Pierre Rondot, 'L'expérience soviétique chez les peuples turcs de l'Asie Centrale', *L'Afrique et l'Asie* (Paris), i (4): 1948, esp. p. 6.
98. The 1959 census in the Soviet Union found out that more than twenty-one millions spoke Turkic languages in the Union. See *Central Asian Review*, viii (4): 1960, pp. 362–75.
99. See, e.g., G.E. Wheeler, 'Cultural developments in Soviet Central Asia', *Journal of the Royal Central Asian Society* (London), xli (3 and 4): July Oct. 1954, pp. 179–89.
100. Examples in Michael Rywkin, *Russia in Central Asia*, 1963, pp. 119 ff; and Allworth, *Uzbek literary politics*, pp. 33, 56, 112, 114, 118, 147, 229, 245, 249. For a diametrically opposed approach see G.L. Imamdzhanova, *Natsional'naya gosudarstvyennost' Uzbyekistana i yeyo falsifikatori*, 1977.
101. See H.S. Dinerstein, 'The Sovietization of Uzbekistan: the first generation, *Harvard Slavic Studies*, iv: 1957, pp. 499–513; G.Z. Imamdzhanova, passim.

102. Examples in Bennigsen and Quelquejay, *Les mouvements*, pp. 155, 167–71, 196–7. See also Tillett.
103. For examples see Hostler, *Turkism*, pp. 160–8; Olaf Caroe, *Soviet Empire: the Turks of Central Asia and Stalinism*, 2nd edn, chs 9 and 10.
104. For an instance of the Soviet propaganda counter-attack, cf. O.A. Sikhariyeva, *Islam v Uzbyekistanye*, 1960. See also *Central Asian Review*, XIV (2): 1966, p. 108.
105. For the recent situation, cf. Alexandre Bennigsen, 'Islam in the Soviet Union', *Soviet Jewish Affairs* (London), IX (2): 1979, pp. 3–14. Essentially the same article appeared, in French, in *L'Afrique et l'Asie Modernes* (Paris), 120: 1979, pp. 3–24.
106. See Mende, pp. 166–7.
107. Examples in Fernau, p. 253.
108. Cf. Richard Pipes, 'Muslims of Soviet Central Asia: trends and prospects', *Middle East Journal* (Washington, D.C.), IX (2): Spring 1955, pp. 147–62; IX (3): Summer 1955, pp. 295–308.
109. This is, essentially, for written work. For other activities, there is a vast literature, see, e.g., A. Bennigsen and C. Lemercier-Quelquejay, *Islam in the Soviet Union*, passim.
110. Prime Ministry State Institute of Statistics, *1979 Statistical Yearbook of Turkey*, 1979, p. 29, table 20.

2

PAN-TURKISM IN THE OTTOMAN
EMPIRE: GENESIS AND FLOWERING

While any attempt to periodise Pan-Turkism in the Ottoman Empire
and Turkey inevitably suffers from the shortcomings inherent in
trying to compress human thought into finite dates, it may still possibly be suggested that the initial stage of active Pan-Turkism in the
Ottoman Empire began early in the twentieth century and developed
swiftly, reaching one of its peaks during the final days and subsequent
dismemberment of the Empire. It was then manoeuvred to the
sidelines (although not obliterated) during the early years of the
Republic of Turkey, replaced by another ideology sponsored by this
new state. The rise of Pan-Turkism during the last decades of the
Ottoman Empire was brought about, on the one hand, by specially
propitious conditions, and by the impact of intellectuals from within
the Empire itself and from the ranks of the Outside Turks, on the
other hand.

During the latter part of the nineteenth century, as one aspect of
the self-questioning about their identity which was prevalent among
many Ottoman intellectuals, writing about nationalism — or at least
having a bearing on it — began to appear in both prose and poetry.
Perhaps the most obvious characteristic of these writings was that
they were mostly secularist-oriented, veering away from the assumption that Islam was a sufficient bond between the inhabitants of the
Empire, notwithstanding the fact that Pan-Islamism was an official
policy, actively initiated by Sultan Abdul Hamid II himself (and in
existence even before his reign[1]). For many people, the term 'Turk'
had a somewhat derogatory connotation at that time, hence certain
intellectuals opted for an 'Ottomanist' type of nationalism;[2] although
others favoured a 'Turkist' one. While Westernisation was making
headway, from the 1840s, particularly among the educated, debate
concerning the relative importance (and political advantages) of Pan-
Islam, Ottomanism and Turkism continued for many years[3] in various
journals in Turkey (such as *Türk Yurdu*, *İctihad*, *Mecmua-ı Ebuzziya*,[4]

and more particularly in *Turan*, published at first in Salonica and then, after its capture by the Greeks in 1912, in Istanbul).[5]

At first, even Turkism (which rehabilitated such terms as 'Turk' and 'Turkish' and gave them new dignity) was generally understood by intellectuals within the Empire to apply solely to the nationalism (in the broadest sense) of the Ottoman Turks; hence, it had been considered different from Pan-Turkism,[6] the ideology evolving among the Outside Turks at approximately the same time. This does not imply that Turks living within the Ottoman Empire were not affected by their kinsmen's sufferings — when the Russians advanced into Central Asia during the 1860s, for example, or when the Turks had to flee Bulgaria in the 1870s. The well-known story of Ali Suavi (1839–78), 'an enlightened theologian'[7] who attempted to incite Istanbul's population for the sake of Turkism (and was tried and hanged as a result), illustrates such concern.[8] In later years, Pan-Turkists considered him as a hero and a pioneer of their cause.[9] Nevertheless, there were only a few such incidents during the nineteenth century. Later, however, during the early twentieth century, Ottoman Turkish interest in the Outside Turks grew to such an extent that the terms 'Turkism' and 'Pan-Turkism' were often confused with one another and used interchangeably. Notwithstanding this confusion in terminology, the major importance of Turkist proponents, as far as this study is concerned, lies in their having familiarised an entire generation of readers in the Ottoman Empire with the problematics of nationalism.

Although the development of Turkism will not be examined in detail here, certain salient points, bearing upon our own topic, will be mentioned briefly,[10] of which the most relevant may be the evolution of Turcology in the Ottoman Empire. In the latter part of the nineteenth century, partly under European impact, there developed in the Empire much interest in Turkish studies.[11] Native scholars 'rediscovered' their past history,[12] the riches of their language and the beauty of their literature.[13] Although interpretations and conclusions obviously varied, many historians and linguists found their research was uncovering a past going back hundreds and even thousands of years, embracing other peoples of kindred origins. It was not merely coincidental that Necib Asım (1861–1935) translated Léon Cahun's *Introduction à l'histoire de l'Asie. Turcs et Mongols des origines à 1405* (published in 1896) from the French during the later years of Abdul Hamid's reign, adding several important sections written in a Turanian vein.[14] Asım glorified the Mongols and their exploits, declaring the Turks to be their descendants. This book was read by Nazım Bey, secretary-general of the Committee of Union and

Progress[15] and probably by other Committee leaders as well; it must have had some bearing on the Committee's subsequently opting for Pan-Turkism. Among certain Turks, this work and others served to increase pride in Turkish origins[16] and heritage (in contrast with Ottoman and Muslim roots) and foster a yet unknown sentiment of nationalism. In addition, such publications stimulated interest in kindred peoples, mostly those of Central Asia, whose history, language or literature had an affinity with those of the Turks themselves. Thus the bases for cultural Pan-Turkism were laid down, chiefly in the late nineteenth and early twentieth centuries — that is, at approximately the same time that Pan-Turk ideology was making headway among the Tatars and other Turkic groups in Russia. It is therefore hardly surprising to note that, in 1900, the writer Mehmet Necip addressed to the journal *Âhenk* (Harmony), edited by Mehmet Şeref, a long letter asserting that 'the ideas and sentiments of Turkism will unite the Turks.'[17]

In a no less direct way, the message of Pan-Turkism was — as a by-product of Turkish nationalism and at first developing simultaneously with it — [18] being increasingly propagated in the Ottoman Empire by other intellectuals. Turkish nationalists were first captivated by the Pan-Turk ideal as a by-product of their own linguistic, historical and literary studies, then came to appreciate Pan-Turkism for its own sake. For instance, Şemsettin Sami (1850–1904),[19] compiler of a well-known dictionary, *Kâmûs-i Türkî*, argued as early as 1880, in an article on the 'Lisan-ı Türkî-i Osmanî',[20] that there was no such language as 'Ottoman'. Considering Turkic linguistic boundaries, he concluded that 'the name "Turk" is an appellation for an important nation extending from the shores of the Adriatic Sea to the frontiers of China and the inner parts of Siberia.'[21] Sami concluded further that there exists a strong bond, in language and history, between the Turks in the Ottoman Empire and those living in a large area of Turkestan. This theory and others were frequently discussed in private (and then in public) meetings and in the press at that time. Passionate arguments were devoted to such issues as 'What is a nation?', 'What is race?' or 'Turkism and religion'.

There is a vast amount of literature on Turkism, with implications for Pan-Turkism, comprising not only scholarly works and intellectual exercises in periodical journals and books, but also various alternative modes of written expression. The works of Ömer Seyfeddin exemplify the multi-faceted approach adopted by many people in Turkey before the First World War. A dedicated writer in the field of Turkish nationalism, Seyfeddin, or Seyfettin (1884–1920),[22] was born to Caucasus Turk parents in a village near Balikesir, Turkey.

He was active in Pan-Turkist circles during his military service, then
turned to literature, writing poems and articles for *Genç Kalemler,
Halka Doğru, Türk Yurdu* and *Zeka,* and stories for *Yeni Mecmua,
Büyük Mecmua* and others. Just before the First World War, Seyfeddin published his *Millî tecrübelerden çıkartılmış amelî siyaset*[23] (Practical politics/policy deriving from national experiences). Seyfeddin's
thesis was that in the Ottoman Empire there lived at least 30 million
people, divided up as follows: 16 million Turks, 9 million Arabs, 1.5
million Greeks, 1.5 million Armenians, and fewer than 500,000 Jews.
The Turks did not have any other national home elsewhere, as the
Greeks did. Seyfeddin opted for the progress of both Turks and Arabs,
two groups of the same faith with no essential conflicts. As he saw
it, the Turks did not want to Turkify the minorities, but rather to let
them live as they wished, provided that the Turks themselves would
rule. He felt that the Turks ought to learn from past experience and
adopt only a Turkish/Islamic policy. Another of Seyfeddin's works,
Yarınki Turan devleti (Tomorrow's Turan State), published soon
afterwards,[24] is a vision of the future Turan, again based upon Turco-
Arab cooperation, but essentially hoping for an extensive Turkish
union, stretching from Anatolia to Turkestan.

Seyfeddin's approach, although systematic in nature (excepting
his statistics), most probably did not satisfy those Pan-Turkists who
considered Turkish unity, rather than Turkish-Arab cooperation, to
be a source of much desired power. Such views became even more
widespread following Arab opposition and revolt during the First
World War and separation from the Ottoman Empire in its final days.
The views of these Pan-Turkists were rather accurately reflected in
an anonymous pamphlet, entitled *Mekteb çocuklarında Türklük
mefkûresi* (The ideal of Pan-Turkism — for school-children),[25] in
which the author argues for Turk, rather than Arab, predominance in
the Ottoman Empire, citing as proof the excellence of the Turks and
their language, common to 100 million people.[26]

Among other nationalist writers of the same generation, the widest
appeal may have been generated by the renowned poet Mehmet Emin
Yurdakul (1869–1944).[27] A collection of his nationalist poems, which
had appeared in various magazines both before and during the First
World War, was published in 1918 under the thought-provoking title
Turana doğru (Towards Turan).[28] It strove to stir up the reader's
patriotic sentiments and simultaneously awaken his pride in his own
race. The poem 'Ey Türk uyan!' (Wake up, Oh Turk!) began as
follows: 'Oh, race of the Turks! Oh, children of iron and of fire! Oh,
the founders of a thousand homelands,[29] oh, the wearers of a thousand
crowns!'[30] The poem 'Irkımın türküsü' (Song of my race) began with

the words 'We are Turks of an Oghuz race.'[31] Several poems were dedicated to 'the dear women of Turan',[32] while another, entitled 'Han'ın sazına' (The *saz*[33] of the Khan) started with 'To my Tatar brethren'.[34]

The Pan-Turk connotations in Mehmet Emin's poetry are unmistakable, as they are in Halide Edib's novel *Yeni Turan* (The new Turan), first published in 1912, and translated several years later into German as *Das neue Turan: ein türkisches Frauenschicksal*.[35] The author (1884–1964) was renowned in both Turkish letters and public life (and one of the very first Turkish women to make her mark successfully in those fields). In this novel of the future, she envisaged the coming struggle between a political party, New Turan, vying for power with an Ottomanist party. The former would be all-Turkish in its strong-minded Turkish nationalism, preaching a return to the past with emphasis upon the original Turkish customs, foods and clothing. The most telling words in this context were most likely those of Ertuğrul Bey, one of the leaders of the New Turan party.[36] Defending the decentralisation advocated by his party, even at the risk of breaking up the Ottoman Empire, he declared: 'Do not fear that the loss of other nationalities spells our own downfall. There are between eighty and one hundred million people of Turkish origin in the world today. This steadily growing Turkish bloc is of excellent vitality, and will persist and increase . . . It should aim at using its power and energy, which gush forth from the depths of the people's spirit, to establish an everlasting nation.' Halide Edib's novel stated that Pan-Turkism — which she persisted in calling 'Turanism' — would be victorious, as it bore both social and political progress and would enable the Turks to decide their own destiny.

Scholarly studies, numerous articles and poems by Mehmet Emin and others, novels such as *Yeni Turan*, together with the military defeat of the Ottoman Empire in Libya and the Balkans — concurrent with plotting and revolt by various non-Turkish communities in the Empire, whose own nationalism was developing in autonomous or even secessionist patterns[37] — served to convince a growing number of thinking Turks of the merits of Pan-Turkism as a practical last resort. Such developments also aided in popularising both the concepts and terms of Pan-Turkism. A Turcologist of the calibre of Mehmet Fuad Köprülü (Köprülüzade) found it fashionable to use the title *Turan* for a school primer which he had written.[38] An equally patriotic Turk, Mehmet Ali Tevfik, did not hesitate to entitle his memoirs *Turanlının defteri* (The notebooks of a Turanian), first published in 1330/1914.[39] In this volume he recorded the thoughts of a nationalist more interested in the immediate future of Rumelia than in Pan-Turkism. However, he also displayed pride in the Turkish race, 'always indifferent to the bullets directed at it' — and described his visions of Turan.

This juxtaposition of Turkism and Pan-Turkism became increasingly evident during and immediately after the First World War. There was an obvious difference in scope between the two ideologies: the basic approach of many Turkists was that Pan-Turkism was just another ingredient in their overall approach to nationalism, while Pan-Turkists generally considered Turkism as a pillar of faith in their interpretation of a wider-embracing nationalist doctrine. On the other hand, both Turkists and Pan-Turkists had very much in common, especially in their attitudes towards the past and their optimism regarding the future. Some Turks, appraising the Ottoman Empire's political and military situation realistically, saw Pan-Turkism as perhaps the only feasible means of saving the Empire; those who dreamed of a greater future role for the Turks considered Pan-Turkism the key to success. Thus, an intellectual like Mehmet İzzet, writing in *Hayat*,[40] saw 'the role of the Turk' as 'domination' (*Hakimiyet rolü*), to be achieved only through an appeal to 'the race of the Turks'. Hence as an increasing number of Turks became familiar with the basic tenets of Turkism and Pan-Turkism, two past-oriented ideologies based upon a concept of a more comprehensive ethnic unity, there was no little confusion between interpretation of the two respective terms. Most probably the phonological similarity between *Türklük* (Turkism) and *Türkçülük* (Pan-Turkism) added to this confusion. The two terms were indeed used interchangeably during and after the First World War.[41] It is therefore hardly surprising that Celal Nuri (1877–1939), a noted Turkish journalist and intellectual,[42] writing in May 1918 (while the Ottoman Empire was still at war), confessed frankly that he saw little difference between Turkism and Pan-Turkism.[43]

One person largely responsible for this terminological mixup was a Jew from Serres, near Salonica, Moïse Cohen (in Turkish: Moiz Kohen), writing under the pseudonym Tekin Alp, which he later adopted as his own name. Although he was not solely responsible for the confusion,[44] he certainly was instrumental in causing it. As he was an ardent Pan-Turkist, he probably did so intentionally. One of the less-known, but influential, figures of Pan-Turkism, Tekin Alp (1883–1961) deserves more attention than he has received hitherto.[45]

He considered and adopted several ideologies (ranging from Ottomanism to Pan-Turkism to Kemalism) during his lifetime, and was a dedicated Pan-Turkist before and during the First World War. An able and prolific journalist, Tekin Alp fought for Pan-Turkism in his articles and books, some of which appeared, in addition to Turkish, in German, English and French, being among the very first to familiarise Europeans with details of the objectives and methods of Pan-Turkism. A 35-page article of his, 'Les Turcs à la recherche d'une âme nationale', was published in Paris in 1912.[46] It may well have been the first detailed study of the general situation in the Ottoman Empire, written from a Pan-Turk point of view, to appear in a non-specialised magazine in a European language. Of particular relevance to our current discussion is Tekin Alp's book *Türkler bu muharebede ne kazanabilirler?* (What can the Turks gain in this warfare?), first published in Turkish in 1914.[47] A more extensive version was translated into German[48] the following year, then into English two years afterwards.[49] In this book, he argued persuasively that the new Turkish nationalism had thrust aside both Pan-Islamism and Ottomanism.[50] Tekin Alp examined this type of nationalism, which he called 'Turkism', emphasising its Pan-Turk elements (which it indeed comprised then). He called upon the movement to become as irredentist as its successful Italian and Romanian counterparts;[51] this was apparently the first cogent public appeal for Turkish irredentism. Furthermore, he implied more than once that true, meaningful Turkism really meant Pan-Turkism,[52] virtually equating the two ideologies with one another.

While Tekin Alp may have been largely responsible for European perceptions of Pan-Turkism,[53] he was much less influential within the Ottoman Empire itself, where, after all, he was merely one of many political writers. Within the Empire, Pan-Turk propaganda — and close association of Turkism with Pan-Turkism — was promulgated to a great extent by the numerous Outside Turks who had emigrated to Turkey during the last decade before the start of the First World War, either of their own free will or as political refugees. Some came from Czarist Russia, where the regime was too absolutist, others from Ottoman territories lost in war. Not a few enrolled as students, chiefly in Istanbul, at Ottoman institutions of higher learning. Some added an ingredient to the intellectual ferment that must have made Istanbul an exciting place at that time. A number of active groups sprang up: e.g. associations of Tatar immigrants, of students originating from Russia, of students from the Crimea, and of the Bukharan Benevolent Society.[54] There were a large number of immigrants, particularly from the Czarist Empire; one source made the over-estimation that there were more Tatars in the Ottoman Empire than in the Crimea.[55] They were readily accepted by Ottoman Turks as equals; indeed, some of the more prominent immigrants, such as Gasprinsky, Akçura and Ağaoğlu, were coopted into Young Turk or

other circles.[56] Although not all Outside Turks were dedicated to
Pan-Turkism, many of the more prominent were so, and applied
themselves actively to propagating its principles among Turks in the
Ottoman Empire.

Among these Outside Turks, Ali Hüseyinzade (1864–1941), an
Azeri physician, politician and writer,[57] came to lecture at the Military
School of Medicine in Istanbul.[58] His poem *Turan* soon became a
manifesto for Pan-Turkists.[59] Yet another Azeri Turk, even more
indefatigable, was Ahmet Ağaoğlu (formerly Agayev, 1869–1939).[60]
Having rounded out his local education by studying in St. Petersburg
and Paris, Ağaoğlu devoted himself, on his return to Russia, to
journalistic activity, emphasising Islam rather than Pan-Turkism. The
greatest obstacle to Azeri harmony at the time was the Sunnite-Shiite
rivalry, which he strove to moderate and bridge over. Increased
Russian supervision of the press, on the one hand, and enthusiasm
over the 1908 Young Turk Revolution, on the other, induced Ağaoğlu
to emigrate to Turkey, where he became an Ottoman subject and was
soon appointed Inspector of Education in Istanbul.[61] In Turkey,
Ağaoğlu became an active polemicist for Pan-Turkism, ceaselessly
lauding its merits in such journals as *Türk Yurdu*, *İctihad*, *Halka
Doğru*, and others.[62] In a lengthy polemic with Süleyman Nazif,
former Governor of Trebizond, published in *Türk Yurdu*, Ağaoğlu
staunchly upheld the unity of Turkish civilisation throughout history,
and the oneness of Turks within and without the Ottoman Empire,
all of whom he considered brethren. Such views, expounded by the
likes of Hüseyinzade, Ağaoğlu, Akçura and other Outside Turks
living in the Ottoman Empire or in Europe, had a cumulative effect
upon many people in Turkey. This influence became even more
pronounced after 1908, once official Hamidian censorship was lifted,
as the Young Turk authorities tended to favour nationalist propaganda. Soon, local Turks joined the immigrants in such pro-Pan-Turk
magazines as the Istanbul *Tanin*, edited by Hüseyin Cahid.[63]

The plethora of Pan-Turk arguments, both written and oral, pre-
dictably displayed a certain divergence of opinions, as there was no
one supreme authority to lay down the doctrine of Pan-Turkism. The
above-noted confusion between Turkism and Pan-Turkism constitutes but one aspect of this. Pan-Turk strategy and tactics required
systematisation, but it was some time before the right person for the
job presented himself. During the first quarter of the twentieth century, several people attempted to analyse and systematise Pan-
Turkism; the first to attack the problem methodically was Ziya
Gökalp. He was virtually the only person who enjoyed sufficient
general appeal among the intellectuals in order to propagate Pan-

Turkism more widely. Gökalp has been considered by some of his admirers as the Grand Master of Pan-Turkism in Turkey. His renown was not necessarily a function of the quantity of his writings on Pan-Turkism, which comprised only several poems and articles,[64] and a few pages in his last book. Rather, it was earned through his attempt to analyse and systematise Turkish thought on Pan-Turkism and his prestige in rendering his interpretation sufficiently authoritative.[65]

Ziya Gökalp (1876–1924),[66] a native of Diyarbakir and essentially a self-taught man, had had a tumultuous career in the nationalist movement, first in the ranks of the Young Turks, where he was a member of the Central Council of the Committee of Union and Progress from 1908 to 1918,[67] then as a supporter of Mustafa Kemal and the movement he headed. He had also taught sociology at the University of Istanbul. Gökalp's main impact on society came about through his day-to-day contacts with people in Salonica and then in Istanbul, as well as through his impassioned poems, some of the most patriotic and Pan-Turk-oriented of which were later collected in his *Kızıl Elma* (Red Apple or Golden Apple), a term borrowed from old Turkish myths.[68] Of these poems, 'Turan', written in 1911, was a resounding call for Pan-Turkism: 'For the Turks, Fatherland means neither Turkey, nor Turkestan; Fatherland is a large and eternal country — Turan!'[69] Three years later, this romantic appeal acquired political connotations; when the First World War broke out, his poem 'Kızıl Destan' (Red epic) called for the destruction of Russia, in unequivocal Pan-Turk terms. No less influential were Gökalp's numerous articles in manifold journals, a part of which were later collected in several volumes.[70] As indicated earlier, only a few focused on Pan-Turkism, although many explored nationalism in general and Turkish nationalism in particular, touching on Pan-Turkism either directly or indirectly.[71] Employing sociological tools for cultural definitions, he seriously attempted to analyse the basic concepts of the relevant terms and their implication for Turkey. One example is his methodical discussion of 'nation',[72] in which he opted for the common bond of culture and sentiment (thus, presumably, including all Turks, near and far, in his own concept of nation). One year before his death, Gökalp summed up his own views on nationalism and Pan-Turkism in what is very probably his *magnum opus*, entitled *Türkçülüğün esasları* (The Principles of Turkism). Partly based on several of his previously-published articles, this work was first published in Ankara in 1923 and reprinted several times since. A meticulous English translation appeared forty-five years later.[73] In the context of our study, the main importance of this book lies in its serious attempt to systematise the discussion on Turkism

and Pan-Turkism; most scholars who dealt with the subject subsequently utilised Gökalp's work as a point of departure.

Examining various criteria for identifying and defining a nation,
Gökalp, as in several earlier articles of his, reached the conclusion
that 'a nation is not a racial or ethnic or geographic or political or
volitional group but one composed of individuals who share a common language, religion, morality, and aesthetics, that is to say, who
have received the same education'.[74] On the basis of this cultural
approach, he re-examined Turkism and other relevant terms.[75] Since
Turks could now be assumed to have only one language and one
culture, Gökalp perceived three levels among them: (*a*) the Turks in
the Republic of Turkey, a nation according to cultural and other
criteria; (*b*) the Oghuz Turks, referring also to the Turkmens of
Azerbayjan, Iran and Khwarizm who, although dispersed throughout
these three areas as well as within Turkey itself, essentially have one
common culture which is the same as that of the Turks in Turkey —
all these four forming Oghuzistan; and (*c*) more distant, Turkic-speaking peoples, such as the Yakuts, Kirghiz, Uzbeks, Kipchaks and
Tatars, possessed of a traditional linguistic and ethnic unity, having
affinity — but not identity — with the Turkish culture. All these form
Greater Turkestan, or Turan (in whose scope, Gökalp contended, there
was no place for such alien groups as Hungarians and Finns). According to Gökalp, only the first of these levels, 'Turkeyism', had
become reality, or the Republic of Turkey; the second, 'Oghuzism',
might be possible at some future date; while the third, 'Turanism'
with its 100 million people, remained a vision for the distant future.[76]

One has here minimum, intermediate, and maximum programmes
for the future Turan.[77] The approach of Gökalp to those three levels
indicated a certain retreat from his own earlier warm support of
Pan-Turk ideals, as his attitude to Pan-Turkism had become less
ardent since the defeat of the Ottoman Empire in 1918. This change
in outlook was probably a concession to the realities of the day, in
which the new Republic of Turkey was beginning to concentrate on
its own problems, shying away from the foreign ventures which had
plagued the late Ottoman Empire. However, the fact remained that
Gökalp by no means despaired of 'Oghuzism' and 'Turanism'. On
the contrary, he declared that Turan had been a reality during the
times of Mete, Genghiz and Tamerlane and that the national state of
Turkey, which nobody had considered feasible previously, did indeed
become a reality after all.[78] Pan-Turkist advocates thus concluded
that their vision too could well materialise, and many chose to continue the struggle.[79]

Meanwhile, following the Young Turk Revolution, Pan-Turkists began to organise in the Ottoman Empire. Before that time, such activity was patently dangerous, as Abdul Hamid II and his ubiquitous spies were suspicious of any form of organisation. After 1908, the new regime was more amenable to allow Pan-Turkist organisation, subsequently favouring it, in fact. Furthermore, the increasing presence of Outside Turk émigrés provided an added impetus to such organisation; several of the aforementioned societies they had set up in the Ottoman Empire could serve as natural nuclei for more specifically Pan-Turkist associations. The various organisations established at that time hardly ever had a clearly-enunciated Pan-Turkist character. Rather, they were scholarly or nationalist groupings which adopted and maintained Pan-Turk policies, largely thanks to the central role played by certain Pan-Turkists amongst them.

The first of these associations, set up in Istanbul in December 1908, soon after the Young Turk Revolution, was *Türk Derneği* (The Association of Turks).[80] Its statutes (*Türk derneği nizamnamesi*) unequivocally stated that the Association intended to concentrate on scholarship alone[81] — obviously alluding to Turcology and implying that politics would be avoided. The statutes went on to specify the Turkish studies envisaged: to study and impart all the written works and activities, past and present, of the Turkish peoples in archaeology, history, linguistics, literature, ethnography, ethnology, sociology, civilisation, and the old and new geography of Turkish lands. It is self-evident that nationalism and Pan-Turkism were implied in the above statutes, hardly surprising in that the Association's founders included such well-known Pan-Turkists as the above-mentioned Necib Asım and Yusuf Akçura (the latter presided over the Association's first meeting), as well as kindred souls such as Veled Çelebi,[82] Rıza Tevfik, Emrullah Efendi,[83] Bursalı Tahir,[84] Ahmet Midhat,[85] Fuad Raif, and Ahmet Ferit. As the Association's avowed aims were academic, non-Turks too were coopted into it; among the founders was an Armenian, Agop Boyacıyan. In addition, several foreign scholars joined in and a Hungarian section was set up in Budapest. The Turks who adhered to the Turkish membership rolls of *Türk Derneği* soon included such committed Pan-Turkists as İsmail Gasprinsky, Ahmet Ağaoğlu, Ali Hüseyinzade, Mehmet Emin Yurdakul, Mehmed Fuad Köprülü[86] and Fuad Sabit.[87] The Association published a monthly, *Türk Derneği* of which seven issues appeared;[88] it reported the proceedings of meetings and debates, and published papers by local and foreign contributors. Subjects considered included: Turkish and Turkic languages, the proverbs of the Kazan Turks, the handicrafts of the Turkmens, the history of Tatar literature, and the discovery of Turkish antiquities. In addition to the

Association's headquarters in Istanbul, branches were set up in Rusçuk, Izmir, Kastamonu, and even in Budapest. By the time it had disbanded in 1911–12 (chiefly due to some of its most active members leaving Istanbul), the Association had a total of sixty-three dues-paying members.[89] Although *Türk Derneği* was not a political society, but rather a small elitist group of intellectuals, its meetings and journal had definite undertones of cultural Pan-Turkism.

These characteristics were carried over into another society, set up in the summer of 1913, which was in more than one way a sequel to it. Named *Türk Bilgi Derneği* (Association for Turkish Knowledge), it intended to serve as an Academy of Arts and Sciences, with semi-official status under the patronage of the Young Turks' Committee of Union and Progress and subsidised by the state.[90] It established sections, as in other Academies, and published a scholarly journal, *Bilgi Mecmuası* (Journal of Knowledge), of which six issues appeared in Istanbul. This journal[91] and other sources not only describe the scholarly activities of the founders and members of this association, but also reveal that several active Pan-Turkists moved over from the *Türk Derneği* to it. The President of *Türk Bilgi Derneği* was Emrullah Efendi, while the Chairman of the Turcology section was Necib Asım and its members, at various times, were Yusuf Akçura, Ahmet Ağaoğlu, Ömer Seyfeddin, Mehmed Fuad Köprülü and others noted for Pan-Turkist activities and interests. The association appears to have petered out during the time of the First World War, as some of its members devoted their energies to other societies.

In August 1911, an association called *Türk Yurdu* (The homeland of the Turks) was founded in Istanbul. *Türk Yurdu* or *Türk Talebe Yurdu* (*Le Foyer des Étudiants Turcs*)[92] was also the name of a separate organisation of Turkish students abroad — mainly in Switzerland, France and Germany — which, since it included a large proportion of Outside Turks among its hundreds of members,[93] had definite Pan-Turk tendencies.[94] The students' organisation appears to have continued to exist throughout the years of the First World War; in 1919 it issued a patriotic pamphlet defending the cause of Turkey.[95] Other publications of the *Türk Yurdu* organisation and the affiliate it established, the Turkish Congress at Lausanne, included *Greek atrocities in the Vilayet of Smyrna* and *Smyrna au point de vue économique, géographique etc.*, as well as the English-language *Turkey: a Monthly Organ of the Turkish Congress at Lausanne*,[96] which supported both Mustafa Kemal's struggle and the independence of the Crimea and of Russian Azerbayjan — all in a Pan-Turk spirit.

The Istanbul *Türk Yurdu* Association comprised more mature persons, chiefly intellectuals, with a fair sprinkling of those noted for

Pan-Turk sympathies, such as Mehmet Emin Yurdakul, Yusuf Akçura, Ahmet Ağaoğlu, Ali Hüseyinzade, Ali Muhtar[97] and others.[98] Later on, Ziya Gökalp was also coopted. The Association's objectives were defined as raising the cultural level of the Turks, but a no less important aim was to set up a meeting-ground for nationalists (and Pan-Turkists) to join forces, a feat which the *Türk Derneği* had failed to achieve.[99] The association petered out, several months after its foundation, when members joined the *Türk Ocağı* (see below). Its most durable contribution was most probably its journal, *Türk Yurdu*, which began publication late in 1911 and (along with its supplement *Halka Doğru*) was the most important organ of Pan-Turkism in the Ottoman Empire for several years. This journal and its editor, Yusuf Akçura, will be dealt with in greater detail below.

The most durable and important of all organisations with Pan-Turk proclivities of those days was the *Türk Ocağı* (Hearth of the Turks), first set up in June 1911 by medical and other students as a semi-secret club. Mehmet Emin Yurdakul, Ahmet Ferit, Ahmet Ağaoğlu, Fuat Sabit, Yusuf Akçura and Mehmet Ali Tevfik[100] were invited to join and direct the organisation.[101] These personalities provided considerable élan; by March 1912 they had reorganized the club's structure and launched it on the road towards becoming a country wide affiliation of clubs,[102] with the journal *Türk Yurdu* as its organ. Its growth was encouraged by several of the Young Turk leaders who were quick to realise its potential; these came to lecture before it and offered generous donations.[103] Most probably, those members of the Committee of Union and Progress who admired German organisation — Enver, in particular — decided to improve *Türk Ocağı* organisationally and use it politically.[104] Other public figures soon joined, making it a broader society and giving it even more prestige. Among these were Ziya Gökalp and Halide Edib. The former provided a sort of personal link with the Committee of Union and Progress; the latter succeeded in passing a resolution making women eligible for membership.

The objectives of the *Türk Ocağı* were defined, in its statutes, as 'Working for the national education of the Turkish people and raising its intellectual, social and economic level, for the perfection of the Turkish language and race'.[105] Another clause insisted that the association keep out of party politics.[106] It did succeed in doing so for a time, largely directing itself towards youth activities, opening additional branches and recruiting new members. *Türk Ocağı* strove to educate the people in a nationalist spirit and teach them to esteem their cultural heritage. It set up clubs, held evening courses and other classes, provided free lectures and arranged literary and artistic soirées; published books and magazines; and assisted needy students with lodgings and medical care. Social activities and sports were also instituted at a later date.[107] One of its least heralded acts was to welcome to Turkey, and assist, refugees of Turkic origin from Russia, particularly after the 1917 Revolution; refugees were greeted warmly by the President of the *Türk Ocağı*, Hamdullah Suphi Tanrıöver (1886–1966),[108] on various occasions.[109] An even less commonly-known fact is that agents from among the most trusted members of this association were despatched to mobilise support for Pan-Turkism during the First World War.[110] Soon there were 'hearths' in every city, town and major village, as well as in many schools and public organisations throughout the Empire. In 1914 the association had sixteen hearths in the Ottoman Empire, with a total membership of over 3,000. The Istanbul hearth, evidently the largest, comprised more than 1,800 members, including about 1,600 students and former students at institutions of higher learning, several of whom were physicians. In the 1920s, membership reached about 30,000.[111]

A parallel (and closely connected) organisation was the association of *İzci*, or boy scouts,[112] under the patronage of Enver himself. A British intelligence report describes them as follows:[113]

The members of this organization received a military training, fitting them for eventual employment as N.C.O.'s. Their badges, scout-names and titles were purely Turkish and pre-Islamic. Ali and Mehmed became Aksonkor and Timur-tash. The 'white wolf', which gave birth to Oghoz, the legendary ancestor of the Turkish people, figured, in spite of the Islamic prohibition, on standards of the İzcis, who were led by their Başbuğ (Emir),[114] and marshalled by Ortabeys and Oymakbeys; said prayers not to Allah, but to Tanrı; were taught to regard all Turanians as their brethren; and cheered, not the Khalif or Padishah, but the 'Hakon' of the Turks.

Türk Ocağı was essentially an association for nationalist culture, not for Pan-Turk propaganda. However, from the very start it was earmarked for Turks only (even other Muslims were not accepted); personalities such as Gökalp, Akçura and others lectured to members or contributed to the *Türk Yurdu* (a journal which many members read). This ensured that a sizable dose of Pan-Turkism filtered through to the *Türk Ocağı* membership, well into the 1920s (the clubs were closed down in 1931, because of changes in government policies, as indicated below).[115] During that period, this association and its journal largely succeeded in absorbing Pan-Turkism into the nationalist doctrine of Turkism.[116] As Ziya Gökalp phrased it, 'All Turkists . . . met and worked together in the *Türk Yurdu* and *Türk Ocağı* ambience.[117]

It has probably been noticed that persons known for their Pan-Turk leanings often belonged to several of the above societies, sometimes simultaneously. In the late Ottoman Empire, it was not uncommon for people to join more than one organisation, in order to open up new avenues for intellectual activity or political participation — in this case, better to serve the cause of Pan-Turkism. Such multi-faceted activity is best exemplified by Yusuf Akçura, or Akçuraoğlu (1876–1935),[118] previously mentioned[119] as a fighter for Pan-Turkism among the Tatars of the Czarist Empire, both in his own journal *Kazan Muhbiri* and several others. Educated in Russia, Istanbul and the École des Sciences Politiques in Paris, he participated in various congresses of Russia's Turkic and Muslim groups, often playing a leading role. We have had an occasion to discuss[120] his attempt in 1904 to systematise Pan-Turkism, by weighing it against Ottomanism and Pan-Islamism.[121] Having left Russia in 1908, he was active before and during the First World War in various organisations of Outside Turks, located in Western Europe.[122] However, it was mainly in the Ottoman Empire that his Pan-Turkist activity, in his more mature years, left a strong imprint on this movement. There was hardly a nationalist organisation sympathetic to Pan-Turkism (including those mentioned above), of which he was not one of the founders, or at least a very active member;[123] there was hardly a periodical of importance to which he did not contribute. His most lasting contribution to the cause of Pan-Turkism may well have been the weekly (for a while, fortnightly) he edited from 1911, *Türk Yurdu*, which made him so famous that in 1913 the prestigious Orientalist periodical, *Revue du Monde Musulman*, of Paris, declared that 'Akçura's renown is equal to that of Jamāl al-Dīn al-Afghānī',[124] the famed Islamist thinker and fighter.

A dedicated Pan-Turkist throughout his life, Yusuf Akçura left Russia for Turkey in 1908 — both because he faced probable arrest in his country of origin and because of his hopes for the new Turkish regime. He began teaching Turkish political history at the Darülfünün and other institutions of higher learning in Istanbul, and was an indefatigable organiser, writer and lecturer. As indicated above, he was a founder or at least a very active member in such societies as *Türk Derneği, Türk Bilgi Derneği, Türk Yurdu,* and *Türk Ocağı* and others, thereby furthering the cause of Pan-Turkism. In addition to writing a number of books and articles,[125] he contributed to many literary journals and other periodicals. Akçura's outstanding efforts during his six-year term[126] as editor of *Türk Yurdu* made that periodical not only a leading journal of Pan-Turk propaganda[127] but also gave it a prestige which led some of the foremost Turkish intellectuals of the time to contribute and which reached a readership of thousands.[128] As the main forum for Pan-Turkists, *Türk Yurdu* overshadowed the other periodicals with Pan-Turk leanings, published in Istanbul, such as the weekly *Büyük Duygu* (The great sentiment) in

1913;[129] in the provinces, e.g. *Türk İli, Turan, Türk Dili* — the last published in Macedonia;[130] — and in the Czarist Empire. Many people too must have read *Türk Yurdu's* literary supplement, *Halka Doğru* (Towards the People), also partly committed to Pan-Turkism, and edited by a writer close to Pan-Turkist circles, Celal Sahir (1883–1935). *Halka Doğru* appeared in Istanbul as a weekly from 11 April 1329/1913.[131] Several days after *Halka Doğru* closed down, in April 1914, Celal Sahir started editing another weekly supplement to *Türk Yurdu*. Entitled *Türk Sözü* (The word of the Turks), it appeared in Istanbul from 13 April 1330/1914.[132] Its banner was 'To go to the people and to work for the people'.[133] Special emphasis was laid in such issues on reports from, and articles about, the 'World of the Turks',[134] in a Pan-Turk spirit. Contributors to *Türk Yurdu* and to its supplements comprised not only such dedicated Pan-Turkists as Akçura, Ziya Gökalp, Ömer Seyfeddin, Mehmet Emin Yurdakul, Ahmet Ağaoğlu, Ali Hüseyinzade, Ali Canip (1887–1967), Mehmed Fuad Köprülü and Mehmet Ali Tevfik, but such personalities as Halide Edib — all of whom must have increased the appeal of these journals. Lastly, Akçura lectured frequently at scholarly conventions, literary gatherings and popular meetings on historical topics or those related to Turkish civilisation, injecting Pan-Turkism into his speeches whenever possible.

On its foundation, the *Türk Yurdu* weekly set itself in its platform several objectives, suggested by Akçura, as follows:[135] to mould the journal, as to both language and subject-matter, in such a way as to ensure maximum readership within the Turkish race; create an ideal acceptable to all the Turks; select topics which, rather than being political, would serve to enrich the knowledge of the Turks and raise their morale; strive to acquaint all members of the Turkish race with events and intellectual trends in the world of the Turks, particularly those which would encourage them to love and esteem one another; defend the political and economic interests of the Turkish elements in the Ottoman Empire, without taking sides in the inter-party struggle; fight the lack of ideals and pessimism, striving for the progress and strengthening of the Turkish national spirit among the Ottoman Turks; and defend the interests of the world of the Turks as a basic principle in the conduct of foreign affairs. These objectives were indeed pursued by the journal, focusing on an explicit advocacy of Pan-Turkism — moderate at first, but more aggressive in subsequent years,[136] passing from a call for solidarity to an appeal for action.

This primacy of the interests of 'the race of the Turks' and 'the world of the Turks' obviously constituted Akçura's own conception of Pan-Turkism and Pan-Turk policy, as elaborated in his books,

articles and lectures. His vision of Pan-Turkism considered the world
of the Turks as one indivisible entity, with evident signs of both
cultural ties (language, history, customs) and material bonds (blood,
race).[137] The term 'Turk' referred to all those of Turkic origin, i.e.,
the Tatars, Azeris, Kirghiz, Yakuts and others.[138] To all these, Akçura
applied the term of 'nation' (*millet*) and argued persuasively for joint
action in a common cause. His own articles and others appearing in
Türk Yurdu constantly and insistently high-lighted the problems and
hopes of the Outside Turks, on the one hand, and on the other,
continued to fight rival ideologies — such as Pan-Islamism and
Ottomanism — which could endanger and weaken a common Pan-
Turkist effort.[139] Akçura's greatest contribution to the Pan-Turkist
struggle, in addition to his preaching cultural Pan-Turkism, was perhaps his insistence on the movement's political role, centred in the
Ottoman Empire — with Russia and Pan-Slavism as its past and
future enemies. Thanks to him, for most Pan-Turkists in his time and
later, both cultural and political Pan-Turkism became the obvious
platforms to fight for, as this combination provided the only plan of
action which held promise of success.[140]

The discourses and arguments about Pan-Turkism during the last
years of the Ottoman Empire were obviously not conducted in a
vacuum. Among the Outside Turks in Czarist Russia, Pan-Turkism
remained largely intellectual, as the state opposed it and the Turkic
peoples did not organise well enough until it was too late. In the late
Ottoman Empire, however, Pan-Turkism was well-regarded by an
important part of the state's political leadership; consequently, the
movement organised more meaningfully under the favourable conditions created.

As indicated above, Pan-Turkism was only one of several
ideologies propounded in that market-place of ideas which was the
Ottoman Empire in its last generation. Pan-Turkism's historic chance
arrived shortly before and during the First World War, when it was
adopted as a guiding principle of state policy by an influential group
among the Young Turks who were determining the Empire's destiny.
The Young Turks' main political organisation, the Committee of
Union and Progress,[141] had in fact displayed some written commitment (as part of their active propaganda campaign)[142] to the problems
of Turkic groups in the Caucasus, Crimea and Azerbayjan.[143] In
1906–7, the Committee again voiced its concern over the fate of these
groups,[144] continuing to do so throughout their rule of the Empire.[145]
At this point, it should be emphasised that at no time did Pan-Turkism
completely replace other well-established state ideologies or *Weltan-
schauungen* within the Committee; rather, Pan-Turkism simply over-

shadowed alternative theories for a time and provided guidelines for policy-making. Thus, for example, the trend towards Westernisation (chiefly in terms of material culture), initiated during the nineteenth century, was pursued further. The crucial problem facing the new regime however concerned their attitude towards nationalism.[146]

The Committee of Union and Progress could hardly adopt as their central policy the Pan-Islamism cherished and nurtured by their arch-enemy, the Sultan Abdul Hamid II.[147] On the other hand, they must have perceived that the achievements of Pan-Islamism were rather modest;[148] moreover, they could never pretend to attain the authority and prestige of the Sultan-Caliph among Muslims. There is also substantial doubt as to the devoutness in Islam of many of the Young Turks; but, nevertheless, their leaders generally appear to have been wary of openly disclaiming Islam, so as not unnecessarily to antagonise Muslims in the Ottoman Empire. In addition, Islam could be used as political blackmail against certain Powers, particularly Great Britain.[149] Therefore, the Young Turks continued to engage the activities of the Sultan's agents — within the Empire as well as among foreign Muslim communities — not infrequently employing Islam as a cover-up for other activities.[150]

The first choice of the Young Turk leadership for a policy which would downgrade Pan-Islamism[151] was Ottomanism; namely, a concerted effort to induce all the Empire's inhabitants to feel that they were citizens, equal in their rights and obligations, and faithful and dedicated to their *vatan* (Fatherland), a term often employed by official circles after the 1908 Young Turk Revolution. This was to be achieved by amalgamating all peoples in the Empire under a centralised Turk leadership.[152] It is hardly surprising, therefore, that the Turkish elites were wary of losing their special standing, while non-Turks in the Ottoman Empire,[153] correctly assuming that they were to be Turkified, first demurred[154] and then loudly protested.[155] The strong policy of Turkification worried even some of the oldest friends of the Ottoman Empire, such as Frederic Harrison, a public figure in Great Britain and a former President of the Eastern Question Association; on 17 July 1911, he sent a letter to the Turkish press, warning that this policy was alienating Turkey's staunchest supporters abroad.[156]

Only after its disappointment with Ottomanism did the Young Turk leadership turn more definitely to Pan-Turkism, although they did not discard Ottomanism entirely and continued the policy of Turkification.[157] Rather, Ottomanism and Pan-Islamism[158] were downgraded and applied only intermittently, whenever occasion demanded.[159] This situation continued even while the Ottoman Minister for Foreign Affairs was assuring foreign diplomats that his Government had decided to abandon all Islamic propaganda absolutely.[160] In practice, the attitudes of rank-and-file members of the Committee of Union and Progress towards Islam — and Pan-Islamism — varied considerably.[161] However, the top leadership was pragmatic in its approach. Sir Harry Luke described the situation well:

He[162] and his colleagues envisaged the three policies being pursued simultaneously and side by side, each one being emphasized in whatever place, at whatever time, it was the most appropriate policy to apply. Ottomanism continued to be the keynote of internal politics; Turkish nationalism, the keynote of relations with the Tatars of Russia, some of whom were beginning to manifest sentiments of sympathy with their cousins in Turkey in their time of trouble; Pan-Islam, that of relations with the Arabs and other non-Turkish Moslems within the Empire and of the Moslem peoples of North Africa and elsewhere outside it.[163]

There were evidently contradictory elements in such multi-faceted propaganda, impressing some people and alienating others at the same time. One example of how this liability was turned into an asset dates from 1910, when a pamphlet in Turkish by Sheikh Muriddin Urusi (pseudonym of Ahmet Hilmi) was printed and distributed in Turkey and abroad, in tens of thousands of copies — a figure which presupposes government subsidies and management.[164] The pamphlet is a rousing address calling on all Muslims to stand together, especially those of Bukhara, Kashgar, India, Iran, China, Kazan, Crimea and the Caucasus;[165] it thus constituted an appeal to Turkic groups there, as a part of a more general call on all Muslims, to stand together. Simultaneously, Muslim Turks abroad, e.g. from Turkestan, were called upon to visit Istanbul — and did so.[166] Later, in 1913, during the Balkan wars, support was drummed up among Muslims in India and elsewhere to impress on the British Government that they had espoused the Turkish cause as their own and endorsed it.[167]

As public controversy continued regarding the relative merits of the three ideologies,[168] it became increasingly clear that Pan-Turkism was in the ascendant. Earlier, Abdul Hamid II's Pan-Islamism had hardly deterred Muslim subjects of his — such as the Arabs or the Albanians — from striving to achieve their national aspirations at the Empire's expense; Pan-Islamism had also failed to recruit much Muslim support abroad. The Young Turks, too, soon found out that Ottomanist propaganda barely hindered the nationalist/separatist activities and aspirations of the above-mentioned groups, or those of the Bulgarians, Serbs, Greeks, Armenians and others. Loyalties to Islam and the Ottoman Empire had failed to check ethnic nationalism.

The repeated defeats of the Ottoman Empire in the Libyan and Balkan wars further aroused patriotic feelings among Turks in the Empire and abroad.

The obvious response to separatist nationalism and centrifugal tendencies was a grand design for Turkish nationalism.[169] Goaded on by this situation, several of the Young Turk leaders began to support increasingly the Pan-Turk option, as a way to offset the Empire's African and European losses by intense Turkification at home as well as a purposeful orientation towards the Turkic groups in Asia,[170] which ultimately could also assist the recovery of recently lost territories. A characteristic expression of these sentiments was voiced by Halil Bey, an influential member of the Committee of Union and Progress; on assuming the presidency of the newly-elected Ottoman Chamber on 19 May 1914, he delivered an eloquently irredentist speech:

I address myself, from this high pulpit, to my nation. I recommend that it does not forget Salonika, the cradle of liberty and of the Constitution, green Monastir, Kosova, Scutari of Albania, Janina and the whole of beautiful Rumelia. I ask our teachers, journalists, poets and all our intellectuals to remind continuously our present generation and the future ones, via their lessons, writings and moral influence, that beyond the frontiers there are brethren to be liberated and bits of the Fatherland to be redeemed. This is the only way to avoid repeating the errors which have brought about our defeats and calamities.[171]

Earlier, several resolutions had been passed at the annual conventions of the Committee of Union and Progress, promoting the Turkish language for assimilation of non-Turks in the Empire and encouraging the immigration to Turkey by Turkic groups in the Caucasus and Turkestan.[172] Although deliberations were held *in camera* and many resolutions remained secret, British and French consular agents in Salonica and elsewhere acquired sufficient information to provide a fairly clear picture of convention proceedings. In the second annual convention, which met in Salonica in November 1910, it was decided that the Turkish language be employed in all schools throughout the Empire, aiming at denationalisation of all non-Turkish communities and instilling of patriotism among the Turks. Other resolutions called for encouragement of immigration to the Empire by Turks and other Muslims from abroad,[173] particularly from the lost provinces of Bosnia and Herzegovina, to be settled near the railway lines.[174] Pan-Islamic propaganda was to be pursued on two levels — the religious and the nationalist[175] (the latter implying Pan-Turkism).

The secret decisions of the third annual convention of the Committee of Union and Progress, which met in Salonica during September-October 1911, were reportedly even more extreme: universal advancement of the Turkish language; organisation of the Turks in Bulgaria, Romania, Bosnia and Herzegovina, putting them in contact with one another and with the Committee of Union and Progress; forming branches of the Committee[176] in all countries inhabited by Muslims, especially Russia and Iran; and institution of an annual gathering of delegates from all Muslim countries in Istanbul.[177] Intensification of Pan-Turk trends in the ruling circles at that time may well have been brought about, at least partly, by the in-penetration of quite a few of the leading Pan-Turkist immigrants, such as Ali Hüseyinzade, who became a member of the Central Council of the Committee of Union and Progress in 1911.[178]

Orientation towards Muslim and Turkic kindred groups was reaffirmed as official policy at the September-October 1913 annual convention of the Committee of Union and Progress.[179] Since then and during the First World War, the cultural and economic policy of Turkification throughout the Empire was to be intensified even further;[180] and the use of Pan-Turkism as a political tool[181] was followed without any letup, internally and externally — although, at times, still cloaked in the guise of Pan-Islamism (in India, for instance[182]). Yet another example of the scope of the movement's activities is provided by Pan-Turk interest in Cyprus at that time. In 1914, a Young Turk Party was active in British-governed Cyprus, siding with the Ottoman Empire and Germany against Great Britain.[183] Three years later, several Turkish Cypriots became active Young Turk sympathisers and propagandists.[184] In addition, Turkish Cypriot members of the Legislative Council in Cyprus, whose attempts to have the island reunited with the Ottoman Empire had formerly been brief and sporadic, began raising their demands more insistently.[185]

Belief in the ethnic identity of Ottoman and Eastern Turks — and support for self-determination of the latter — was among the main principles adopted by Pan-Turkists at that time. Shortly before and during the First World War, about half the people of Turkish stock were believed to be under Czarist domination.[186] Pan-Turkism thus played a substantial role in both Ottoman and German propaganda campaigns against Russia. During those years, Pan-Turk sentiments appeared not only in journals such as *Tasvir-i Efkâr* and *Sabah*, or in government organs, such as *Tanin*, but also in Opposition newspapers, including *Ikdam* and *Zaman*.[187] Many of the people to whom these campaigns were directed were Muslims; hence, Pan-Turk propaganda often continued to be coloured by an Islamic (and, sometimes, Pan-Islamic) element.

Propaganda and organisational activity abroad were evidently carried out by special agents. Information available on this subject is scarce and less reliable than data pertaining to the Ottoman Empire itself. In any event, however, it appears that by 1911 the Committee of Union and Progress had succeeded in establishing several branches in the Caucasus and in Turkestan, seven of them reportedly among the Tatars. A secret resolution of the Committee's third annual convention in 1911 was aimed at increasing the number of branches[188] and despatching more agents to the Muslims of Turkestan, Iran, India, the Caucasus and Egypt.[189] Some of these agents, of course, had already been active somewhat earlier, spreading Pan-Islamic, or Pan-Turk, propaganda (or both). For instance, early in 1910 Enver Bey, Ottoman Consul-General in Tabriz, was reported to be plotting with the Karadağ Khans in Azerbayjan, offering them Turkish protection through the good offices of Cemil Bey, a member of the Committee of Union and Progress.[190] According to more detailed reports, recorded in early 1911 by the British Vice-Consul at Van, Captain L. Molyneux-Seel, three 'Inspectors' — Kara Bey, Hilmi Bey and Abdül Kader — sent by the Committee of Union and Progress, arrived at Van towards the end of 1910. All three were emissaries of a secret organisation headed by Talat himself, who had issued a special passport to their leader, Kara, supplying them with ample means from a secret fund. Kara, an associate of Ahmet Ağaoğlu, seemed to have been a man of some renown. From his conversations with Kara and other sources, Molyneux-Seel learned that these three were acting in the interests of Pan-Islamism, although details of their activities related just as much to Pan-Turkism as well. Kara had spoken at length of the Ottoman Empire's need for a strong army and strong Pan-Islamic bonds. Firearms and ammunition, acquired in Germany, were being forwarded to Trebizond and thence via Erzerum and Beyazit to Tabriz, where they were divided up and despatched by three separate routes, two of which led to Turkestan and the third, via Seistan, to Afghanistan and the Indian frontier. Emissaries travelled to India via Tehran and Seistan, returning via Kashmir and Russian Turkestan.[191] Other emissaries were despatched at about the same time to Chinese Turkestan in order to spread Pan-Turk and Pan-Islamic propaganda there.[192] Still others were sent by the Committee of Union and Progress to Albania and Afghanistan (where there was a sizable minority of Turkic origin). In 1910, three agents, all of them army officers, were sent to Afghanistan to preach Pan-Turkism, and by 1913 their number had increased to fifteen. Several other agents were propagating the Ottoman Turkish language in Russian Azerbayjan and among the Volga Tatars,[193] probably combining this effect with ideological indoctrination. Concurrently, Ottoman embassies and consulates were ordered to take part in this propaganda campaign.[194]

The main thrust of officially-inspired Pan-Islamic and Pan-Turk propaganda was directed against Russia, however — a fact which Russian authorities well knew.[195] Its only logical follow-up was an effort to break down the Czarist Empire, a joint objective of both the Ottoman Empire and Germany.[196] Indeed, the above-mentioned Halide Edib, a highly knowledgeable observer at that time, suspected that Germany had signed the 1914 secret treaty with the Ottoman Empire not so much because it counted on Turkey's military capabilities as because of the likely effects of Pan-Islamism and Pan-Turkism in hampering the Allies' war effort.[197] Of course, not all Committee of Union and Progress leaders took Pan-Turkism seriously (they often differed on various issues[198]); some considered it fanciful and impracticable. Cemal Pasha, for example, inclined towards intensifying Turkification and relying on the Turks of the Ottoman Empire:

Young Turkey realized that among the various Ottoman elements which were struggling for the advancement of their respective nationalities the Turks alone were isolated . . . so they, too, began to work for a great national revival in knowledge, education and virtue. The Committee of Union and Progress had no right to put any obstacle in their way . . . Speaking for myself, I am primarily an Ottoman, but I do not forget that I am a Turk, and nothing can shake my belief that the Turkish race is the foundation stone of the Ottoman Empire . . . in its origins the Ottoman Empire is a Turkish creation.[199]

Even, so, Cemal went along with his colleagues in supporting Pan-Turkism. It seems that all three policy-makers — Enver, Talat and Cemal[200] — eventually perceived the advantages of Pan-Turkism under those circumstances.[201] Of these, Enver (1881–1922) had the most definite ideas in favour of Pan-Turkism and its crucial future role[202] as an expansionist policy[203] and he was the one largely responsible for its adoption as a state policy.[204]

Enver's passion for Pan-Turkism as a political and military ideal is corroborated by an unexpected and independent source, the renowned French writer André Malraux. In *Les Noyers de l'Altenburg*, published in 1948, Malraux devoted a long chapter to the activities of his father, an Alsatian who had served for six years in the German Embassy in Istanbul and who had become one of Enver's closest and most trusted advisers.[205] As Malraux tells it, his father had become obsessed with the idea of Turan and had collaborated closely with Enver in the matter. Even before the war in Libya, Enver had coopted Muslim activists from among the Turkic groups in the Czarist Empire into the Young Turk circles. Even at that time, Enver envisaged a union of all Turkic peoples from Edirne (Adrianople) to the Chinese oases along the road of the silk-trade. He allegedly was unconcerned

about Greece and Serbia having achieved their independence, so long
as a substitute empire, with its capital in Samarkand, could be set up.
As soon as peace had been secured in the Balkans, Enver's emissaries
contacted the Emirs of Bukhara and Afghanistan, as well as the Khans
of Russian Turkestan. The older Malraux was indeed despatched to
Afghanistan for this very purpose. He returned very much in doubt
about the real existence of Turan; but Enver, for whom Turan had
become an *idée fixe*, would not listen to him.

While a part of the above account may be fanciful — especially
regarding his dream about Samarkand — all available evidence
indicates that Enver did take certain practical steps to bring about the
materialisation of Pan-Turkism. The above Tekin Alp, who had
moved from Salonica to Istanbul in 1912 and maintained close connections with Young Turk circles, reported that Enver had established
relations with such well-known Outside Turk activists as İsmail
Gasprinsky, Fatih Kerimof and Arif Kerimof.[206] It is even more
certain that, shortly before the outbreak of the First World War, Enver
set up the *Teşkilât-ı mahsusa* (Special organisation), a secret service
whose agents, all volunteer officers, carried out Pan-Turk and Pan-
Islamic propaganda beyond the Ottoman frontiers, chiefly among
Turkic groups.[207] The organisation remained under Enver's control
until the end of the First World War.[208] It probably remained separate
from, and in competition with, Talat's net of agents. A number of the
former may have been among the agents carrying on Pan-Turk
propaganda before the First World War, as indicated above.[209] During
the war, many were sent to Iran, Afghanistan, India and elsewhere.[210]
Russian sources indicated that they criss-crossed Transcaucasia.[211]

The very entry of the Ottoman Empire into the First World War
on the side of the Central Powers[212] has been considered by some
informed observers to have been largely motivated by Enver's Pan-
Turk and anti-Russian designs;[213] there was hardly any doubt by then
of Pan-Turkism's anti-Russian thrust.[214] Other members of the
government hesitated and prevaricated (as Talat, then Minister of
Interior, has related in his memoirs[215]). A few weeks before hostilities
broke out, the British Consul in Batum reported the concentration of
Ottoman troops on the border, the seizure of goods belonging to
Russian traders, as well as general harassment.[216] Very possibly, there
was some German encouragement;[217] the German Ambassador, von
Wangenheim, did promise the Grand Vizir support for changes in
Turkey's eastern frontier.[218] In a confidential letter to the Grand Vizir,
dated 6 August 1914, von Wangenheim referred to the secret 'Treaty
of Alliance', signed four days earlier, writing as follows: 'Germany
takes upon itself to strive for a rectification of Turkey's eastern

frontier, which would enable it to have a direct contact with the Muslim elements in Russia.' The Germans were evidently interested in exploiting Pan-Turkism and Pan-Islamism[219] both in order to weaken Russia and to secure some hold over Central Asia's immense economic wealth.[220] It is nevertheless an exaggeration to surmise that Pan-Turkism was merely a camouflage for German imperialist designs in Central Asia,[221] or that Pan-Turkism was merely a tool of the Germans.[222] It is possible, indeed, that the Germans may well have promised Enver 'the liberation of the Caucasus and of Turkestan', if the Ottoman Empire joined their side in the war against Russia.[223] Later, German publications continued to support the Pan-Turk idea, favouring the feasibility of a Caucasus freed from 'Russian domination' and united under Tatar leadership, for example.[224]

The proclamation issued by the Young Turks on the entry of the Ottoman Empire into the war lends some support to the assumption of German encouragement for Pan-Turkism. Among other points, it included the following statement: 'Our participation in the World War represents the vindication of our national ideal. The ideal of our nation and our people leads us towards the destruction of our Muscovite enemy, in order to obtain thereby a natural frontier to our Empire, which should include and unite all branches of our race.'[225] Furthermore, the declaration of *Jihad* by Şeyhül-İslam, although imbued with a Pan-Islamic spirit and appealing for the cooperation and assistance of all Muslim peoples, specifically mentioned those Muslims living in the Crimea, Kazan, Turkestan, Bukhara, Khiva, India, China, Afghanistan, Persia, Africa and other countries.[226] The insistence on Muslims of Turkic stock could hardly be fortuitous; it cleverly combined Pan-Islamism and Pan-Turkism.[227]

Several of the steps taken by the leadership of the Committee of Union and Progress during the war itself[228] — with Enver in a very powerful position as Minister of War[229] — are virtually inexplicable outside the context of commitment to Pan-Turkism. The abortive offensive in the Caucasus in late 1914 and early 1915 was a first sign of this commitment. In addition, the strong-handed exile of the Armenians may be partly seen as motivated by the wish to eliminate a barrier between Turkey and several Turkic groups in Russia living near the frontiers. The Czarist Government's advocacy, before the war, of the establishment of an Armenian autonomous unit and the support given to this idea by certain Armenian groups,[230] further aroused Pan-Turkist suspicions.[231] During the early war years, Turkish agents — together with German ones headed by Dr Werner Otto von Hentig — were busily recruiting support among the Turkic groups in Central Asia.[232] In 1915 and 1916, thousands of Pan-Turk and Pan-Islamic pamphlets were distributed in Afghanistan and in Russian and Chinese Turkestan.[233] In August 1915, a joint Turco-German mission arrived in Kabul, where it was active until May 1916, leaving then for Herat and other border areas, including Khybar; there they engaged in Ottoman and Pan-Turk propaganda until the war was nearly over.[234] During the later part of the war, various independent reports noted intensification of Ottoman-inspired (and, largely, German-coordinated) activity and propaganda in Central Asia. In 1917, Turkish agents were arousing Pan-Turk sentiments in Bukhara,[235] while in the Caucasus they were busy transporting money and firearms.[236] During the same year, these activities nearly reached the farthest limits of the Russian Empire,[237] soon spreading to the borders of China: Russian Turkic groups appealed to the Chinese Resident in Sinkiang (Chinese Turkestan) to support the Ottomans.[238]

In the last year of the war, with so much hanging in the balance, this propaganda intensified even more throughout Russian Central Asia, Afghanistan and Turkestan.[239] Employing the Turkish-Turkic *lingua franca* previously devised by Gasprinsky, a concentrated effort was made to forge links between the Outside Turks and the Ottoman Empire. Although the Islamic element was also utilised to the fullest extent, increasing emphasis was laid upon Pan-Turkism and its political implications.[240] Major F.M. Bailey, entrusted by the British authorities in India with a confidential mission to Bukhara and Turkestan, has described in his manuscript diary how, in 1918, Turkish officers there were busily spreading Pan-Turk propaganda.[241] At the same time the Germans, for their part, trained in Berlin a number of Pan-Turk agents, too, for instance from the Azerbayjan Turks.[242] Yusuf Akçura, Ali Hüseyinzade and other emigrants from Russia and active Pan-Turkists, also went to Budapest, Vienna, Berlin and Sofia in 1915 and Lausanne and Zurich in 1916, for a similar purpose (probably with the approval of the Ottoman Government).[243]

In the meantime, however, the course of the war, which was to determine (among other matters) the fate of Pan-Turkism, went on. With Russia in revolution, the 'Sick Man' found himself less sick than his northern neighbour.[244] It is significant that in 1917–18 the Ottoman High Command, very probably at Enver's own request, transferred units badly needed on the Syrian and Mesopotamian fronts for a thrust into Southern Russia up to Baku (Caucasus Ottoman forces were increased to six divisions). The campaign succeeded,[245] but hastened the collapse of Ottoman armies in Syria and Mesopotamia and the subsequent Ottoman defeat. This again indicates the Pan-Turk commitment of Enver and his associates.[246] Early in 1918, in line with this approach, the Turkish delegation at Petrograd encouraged the separatist tendencies of Russia's Turkic groups, in the hope of attaching Transcaucasia to the Ottoman Empire.[247] At the same time, every effort was made to recruit the support of the Turkic groups themselves. Thus the Tatars helped in seizing the telegraph and railway lines between Baku and Tiflis in cooperation with the Ottoman forces,[248] while the pro-Turk *Müsavat* Party[249] in Azerbayjan[250] actively aided the Pan-Turk cause.[251]

Their military victories achieved, the Turks set up pro-Turkish governments in the Northern Caucasus.[252] Not unexpectedly, in October 1918 Enver ordered Nuri, Ottoman commander in Baku, to clear Azerbayjan of Russians and Armenians, in order to ensure Turkish-Turkic territorial continuity;[253] a few days later, foreseeing the eventuality of withdrawal if peace were concluded, he ordered that Turkish officers be left in command of Azerbayjan and Northern Caucasus troops.[254] As one British diplomat speculated at the time, it certainly appeared that the Young Turk leadership proposed to establish an alternate Turkish-Turkic empire, extending to the east and northeast of Istanbul.[255] Indeed, even after the armistice, serious efforts were made to keep the Northern Caucasus or Russian Azerbayjan, or both,[256] linked with the Ottoman Empire. Additional Turkish officers were despatched to Azerbayjan[257] and known Pan-Turkists were encouraged to remain there for the good of the cause.[258] In 1919, Turkish officers continued fighting in the Northern Caucasus (this time against the British Expeditionary Force)[259] and local inhabitants from among the Turkic groups were coopted for propaganda and resistance.[260] Simultaneously, Captain Mehmet Kasım, Ottoman Delegate to Afghanistan, disseminated Turkish-language leaflets throughout Central Asia, calling upon all Turks and all Muslims to join forces in order to 'save Turkistan and assist in freeing the Holy Islamic centres and the Ottoman dominions'.[261] Indian Muslims at home and abroad recruited support for the continued existence of the Ottoman Empire.[262] During 1919 and the years immediately following, Turkish military officers, policemen and political agents continued to infiltrate the Caucasus and Azerbayjan, fanning Pan-Turk and Islamic sentiments through skillful exploitation of local apprehensions about the new regime in the Soviet Union.[263] Indeed, Pan-Turkism seemed to have lost but little of its irredentist drive through the Ottoman Empire's defeat.[264]

Lastly, the arrival of Enver himself in Central Asia in 1921, his command of the Basmachi forces[265] and his assumption of the title of 'Emir of Turkestan'[266] appeared to many as the realisation of the Pan-Turk ideal, which enjoyed a growing popularity and succeeded in winning many recruits.[267] Several local and foreign observers agreed at the time that although the Central Asian population may not have shown excessive interest in Pan-Turkism after all,[268] there was no doubt concerning Enver's own sincerity in the matter.[269] He considered it feasible to unite all Turkic elements in Bukhara (and possibly elsewhere), as the basis for a Turkic-Turkish empire.[270] This is borne out by Enver's ultimatum to the Government in Moscow, delivered via Narimanov, President of the Council of Azerbayjan, in which he reaffirmed 'the unshakable will of the people of Bukhara, Turkestan and Khiva to live free and independent; this independence must be acknowledged by Soviet Russia.'[271] To achieve this aim, Enver intended to organise anti-Bolshevik revolts wherever and whenever possible, raising the combined banners of Pan-Turkism and Pan-Islamism to provide an ideology competing with that of the Bolsheviks.[272] This struggle conditioned his relations with the Soviet authorities[273] and most of his other activities towards the end of his life.[274] It was only Enver's death in battle on 4 August 1922[275] which put an end to this course of events, although his lieutenant, Hacı Sami Bey (alias Selim Pasha) continued the battle for a time in Eastern Bukhara;[276] but he too was defeated and had to retreat to Afghanistan in June 1923, where he went on with what he himself frankly labelled 'Pan-Turk propaganda'.[277] The Enver legend lived on,[278] however, fed by the verse of Bukharan and other poets.[279] It was revived, from time to time in Turkey too,[280] and even lived on in Western Europe among those who had known him.[281] Cemal, another member of the erstwhile ruling Triumvirate, was assassinated in Tiflis at about the same time, after having failed to arouse a nationalist Pan-Turkist movement in Turkestan.[282] Thus ended the Pan-Turk dream of the Young Turks.

NOTES

1. See D.E. Lee, 'The origins of Pan-Islamism', *The American Historical Review*, XLVII (2): Jan. 1942, pp. 278–87. J.M. Landau, *The Politics of Pan-Islam*, 1990, ch. 1.
2. For an evaluation of Ottomanism, cf. R.H. Davison, 'Turkish attitudes concerning Christian-Muslim equality in the nineteenth century', *The American Historical Review*, LIX (4): July 1954, pp. 844–64.
3. For example see Timur Taş, 'İslamiyet karşında milliyetler: Türklük', *İctihad* (Istanbul weekly), IV (68): 30 May 1329/1913, pp. 1488–93. For an analysis, cf. Bernard Lewis, 'The Ottoman Empire and its aftermath, *Journal of Contemporary History* (London), XV (1): Jan. 1980, esp. pp. 27–9.
4. For a non-Turk evaluation of these three, and more especially of Pan-Turkism, see X, 'Les courants politiques dans la Turquie

contemporaine', *RMM*, XXI: 1912, pp. 158–221; G.G. Arnakis, 'Turanism, an aspect of Turkish nationalism', *Balkan Studies*, I: 1960, pp. 19–32.

5. Several issues of *Turan*, dating from 1914–15, may be consulted in the Tarık Üs library, Istanbul.

6. Cf. Niyazi Berkes, *The development of secularism in Turkey*, 1964, pp. 344 ff.

7. In the words of E.G. Mears, *Modern Turkey*, 1924, p. 481.

8. Cf. a detailed analysis of Suavi's ideas in Şerif Mardin, *The genesis of Young Ottoman thought*, 1962, ch. 12. See also S.J. Shaw and E.K. Shaw, *History of the Ottoman Empire and modern Turkey*, II, pp. 157–8; H.F. Gözler, 'Ali Suavi'yi tanımalıyız', *TK*, 64: Feb. 1968, pp. 236–47.

9. See, e.g., H.F. Gözler, 'Suavi'de zulme isyan duygusu', *Orkun* (Istanbul), 33: 18 May 1951, p. 5; and Erhan Demirutku, 'Ülkücü Ali Suavi', *Ötüken* (Istanbul), 77: May 1970, pp. 12–13.

10. For additional details see Bayur, vol. I, part 2, esp. pp. 19–22; David Kushner, *The rise of Turkish nationalism 1876–1908*, esp. pp. 7 ff.

11. For examples and details cf. B. Lewis, *Emergence*, pp. 339 ff.

12. Oh history writing in Turkey and the rise of nationalism, see id., 'History writing and the national revival in Turkey', *Middle Eastern Affairs (MEA)* (N.Y.), IV (6–7): June–July 1953, esp. pp. 218–24.

13. Examples in Ziya Gökalp, *The principles of Turkism* (transl. by R. Devereux), pp. 2 ff and H.N. Orkun, pp. 50 ff.

14. Details in Akçura, *Türkçülük*, pp. 113–18; Orkun, pp. 51–3; Hostler, *Turkism*, p. 141.

15. FO 395/16, file 100207, the memorandum on *The Neo-Turanian movement in Turkey*, drawn up by the [British] Arab Bureau, dated Cairo, May 1916.

16. Several non-Turks were also interested, at just the same time, in the origins of the Turks — sometimes reaching different conclusions. See, e.g., E.H. Parker, 'The origins of the Turks', *The English Historical Review* (London), XI: 1896, pp. 431–45.

17. 'Türkleri birleştirecek olan Türklük fikir ve duygusu . . . ' See H.N. Orkun, p. 54.

18. As correctly pointed out, regarding the first two decades of the 20th century, by Mohammad Sadiq, 'Türkçülük cereyanı — Türk milliyetçiliğinin eşiğinde (1908–1918)', *Türk Kültürü Araştırmaları* (Ankara), III–VI: 1966–9, pp. 5–18.

19. For whom see, among others, Akçura, *Türkçülük*, pp. 109–113; Osman F. Sertkaya, 'Şemsettin Sami ve Kâmûs-i Türkî-si', *TK*, 56: June 1967, pp. 577–81.

20. *Hafta*, I (12): 1 Zilhicce 1298, pp. 176–81.

21. 'Türk ismi ise Adriatik Denizi savahilinden Çin hududuna ve Sibiryanın iç taraflarına kadar münteşir olan bir ümmet-i azimenin unvanıdır'.

22. For his numerous writings, *cf.* Millî Kütüphane — Okuyucu Hizmetleri Bölümü, *Ölümünün 50. yıldönümü münasebetiyle Ömer Seyfeddin bibliyografyası*, 1970. About him, see Ali Canip Yöntem, *Ömer Seyfeddin'in hayatı ve eseri*, 1935; K.H. Karpat, 'Ömer Seyfeddin and the transformation of Turkish thought', *Revue des Études Sud-Est Européennes* (Bucharest), x: 1972, pp. 677–91; Yalçın Toker, *Ömer Seyfeddin*, 1973; and A.D. Dzhyeltyakov, 'Pantyurkizm i Ömer Seyfeddin', *Vostokovyedyeniye* (Leningrad), VII: 1980, pp. 180–8.

23. Reissued, in Latin characters, by Sakin Öner, with the same title, 1971.

24. It was first published in Istanbul in 1330 (1914), then reprinted, in Latin characters, several times, since 1958, including one edited by Sakin Öner, ibid., as a sequel to Seyfeddin's other work.

25. Published in Istanbul, this work carries no date; it appeared in the First World War years.

26. Esp. on pp. 10–19.

27. On whom see Akçura, *Türkçülük*, pp. 134–58; Fethi Gözler, 'Mehmet Emin Yurdakul', *TK*, 136–8: Feb.–Apr. 1974, pp. 219–27.

28. First published in Istanbul, 1334/1918. Reprinted in Latin characters, under the same title of *Turan'a doğru. Ey Türk uyan* (Towards Turan. Wake up, oh Turk), 1973.

29. In Turkish *yurt*, which designates both home and native country.

30. 'Ey! Türk ırkı. Ey! demir ve ateşin evlâdı, Ey! Binlerce yurt kuran, Ey! binlerce taç giyen.'

31. 'Biz Oğuzlar soyu olan Türkleriz.' The Oghuz had a specially-favoured standing in the view of Pan-Turkists at the time.

32. 'Turanın aziz kızları.'

33. A *saz* is a musical instrument.

34. 'Tatar kardeşlerime.'

35. Translated by Friedrich Schrader, 1916. The best study of Halide Edib is İnci Enginün's *Halide Edib Adıvar'ın eserlerinde doğu ve batı meselesi*; for an analysis of *Yeni Turan*, cf. pp. 127–60.

36. German translation, pp. 66–7. Translation of this quotation — mine.

37. W.W. Haddad and W. Ochsenwald (eds), *Nationalism in a non-national state: the dissolution of the Ottoman Empire*.

38. *Turan'a kitabı. Ahlâkî ve medenî musahebeler*, 1333.

39. Then reprinted, in Latin characters, under the same title, n.d. [1971].

40. 'Türk'ün rolü' (The role of the Turk), *Hayat* (Ankara weekly), 50: 10 November 1927, pp. 3–4.

41. Cf. E.Yu. Gasanova, *O kontsyeptsii Tyurkizma v idyeologii Mladoturok*, repr. from: *Premier Congrès des Etudes Balkaniques* (Sofia, 1966), *Communications de la Délégation Soviétique*, Moscow, 1966, pp. 1 ff.

42. For whom see Akçura, *Türkçülük*, p. 237; and Admiralty Staff, Intelligence Division, *Personalities in Turkey*, 2nd edn, 1916, p. 11. A copy of the latter is in the India Office, L/P&S/20, file c. 132.

43. 'Fakat Türkçülük? Zannederim ki bu mefhumun benim anladığım

Türklükten (çendân) (okadar) farkı yok.' See Celal Nuri, 'Türkçülük ve halkçılık', *Edebiyat-ı Umumiye Mecmuası*, 36–37: 2 Recep 1336/11 May 1918.

44. As Berkes, p. 344, thinks.
45. J.M. Landau, *Tekinalp, Turkish Patriot*, 1984.
46. *Mercure de France*, 16 Aug. 1912, pp. 673–707. This article is signed with a pseudonym, P. Risal.
47. The Ottoman date is 1330.
48. Tekin Alp, *Türkismus und Pantürkismus*, 1915.
49. *The Turkish and Pan-Turkish idea*, 1917.
50. *Türkismus und Pantürkismus*, pp. 4 ff.
51. Ibid., pp. 73–7.
52. Ibid., pp. 16–26.
53. Cf. Hostler, *Turkism*, p. 115.
54. L.B. (Bouvat?), in *RMM*, x: Jan. 1910, p. 106; Hostler, *Turkism*, p. 146.
55. Fernau, p. 246.
56. Ibid., pp. 247–8.
57. Already mentioned in ch. 1 of our study, pp. 13, 15.
58. See on him Richard Hartmann, 'Zija Gök Alp's Grundlagen des türkischen Nationalismus', *Orientalistische Literaturzeitung* (Leipzig), XXVIII: 1925, pp. 578, 583.
59. Akçura, *Türkçülük*, pp. 181–9; Zenkovsky, passim; H.N. Orkun, pp. 67–8; İ.A. Gövsa, *Türk meşhurları ansiklopedisi*, s.v. 'Turan, Ali Hüseyin-Hüseyinzade'; Hostler, *Turkism*, p. 142.
60. For his career and writings, see his son's memoirs, Samet Ağaoğlu, *Babamdan hatıralar*, 1940, and *Babamın arkadaşları*, 3rd edn, 1969, which lists (p. 214) Ahmet Ağaoğlu's publications. Cf. *RMM*, XXIII: 1913, pp. 203–4; Akçura, *Türkçülük*, pp. 189–208; FO 371/13092, E 247/247/44, 'Notes on leading Turkish personalities', compiled by Helm, enc. in Sir George R. Clerk's (British Ambassador to Turkey) no. 16, Confidential, to Sir Austen Chamberlain, dated Constantinople, 11 Jan. 1928; H.N. Orkun, pp. 67–9; Gövsa, s.v. 'Ağaoğlu, Ahmet'.
61. L.B., in *RMM*, x: Jan. 1910, p. 106.
62. For an evaluation of his political and journalistic activity at that time, cf. FO 195/2452, no. 928, copy of a report dated Pera, 24 Feb. 1913, enclosing the translation of an article by Ağaoğlu.
63. See M.R. Kaufmann, *Pera und Stambul*, Weimar, Kiepenheuer, 1915, p. 198.
64. N. Berkes, in the preface to his *Turkish nationalism and Western civilization*, p. 8, correctly observes that Gökalp devoted only two essays exclusively to Pan-Turkism. However, Gökalp did refer to it in many others (as Berkes's own selection demonstrates), as well as in his poems, books and, most probably, conversations.
65. Among his disciples one may count, e.g., Köprülü, already mentioned. See Ali Galip Erdican, *Mehmet Fuat Köprülü: a study of his contribution to cultural reform in modern Turkey*, 1974, pp. 6 ff.

66. Among the earliest European evaluations of Gökalp (still worthwhile consulting) are Ettore Rossi's 'Uno scrittore turco contemporaneo: Ziyā Gök Alp', *OM*, IV (9): 15 Sep. 1924, pp. 574–95; and J. Deny's 'Ziya Goek Alp', *RMM*, LXI: 1925, pp. 1–41. The best work about him remains Uriel Heyd's *Foundations of Turkish nationalism*, 1950. Berkes has dealt with Gökalp and published a very useful selection of his works in his *Turkish nationalism and Western civilization*. See also Nami Duru, *Ziya Gökalp*, 1948; Ali Nüzhet Göksel, *Ziya Gökalp, hayatı ve eserleri*, 1948; H.N. Orkun, pp. 71–7; Shaw and Shaw, II, pp. 301–4.

67. For Gökalp's connections with the Committee, cf. E.B. Şapolyo, *Ziya Gökalp, İttihadı terakki ve meşrutiyet tarihi*, 2nd edn, Istanbul, İnkilâp ve Aka, 1974, esp. part 2.

68. Details in Fernau, p. 248.

69. 'Vatan ne Türkiyedir Türklere, ne Türkistan, Vatan büyük ve müebbet bin ülkedir: Turan!'
For an analysis of the poem 'Turan', see Mehmet Kaplan, in his *Edebiyatımızın içinde*, pp. 77–82, reprinted from *Bozkurt*, 3 May 1972, pp. 33–5.

70. A bibliography of his works was published by İsmet Binark and Nejat Sefercioğlu, entitled *Doğumunun 95. münasebetiyle Ziya Gökalp bibliyografyası: kitap, makale*. It covers 436 items by Gökalp.

71. See M. Tayyib Gökbilgin, 'Ziya Gökalp'e göre Halkçılık, Milliyetçilik, Türkçülük', *Islam Tetkikleri Enstitüsü Dergisi* (Istanbul), VI (3–4): 1976, esp. pp. 210–11.

72. 'Millet nedir', *Yeni Mecmua*, 70: 15 Feb. 1339/1923.

73. Ziya Gökalp, *The principles of Turkism*, transl. by Robert Devereux, 1968. Some extracts have been rendered into German and analysed by R. Hartmann, in *Orientalistische Literaturzeitung*, XXVIII: 1925, pp. 583–610.

74. Gökalp, Devereux translation, p. 15.

75. Ibid., pp. 17 ff.

76. See also Heyd, pp. 126–30, where he lists several of Gökalp's press-articles relating to Pan-Turkism.

77. A minimum plan for a 'Small Turan' and a maximum one for a 'Great Turan' had already been broached, about a dozen years earlier, by Tekin Alp, in his book *Turan* — as rightly pointed out by A.S. Tvyeritinova, 'Mladotyurki i Pantyurkizm', *Kratkiye Soobshchyeniya Instituta Vostokovyedyeniya*, XXII: 1956, esp. pp. 68–9. Most probably, these matters were being debated within Pan-Turkist circles in those years.

78. Gökalp, Devereux translation, pp. 20–1.

79. Cf. C. Savaş Fer, 'Hesap veriyoruz!', *Gök Börü* (Istanbul), 1: 5 Nov. 1924, esp. p. 3. For Gökalp's contribution to Pan-Turk ideology, see also a series of articles by A.N. Kırmacı, 'Türkiyede aşırı akımlar: Milliyetçilik-Irkçılık-Turancılık', *Vatan* (Istanbul daily), 24–27 Nov.

1960. For attacks on him (from an Islamist point of view), because of this contribution, cf. H.M. Genç, *Islâmî açıdan Ziya Gökalp ve Türkçüler.*

80. For this association, see Akçura, *Türkçülük*, pp. 209–12; Julius Germanus, 'Türk Darnay', *Keleti Szemle* (Budapest), x: 1909, pp. 341–4; H.N. Orkun, pp. 85–7; T.Z. Tunaya, *Türkiyede siyasî partiler, 1859–1952*, pp. 376–7; Bayur, vol. IV, part 2, pp. 400–1; Lewis, *Emergence*, pp. 343–4.

81. 'Sırf ilim ile uğraşır bir cemiyet.'

82. On whom see Akçura, *Türkçülük*, pp. 118–22.

83. Cf. ibid., p. 126.

84. Ibid., pp. 126–9.

85. Ibid., pp. 77–9.

86. For Köprülü (1890–1966), already mentioned, see the special issue of *TK*, 47: Sep. 1966.

87. Akçura, *Türkçülük*, pp. 210–11.

88. A set may be consulted in Atatürk Kitaplığı, Istanbul. On this journal, see Carl Brockelmann, *Das Nationalgefühl der Türken im Licht der Geschichte*, p. 15.

89. So we are informed by Akçura, *Türkçülük*, p. 210.

90. See Tekin Alp, *Türkismus und Pantürkismus*, pp. 31–2. Cf. H.N. Orkun, p. 87; Valentine Chirol, 'Islam and the war', *Quarterly Review* (London), CCXXIX (455): Apr. 1918, p. 512.

91. Chiefly, *Bilgi Mecmuası*, 6: Apr. 1330/1914, pp. 646–9.

92. For the name cf. *RMM*, XXII: Mar. 1913, p. 215.

93. According to Tekin Alp, *Türkismus und Pantürkismus*, p. 31.

94. Acc. to Halide Edib's *Memoirs* (see Select Bibliography), this students' organisation was established in 1910. However, their statutes, *Yurducular yasası*, Geneva, n.d. [1914], mention 1911 as the date of foundation.

95. Turc Yourdou, *La Turquie moderne*, Geneva. 1919. A copy may be consulted in the Middle East Collection, at the Marriott Library, University of Utah, Salt Lake City.

96. Issues 1–13: Feb. 1921–Apr. 1922 may be consulted at the Colindale Newspaper Library, London.

97. For whom see Akçura, *Türkçülük*, p. 235.

98. For the Istanbul *Türk Yurdu* Association, see ibid., pp. 212–14; H. Edib's *Memoirs*, pp. 321–2; H.N. Orkun, p. 87; Tunaya, p. 377.

99. See Shaw and Shaw, vol. II, p. 289.

100. Mentioned above as the author of *Turanlının defteri.*

101. Cf. H. Edib's *Memoirs*, p. 333; Akçura, *Türkçülük*, pp. 215 ff; M.E. Erişirgil, *Türkçüler devri, milliyetçilik devri, insanlık devri*, pp. 67–71.

102. For the *Türk Ocağı*, see H. Edib's *Memoirs*, pp. 323–5; Tekin Alp, *Türkismus und Pantürkismus*, pp. 27–31; Akçura, *Türkçülük*, pp. 214–20; Réchid Safvet, *Les Türk-Odjaghis*, Ankara, 1930 — the author was an indefatigable Pan-Turkist activist, cf. FO 424/280, E 127/127/44,

'Notes on leading Turkish personalities', enc. in Percy Loraine's no. 1, Confidential, dated Ankara, 1 Jan. 1936. See also Erişirgil, pp. 67 ff; Tunaya, pp. 378–86; Shaw and Shaw, vol. II, pp. 309–10; Bayur, vol. IV, part 2, pp. 405–6.

103. E.g. a grant of TL (Turkish pounds) 50,000 from the Ministry of Evkaf, in 1917, for Pan-Turk publications, acc. to 'The racial propaganda in Turkey', *The Near East* (London): 30 Mar. 1917, p. 507. This information was however part of war-propaganda and ought to be treated with due caution. See also the data in Agâh Sırrı Levend, 'Türk ocaklarından halkevlerine', *Ulus* (Ankara daily), 17 Jan. 1951, p. 2.

104. Cf. the well-informed typewritten articles on 'Turkish nationalism', in FO 395/47, file 98089, no. 214716, dating from Oct. 1916.

105. For the statutes, cf. Tunaya, pp. 383–6. See also Tekin Alp, *Türkismus und Pantürkismus*, p. 27; Akçura, *Türkçülük*, pp. 214–15.

106. These were very much in the public eye then. On the parties in those years, cf. T.Z. Tunaya, *Hürriyetin ilânı: ikinci meşrutiyetinin siyasî hayatına bakışlar*, 1959, esp. pp. 31–52.

107. See the report of the Fourth Convention of *Türk Ocağı* in *Büyük Mecmua* (Istanbul), 6: 24 Apr. 1335/1919, p. 87.

108. On whom cf. Akçura, *Türkçülük*, pp. 221–3; the special issue dedicated to his memory by *Türk Yurdu* (New Series), VI (2): Feb. 1967, and by *TK*, 45: July 1966; B.G. Gaulis, *La question turque*, 1931, pp. 206–11; K.H. Karpat, *Turkey's politics: the transition to a multi-party system*, pp. 62, 255–6, 276, 280, 381. See also below, p. 77.

109. See Peyami Safa, *Türk inkilâbına bakışlar*, n.d. [1938], pp. 73 ff.

110. In one instance, a circular letter of theirs was seized in Medina, in 1917 — cf. FO 395/139, file 15725, no. 144185, a decyphered message from Sir Reginald Wingate to the Foreign Office, dated Ramleh, 21 July 1917.

111. Tekin Alp, *Türkismus und Pantürkismus*, pp. 27–31; H.N. Orkun, p. 93; D.E. Webster, *The Turkey of Atatürk*, 1939, pp. 28, 74. See also below, ch. 3 of our study.

112. The Arab Bureau [of the British] in Egypt referred to them as 'The New Turan' (*Yeni Turan*), see the Bureau's *The Arab Bulletin*, 26: 26 Sep. 1916, p. 268.

113. FO 395/16, file 100207, memorandum on *The Neo-Turanism movement in Turkey*, drawn up in May 1916 by the above Arab Bureau in Cairo. See also Chirol, in *Quarterly Review*, CCXXIX (455): Apr. 1918, p. 512.

114. Probably, Enver himself.

115. See below, ch. 3 of our study, p. 77.

116. Cf. Berkes, *The development*, p. 346.

117. *Principles of Turkism*, Devereux's translation, p. 10.

118. Acc. to another version, he was born in 1879. Despite his impressive role in the Pan-Turkist movement in Czarist Russia, the Ottoman Empire and (to a lesser degree) in the Republic of Turkey, the only

scholarly book about him is François Georgeon's recent *Aux origines du nationalisme turc: Yusuf Akçura (1876–1935)*. A Ph.D. thesis on Akçura, by David Thomas at McGill University, remains in manuscript. The best source is still Akçura's autobiographical account, part of the *Türk yılı 1928*, reprinted in his *Türkçülük*, pp. 161–81 (this volume comprises, also, an essay on Akçura by the editor, Sâkin Öner) and his own numerous articles in *Türk Yurdu* and elsewhere. See also Muharrem Feyzi Togay's monograph, *Yusuf Akçura'nın hayatı*, 1944; Hostler, *Turkism*, pp. 143–6; X, 'Le Panislamisme et le Panturquisme', *RMM*, XXII: Mar. 1913, pp. 193 ff; S.M. Arsal, 'Dostum Yusuf Akçura', *TK*, 174: Apr. 1977, pp. 346–54.

119. See above, ch. 1.
120. Ibid., p. 14.
121. For his intellectual formation in Russia and France and his *Üç tarz-ı siyaset*, see Thomas, in *Journal of Turkish Studies*, II: 1978, pp. 127–40. Cf. *RMM*, XXII: 1913, pp. 198 ff; Enver Ziya Karal, *Osmanlı tarihi*, vol. VIII: 1962, pp. 561 ff.
122. H.Z. Ülken, *Türkiyede çağdaş düşünce tarihi*, 1966, vol. I, p. 428. On these organisations see also Eugen Oberhummer, *Die Türken und das osmanische Reich*, 1917, p. 94. The author was a geographer with personal knowledge of the Ottoman Empire.
123. Ülken, vol. I, p. 333.
124. 'Le Panislamisme et le Panturquisme', *RMM*, XXII: 1913, p. 193. Cf. ibid., pp. 193–4, 198–200, for his life and activities.
125. List by Sâkin Öner, in his introduction to Akçura, *Türkçülük*, pp. 26–30. Cf. Samet Ağaoğlu, *Babamın arkadaşları*, 3rd edn, p. 214.
126. Later, Ahmet Ağaoğlu seems to have taken over — acc. to L.T. Stoddard, 'Pan-Turanism', *The American Political Science Review*, XI (1): Feb. 1917, p. 19.
127. See Bertrand Bareilles, who comments on the journal's intensive Pan-Turk campaign, in his *Les Turcs: ce que fut leur empire*, 1917, p. 264. Bareilles lived in Turkey during the Young Turk Revolution and the immediately following years; acc. to R.H. Davison, in *Tarih Dergisi* (Istanbul), XXXII: Mar. 1979, p. 642, Bareilles lived there from the mid-1890s to 1914.
128. Which may have induced the Young Turks to participate in its financing — acc. to Şerif Bilgehan 'Türkiyede (Türkçülüğün) geçirmiş olduğu merhaleler', *Tanrıdağ* (Istanbul), 1st series, 5: 5 June 1942, p. 10.
129. Of which seven issues appeared, 2 Mar.–23 May 1329 (1913).
130. Cf. *RMM*, XXII: 1913, p. 218.
131. The mast said it was published by the *Türk Yurdu* Association. The Beyazıd Library in Istanbul has a set of the first year's 52 issues, 11 April 1329 to 3 April 1330 (probably all that appeared). See on this journal Brockelmann, pp. 15–16.

132. My private collection has issues 1–16: 12 Apr. 1330/1914–24 July 1330/1914 (all published?).
133. *Halka doğru gitmek, halka için çalışmak.*
134. *Türk dünyası.*
135. Acc. to Akçura's own account, in his *Türkçülük*, pp. 213–14. For this programme and reactions to it, cf. Bayur, vol. IV, part 2, pp. 401–3; a more detailed analysis of the journal in Paul Dumont, 'La revue *Türk Yurdu* et les Musulmans de l'Empire Russe', *Cahiers du Monde Russe et Soviétique*, XV (3–4): July–Dec. 1974, pp. 315–51; and Masami Arai, 'Between state and nation: a new light on the journal *Türk Yurdu*', *Turcica*, XXIV: 1992, pp. 277–95.
136. Dumont, p. 323.
137. Akçura, *Türkçülük*, pp. 23–6 and passim.
138. Cf. ibid., pp. 33 ff.
139. Examples in Bayur, vol. I, part 2, pp. 413–36.
140. Even in the view of such Westernised Turks as Niyazi Berkes, who had no special sympathy for Pan-Turkism, this appeared more effective in terms of policy than either Pan-Islamism or Ottomanism. See Berkes, in *The Middle East Journal*, VIII: Autumn 1954, p. 381.
141. A great deal has been written on it. See, *inter alia*, the contemporary appraisal by D. Imhoff, 'Die Entstehung und der Zweck des Comités für Einheit und Fortschritt', *Die Welt des Islams* (Berlin), I (3–4): 1913, pp. 167–77. Cf. Yu.A. Pyetrosyan, *Mladotyuryetskoye dvidzhyeniye*, Moscow, Nauka, 1971; Feroz Ahmad, *The Young Turks: the Committee of Union and Progress in Turkish Politics, 1908–1914*; Mustafa Ragıb Esatlı, *İttihat ve terakki tarihinde esrar perdesi*, 1975.
142. For which see Yu.A. Pyetrosyan, 'Iz istorii propagandistskoy dyeyatyel'nosti Mladoturok v Emigratsii', *Narodi Azii i Afriki*, 1963, part 4, pp. 184–8; Ş.A. Mardin, *Jön Türklerin siyasî fikirleri, 1895–1908*.
143. Cf. the materials indicated by Dumont, in *Cahiers du Monde Russe et Soviétique*, XV (3–4): July–Dec. 1974, p. 316.
144. Bayur, vol. I, part 1, pp. 349–51; cf. ibid., vol. II, part 4, pp. 406 ff.
145. Although their first programme, after the 1908 Revolution, stressed Turkism (in education, etc.) rather than Pan-Turkism. See A. Sarrou, *La Jeune Turquie et la révolution*, pp. 40 ff.
146. Yu.V. Marunov, 'Politika Mladoturok po natsional'nomu voprosu (1908–1912)', *Kratkiye Soobschchyeniya Instituta Vostokovyedyeniya*, XXX: 1961, pp. 161–72.
147. On Pan-Islamic propaganda during the later years (1904–8) of Abdul Hamid II's reign, see the documents in India Office, R/15/5, file 62, 'Pan-Islamic Propaganda'.
148. On the failure of Pan-Islamic activity to achieve tangible results, see Chirol, in *Quarterly Review*, CCXXIX (455): Apr. 1918, pp. 489 ff; Shaukat Ali, *Pan-movements in the Third World: Pan-Arabism, Pan-*

Africanism, Pan-Islamism, pp. 198 ff. But contrast the estimate of M. Larcher, *La guerre turque dans la guerre mondiale*, pp. 7–16.

149. 'Exploiting the crescent: Pan-Islamic aims', *The Times* (London), 27 Apr. 1915.

150. For its continuing use by the Committee of Union and Progress, see the contemporary evaluation of Muçafir, *Notes sur la Jeune Turquie*, pp. 81–8; René Pinon, *L'Europe et la Jeune Turquie*, pp. 134–6; R.L. Shukla, 'The Pan-Islamic policy of the Young Turks and India', *Proceedings of the Indian History Congress, 32nd session*, part 2, 1970, pp. 302–7.

151. An example of the press-campaign in this sense was Hüseyin Cahit's editorial in *Tanin* (Istanbul) of 23 Sep. 1911, in which he attacked all those harping on the Pan-Islamic theme in the Ottoman press, accusing them of sinister intentions to divert Ottoman foreign policy into the wrong direction. Significantly, he criticised most severely those 'who are not children of this land by their origin'. See also FO 371/1262, file 38360, enc. 1 in British Ambassador Gerard Lowther's no. 653, to Sir Edward Grey, dated Constantinople, 27 Sep. 1911.

152. For a contemporary account of Ottomanism via Turkification, see Muçafir, pp. 36–55. On Ottomanism as a policy and its failure cf. Pinon, pp. 122 ff.

153. See Elie Kedourie, *England and the Middle East: the destruction of the Ottoman Empire, 1914–1921*, 1956, pp. 59 ff.

154. Cf. Schrader, in the introduction to his German translation of Halide Edib's *Yeni Turan (Das neue Turan)*, p. vi.

155. Joseph Pomianowski, *Der Zusammenbruch des Ottomanischen Reiches: Erinnerungen an die Türkei aus der Zeit des Weltkrieges*, 1928, pp. 28–30. The author was in Turkey during the war.

156. Text in FO 371/1320, file 4, no. 28361.

157. Details in Edwin Pears, 'Turkey, Islam and Turanianism', *The Contemporary Review* (London), cxiv: Oct. 1918, esp. pp. 374 ff.

158. For the downgrading of Islam in favour of Pan-Turkism, see ' "Turanian" and Moslem: the Turkish apostasy', *The Near East*, 20 Apr. 1917, pp. 567–8. This however was war propaganda and, consequently, should be treated with due caution.

159. This went on during the First World War, too, as observed in Turkey by Harry Stuermer, *Two war years in Constantinople*, esp. chs 7–8. Pan-Islamic propaganda emphasised the duty of every Muslim to assist the Ottoman Empire, the largest independent Muslim state. See the Historical Section of the Foreign Office, *The Pan-Islamic movement*, esp. pp. 64–72.

160. FO 371/1497, file 32941, Marling's no. 646, Confidential, to Grey, dated Constantinople, 31 July 1912.

161. Toynbee, *Report on the Pan-Turanian movement*, esp. pp. 9–10, 23. This was an issue which was to trouble Pan-Turkists for a long time.

162. Enver Pasha.

163. *The making of modern Turkey*, p. 157.
164. India Office, L/P&S/20, 'Asiatic Turkey and Arabia, 1910', Lowther's no. 715, to Grey, dated Constantinople, 9 Oct. 1910.
165. An English translation of this pamphlet is enclosed with Lowther's above despatch.
166. See Lowther, in his above despatch.
167. Cf. India Office, L/P&S/10/306, file 4287/1912, 'Balkan War'.
168. Cf. a pamphlet by Edhem Nejad, *Türklük ne dir ve terbiye yolları* (What is Turkism — and the ways of education), published *c*. 1914, in which the author put together many of the relevant arguments.
169. See, e.g., M. Haireddin, 'Das Urteil eines Türken', *Zeiten und Völker* (Stuttgart), 12: 1912, pp. 290–1. Also Masami Arai, *Turkish nationalism in the Young Turk era*, 1992.
170. Karpat, *Turkey's politics*, esp. pp. 24 ff. For the veering of the Committee of Union and Progress toward Pan-Turkism cf. 'Turkey, Russia and Islam', *The Round Table*, Dec. 1917, pp. 110 ff. See also Larcher, pp. 21 ff.
171. A French translation appeared in *La Turquie* (Istanbul), 21 May 1914; the translation into English is mine. This was enclosed in FO 371/2134, file 21624, Sir L. Mallet's no. 363, Confidential, to Grey, dated the same day.
172. Luke, p. 166; Hostler, *Turkism*, p. 99.
173. Indeed, soon afterwards, the *Vali* of Van, visiting Tiflis, offered inducements, on behalf of the Ottoman Government, to Muslims (very probably comprising the Turkic groups) in the province of Tiflis, to emigrate into the Ottoman Empire. See FO 371/1245, file 6158, the report of the British Vice-Consul, Captain L. Molyneux-Seel, dated Van, 9 Jan. 1911.
174. Pinon, p. 129.
175. FO 371/1000, 926/44844, Findlay's no. 158, Secret, to Grey, dated Sofia, 7 Dec. 1910, and enclosure (report by Choublin, French Consul-General in Salonica). FO 371/1017, file 41308, British Consul-General H.H. Lamb's report no. 163, to Marling, dated Salonica, 16 Dec. 1910, enc. in Marling's no. 911, Confidential, to Grey, dated Constantinople, 20 Dec. 1910.
176. At the time, it had 4,800 branches with 135,000 members, acc. to *The Times*, 3 Oct. 1911. Probably most, but not all, were in the Ottoman Empire — see below.
177. FO 371/1263, file 51124, information supplied to H.C. Woods (on a mission to the Balkans) by the Bulgarian Consul-General in Salonica, in December 1911, and passed on by him to the Foreign Office in London. See also *The Times*, 3 Oct. and 27 Dec. 1911.
178. Cf. C.J. Walker, *Armenia: the survival of a nation*, p. 191. The book is strongly opposed to Pan-Turkism.
179. See Bayur, vol. IV, part 2, p. 410. The resolutions concerning Turkification, passed at the 1913 convention, seem however to have been more

moderate than the previous ones — at least acc. to FO 371/1846, file
48679, Marling's no. 874, Confidential, to Grey, dated Constantinople,
20 Oct. 1913.
180. Cf. the evidence of Stuermer, chs 7 and 8.
181. See the three anonymous articles (prob. written by A.J. Toynbee) in
The Times, 3, 5 and 7 Jan. 1918. For the rejoinder of the *Frankfurter
Zeitung*, cf. *The Times*, 4 Feb. 1918.
182. FO 882/15, V. Vivian's memorandum, dated 30 July 1917, preserved
in the files of the [British] Arab Bureau, Egypt.
183. CO 67/173, file 35985, High Commissioner H. Gould-Adams's confidential despatch to Lewis Harcourt (Secretary of State for the
Colonies), dated Troodos, 4 Sep. 1914.
184. CO 67/192, file 31495, M. Stevenson's (Officer Administering the
Government) secret despatch to Viscount Milner (Secretary of State
for the Colonies), dated Nicosia, 6 May 1919.
185. CO 69/27, pp. 100–1 of the Minutes, for 31 Mar. 1911. CO 69/33,
pp. 204–5 (= *Cyprus. Minutes of the Legislative Council of the session
of 1917*, vol. XXIX: 1917; Nicosia, Government Printing Office, 1918),
for 6 June 1917.
186. Oberhummer, p. 17.
187. Czaplicka, pp. 9–18, 119.
188. See above.
189. *The Times*, 3 Oct. 1911.
190. FO 371/945, file 3, no. 2531, confidential cable from Sir G. Barclay
to Grey, dated Tehran, 23 Jan. 1910.
191. FO 371/1245, file 6158, Molyneux-Seel's two despatches to Marling,
dated Van, 9 and 23 Jan. 1911, respectively.
192. FO 395/93, file 2399, no. 56191, Edward E. Lang's letter to Sir Arthur
Hirtzel, dated London, 5 Mar. 1917.
193. British Military Attaché G.E. Tyrell's no. 6 to Ambassador Lowther,
dated Constantinople, 10 Jan. 1910, reprinted in 'Further correspondence respecting the affairs of Central Asia, 1910', p. 2. L.W.
Reynolds's no. 37, to the India Office, dated Simla, 14 Apr. 1913,
reprinted in 'Further correspondence respecting Russia and Central
Asia, 1913', pp. 31–2. Both reprints are available in the India Office.
194. Details in Marunov, 'Pantyurkizm i Panislamizm Mladoturok', *Kratkiye Soobshchyeniya Instituta Narodov Azii*, XLV: 1961, esp. pp. 45 ff.
195. Examples in FO 371/1213, file 46, summary of Sir G. Buchanan's
despatch no. 494, dated St. Petersburg, 18 Dec. 1910, reporting his
conversation with Stolipin. Cf. FO 371/1262, file 40898, Sir Edward
Grey's no. 266 to O'Beirne, dated London, 24 Oct. 1911, summarising
a conversation the Russian Ambassador to London had had with Sir
A. Nicolson at the Foreign Office, the previous day. See also
Marunov's article, mentioned in the preceding footnote.
196. Oberhummer, pp. 94–5; Czaplicka, pp. 9–18, 119.

197. Halide Edib, *Conflict of East and West in Turkey*, p. 94. On the treaty itself and its Pan-Turk implications, see below.
198. Cf. G.Z. Aliyev, 'O vnutryennikh protivoryechiyakh v partii "Ittikhad ve Terakki" ', *Kratkiye Soobshchyeniya Instituta Narodov Azii*, LXXIII: 1963, pp. 125–31.
199. Djemal Pasha, *Memories of a Turkish statesman, 1913–1919*, pp. 251–2.
200. On these three, see the contemporary characterisation of Henry Morgenthau, *Secrets of the Bosphorus: Constantinople, 1913–1916*, chs 10, 15, 25. Cf. Jean-Paul Garnier, *La fin de l'empire ottoman: du Sultan Rouge à Mustafa Kemal*, 1973, pp. 126–9.
201. See Pomianowski, pp. 29–30.
202. Details in Şevket Süreyya Aydemir, *Makedonya'dan Orta Asya'ya Enver Paşa*, 2nd edn, esp. vol. II, ch. 12.
203. See Feroz Ahmad, *The Young Turks*, pp. 154–5.
204. Cf. D.A. Rustow, 'Enwer Pasha', *EI²*, vol. II, p. 699.
205. André Malraux, *Les noyers de l'Altenburg*, pp. 46–75. These pages have been translated into Turkish by Sabahattin Eyüboğlu, as *Turan yolu*, Istanbul, 1965.
206. See his *Türkismus und Pantürkismus*, pp. 11–12.
207. See, e.g., the evidence offered by one of those agents, Hüsameddin Ertürk, in his memoirs, later edited by Samih Nafiz Tansu as *İki devrin perde arkası*, 3rd edn, Istanbul, Ararat Yayınevi, 1969, pp. 115–16. On the organisation itself cf. Ergun Hiçyılmaz, *Belgelerle Teşkilat-ı mahsusa*, Istanbul, Ünsal Kitabevi, 1979; Doğu Ergil, 'A reassessment: the Young Turks, their politics and anti-colonial struggle', *Balkan Studies* (Salonica), XVI (2): 1975, pp. 70–1.
208. D.A. Rustow, 'The army and the founding of the Turkish Republic', *World Politics* (Princeton), XI (4): July 1959, pp. 518–19.
209. See above, ch. 2 of our study.
210. India Office, L/P&S/10/472 and 473, file 3443/1914, parts 1 and 2, chiefly referring to the years 1915–16.
211. See Ye.K. Sarkisyan, *Ekspansionistkaya politika Osmanskoy Impyerii v Zakavkaz'ya*, ch. 2.
212. For the course of events leading to this, see the personal account of the Ottoman Ambassador to Berlin, M. Moukhtar Pacha, *La Turquie, l'Allemagne et l'Europe*, ch. 6.
213. Cf. Ahmed Emin, *Turkey in the world war*, New Haven, Yale University Press, 1930, pp. 64–9.
214. See 'Le mouvement Pantouranien', *L'Asie Française*, XVII (171): Oct.–Dec. 1917, p. 174.
215. 'Posthumous memoirs of Talaat Pasha', *Current History* (N.Y.), XV (2): Nov. 1921, pp. 287 ff.
216. FO 371/2096, file 61356, no. 61356, Consul Stevens's no. 64, to the Foreign Office, dated Batum, 25 Sep. 1914. Cf. FO 371/2147, file

74733, no. 74733, Stevens's no. 70, to the Foreign Office, dated Batum, 29 Oct. 1914.

217. Emil Lengyel, *Turkey*, N.Y., Random House, 1941, p. 313; Hostler, *Turkism*, p. 150.

218. Text of this letter in Carl Mühlmann, *Deutschland und die Türkei, 1913–1914*, pp. 96–7 (translation mine). Cf. Lothar Krecker, *Deutschland und die Türkei im zweiten Weltkrieg*, p. 207; Ulrich Trumpener, *Germany and the Ottoman Empire*, passim, esp. pp. 113–14.

219. M. Alishan, 'Berlin to India', *Asia: Journal of the American Asiatic Association* (N.Y.), XVIII (5): May 1918, esp. pp. 359–60.

220. FO 371/3391, file 3828, no. 122038, Major P.T. Etherton's memorandum on *Central Asia: the Pan-Turanian movement*, dated Kashgar, May 1918. For the German war objectives in this area, see H.S.W. Corrigan, 'German-Turkish relations and the outbreak of war in 1914: a reassessment', *Past and Present* (Oxford), 36: Apr. 1967, pp. 144–52; Charles D. Sullivan, *Stamboul crossings: German diplomacy in Turkey, 1908–1914*, ch. 7.

221. As suggested in 'Russia, Germany and Asia', *The Round Table*, XXXI: June 1918, esp. pp. 557–8. The precise reasons for the Ottoman Empire's joining the war as an ally of Germany are still in some doubt. The best analysis may be that of Ulrich Trumpener, 'Turkey's entry into World War I: an assessment of responsibilities', *The Journal of Modern History* (Chicago), XXXIV (4): Dec. 1962, pp. 369–80.

222. See 'Le fanatisme Panturc', *L'Asie Française* (Paris), XVII (169): Apr.–June 1917, pp. 72–4; René Pinon, 'The Young Turk policy in Asia', *Current History* (N.Y.), XI (2): Nov. 1919, esp. pp. 334–5.

223. Cf. Victor Bérard, *Le problème turc*, 1917, pp. 110–12. Bérard spent some time in Istanbul before the First World War.

224. See Michael v. Tseretheli, in *Korrespondentzblatt der Nachrichtenstelle für den Orient* (Berlin), 3: 4 Nov. 1916. An English translation is enclosed in FO 371/2823, file 249544, no. 249544.

225. Quoted by Luke, p. 161.

226. Cf. Hostler, *Turkism*, p. 147.

227. French translation in *La Turquie*, 26 Nov. 1914, of which a copy is available in FO 371/2147, file 82892. More details about this propaganda in G.W. Bury, *Pan-Islam*, London, Macmillan, 1919.

228. For a detailed objective analysis of the Ottoman Empire in the First World War, see Larcher.

229. FO 371/2143, file 60266, no. 60278, Sir L. Malet's confidential cable, to Grey, dated Istanbul, 16 Oct. 1914.

230. Examples in FO 371/1778, file 543, no. 8875 (for the year 1913).

231. For the views of the Armenians in this matter, see Simon Vratzian, *Armenia and the Armenian question*, Boston, Hairenik, 1943, pp. 32 ff. Cf. Firuz Kazemzadeh, *The struggle for Transcaucasia (1917–1921)*, 1951, pp. 84 ff.

232. Bérard, *Le problème turc*, pp. 104–8; Alexander Henderson, 'The Pan-Turanian myth in Turkey today', *The Asiatic Review* (London), XLI: 1945, esp. p. 90.

233. Cf. FO 371/2320, file 4660, no. 103362, British Consul-General P.M. Sykes no. 493–13, confidential, to the Secretary of the Government of India, dated Kashgar, 31 May 1915. FO 371/2654, file 2654, no. 39502, British Consul-General George Macartney's no. 42 to Sir John Jordan (British Minister in Peking), dated Kashgar, 22 Dec. 1915. Ibid., file 39502, no. 88937, Macartney's cyphered cable no. 4, to Jordan, dated Kashgar, 13 Apr. 1916, and enc. Ibid., no. 93813, Jordan's no. 103, to Grey, dated Peking, 20 Apr. 1916, and enc. Ibid., no. 100333, India Office's very confidential message to the Under Secretary of State for Foreign Affairs, dated 25 May 1916.

234. Lal Baha, 'Activities of Turkish agents in Khyber during World War I', *Journal of the Asiatic Society of Pakistan* (Dacca), XIV (2): Aug. 1969, pp. 185–92.

235. FO 371/3057, file 103481, Captain N.N.E. Bray's report to Lieut.-Col. C.E. Wilson, dated Jedda, 27 Mar. 1917, enc. in Wilson's no. J.P. 11/4, secret, to Gen. Sir Reginald Wingate, dated Jedda, 27 Mar. 1917.

236. Acc. to an intercepted letter from Tiflis, dated 11 Aug. 1917 — see FO 395/109, file 204738, no. 217122.

237. Naval Staff — Intelligence Department, *A manual on the Turanians and Panturanianism*, 1918, pp. 222–3.

238. See Alishan in *Asia: Journal of the American Asiatic Association*, XVIII (5): May 1918, p. 360.

239. FO 371/3296, file 676, nos 676, 1919, 8818, 11750, 14682, dated Dec. 1917 to Jan. 1918. FO 371/3303, file 3172, no. 7716, Sir J. Jordan's cyphered cable no. 40, dated 12 Jan. 1918. Ibid., no. 54088, cable no. P–11C, from the British Consul-General in Khorasan, to the Secretary in the Government of India, dated Meshed, 23 Jan. 1918, and cable no. 16-C, from the same to the same, dated 26 Jan. 1918. Ibid., no. 61829, Jordan's no. 50, to Balfour, dated Peking, 29 Jan. 1918. FO 371/3393, file 6554, no. 6554, British Ambassador Horace Rumbold's no. 13, to Balfour, dated Berne, 4 Jan. 1918. Ibid., no. 32551, Rumbold's no. 113, to Balfour, dated Berne, 13 Feb. 1918. Ibid., no. 37147, Rumbold's no. 136, to Balfour, dated Berne, 19 Feb. 1918.

240. FO 395/16, file 100207, 'The Neo-Turanian movement in Turkey', memorandum drawn up by the Arab Bureau, Cairo.

241. 'Major Bailey's Russian diary 1918–1920', esp. pp. 90 ff. This manuscript is deposited in the India Office, under MSS. Eur. C. 162.

242. FO 371/3399, file 35096, no. 35096, secret circular of the War Office, dated Geneva, 12 Feb. 1918. Cf. FO 371/3391, file 3828, no. 3828, Sir G. Buchanan's cyphered cable no. 48, to the Foreign Office, dated 6 Jan. 1918. FO 371/3300, file 2242, no. 19010, Stevens's cyphered cable no. 14, dated Tiflis, 28 Jan. 1918.

243. Details in Marunov, in *Kratkiye Soobshchyeniya Instituta Narodov Azii*, XLV: 1961, pp. 52 ff; Georgeon, pp. 78–80.
244. As *The Times* of 3 Jan. 1918 put it, in an article on 'The Turk militant'.
245. For a detailed description and analysis of this campaign, cf. Larcher, pp. 365–427.
246. For further details, see Gotthard Jäschke, 'Der Turanismus der Jungtürken: zur Osmanische Aussenpolitik im Weltkriege', *Die Welt des Islams*, XXIII: 1941, pp. 1–53. See also Wipert, in *Der Neue Orient*, VI (4): Dec. 1922, pp. 207 ff.
247. FO 371/3400, file 37581, no. 37581, Intelligence Bureau — Department of Information's *Weekly Report on Turkey and Other Moslem Countries*, no. ETW/001, dated 27 Feb. 1918.
248. FO 371/3300, file 2242, no. 19010, General Dunsterville's cable no. G6, dated 7 Mar. 1918.
249. On which see FO 371/3866, file 150, no. 159294, confidential memorandum to Lord Curzon, dated 26 Nov. 1919.
250. By which we refer throughout to Russian Azerbayjan (not to the Iranian).
251. FO 371/3301, file 2242, no. 86031, Marling's cyphered cable no. 407, dated Tehran, 13 May 1918.
252. FO 371/3415, the Director of Military Intelligence's no. B. 1/784 (M.I.2), secret, to the Under Secretary of State for Foreign Affairs, dated 10 Nov. 1918.
253. FO 371/3388, file 1396, no. 173495, the Director of Military Intelligence's no. B. 1/565 (M.I.2), secret, to the Under Secretary of State for Foreign Affairs, dated 15 Oct. 1918. This was realised even earlier at the Arab Bureau in Cairo, see 'Pan-Turan and the Arabs', *The Arab Bulletin*, 74: 24 Dec. 1917, pp. 507–9.
254. FO 371/3388, file 1396, no. 174496, the Director of Military Intelligence's no. B. 1/594 (M.I.2), to the Under Secretary of State for Foreign Affairs, dated 18 Oct. 1918, and enclosed memorandum. See also FO 371/3413, file 171726, internal Foreign Office correspondence, dated Oct. 1918; FO 371/3259, file 8, no. 83711, Marling's cyphered cable no. 396, dated Tehran, 9 May 1918.
255. Rumbold thought that it was meant to stretch from Constantinople to Tibet. See FO 371/3393, file 6554, no. 37147, Rumbold's no. 136, to Balfour, dated Berne, 19 Feb. 1918.
256. British Intelligence was practically certain that the Ottoman Empire was then working to form one unified government in the Northern Caucasus and Azerbayjan. See FO 371/3262, file 8, no. 175475, the Director of Military Intelligence's no. I/601 (M.I.2), dated 18 Oct. 1918; this is termed 'a reliable report from a very secret source.'
257. FO 371/3416, file 187338, nos 208036 and 211760, dated, respectively, 8 and 18 Dec. 1918; the second mentioned 150 Turkish officers.
258. For instance, referring to Mehmet Resulzade, see FO 371/3413, file 171726, Oct.–Nov. 1918.

259. FO 371/3663, file 1015, no. 135368, cable dated 26 Sep. 1919, forwarded from the War Office to the Foreign Office.
260. Jacques Kayaloff, 'From the Transcaucasian past: two documents about Turkish resistance in 1918', *Journal of Asian History* (Wiesbaden), VI (2): 1972, esp. pp. 129 ff.
261. Extracts, in English translation, appeared in *The Arab Bulletin* (Ramleh, Egypt), 114: 30 Aug. 1919, p. 143.
262. One example is Shaikh Husain Kidwai of Gadia, *The future of the Muslim empire: Turkey*, n.d. [prob. 1919].
263. FO 371/3662, file 1015, no. 115218, Lt.-Col. T. Bridges's secret report, dated 26 July 1919, enc. in the Director of Military Intelligence's no. B. I/4881 (M.I.2) to the Acting Under Secretary of State at the Foreign Office, dated 11 Aug. 1919. FO 371/5165, E 1509/262/44, Intelligence Report of the British G.H.Q. in Istanbul, no. 2737, weekly report no. 55, for the week ending 11 Feb. 1920, esp. App. D. FO 371/4161, file 521, no. 173267, the Director of Military Intelligence's weekly report no. 47, for the week ending 18 Dec. 1919, sent to the Secretary of State for Foreign Affairs on 23 Jan. 1920. *The Times*, 20 Mar. 1920.
264. See *The rise of the Turks. The Pan-Turanian movement*, prepared and printed by the Foreign Office, 1919, esp. pp. 28 ff. A copy of this booklet may be consulted in the India Office, under L/P&S/20–C.191.
265. FO 371/8073, N 3621/6/97, Hodgson's no. 203, confidential, to Curzon, dated Moscow, 10 Apr. 1922. Cf. Caroe, 2nd edn, ch. 7 ('Enver and the Basmachis').
266. Castagné, *Les Basmatchis*, p. 50; Karl Stählin, *Russisch-Turkestan gestern und heute*, p. 21.
267. Park, p. 163. On Enver and the Basmachis see also 'The Basmachis: the Central Asian resistance movement, 1918–24', *Central Asian Review*, VII (3): 1959, esp. pp. 242–6.
268. FO 371/8038, F 2073/2073/10, British Consul-General Lt.-Col. P.T. Etherton's no. 42–1922, to the Secretary to the Government of India, dated Kashgar, 3 Apr. 1922. FO 371/8075, N 10281/6/97, C.P. Skrines's (Offg. British Consul-General, Kashgar), no. 101, secret, to the Secretary to the Government of India, dated Kashgar, 14 Sep. 1922.
269. E.g., the Persian Minister to Kabul was certain about Enver's Pan-Turk 'designs' in Turkestan. See FO 371/8074, N 5478/6/97, Colonel Humphry's cyphered cable no. 28, to the Foreign Office, dated Kabul, 29 May 1922.
270. Castagné, *Les Basmatchis*, pp. 46 ff. See also Yamauchi Masayuki, *The green crescent under the red star: Enver Pasha in Soviet Russia 1919–1922*, 1991.
271. The ultimatum has appeared in a French translation by Castagné, pp. 49–50 and in *RMM*, LI: Oct. 1922, pp. 229–30.
272. As cannily analysed at the time in a report of the British Intelligence Service, see FO 371/8179, N 10682/246/38, Intelligence Service Report no. Misc. 15, secret, dated 23 Aug. 1922.

273. Cf. detailed report in FO 371/7947, E 6421/3873/44, most secret, dated 22 June 1922.
274. For which see FO 371/8179, N 9461/246/38, most secret, dated Foreign Office, London, 23 Oct. 1922. Cf. *OM*, II (4): 15 Sep. 1922, pp. 240–2.
275. FO, ibid. Also FO 371/9288, N 8951/153/97, *Meshed Intelligence Diary*, no. 76, for the period ending 17 Sep. 1923. Cf. Castagné, *Les Basmatchis*, pp. 60–1; Louis Fischer, 'The end of Enver Pasha', *The Virginia Quarterly Review* (University of Virginia), VI (2): April 1930, pp. 232–9; P.R. Ali, 'Enver Pasha his status in modern Turkish history', *Egyptian Historical Review* (Cairo), XXII: 1975, esp. pp. 24–7.
276. Cf. *Central Asian Review*, VII (3): 1959, p. 246.
277. He even sent agents to work for Pan-Turkism among the Turkmens of Transcaspia and the Turkic elements on the Caucasian frontier. See India Office, L/P&S/12/2274, Collection 10/2, report of the British military attache in Meshed, no. 949, secret, to the Chief of the General Staff, Army Headquarters, Delhi, dated Meshed, 30 Nov. 1924.
278. Details in Aydemir, 2nd edn, vol. III, esp. chs 9–12. Cf. Hostler, *Turkism*, pp. 148–56; Kurt Okay, *Enver Pascha, der grosse Freund Deutschlands*, 1935; Cemal Kutay, *Enver Paşa Lenin'e karşı*.
279. Stählin, pp. 21 ff. See also, for a detailed account of Enver's activities and battles in Central Asia, Tekin Erer, *Enver Paşa'nın Türkistan kurtuluş savaşı*.
280. E.g. in Abdullah Receb Baysun's *Türkistan millî hareketleri*, 1943, pp. 51–135.
281. For an example, see L.A. Springer, 'The romantic career of Enver Pasha, leader of the Young Turks and ally of the Kaiser', *Asia: Journal of the American Asiatic Association*, XVII (6): Aug. 1917, pp. 457–61.
282. Cf. Caroe, 2nd edn, pp. 122–3.

3

PAN-TURKISM IN THE REPUBLIC OF TURKEY: THE LATENT STAGE

The defeat and break-up of the Ottoman Empire discredited the main political ideologies which had been prevalent during its later years. Ottomanism had lost its very *raison d'être*; and neither Pan-Islamism nor Pan-Turkism had succeeded in saving the Empire. The latter also lost its foreign ally, as the new German state displayed no interest. Various Turkish organisations in Europe did address letters to different governments and to the Peace Conference, continuing to adduce Pan-Turk arguments for the Ottoman Empire's participation in the First World War.[1] However, Turkey's future was to be determined within its own borders. Although some Pan-Turkists (possibly in contact with Enver[2]) were still active in Turkey, the country's War of Independence, so capably led by Mustafa Kemal, aroused the support of the population by emphasising patriotism — the defence of land and home against invaders — above all other sentiments.[3] It should hardly have been surprising, therefore, that on establishing the Republic of Turkey in 1923, Mustafa Kemal exerted considerable efforts to endow it with a new conception of nationalism.

Evidently, ideologies do not simply disappear on orders from above: in this case not a few ideas of the Young Turks and their era (for instance, several of Ziya Gökalp's teachings) carried over into the Republic.[4] Thus several elements of the Turkism and Pan-Turkism of the late Ottoman Empire passed to the new ideology.[5] Nevertheless, the nationalism envisaged by Mustafa Kemal — which consequently became state doctrine in the Republic — had an essentially different orientation. As early as 1921, during the War of Independence, Mustafa Kemal, speaking at Eskişehir, declared: 'Neither Islamic union nor Turanism may constitute a doctrine, or logical policy for us. Henceforth the Government policy of the new Turkey is to consist in living independently, relying on Turkey's own sovereignty within her national frontiers.'[6] The new approach regarded the national *internal* interests of the new Republic as the most important of all considerations, and indeed the only relevant ones. Mustafa Kemal reiterated this view on several occasions, including it within his six-day speech in 1927.[7] All this made sense to Mustafa Kemal and his advisers not only because patriotism had vindicated itself remarkably, while other ideologies had failed, but also because Turkey, badly ravaged by war, needed to concentrate its efforts on its own reconstruction. Turkey was now a smaller and fairly homogeneous state, as compared to the huge multi-national Ottoman Empire; hence the option appeared more feasible. A self-centred policy would also prove advantageous in foreign relations, as the renouncing of Pan-Turk ideals would assist in normalisation of relations with the Soviet Union — a policy which Mustafa Kemal prudently pursued.[8] Not accidentally, perhaps, this withdrawal from Pan-Turkism coincided with Lenin's abandonment of Pan-Slavism.[9]

With very few exceptions, such as in the case of the Syrian district of Alexandretta annexed by Turkey in the late 1930s and renamed Hatay, political Pan-Turkism, particularly its irredentist element, was officially frowned upon and discouraged.[10] One may even say that the wave of reforms in Turkey raised a barrier between the local Turks and others.[11] Interest shown in the areas inhabited by Turkic groups[12] was always minimal and discreet on the official level. While the Turkish authorities, during the 1920s and 1930s, did encourage Turks from other countries to emigrate to Turkey,[13] for instance from Cyprus between 1934 and 1936,[14] or from the Balkans,[15] this need not be interpreted in a Pan-Turk context;[16] rather, it represents a desire to recoup the loss in population sustained during the First World War and the War of Independence. Then, during the 1930s, although several associations with Pan-Turk leanings were active outside Turkey — with such suggestive names as *Turan* or *Altın Ordu* (The Golden Horde) in Bulgarian Thrace[17] or *Kardeş Ocağı* (The hearth of brethren) in Cyprus, where it was supported by the Turkish newspapers *Söz* and *Ses*[18] — there is no evidence to suggest that the Government of Turkey itself officially supported them. Indeed, during the 1930s government circles expressed reservations about these manifestations.[19]

Kemalism[20] consistently displayed considerable talent in assimilating the immediate past and shaping a new future. Whenever possible, proponents of the doctrine convinced potential rivals, accommodated existing institutions and absorbed diverse ideological elements, including those of Pan-Turkism, as a few examples will demonstrate.

Firstly, Halide Edib, whose novel *Yeni Turan* had inspired the Pan-Turkists[21] and who, early in 1920, was still proclaiming to the Istanbul crowds, at a large meeting organised by the *Türk Ocağı*, that

Azerbayjan's independence was the first step in the Pan-Turk programme (also to include the Crimea, Khiva, Tashkent and Bukhara),[22] subsequently abandoned Pan-Turkism. And Mehmet Emin Yurdakul re-edited some of his poems to read *vatan* (Fatherland) instead of *Turan*. Then Ahmet Ağaoğlu accepted the official position of Director of the Press Bureau in Ankara, in June 1921 (he was later elected to the Grand National Assembly in 1923 and 1927).[23] As early as 1923, Ağaoğlu, still Director of the Press Bureau, impressed a visiting French journalist with his devotion to Mustafa Kemal. It was remarkable to note that he — of all people — had told her: 'Ankara is nationalist, renouncing the pretensions of the old Ottoman Empire; it wishes to establish a modest Turkish national home, restricted to the ethnographic Turkish frontiers . . . for that, she needs peace'.[24] Ağaoğlu also expressed these views in the press of that time.[25] Five years later, Yusuf Akçura proclaimed that the Republic of Turkey was the embodiment of all Pan-Turkism's desires.[26] Without abjuring Pan-Turkism, Akçura — as a Member of the Grand National Assembly and a professor of history — had to identify with the new regime; never having been a member of the Committee of Union and Progress, he could join with relative ease. Tekin Alp and several others had also meanwhile become fervent Kemalists; Tekin Alp, in fact, became the author of a standard work on Kemalism.

Secondly, a rather similar process occurred with respect to *Türk Ocağı*, commonly known during the Republican period as *Türk Ocakları*[27] (that is, Hearths of the Turks), the only effective organisation that Pan-Turkists had established within the Ottoman Empire.[28] It had participated in the war effort through dissemination of political propaganda within the Empire and had reportedly even set up branches in the Caucasus and Turkestan.[29] In 1917, the organisation's emissaries spread Pan-Turk propaganda in the Arabian Peninsula.[30] When the war ended, its leaders joined forces with the *Teceddüd* (Regeneration) political group led by an ex-member of the Committee of Union and Progress, İsmail Cambolat, thereby striving for a joint impact upon local politics.[31] Many of the organisation's members met in Istanbul on 11 March 1919, unanimously adopting a resolution which was later presented as a petition to the British High Commissioner (for transmission to the victorious Allies). This petition protested the projected dismemberment of the Ottoman Empire and averred that it had gone to war only against its hereditary enemy, Russia.[32] Late in April 1920, the organisation reaffirmed its support for Azerbayjan's struggle for independence and for close ties with Turkey.[33] In the next few years, however, its activities were frozen; it reopened only in 1924.

The President of the *Türk Ocakları*, Hamdullah Suphi Tanrıöver, already mentioned,[34] had never been one of the leading Pan-Turkists, although he was acceptable to them.[35] During the First World War, he had indeed shown some sympathy with Pan-Turkism — when it was fashionable to do so — and had even written an article in favour of it for *Türk Yurdu* in 1915.[36] Otherwise, he showed himself to be a nationalist Turk, a Turkist rather than a Pan-Turkist, as his articles[37] and speeches[38] indicate (rare exceptions notwithstanding[39]). It was not difficult for Tanrıöver, a gifted orator, to persuade *Türk Ocakları*, from the mid-1920s on, to adopt the nationalist ideology that had become the official state doctrine,[40] especially as initiated and recommended by Mustafa Kemal himself. At the first congress of the 'new' hearths, convened in Ankara in 1924 (with representatives of 135 hearths present), Tanrıöver determined that the main objective of *Türk Ocakları* was to preserve Turkish culture and defend Kemalist reforms. The organisation did indeed concentrate its efforts increasingly on cooperating with the Republican People's Party, in both larger and smaller population centres, working for modernisation of Turkey. For *Türk Ocakları*, this involved an intensive westernisation campaign, expressed in terms of modernised education, the establishment of reading-rooms and libraries with French and English (in addition to Turkish) journals and books and the introduction of Western music, theatrical performances and sports activities.[41] By 1930, the organisation even had its own printing press in Ankara. Membership, which in 1925 had been 30,000 (in 217 hearths), remained fairly steady, even increasing by 1930 to about 32,000, dispersed among 257 hearths throughout Turkey.[42]

Despite *Türk Ocakları's* commitment to Kemalism, Pan-Turk tendencies continued to manifest themselves in the organisation. For example, Pan-Turk articles continued to appear in *Türk Yurdu*, such as those contributed by Ayaz İshakî, a Tatar and active Pan-Turkist, in November 1925.[43] In consequence, Tanrıöver, no doubt on instructions from the Government, amended the organisation's constitution in 1927, limiting 'the field of operations of the Turkish Hearths to the frontiers of the Republic of Turkey'.[44] Nevertheless, Pan-Turk demands continued to be voiced among members; as late as 1930, requests were still being received from Turkic groups in Azerbayjan, Turkestan and Bulgaria who wished to set up branches of *Türk Ocakları* in their respective areas.[45] It was hardly surprising, therefore, that the organisation was dissolved in March 1931,[46] and replaced by another, the *Halk Evleri* (Peoples' Homes), totally committed to the new state ideology and to its propagation.[47]

Thirdly, certain elements of cultural Pan-Turkism were incor-

porated into the new nationalist ideology[48] known as Kemalism[49] —
although, as indicated above, the irredentist motif was avoided,[50] and
no political decisions were based on Pan-Turkism.[51] The Kemalists,
like the Turkists of the two preceding generations, studied and researched the glorious past of the Turks since their earliest origins —
concentrating upon language, literature, history, geography, and related domains. Once again, it was hoped that the new Turkish nation
would be provided with a past of its own, of which it could rightly
be proud; then, once an appropriate sense of direction was added, it
would guide the nation towards a future based on their past. Examples
of this approach are numerous, in several areas,[52] particularly with
respect to the purification of the Turkish language and the re-writing
of history. In the former discipline, systematic elimination of Arabic
and Persian words was interpreted by Pan-Turkists (such as Mehmet
Asım, writing in *Vakit*, in 1925[53]) as a step in the direction of creating
a language common to Turks in Turkey and abroad.[54] In the latter
case, new writings indicated that the place of origin of all Turks was
on the Altai plateau in Central Asia, whence they spread civilisation
to the world.

Writers, accordingly, continued the pre-war tradition of demonstrating the historical unity of all Turks. For example, in the early
1920s there appeared a book by Cami (pseudonym) entitled *Osmanlı
ülkesinde Hristiyan Türkler* (The Christian Turks in the Ottoman
countries),[55] which examined the early history of the Turks from a
Pan-Turk view-point, its title notwithstanding. An even more relevant
work was the new, four-volume history text for all Turkey's secondary (senior high) schools (*lise*), prepared by the respectable Turkish
Historical Society (*Türk Tarih Kurumu*) at the request of the Ministry
of Education.[56] The first volume, printed in 1932, put forth observations which may have had Pan-Turk connotations (as the Soviets
believed[57]), including the claim that the ancient Turks had already
possessed the idea of nationality; the concept of 'Turkish race' and
so forth.[58] Such ideas occasionally penetrated *Ülkü* (Ideal), the sedate,
officially-inspired monthly of the above-mentioned People's Homes
(published since February 1933), although this is hardly an indication
of Pan-Turk sympathies; rather, it provides additional evidence of the
absorption of Pan-Turkism into the official state ideology.[59] The
earlier confusion between Turkism and Pan-Turkism[60] seemed to be
resolving itself by the fusion of the latter into the former. Even the
official policy of encouraging the Turkic-speaking minorities in Bulgaria and Greece to emigrate to Turkey[61] was regarded in the light
of the interests of the Republic of Turkey. Similarly, Law 2510,

passed in 1934, provided the means for assimilating Turkish nationals of non-Turkish culture into Turkey, on the one hand, and, on the other, for absorbing and settling immigrants of Turkish culture arriving from abroad.[62]

Under such circumstances, Pan-Turkists in the Republic of Turkey found themselves in a situation radically different from the one they had become accustomed to in the late Ottoman Empire, when their ideologies had in fact been adopted for a time by the leadership of the Committee of Union and Progress. Only confirmed optimists could have agreed with Dr Arın Engin, a dedicated Pan-Turkist, whose motto, as expressed in one of his books,[63] was that 'Atatürk is not merely the Father of Turkey's Turks, but of all Turkdom' — implying that he is the father of all Outside Turks as well. The attitude of the authorities in the Republic of Turkey was hardly such as to encourage Pan-Turkism, but this was only one of the difficulties facing Pan-Turkists. Another was the changed situation in the world after the Versailles Peace Conference and the 1923 Lausanne Conference. Besides the Outside Turks living in Iran, the Soviet Union and China, already there before the war, a large number had joined this status in former Ottoman possessions, such as Irak, Syria, Romania, Bulgaria, Yugoslavia, Greece and Cyprus. The broadening scope of this issue posed new challenges for Pan-Turkism's irredentism at a time when the movement was least capable of coping with them.[64] Yet another handicap was occasioned as many leading Pan-Turkists passed into the service of the Republic, as mentioned above. In addition, several leading Pan-Turkists died during the first two decades of the Republic: Gökalp died in 1924, Necib Asım, Yusuf Akçura and Ahmet Ağaoğlu in the 1930s, Ali Hüseyinzade in 1941, and Mehmet Emin Yurdakul in 1944.

All things considered, Pan-Turkism was more latent than visibly active during those first twenty years from the Republic's foundation in 1923 until that turning-point during the Second World War when new hopes stirred the Outside Turks and Pan-Turkist circles within Turkey to renewed optimism and action. During that time, what limited organisation there was[65] existed mostly to help emigrants, materially and culturally. Pan-Turkists in Turkey limited themselves chiefly to literary and journalistic activity, ostensibly within the officially-imposed parameters, but actually seeking every legal or semilegal loophole, first, to highlight the situation of the Outside Turks as a cause common to Turkey's Turks as well; and, secondly, emphasising the political character of this bond. These features essentially differentiated the Pan-Turkist publications from those following the official Kemalist line. No wonder, then, that in the late 1920s and early 1930s several periodicals of the Outside Turks in Turkey were closed down and the importation of others from Europe was banned.[66]

During the first two decades of the Republic, Pan-Turk periodicals published abroad had a very definite political character, while many of those issued in Turkey prudently kept to the cultural level, at least during the lifetime of Mustafa Kemal (who died in November 1938). It is highly unlikely that this two-pronged approach to Pan-Turkism was masterminded by any particular organisation; rather, it appears to have been due to force of circumstances. The following is a summary of some of the main topics considered in this literature, accompanied by an analysis of its characteristics and trends.

Pan-Turk literature published outside Turkey after the First World War (some of which undoubtedly found its way into Turkey as well) was largely political in nature, not only because it appeared in countries which did not impose press censorship, but also because it was almost invariably written and sponsored by Outside Turks, refugees from the Soviet Union, who enjoyed political involvement in the fortunes of Pan-Turkism.

During this period, several periodicals of Pan-Turk character were published in Europe. Most were issued irregularly (probably because of the expenses involved), but there were two exceptions: *Turan Mecmuası*, published in Budapest, and *Prométhée*, an anti-Soviet journal originating in Poland.

Turan Mecmuası (The magazine of Turan), already mentioned briefly,[67] was not a Pan-Turk journal in the strict sense; rather, it was a Turanian publication, issued by Hungarians who considered themselves part of the Turanian race,[68] and several of whom belonged to a society named *Turan*, established early in the twentieth century and subsidised by the Hungarian Government.[69] Although primarily concerned with scholarly research into Turanian languages, history and folklore, *Turan* also had definite political objectives. Indeed, its ultimate goal was the establishment of a Turanian state in the area roughly defined as 'the territory between the Volga, the Caspian Sea, Iran and the Altai Mountains'.[70] This, the society's leaders claimed, was not only feasible due to the ethnic ties among the peoples in this area, but also viable economically, thanks to its natural resources. This was expressed in a series of studies on Turkism, by László Rásonyi[71] and others. The society's organ, *Turan*, which began publication in 1913 as a quarterly, was mostly in Hungarian, but had several pages in Turkish as well, particularly in the early years. Later, articles in German and French were added. The first issue's masthead read 'The Turan journal — Monthly of the Turan Society'.[72] From 1918 it proclaimed, in German and Hungarian, that *Turan* was 'a periodical for East-European, Near- and Middle-Eastern Studies'. From 1924, it also included a more detailed French legend, claiming that the journal deals with 'the history, ethnography, political situation and literature of the Turanian peoples, as well as their cultural aspirations and historical bonds with Western lands'.[73] The journal strove to convince its readers of the practical relevance of the Turanian ideology, particularly in the light of its claim that Turanians numbered 610 million.[74]

It was evident that the Turan society and its publications constituted an expression of the isolation felt by the Hungarians in what appeared to them as a hostile environment, as well as a manifestation of their search for potential allies. To a great extent this was also the feeling of those Polish circles which published the other long-term inter-war periodical, *Prométhée*. This was the organ of the Promethean League, a semi-clandestine anti-Soviet association, established and sponsored by President Pilsudsky, the Polish Ministry for Foreign Affairs and the General Staff as an umbrella-organisation to provide financial assistance and political co-ordination for anti-communist governments-in-exile.[75] All those who had suffered at the hands of the Soviets were considered as their natural allies against the Soviet peril; among these, the Outside Turks held a prominent position. The association's bulletin, *Prométhée: Organe de Défense Nationale des Peuples du Caucase et de l'Ukraine* was published monthly in Paris from November 1926 to April 1938.[76] Turkestan was subsequently added to its masthead and the publication was ultimately named *Prométhée: Organe de Défense Nationale des Peuples Opprimés de l'U.R.S.S.* Well-known Pan-Turkists, such as Resul-Zade, Mirza-Bala and others, contributed articles about the strong sentiments for independence and for a Pan-Turk union in Azerbayjan, the Caucasus and Turkestan. Polish financial aid to Pan-Turkist organisations may well have continued even during the Second World War;[77] this subject, however, lies beyond the scope of our immediate concern.

Most Pan-Turk publications issued outside Turkey during the period under discussion, appeared in Western (more rarely, Eastern) Europe, subsidised in part by the Promethean League. Periodicals included:
(1) *Yeni Turan* (The new Turan), monthly organ of the Hearth of Turan in Finland, appearing in Tampere and then in Helsinki, from November 1931,[78] in Turkish and Finnish. Its publisher was Abdullah Ahsan. First and foremost an anti-Soviet periodical, it was also definitely concerned with the Outside Turks everywhere and, no less, with Pan-Turkism—about which it printed poems and articles.

82   *Pan-Turkism*

(2) *Kurtuluş* (Liberation), an Azerbayjan monthly in Turkish, organ of the *Müsavat* Party, appearing in Berlin from November 1934 to July 1939, edited by Hilâl Münşi and Mehmet Emin Resul-Zade.[79] The latter was already known for contributing articles and stories to the periodical press in Turkey that showed sympathy to Pan-Turkism.[80]

(3) *Şimalî Kafkasya*, subtitled *Syevyerniy Kavkaz — Le Caucase du Nord — Northern Caucasus*, monthly organ of the Popular Party of the people of the Caucasus, published in Warsaw from May 1934 to June 1939, in Russian and Turkish. The editor was throughout Barasbi Baytugan. Articles promoted 'the unity of the Caucasus' (which, according to the map on the back cover of all issues, extended from Kuban to Baku) and carried both information about the region, past and present, and Pan-Turk anti-Soviet articles — some fictional, others based on research.[81]

(4) *Yaş Türkistan* (Young Turkestan), organ of the National Council of Turkestan, issued in Berlin as a monthly from December 1931 to June 1939, in Turkestanian; its life-and-soul was Mustafa Çokay.[82]

(5) *Yeni Millî Yol* (The New National Road), organ of the National Idel[83] Ural Committee, published in Berlin in Tatar Turkish.

(6) *Emel Medjmuası* (sic) (The journal of hope), monthly of the Crimean Turkish Committee, put out in Pazarcık (Romania) in Crimean Turkish, from January 1930 to 1941; its publisher-editor was a local lawyer, Müstecib H. Fazıl.[84]

(7) The monthly *Türkistan* (entitled, in French, *Turkestan. Revue Nouvelle. Organe de défense nationale de Turkestan*), published during 1934–5, in France, in Turkish (but in Arabic script[85]) and mainly concerned with Turkestan and its suffering under the Soviets. Its editor-publisher was the above-mentioned Mustafa Çokay (or Çokayoğlu),[86] a nationalist who had to flee from Khokand before the advance of the Red Army in February 1918.[87] He settled in Paris and continued to struggle for the cause of Turkestan, particularly on behalf of its Uzbeks and Turkmens. A sample of his publications is provided by his *Chez les Soviets en Asie Centrale*, printed in Paris in 1928 (he enlarged it, in Russian, seven years later[88]). This combined strongly-worded accusations against Soviet rule in Turkestan with a Pan-Turk-inspired appeal for its independence.

At the December 1931 General Islamic Congress in Jerusalem, two booklets in Arabic were presented, separately, and subsequently published by, respectively, Said Şamil, Head of the National Defence Committee for the Northern Caucasus[89] and Ayaz İshakî. The latter was a Kazan Turco-Tatar nationalist (1878–1954),[90] who had assisted

Akçura in setting up *Kazan Muhbiri*,[91] participated in the all-Muslim Congress of 1905,[92] been active in attempts to unite all Turco-Tatars, and later contributed Pan-Turk articles to *Türk Yurdu* in the era of the Republic.[93] In 1931 he headed the Independence Committee for the Muslims of Idel Ural.[94] Although the grievances brought up by Şamil and İshakî were presented on behalf of Muslims in the Soviet Union, they evoked Pan-Turk arguments as well.

Somewhat later, Basry Bey, a Yugoslav Turk of Albanian origin, formerly close to Young Turk circles, in his *Le Monde Turc et l'avenir de sa mission historique (l'illusionisme moscovite et la réalité turque)*, published in 1932, launched an appeal for the unity of all Turks. This call for unity was summed up toward the end of the book, as follows:[95]

Since the revolution broke the force of the Czar's armies, Central Asia has unceasingly looked not towards Moscow but towards Asia Minor. In any event, there is continuity between these two Asias: From the most remote deserts of Mongolia, through Samarkand, Bukhara, Baku, Ganja and Ankara, up to Istanbul and Edirne, the Turks, filled up with a new hope, join hands together. This force, which has gained momentum, leads to the inevitable union of all these proud peoples, towards a Federation of all Turkeys!

A few years later, in 1938, two politically-active Azeri Turks, writing in what was clearly a Pan-Turk style, attempted to mobilise public support for their cause. The first such work was Mehmet-Zade Mirza-Bala's (1898–1959) *Millî Azerbaycan hareketi Millî Az. Müsavat Halk Fırkası tarihi* (The national movement of Azerbayjan: the history of the national Azerbayjan *Müsavat* People's Party), a voluminous study probably intended for readers in Turkey, as it was written in Turkish. The second, published in German and, hence, probably intended for European consumption, was *Das Problem Aserbeidschan*, the text of a lecture by M.E. Resul-Zade (1884–1955),[96] on the twentieth anniversary of Azerbayjan's Declaration of Independence (28 May 1918).[97]

Two years later, H.M. Ahmad, writing in Germany during the early days of the Second World War, energetically supported Pan-Turkism — in Turanian guise — in his 1940 *Kampf um leere Räume: Turan — Turkestan — Tibet*. He argued persuasively that Turks and Mongols belonged to the same race; by joining forces, he said, they could achieve anything they desired.[98] The obvious implication was that the time was right for just such an undertaking.

These are only a few examples of the numerous Pan-Turk-leaning publications issued outside Turkey. An even greater number were printed within Turkey itself, by both Outside and native Turks.

Several of the more characteristic examples of such publications will be considered; these may be classified according to two principal categories — monographs and periodicals.

In 1925, Abdullah Battal-Taymas (1882/3–1969) wrote his *Kazan Türkleri: Türk tarihinin hazin yaprakları* (The Turks of Kazan: sad pages of Turkish history).[99] Although basically a history of the Kazan Tatars — whom the author, characteristically, called 'Turks' — from ancient times to the Soviet era, the book strongly emphasised Tatar cultural activities, promoting the concept of unity of Turkish culture and (not coincidentally) of Pan-Turkism. The style is written with sadness, rather than passion. At the same time, Mehmet Emin Resulzade — whose earlier work, *Azerbaycan Cumhuriyeti, Keyfiyet-i teşekkülü ve-şimdiki vaziyeti* (The Republic of Azerbaijan: the manner of its formation and its actual situation), had already appeared two years previously[100] — now published in 1925 *İstiklâl mefkûresi ve gençlik. Esbab-ı hezimemize bir mütâlaa* (The ideal of independence and youth: a study in the causes of our defeat), a survey of the nationalist movement in Azerbayjan, under Czarist and Soviet rule (until *c.* 1923) and an interpretation of its failure.[101] In 1927, Mehmedzade Mirza-Bala *Azerbaycan Misak-ı Millî* (The National Pact of Azerbayjan) described the nationalist movement in Azerbayjan since 1918, with obvious sympathy for the 'nationalists and Pan-Turkists'.[102] While the author prudently avoided sounding a clear call for action — probably in order not to antagonise his Turkish hosts — the implication was definitely there.

The Outside Turks, actively sustaining the cause of Pan-Turkism in Turkey during the 1920s, were joined by local Turks in the 1930s. At this time, Pan-Turk sympathisers had to express themselves very cautiously. Consider, for example, Aka Gündüz (1886–1958), a man of letters whose articles were published in the press before and during the First World War; a British Intelligence report had described him then as 'an incendiary journalist: strongly Nationalist. Of the Neo-Turanian school'.[103] During the Inter-War period, Aka Gündüz continued to write novels, short stories and plays. These works, many of which were printed in several editions, were replete with local colour and at least hinted at evident Pan-Turk sentiments (as one could not do much more than hint at them then).

Perhaps the very first book to relate directly to Pan-Turkism during this period was Reşit Saffet's *Türklük ve Türkçülük izleri* (Traces of Turkism and Pan-Turkism) of 1930, in which the author collected archaeological and literary traces of the world's Turks to be found in places he had visited or books he had read. The book was part of a series issued by the *Türk Ocakları* organisation;[104] hence, Saffet had

to be doubly careful in his writing, emphasising his Turkism rather
than his Pan-Turkism, two terms he frequently confused, perhaps
intentionally. Pan-Turk sentiments did gush forth,[105] however, in his
discussion of the Turks in Iran,[106] whom he claimed the Iranian
authorities were annihilating. Saffet declared that he did not demand
any of Iran's territory, but that something must be done immediately
to rescue the Turks there. An even more emotional work is Fuat
Şükrü's 1931 *Turan ve Türkler. Şiir* (Turan and the Turks. Poems),
published in the following year. These have a definite Pan-Turk slant,
idealising Turan and expressing longing and admiration for the land,
its natural beauty and sentimental associations.

In another vein, A.A.A. Candar's *Türklüğün kökleri ve yayılışı*
(The roots and spread of Turkism), published in 1934, is in the nature
of a socio-linguistic study. It begins with a chapter on the greatness
of the Turkish race,[107] praising the Turks in a spirit which most
Pan-Turkists would have approved of. Similar sentiments are expressed in Muharrem Feyzi Togay's[108] 1938 *Turanî kavimler ve siyasî
tarihlerinin esas hatları* (The Turanian peoples[109] and the basic lines
of their political history), the text of a lecture to a group of Turkestanian youths, which constitutes more than a mere analysis of Turan
inhabitants. His imagination fired by the aura of the term 'Turan',
Togay insisted that he was speaking not merely about Turan, but
rather about Great Turan,[110] which implied a maximalist Pan-Turk
approach. Even more revealing was his insistence on the unity (or
the union) of Turan[111] — past, present and future — which would
place Turan on the political map.[112] An even more compendious
volume by the renowned Turcologist Ahmed Zeki Velidi Togan,[113]
Bugünkü Türkistan ve yakın mazisi (Contemporary Turkestan and its
recent past), published the following year,[114] was also not merely a
scholarly description and analysis of Turkestan, past and present, but
also a deliberate attempt to emphasise the importance of its future to
the world at large.

The two last-mentioned works appeared, one near the end of
Mustafa Kemal's life, the other after his death. Less than a year later,
the Second World War broke out and Turkey's neutrality allowed
Pan-Turkists a clear perception of world events. Several of them
renewed their activity at that time, including A. Münir Haymana
Yaylalıgıl who, in 1937, had already translated a part of the British
Admiralty's *A Manual on the Turanians and Panturanianism* (1918),
under the suggestive title *Hali hazırın Türk toplulukları ve Pan-
Türklüğe dair* (Concerning the actual present of the Turkish groups
and Pan-Turkism). It was surely not accidental that his title translated
'Turanians' as 'Turkish groups' and 'Panturanianism' as 'Pan-

Turkism'. In 1942, he added a pamphlet entitled *Türkçüleri unut-mıyalım! Çünkü: onlar, buna lâyıkdır* (Let us remember the Pan-Turkists, because they have merited it!). These publications strove to put an end to the discreditation of Pan-Turkism and Pan-Turkists and to enable them to enjoy political respectability once again.

At the very same time, there was also renewed interest in the Outside Turks, whose emigrants were constantly active in Turkey. One example is the fairly detailed biography of İsmail Gasprinsky published in 1934, of which the author was Cafer Seydahmet (Kırımer), another Tatar, an active Pan-Turkist who had settled in Turkey.[115] The number of monographs written by emigrants to Turkey about their brethren, the Outside Turks — generally with Pan-Turk content — increased during the war. For instance, A. Caferoğlu's *Azerbaycan*, published in 1940, pleaded for the independence of Soviet-governed Azerbaijan. In 1942, San'an Azer (pseudonym of M. Sadık Aran) published his *İran Türkleri* (The Turks of Iran). Written by a refugee from the Tabriz area, who claimed to speak for the 5 million Turks of Iran (out of a total population of 10 million),[116] it attacked the persecution of the Turks — especially the repression of the Turkish language and culture, attempting to rouse public opinion in Turkey on their behalf. One year later, in 1943, Abdullah Receb Baysun's *Türkistan millî hareketleri* (The national movements of Turkestan) appeared in Istanbul. The monograph described glow-ingly the national struggle of Turkestan; the Pan-Turk implications were evident.

Pan-Turk writing during the first two decades of the Republic seems to have received its main thrust through journalism. A man like Yusuf Akçura obviously could not be prevented from writing, and his articles appeared in various periodicals, such as *İctihad* (published twice a month in Istanbul), where he even had a regular column, *Siyaset ve İktisat* (Politics and Economics).[117] Other journalists published special volumes of collected articles, which would thus reach a potentially wider audience. Examples of such collected works are Atsız, a leading Pan-Turkist (to whom we shall revert presently), in his 1935 *Türk tarihi üzerinde toplamalar* (Addenda to the history of Turks), in which he attempted to periodise Turkish history along broader Pan-Turk lines, as well as İ.M. Hakkı Baltacıoğlu's 1943 *Türke doğru* (Towards the Turk), which dealt with Pan-Turkism in a prudent but obvious manner.[118]

Eventually, however, several Pan-Turkists began to realise that their cause would best be served by publication of periodicals which were wholly Pan-Turk in nature. The first steps were taken by Outside Turks who had emigrated to Turkey. Thus Azeris put out *Yeni Kaf-*

kasya. Edebî, içtimaî ve siyasî milliyetperver mecmua (New Caucasus: a literary, social and political patriotic journal) which appeared
in Istanbul between 1923 and 1927,[119] in Turkish. Soon afterwards,
there appeared in Istanbul, from 1927 to 1931, somewhat irregularly,
thirty-nine issues of a monthly entitled *Yeni Türkistan* (The New
Turkestan), first in Ottoman Turkish, then in the new Latin script;[120]
it was edited by Ahmed Mecdeddin. This had been joined by *Odlu
Yurt: Millî Azerbaycan fekriyatını tervic eden aylık mecmua* (Fiery
Fatherland: a Monthly Promoting the Concept of a National Azerbayjan), published in Istanbul in Turkish between 1929 and 1931 and
edited by M.E. Resulzade.[121] *Azerbaycan Yurt Bilgisi* ('Civics' of
Azerbayjan — a remarkably innocuous-sounding title), a more
scholarly journal edited by Ahmet Caferoğlu,[122] was issued monthly
in Istanbul from 1932 to 1934, after the former two periodicals had
already ceased publication. It was only from the early 1930s that local
Turks succeeded in issuing their own periodicals in a systematic
manner. From then on, the history of Pan-Turkism has largely been
a function of the publications issued by its adherents. The following
brief survey of such periodicals will aid in identification of the main
trends.

The first such publication is apparently *Atsız Mecmua. Aylık fikir
mecmuası* (Atsız: a Monthly Magazine of Ideas), so named for its
publisher-editor, the above-mentioned Hüseyin Nihal Atsız. It was
published in Istanbul, on a fairly regular basis between 15 May 1931
and 25 September 1932,[123] with Atsız himself contributing many of
the articles. The topics focused on Turkish history and literature, with
considerable attention given to the Outside Turks. The articles were
generally innocuous, dealing with such topics as Uzbek and Turkmen
music,[124] folk-songs of the Kirkuk Turks,[125] popular literature of
Azerbayjan,[126] and the daily life and work of Kazakh women.[127]
However, one series of articles concerned with the statistical data of
Turks living in Soviet lands[128] concluded that there were 16,462,381
such people.[129] These articles were particularly relevant in view of
Atsız's own forcefully-stated opinions[130] that all Turks were of one
race — the Altaic or Turanian — and that they should under no
circumstances forget their traditions.[131] All in all, however, *Atsız
Mecmua* was rather moderate in tone, concentrating on the cultural
life of Turks and Outside Turks, with political views implied, rather
than explicitly voiced. As 1931 was the year that the *Türk Ocakları*
was closed down, it was hardly the most opportune moment for overt
Pan-Turk propaganda. Nevertheless, a start had been made and patterns laid down, to be followed in the future.

The next Pan-Turk periodical to appear was *Orhun. Aylık Türkçü*

Mecmua (Orhun:[132] A Pan-Turk Monthly), published in Istanbul as
a monthly (but irregularly); the first nine issues appeared from late
1933 to 16 July 1934, while the next seven were issued, after a long
interruption, from 1 October 1943 to 1 April 1944.[133] The term
Türkçü, which appeared on *Orhun's* masthead, means 'Turkist' or
'Pan-Turkist', although there is not much doubt that the latter meaning
was intended by the publisher-editor, Hüseyin Nihal Atsız. Although
Orhun did have its share of studies in the Turkish language, literature,
and history, with appropriate comments on the glory of the ancient
Turks, an increasing number of articles of Pan-Turk character, quite
militant in tone, began to appear as well. Most were written by Atsız
himself, thus setting the publication's general tone. For example, he
praised Tatar activity in the Russian *Duma*, arguing that the Tatars
are Turks;[134] another article was devoted to İsmail Gasprinsky, emphasising his activities on behalf of all-Turk union.[135] The cover pages
of several issues[136] showed a map of all Turks in Turkish lands,
extending from the Mediterranean through Central Asia almost up to
the shores of the Pacific. This view was also stressed[137] in Atsız's
writing on Eastern Turkestan, where he dramatically proclaimed
'Turkestan is ours!' and 'All of Turkestan and all the Turkish lands
are ours!'[138] Atsız consistently propounded his theory of racial unity,
the crux of which was that for the Turks, the problem of nationhood
was first and foremost one of blood; that is, one who says 'I am a
Turk' must be of Turkish stock. According to Atsız, the Kipchaks of
Lithuania and the Kirghiz are Turks by blood, while people of 'alien
blood', even if they live in Turkey and speak Turkish, as Jews or
negroes do, are not.[139]

The year 1934 was a bad time for Pan-Turk periodicals. *Orhun*
closed down, as did two other magazines sympathetic to Pan-Turkism
— *Geçit* (Mountain Pass) and *Birlik* (Unity, or Union), the latter an
organ of the students' organisation, the *Milli Türk Talebe Birliği*.[140]
Their place was taken by *Çağlayan. Aylık fikir ve edebiyat dergisi*
(Waterfall: a monthly of ideas and literature), which appeared in
Antalya in December 1935.[141] Its publisher-editor was Sıtkı Tekeli.
The new journal stood for a 'nationalist literature'.[142] This it interpreted as affording an opportunity for nationalist writers to publish
in its pages. Anyway, its nationalism was expressed mildly, probably
due to strict government control. It did, however, occasionally assume
an anti-Russian line.

Following the discontinuation of *Çaglayan*, another monthly
started to appear, entitled *Ergenekon. Gençlik ve fikir dergisi. İlmî-
Edebî-İçtimaî* (*Ergenekon*:[143] a Review for Youth and Thought,
Scientific-Literary-Social), published in Ankara and starting on 10

November 1938. Only three or four issues appeared.[144] The publisher-editor was Reha Oğuz Türkkan who, still young at the time, was already an active Pan-Turkist.[145] We shall have more to say about him later.[146] It was perhaps because of Türkkan's youth that his writing was so aggressive in character. *Ergenekon* had on the cover of each issue the photograph of a *bozkurt*, the wolf of the steppes, which plays an important role in early Turkish lore. Together with the usual number of research articles, the racial concept, previously adopted by Atsız, reappeared in Ergenekon's cover-page slogans: 'The Turkish race above everything!'[147] and 'The Turkish race above any other race!'[148] Türkkan himself roundly attacked communism[149] and the communist regimes. However, in order not to lend credence to accusations of fascism (because of his emphasis on race and his anti-communist stand),[150] Türkkan condemned it as forcefully as he did communism,[151] particularly careful to remind his readers that Mete had been the first Pan-Turkist as well as the first racist, by uniting the ancestors of the Turks;[152] consequently, the Turks — not the Pan-Germanists or Hitler — had been the founders of the first state based upon racism and the first to practise this doctrine.[153]

Yet another Turkist journal, somewhat less pronouncedly Pan-Turkist than either *Atsız Mecmua* or *Ergenekon*, was *Kopuz. Aylık millî sanat ve fikir mecmuası* (Kopuz:[154] a Monthly Journal of National Arts and Ideas), which started publication on 15 April 1979 and ceased to appear early the following year.[155] Its publisher-editor, Cemal Tigin, was less politically-minded than either Atsız or Türkkan; hence *Kopuz* emphasised cultural, rather than political, Turkism and Pan-Turkism. Articles mostly dealt with the history, literature and folklore of the Turks in Turkey and abroad, through the ages — with a moderate Pan-Turk slant. It was briefly revived as *Kopuz. Aylık. Türkçü dergi* (Kopuz: a monthly Pan-Turk journal), appearing in Samsun, in May 1943, with Tevetoğlu as editor.[156]

Longer-lived than other Pan-Turk periodicals appearing in the 1930s was *Bozkurt* (Wolf of the steppes — a symbol of Turkism and Pan-Turkism),[157] also founded by Türkkan, which began publication in Istanbul as a monthly in May 1939. However, the blatantly out-spoken Pan-Turkism of its first two issues (May and June 1939) brought about legal proceedings and the suspension of publication. Following its acquittal, the journal resumed publication in May 1940.[158] It became a weekly on 5 March 1942, appearing irregularly until July of that year. A total of seventeen issues came out.[159] Although the posts of editor and publisher were later assumed by A. Nurullah Barıman and M. Sami Karayel respectively,[160] Türkkan remained the journal's policy-maker and wrote quite a number of its editorials. Several scholars, such as Professor Abdülkadir İnan, contributed to *Bozkurt* and provided it with a certain aura of scholarly respectability. Nevertheless, it was Türkkan and his associates who invested the journal with its aggressively Pan-Turk character. There were some Turanian elements involved, as Finns, Hungarians and Estonians[161] were regarded, besides the Turks and the Turkic groups. However, *Bozkurt's* main concern, overtly and outspokenly,[162] was Pan-Turkism. Like other Pan-Turk journals, previously published, *Bozkurt* combined support for the Turkish race as a unifying concept (and pride in Atila and others who had succeeded in uniting the Turks)[163] with an attack on communism,[164] the enemy of this race (and the enslaver of a part of it). Unlike other journals, however, *Bozkurt* exerted special efforts at rehabilitating Pan-Turkism and restoring its self-respect and special standing in public life. As Nejdet Sançar (brother of Atsız and a prominent Pan-Turkist himself) chided those who suspected the Pan-Turkists of being Fifth Columnists,[165] Türkkan harangued Pan-Turkists that they should reply proudly in the affirmative when asked whether they were of this conviction:[166] He who stands for the holy concept of founding a Turkish state of 65 millions ought to be prepared for this task.[167] Under these new circumstances, Türkkan strove to redefine Pan-Turkism by informing Pan-Turkists what was expected of them:[168] belief in the superiority of the Turkish race and continuous promotion of Pan-Turkism, in every domain. Regarding the latter, he exhorted Pan-Turkists to adhere firmly to the following principles: racism, All-Turk unity,[169] a warlike outlook, morality, proper administration and activism.

Another important Pan-Turk journal was the weekly *Tanrıdağ. İlmî, Edebî, Turkçü. Bu Türklerin dergisidir* (Tanrıdağ:[170] Scholarly, Literary Pan-Turk Journal of the Turks), published in Istanbul from 8 May to 4 September 1942,[171] four days before the death of its editor, Dr Rıza Nur, a veteran intellectual and politician who had contributed to a number of scholarly and Pan-Turk periodicals.[172] *Tanrıdağ*, whose articles were written primarily by Rıza Nur himself, was no less aggressively Pan-Turk by nature than *Bozkurt*. Even the customary Turcological studies had a pronounced Pan-Turk bias. For example, Hüseyin Namık Orkun's[173] article on Vambery stressed the latter's work in Turkish studies as well as his contribution to Pan-Turkism.[174] Halil Yaner, a lawyer, writing about the Danube Turks, appealed to natives of Turkey to be more active in collecting and preserving Turkish cultural works elsewhere.[175] Ahmed Rasim Aras, studying the great Azeris of the fourteenth century AD, left no doubt that he was discussing Azerbaijan Turks.[176] Fiery poems with covert or overt Pan-Turk undertones often appeared in *Tanrıdağ*.[177] Several articles took an even more unequivocal stand: writers discussed 'the Turkish race', its great past and brilliant future,[178] considering its existence to be self-evident. The previously mentioned Nejdet Sançar, true to his militant views on Turkish nationalism and Pan-Turkism, wrote on 'The Turk, the Army, and the War',[179] arguing that the three were — and ought to be — inseparable. This argument is also taken up by Sıtkı Tuncer, whose article 'How should our Nationalism be?'[180] called for a nationalism which is neither peace-loving, nor utopian, as well as Dr İhsan Unaner whose 'Mobilisation for sacrifice'[181] appealed for a greater readiness to make sacrifices. However, it was Rıza Nur himself who set the overall tone of *Tanrıdağ*, both in his selection of contributors and in his own articles, of which the most revealing was the programmatic 'The nationalism of the Turks',[182] published in *Tanrıdağ*'s very first issue. Rıza Nur considered irredentism[183] an important and active element of Turkish nationalism. Following this approach, he identified three major components in Turkish nationalism — Turanism, Pan-Turkism, and Anatolianism.[184] He then argued that the first had merged into the second, the scope of which comprised Turks everywhere, while the third considered Anatolian Turks to be superior. Rıza Nur agreed with this last approach, although he felt that this limitation considerably weakened the impact of nationalism; hence he concluded that 'racial Pan-Turkism'[185] was most viable.

Another periodical of that era, which, like *Tanrıdağ*, clearly advertised its Pan-Turkism on its masthead, was *Gök Börü. Türkçü dergi* (Gök Börü:[186] a Pan-Turk Magazine), published in Istanbul, twice a month, starting on 5 November 1942.[187] Its publisher and director (i.e. editor) was, again, Türkkan, whose former journal, *Bozkurt*, had ceased publication about four months earlier. *Gök Börü*'s motto was the same as that of *Ergenekon*: 'The Turkish race above any other race!' Once again, in addition to various contributions of general Turcological interest by Abdülkadir İnan[188] or by scholars sympathetic to Pan-Turkism, such as the aforementioned Togan,[189] *Gök Börü* also printed more strongly-worded Pan-Turk articles. Several vied with those of *Tanrıdağ* in their support of the 'Turkish race' concept.[190] Considerable affection was shown for the Outside Turks, past and present,[191] with vehement attacks on Communism in general and on the Communists in Turkey in particular.[192] It was obvious, however, that Türkkan himself was, again, responsible for setting the general guidelines of *Gök Börü*. Promising[193] to fight against pernicious ideologies[194] (Communism?), he adopted 'racial Pan-Turkism'[195] and published his own version of Turkish and Pan-Turk nationalism in 'Observations about Pan-Turkism',[196] printed in the first issue of *Gök Börü* and apparently the programme of this journal. Without actually saying so, Türkkan adopted Rıza Nur's division of Turkish nationalism into Pan-Turkism, Turanism and Anatolianism,[197] maintaining that Turanism was concerned solely with a future vision focused upon the Outside Turks, while Anatolianism concentrated only on local ones. Pan-Turkism was thus the only ideology which combined both visions, focusing on both the present and the future, and was consequently the only practicable type of nationalism. In another article, entitled 'Advancing Pan-Turkism',[198] Türkkan called upon all Pan-Turkists to support this ideology and to strive for it proudly. Later, another important and relatively long-lived Pan-Turk journal was *Çınaraltı. Türkçü fikir ve sanat mecmuası* (Under the plane-tree: a journal of Pan-Turk thought and art). A weekly, it appeared in Istanbul from 9 August 1941 to 15 July 1944,[199] reaching no less than 136 issues.[200] Its editorial board was headed by Orhan Seyfi Orhon, a Pan-Turk man of letters;[201] his book *Dün, bugün, yarın* (Yesterday, today, tomorrow), published in 1943, displayed evident sympathy for Pan-Turkism. In general *Çınaraltı* was more moderate than several Pan-Turk periodicals of the time. Its masthead repeated Gaprinsky's famous slogan 'Unity in language, thought and action'.[202] The editors and contributors, admirers of Ziya Gökalp, seemed to favour cultural Pan-Turkism. The first issue's editorial, by Orhan himself, was entitled 'İdeal' (An ideal), and argued that what the Turks most lacked was neither goods nor luxuries (even though it was during war-time) but rather an ideal.[203] Another frequent contributor who wrote about ideals was a retired general, H.E. Erkilet,[204] of whom we shall have more to say later.[205] Erkilet argued, also, that 'every nationalist Turk is a Pan-Turkist and every Pan-Turkist is a nationalist.'[206]

Çınaraltı strove hard to instil a large measure of pure Turkism and the values of Pan-Turkism into its readers. In addition to articles on history, literature, language and education, there were many contributions on the Outside Turks. Following the Pan-Turk fashion of the day, it supported the race theory[207] and attacked Communism,[208] although its major emphasis remained on culture and its crucial importance.[209] Orhon stressed the significance of 'national sentiment',[210] while Erkilet redefined the objectives of Pan-Turkism within a cultural framework.[211] Furthermore, in writing about 'the Turkish national entity',[212] Rebi Barkın argued specifically for cultural unity rather than otherwise. Poems and stories — some of the latter written by another editor, Yusuf Ziya Ortaç — followed the same line. Even contributors like the above-mentioned Hüseyin

Namık Orkun and Nejdet Sançar had, when writing for *Çınaraltı*, to conform to this approach.

Lastly, there was the short-lived *Türk amacı. Türk kültür birliği mürevvicidir* (The objective of the Turks: Propagator of the union of Turkish culture), later renamed *Türk amacı. Türk kültürü birliği dergisidir* (The objective of the Turks: Journal for the union of Turkish culture). It started publication in July 1942 and appeared for hardly more than half a year.[213] As it was published and edited by Ahmet Caferoğlu, a known Turcologist at Istanbul University, *Türk amacı* displayed signs characteristic of a learned periodical, with well-researched articles on the civilisation of the Central Asian Turks, their history, geography, language, literature, economy, music and religion. However, not a few of these and others followed an evident Pan-Turk line. Examples were an article by Muharrem Feyzi Togay (author of a book on Akçura) about Şamil's struggle for the independence of the Caucasus;[214] or another, by V.L. Salcı, on the Turkish tribes in Thrace.[215] The fact was that, although edited by an Azeri emigrant to Turkey, *Türk amacı* exhibited considerable interest in, and affection for, other Outside Turks too, e.g. those in Turkestan, Thrace and elsewhere. While it could not openly preach political action within a Turkey ruled by martial law, during the Second World War, its very publication in those crucial years certainly helped to keep interest in the Outside Turks alive. In general, *Türk amacı* fulfilled the promise, declared in its first editorial,[216] that the journal would struggle for the Turkism (*Türklük*) of the whole Turkish world — a common slogan in Pan-Turkism. This it would attempt to achieve by publishing scholarly research on the great achievements of the Turkish race (*uruk*) throughout history, while focusing on those Turks living apart from one another.

The Pan-Turk periodicals of the 1930s and early 1940s, the most important of which have been considered above,[217] differed in both tone and content from earlier ones. Their tone was more pronouncedly aggressive, foreshadowing the militant style which would characterise them in the later years of and following the Second World War.[218] In addition, the content became increasingly politicised, possibly as a result of changing circumstances. Just as Pan-Turkism had engaged in a three-cornered struggle with Pan-Islamism and Ottomanism during the late Ottoman period, it was now battling with Turanism and self-centred Turkish nationalism (which Pan-Turkists termed 'Anatolianism'), but mainly with the latter since the former had partly merged into Pan-Turkism and was thus of no great significance in Turkey at that time. Since Pan-Turkists were competing with the state ideology, Turkish nationalism, from a position of weakness, many of them adopted racism (*ırkçılık*) as the new cornerstone of their credo. The problem of race in general and that of the Turkish race in particular had been probed by intellectuals during the late Ottoman Empire period, although in a less intensive manner and with various opinions expressed.[219] This was a retreat from the cultural Pan-Turkism advocated by Gökalp (who had condemned racism[220]). This approach had, besides, obvious tactical advantages, because Kemalism, which approved of the glorious past of the Turks, seemed to favour racism (although it basically did not; Kemalism searched the ethnic origins of the Turks and extolled them — but without over-emphasising the superiority of the Turkish race).

One can only speculate to what extent the racist theories of Nazism in the 1930s had an impact on Pan-Turkism's attitude in this respect,[221] particularly as Germany did raise the hopes of Pan-Turkists during the Second World War.[222] During those years, Pan-Turk publications clearly rejected both the charges of fascism[223] and that of German influence upon their own concept of racism: Turkish racism, they argued, was a native invention.[224] They maintained that blood was the best and perhaps the only meaningful bond of the Turkish race,[225] a great and superb one,[226] surpassing all others.[227] The greatest danger was in the mixing of Turkish blood with that of other races. They held that it was the other races, then minorities in the Ottoman Empire, which had brought about its downfall.[228] Various sociologists and physicians attempted to adduce 'proofs' justifying the existence of races and the differences between them.[229] Scientists connected with Pan-Turkist circles, such as Dr Mustafa Hakkı Akansel, also published books examining the alleged evidence favouring race-theories and their application to the Turks.[230]

There is not much to say about the organisation of Pan-Turkism in the stage discussed here. During the first two decades of the Republic, Pan-Turkism was generally latent and its activists were few. Worse still from their point of view, they were deeply divided, vying with one another for leadership (for instance, Atsız versus Türkkan[231]), competing for the support of those Outside Turks who had organised *Landsmannschaften* in Turkey, such as The Turkish Cultural Union, grouping Turks who had emigrated from the Soviet Union, and which published, in 1942, the periodical *Türk amacı* (The goal of the Turks).[232] The Turkish Youth of Turkestan was another such organisation.[233] Moreover, Pan-Turkists were constantly quarrelling about minute points in the interpretation of their ideology. Not unexpectedly, groups formed and reformed around personalities and journals which bound them together for a time, membership being essentially fluid. Several groups maintained a semi-clandestine character, closed not only to outsiders, but at least as much to one another as well. Needless to say, this strife compounded the problem of paucity in numbers and adversely affected Pan-Turkist attempts at political influence. Several groups may be discerned.

The first such group was led by Professor Ahmed Zeki Velidi Togan (1890–1970) who had fought indefatigably for the cause of Pan-Turkism for many years; his numerous books and articles, many of a scholarly character, were not infrequently coloured by his political convictions. Born in Russian Turkestan, he had been active, among a group of Muslim delegates, in the 1916 *Duma*. He then attempted, during the Bolshevik Revolution, to establish an independent Turkestan. His organisation, entitled The Turkestan Nationalist Committee, had its headquarters in Bukhara, with branches in several of the major population centres elsewhere; agents went abroad to recruit support for the nationalist movement in Turkestan. The objective of Togan and his close associates was to set up several independent states in the Caspian area — Bukhara, Khiva, Ferghana and Semirechiye — with the ultimate aim of uniting them[234] in a grand Pan-Turk design. Having failed in this, Togan engaged in Turcological research in Germany, utilising this opportunity to propagate his views on Turkestan and Pan-Turkism.[235] Later, in 1927, he was appointed to the Chair of Turkish History at Istanbul University, never interrupting his Pan-Turk activities. It was apparently because of these pursuits that he had to resign his position in 1932 and go abroad, returning to his Chair only in 1938, when he again busily set about organising a clandestine Pan-Turk society.[236] Togan was to continue indefatigably with his struggle for the national liberation and political union of the Outside Turks; a selection of his numerous articles, entitled *Türklüğün mukadderati üzerine* (About the values of Turkism), published in the last year of Togan's life (1970) and reprinted seven years later, is evidence of his passionate tenacity. In 1940, he wrote a pamphlet entitled *1929–1940 seneleri arasında Türkistanın vaziyeti* (Turkestan's situation between 1929 and 1940) which, in a bitterly anti-Soviet tone, was a fiery appeal for Turkestan's independence.

A second group, also clandestine in part,[237] was led by Hüseyin Nihal Atsız (1905–75), assisted by his brother Nejdet Sançar (1910–75), of whom more later. Born in Istanbul and educated in Turkey, Atsız was a journalist, novelist and poet who earned his living as a teacher. After a lengthy period of relative inactivity among Pan-Turkists during the 1920s, he was the first to publish and edit a Pan-Turk periodical, *Atsız Mecmua*, in 1931–2, then *Orhun* in 1933–4.

Brought to court in 1936 for Turanist activity, he was found not guilty
and continued writing. He used to label himself, ideologically, 'a
racist, Pan-Turkist and Turanist',[238] and considered himself a leader,
even going so far as to affect some of Hitler's mannerisms. The
association Atsız headed was partly clandestine, organised in cells
and reportedly with its own system of correspondence in cypher.[239]
We shall revert later to him[240] and his activities,[241] practically all of
which were dedicated to the cause of Pan-Turkism.

A third group was led by Dr Rıza Nur (1879–1942) and organised
around the journal *Tanrıdağ*. Rıza Nur had had a long career, before
editing *Tanrıdağ*. At first an Ottomanist, he was elected a Member
of Parliament during the Young Turk period and then became active
in the Kemalist movement. However, his overall political philosophy
displayed a strong Pan-Turk streak. He was one of the first, and
possibly the very first, to envisage the setting up of a Pan-Turk
political party.[242] He was a scholar and an intellectual, constantly
writing on matters of cultural interest, chiefly in the area of Turkish
studies. Before editing *Tanrıdağ*, he had already published, in French
and Turkish, a *Revue de Turcologie*,[243] founded in Paris, but issued
in Alexandria (Egypt) between 1931 and 1937.[244] After Rıza Nur's
death, the small group of Pan-Turkists he had been heading appears
to have been taken over by Atsız.[245]

A fourth group was led by Reha Oğuz Türkkan (born 1920), a
former disciple of Togan. Türkkan was born in Istanbul and graduated
from Ankara University's Faculty of Law, subsequently being employed in the Ministry of Justice.[246] His attachment to Pan-Turkism
dated from his student days; as a youngster, in 1936–7, he had already
been active spreading Pan-Turk propaganda. According to his own
memoirs, Türkkan organised two semi-clandestine societies, intended
to influence Turkish officials and others in favour of Pan-Turkism.[247]
He wrote several books, with a definite Pan-Turk bias. One of these,
Türkçülüğe giriş (Introduction to Turkism, or: Introduction to Pan-
Turkism)[248] argued that the union of 20 million Turks in Turkey with
another 100 million abroad — based on common racial characteristics
— was vital for the continued existence of Turkism, and could not
be postponed for long.[249] He also wrote, in 1943, two anti-Communist
pamphlets, *Solcular ve kızıllar* (Leftists and reds) and *Kızıl faaliyet!*
(Red activities!). However, Türkkan is best known for the three
periodicals he launched: *Ergenekon, Bozkurt* and *Gök Börü*. Some of
his articles in these were collected, in 1944, in a volume entitled
Milliyetçilik yolunda (On the road of nationalism). The group which
Türkkan headed had a marked penchant for clandestinity. They used
to refer to themselves as *Bozkurtçu* (Bozkurtists) — alluding both to

their journals and the wolves of the steppes — and were apparently more extreme in their racism than other groups. Türkkan's group had a bitter feud with the one led by Atsız, each accusing the other of not being a real Turk (hence, presumably unfit to speak for Pan-Turkism).[250] In addition, Türkkan accused Atsız and his group of Nazi-style racism, claiming for himself a different, anti-fascist style of racism.[251]

Finally, there was a small group of Pan-Turkists, more oriented towards the past than some of the others, bound by the periodical *Çınaraltı* (1941–45).[252] Its editors, Orhan Seyfi Orhon (1890–1972) and Yusuf Ziya Ortaç (1895/6–1967) were both followers of Gökalp and hence the group tended to downgrade racism and favour cultural Pan-Turkism, although they too enthusiastically advocated a nation of 80 million Turks.[253]

Summing up, one may say that in the first two decades of the Republic of Turkey Pan-Turkism was, on the whole, latent there. Several periodicals issued during the 1920s (usually in Istanbul, fewer in Ankara) along with a few other publications produced since the early 1930s, served as a bond between the sympathisers, barely fanning the flames. These sympathisers were few in number and sharply divided by rival claims to leadership and by heated arguments over the finer points of ideological interpretation.

NOTES

1. See examples in FO 371/4177, file 1883, no. 1883, letter of the Islamic Society, London, to the Foreign Office, dated London, 2 Jan. 1919. FO 371/5201, E 10420/971/44, letter of H. Alitcha, for the Bureau Permanent du Congrès Turc de Lausanne, to Curzon, dated Lausanne, 23 Aug. 1920. Cf. ibid., E 11690/971/44, for Curzon's reaction.
2. For some of these contacts, see Kâzım Karabekir, *İstiklâl harbimizde Enver Paşa ve İttihat Terakki erkânı*, 1967, passim.
3. But Hans Kohn argues, in his *Pan-Slavism*, pp. 202–3, that it was 'Pan-Turanism' that helped the Turks to defeat first the Russian, then the Greek, advance.
4. See Şerif Mardin, *Continuity and change in the ideas of the Young Turks*, 1969, pp. 3 ff; Mohammad Sadiq, 'The ideological legacy of the Young Turks', *International Studies* (New Delhi), XVIII (2): Apr.–June 1979, pp. 177–207. For the continuing impact of Ziya Gökalp, cf. Sabri Mehmed Akural, 'Ziya Gökalp: The influence of his thought on Kemalist reforms', Ph.D. thesis, Indiana University, 1978 (unpublished).
5. Cf. the arguments advanced by D.Ye. Yeryemyeyev, 'Kyemalizm i Pantyurkizm', *Narodi Azii i Afriki*, 1963, no. 3, pp. 58–70, largely

based on a book by A. Engin, *Atatürkçülük ve Moskofluk-Türklük savaşları.*

6. Translation of the above by C.W. Hostler, 'Trends in Pan-Turanism', *Middle Eastern Affairs (MEA),* III (1): Jan. 1952, p. 3. See also Hostler, *Turkism,* p. 109. Cf. 'Il panislamismo e Mustafà Kemāl', *OM,* 1 (8): 15 Jan. 1922, pp. 467–8; see also ibid., I (9): 15 Feb. 1922, pp. 572–3; II (7): 15 Dec. 1922, pp. 402–4; III (4): 15 Sep. 1923, pp. 214–15; III (5): 15 Oct. 1923, pp. 270–1; III (6): 15 Nov. 1923, p. 345.

7. For later years, cf. *OM,* XIII (11): Nov. 1933, pp. 555–7. See also Hostler, *Turkism,* p. 109. Additional examples in Gotthard Jäschke, 'Der Turanismus und die kemalistische Türkei', in R. Hartmann and H. Scheel (eds), *Beiträge zur Arabistik, Semitistik und Islamwissenschaft,* 1944, pp. 468 ff; and B. Lewis, in *Journal of Contemporary History,* XV (1): Jan. 1980, esp. pp. 30–3.

8. For these relations, in the first years after the First World War, cf. 'Les relations Russo-Turques depuis l'avènement du bolchévisme', *RMM,* LII: Dec. 1922, pp. 181–217.

9. Kohn, p. 203.

10. See details in Frank Tachau, 'The search for national identity among the Turks', *Die Welt des Islams* (New Series), VIII (3): 1963, pp. 165 ff.

11. Cf. Herbert Jansky, 'Die "Türkische Revolution" und der russische Islam', *Der Islam* (Berlin and Leipzig), XVIII: 1929, pp. 158–67.

12. See, for the case of Russian Turkestan, in 1923, FO 371/10397, N 1527/21/97, *Meshed Intelligence Diary,* no. 90, for the period ending 31 Dec. 1923.

13. Details in FO 371/44188, R 9943/9943/44, Foreign Office Research Department's memorandum on *Turkey's claims and interests in territories and populations outside her territories,* dated 22 June 1944.

14. CO 67/258, file 5, no. 39915, police report on Cyprus for Dec. 1934. CO 67/277, file 15, J.D. Montagu's (Commissioner of Nicosia) report no. 98 A/1936, dated 8 Feb. 1937, enc. in Governor Richmond Palmer's no. 76, to Ormsby Gore, dated Nicosia, 19 Feb. 1937.

15. CO 67/262, file 2, duplicate of James Morgan's no. 465, to Sir Samuel Hoare, dated Istanbul, 14 Sep. 1935.

16. Cf. FO 371/13090, E 129/129/44, G.G. Clerk's no. 5, confidential, to Sir Austen Chamberlain, dated Constantinople, 4 Jan. 1928; FO 371/13092, E 255/255/44, Chargé d'Affaires Charles Dodd's no. 5, to Chamberlain, dated Sofia, 11 Jan. 1928, and ibid., E 1285/255/44, Clerk's no. 138, confidential, to Chamberlain, dated Constantinople, 6 Mar. 1928.

17. FO 371/16649, C 10014/3/7, J. Waterloo's no. 300, to Sir John Simon at the Foreign Office, dated British Legation, Sofia, 11 Nov. 1933. This is an interesting report on Bulgarian irredentism.

18. CO 67/278, file 5, Governor Palmer's confidential despatch to Ormsby

Gore, dated Nicosia, 29 Oct. 1937; CO 67/300, file 4, official correspondence between 3 Feb. 1939 and 20 Mar. 1940.

19. For instance, in the case of Turkish Cypriot sentiments for Turkey and Pan-Turkism, the Acting Foreign Minister of Turkey, Şükrü Kaya, assured Storrs, then Governor of Cyprus, that he expected them to be loyal to the British Crown. See CO 67/247, file 98649, Storr's no. 201, to Sir Philip Cunliffe-Lister, dated Nicosia, 25 Apr. 1932. Later, Minister Aras told Percy Loraine, British Ambassador to Turkey, that 'there was no attempt by Kemalists to organise minorities in other people's territories . . . there was no grain of ambition or aspiration in the Turkey of to-day to recover any of her former island properties'. See CO 67/291, file 101, no. 90437, copy of Loraine's personal and secret letter to Palmer (Governor of Cyprus), dated Istanbul, 1 Sep. 1938, and enclosed minute.
20. For this new ideology, see in the following pages.
21. See above, ch. 2 of our study, p. 33.
22. Report from Istanbul in the *Morning Post* (London), 9 Feb. 1920. Her address was followed by Akçura's strongly Pan-Turk speech, see René Pinon, 'L'offensive de l'Asie', *Revue des Deux Mondes* (Paris), XC: Apr. 1920, pp. 810–11.
23. FO 371/13092, E 247/247/44, *Notes on leading Turkish personalities*, compiled by Helm, enc. in Clerk's no. 16, confidential, to Chamberlain, dated Constantinople, 11 Jan. 1928. See also Georgeon, p. 30, fn. 9.
24. Berthe Georges-Gaulis, *La nouvelle Turquie*, 1924, pp. 230–1; translation mine.
25. Dumont, in *Cahiers du Monde Russe et Soviétique*, XV (3–4): July–Dec. 1974, p. 331.
26. Akçura, *Türkçülük*, pp. 221–3. Prof. Ercümend Kuran, in his 'Türk milliyetçiliğinin gelişmesi ve Yusuf Akçuraoğlu', *TK*, 42: Apr. 1966, pp. 529–30, argues that the military defeats made Akçura despair of political activity in the cause of Pan-Turkism. See also Georgeon, p. 82.
27. That is, in the plural, 'The hearths of the Turks.'
28. See above, ch. 2 of our study, pp. 41 ff.
29. FO 371/4141, file 71, no. 49194, British High Commissioner Admiral Richard Loeb's no. 290/1294, dated Constantinople, 8 Mar. 1919.
30. One of their pamphlets was seized and published in *al-Qibla*, 91: 30 June 1917. See FO 395/139, file 15725, no. 144185, cyphered message from R. Wingate to the Foreign Office, dated Ramleh (Egypt), 21 July 1917.
31. Cf. FO, ibid. For Jambolat, see Admiralty Staff — Intelligence Division, *Personalities in Turkey*, 2nd edn, 1916 (= C.B. 1148), p. 24, which claimed that he had been head of the Secret Service under the Young Turks; and FO 371/7869, E 7840/5/44, Rumbold's no. 680, confidential, to Balfour, dated Constantinople, 1 Aug. 1922.

32. The text of the petition is enclosed in FO 371/4154, file 275, no. 55066, Loeb's no. 395/1702, to Balfour, dated Constantinople, 27 Mar. 1919. For their other activities in 1919, cf. *Büyük Mecmua*, 6: 24 Apr. 1919, p. 87; and 17: 25 Dec. 1919, p. 267.
33. See Jäschke, in *Beiträge*, p. 469.
34. See above, ch. 2 of our study, p. 42.
35. Cf. Akçura, *Türkçülük*, pp. 221–3.
36. Reprinted in Hamdullah Suphi Tanrıöver's collection of articles (1912–29), entitled *Günebakan*, Ankara, Türk Ocakları Ilim ve San'at Neşriyatı, 1929, pp. 71–7 ('Ton sesleri').
37. Collected in *Günebakan*, see the preceding footnote.
38. Collected in his *Dağ yolu*, first printed by Türk Ocakları Hars Heyeti Neşriyatı, 1928; then, in Latin characters, by the same press, vols I–II, 1929–31.
39. Jäschke, in *Beiträge*, p. 473.
40. On his special relationship with the *Türk Ocakları*, see the obituary by İhsan Karlıklı, 'Türkocağı ve Hamdullah Suphi', *Türk Yurdu* (New Series), VI (2): Feb. 1967, pp. 58–61.
41. Details in FO 371/11557, E 6855/6855/44, Geoffrey Knox's report to L. Oliphant at the Foreign Office, dated Ankara, 2 Dec. 1926; FO 371/12322, files E 460/460/44 and E 1215/460/44 dated, respectively, Jan. and Mar. 1927; FO 371/12320, E 3352/257/44, Clerk's no. 398, confidential, to Chamberlain, dated Therapia, 27 July 1927, and enclosures; FO 371/14579, E 1002/1002/44, Clerk's no. 64, confidential, to A. Henderson, dated Constantinople, 20 Feb. 1930, and enclosure; ibid., E 2271/1002/44, Clerk's no. 141, confidential, to A. Henderson, dated Constantinople, 30 Apr. 1930, and enclosure.
42. For 1925, see Agâh Sırrı Levend, in *Ulus*, 17 Jan. 1951, p. 2. For 1930, cf. R. Sefvet, pp. 10–11.
43. Partly translated by E.R. (= Ettore Rossi), in *OM*, VI (4): Apr. 1926, pp. 239–41.
44. Fuller details in Tachau, in *Die Welt des Islams* (N.S.), VIII (3): 1963, pp. 170–5.
45. FO 371/14579, E 1002/1002/44, 'Notes by P.M. Roberts', dated Ankara, 14 Feb. 1930, enc. in Clerk's no. 64, confidential, to Henderson, dated Constantinople, 20 Feb. 1930.
46. On the decision, see Neşter, 'Türkocakları nasıl kapatıldı', *Orkun*, 20: 16 Feb. 1951, pp. 12–13. They were re-established in 1949, but with no commitment whatsoever to Pan-Turkism and with a much weaker organisation.
47. E. Houminer, 'The people's houses in Turkey', *Asian and African Studies* (Jerusalem), I: 1965, pp. 81–121; Karpat, *Turkey's politics*, pp. 380 ff.
48. Ercümend Kuran, in his 'Atatürk ve Ziya Gökalp', *TK*, 13: Nov. 1963, pp. 9–12, discusses the impact of Gökalp on Mustafa Kemal.
49. On which see Suna Kili, *Kemalism*, 1969; D.E. Webster, pp. 163 ff;

R.D. Robinson, *The first Turkish republic*, Cambridge, Mass., Harvard University Press, 1963, pp. 84 ff. For the relation of Kemalism to Pan-Turkism, cf. the useful paper of G.E. Carretto, 'Polemiche fra kemalismo, fascismo, communismo, negli anni '30', *Storia Contemporanea* (Rome), VIII (3): Sep. 1977, pp. 490 ff.

50. The claims of several Western observers, like René Pinon in *Revue des Deux Mondes*, XC: Apr. 1920, pp. 805–15, that Mustafa Kemal was a Pan-Turkist, have never been substantiated.

51. When Turkey's rapprochement to Iran and Irak in 1937 was interpreted as a revival of Pan-Turkism, this was vehemently denied in Turkey. See *The Times*, 19 June 1937; *OM*, XVII (7): July 1937, pp. 320–1.

52. There is a vast literature on this subject. See, e.g., İsmet Giritli, *Fifty years of Turkish political development, 1919–1969; Atatürk devrimleri. I. Milletlerarası simpozyumu bildirileri*, 1975; Lewis, *Emergence*, pp. 250–87. J.M. Landau (ed.), *Atatürk and the modernization of Turkey*, 1984. For a different view, cf. G. Barthel (ed.), *Der Kemalismus und die moderne Türkei*, 1979. (= *Asia-Africa-America*, special issue 5). See also the next footnote.

53. Summarised by L.B. (= Luigi Bonelli), 'Turanismo e lingua turca', *OM*, VI (3): Mar. 1926, pp. 176–7.

54. Cf. Uriel Heyd, *Language reform in modern Turkey*, 1954, and the bibliography he listed; Ettore Rossi, 'La riforma linguistica in Turchia', *OM*, XV (1): Jan. 1935, pp. 45–57; *The new Turkey*, 1938, pp. 91–5.

55. Istanbul, 1338; 120 pp. A second edn, in the Latin script, came out in Istanbul, 1932; 141 pp.

56. See details in Uluğ İğdemir, *Cumhuriyetin 50. yılında Türk Tarih Kurumu*, Ankara, 1973, pp. 15–23.

57. E.g., A. Rafikov, 'Racist ravings in Turkey', *New Times* (Moscow), 37: 7 Sep. 1949, pp. 30–1.

58. Details and examples in İ.H. Danişmend, *Türklük meseleleri*, esp. pp. 6, 7, 12, 42, 93–5, 147, 224–33; Hostler, *Turkism*, pp. 111–12. For a translation of some racially-minded extracts, see F.F. Rynd, 'Turkish racial theories', *Journal of the Royal Central Asian Society*, XXI (3): 1934, pp. 476–87.

59. A spot check of the first volumes of *Ülkü* indicates this. The term 'Turan' does appear in an article on sports in Turkish history (6: July 1933, p. 477), but only as information about the Turan-Iran wars. A rare exception is an article by Reşit Galip (9: Oct. 1933, pp. 164–77), but even this is chiefly to refute 'foreign misconceptions.'

60. See above, ch. 2.

61. See above, at the beginning of ch. 3.

62. For a detailed analysis of this law, cf. India Office, L/P&S/12/4391, Collection 39/4, E 6434/5161/44, James Morgan's no. 489, confidential, to John Simon, dated Constantinople, 13 Oct. 1934, and enc.

63. *'Sosyalist' geçinenlere karşı Atatürkçülük savaşı.*

64. This was particularly so as Turanism became fashionable for a while,

again, attracting Pan-Turkist attention not only to the Finns and the Hungarians, but even to the Bulgarians. See Stoddard, in *The American Political Science Review*, XI (1): Feb. 1917, pp. 19–22.

65. One example was the *Türkistan Gençler Birligi* (Union of Turkestani Youths), established in 1927; cf. Baysun, pp. 192–6.
66. Details in Jäschke, in *Beiträge*, pp. 471–2.
67. See above, introduction, p. 1.
68. It was those circles, most probably, that published such lectures as that by Validi Ahmedzeki (i.e., Ahmet Zeki Velidi Togan), *Die gegenwärtige Lage der Mohammedaner Russlands*, 1930.
69. X, 'Le Panislamisme et le Panturquisme', *RMM*, XXII: Mar. 1913, p. 195.
70. See the interview granted by one of the society's prominent members, Prof. Benedik de Baratoshi, to the British Consul in Tokio, C.J. Davidson, in Nov. 1921. Davidson's report, dated 24 Nov. 1921, is enclosed in FO 371/8073, N 6/6/97, British Ambassador Sir C. Eliot's no. 630, to Curzon, dated Tokyo, 28 Nov. 1921.
71. Known to me only in the Turkish version, *Tarihte Türklük*, 1971.
72. In Turkish: 'Turan Mecmuası — Turanî Cemiyetinin aylık risalesi.' In Hungarian: 'TURÁN A Turáni Társaság Magyar Ázsiai Társaság Follyóirata.'
73. The library of the Turkish Historical Society in Ankara has an incomplete set of this periodical from 1913 to 1934.
74. See, e.g., Alois v. Paikert, 'Der turanische Gedanke', *Turan*, 4–5: April–May 1917, pp. 182 ff; ibid., 6–7: June–Sep. 1917, pp. 291–301.
75. For this association, see details in Hostler, *Turkism*, pp. 157 ff.
76. A set of *Prométhée* may be consulted in the library of the School of Oriental and African Studies, London.
77. Acc. to the captured records of the German Foreign Office, as summarised in FO 371/72543, R 1374/1374/44, Foreign Office Research Department's minutes, dated 13 Dec. 1947; see especially Doc. 215231 in bundle 411.
78. The first nine issues, Nov. 1931–May 1933 (all published?) may be found in the Tarık Üs Library, Istanbul.
79. An incomplete set may be consulted in the library of the School of Oriental and African Studies, London.
80. E.g., a story about the 1892 revolt, in *Zeka*, I (10): 7 Şaaban 1330–9 July 1328 (1912), pp. 163–4.
81. Issues 1: May 1934 to 61–62: May–June 1939 (probably all that was published) may be consulted in the British Library, London.
82. A set may be consulted ibid.; another, almost complete, in the library of the Central Asian Research Institute, London. See, on this periodical, A.Ş. Turan, 'Doğu Türkistan millî mücadelesinde Yaş Türkistan dergisinin hizmetleri', *TK*, 177: July 1977, pp. 581–3.
83. I.e. the Volga.
84. The National Library, Ankara has an incomplete set for the years

1930–5 only. Another Pan-Turk Turco-Tatar magazine, was published, in Pazarcık as well, under the title *Rom ânia. Cotidian independent* (Romania: an independent daily). Edited by İ. Kemal Zandallı, it first came out on 5 August 1921 as a daily, became a weekly in 1925 and continued to appear irregularly at least until 21 July 1936.

85. Several issues from those years may be consulted in the library of the Turkish Historical Society, Ankara.
86. Whose name appears in the monthly *Türkistan* as Moustapha Tchokaï-Oghly.
87. See above, ch. 1 of our study.
88. Mustafa Chokayogli, *Tyurkyestan pod vlast'yu Sovyetov*, 1935; 127 pp.
89. Sa'īd Shāmil, *Bayān ilā 'l-Mu'tamar al-Islāmī 'l-'āmm al- mun'aqad fī Bayt al-Maqdis yawm 27 rajab sanat 1350 Hijriyya 'an ḥālat al-Muslimīn fī 'l-Qafqās.* N.d. [1350]; 10 pp.
90. For İshakî's other works, see Hostler, *Turkism*, p. 227; for his life, cf. ibid., pp. 213–14. See also Hasan Agay, 'Ayâz Ishakî'nin kısa hayat hikâyesi', *TK*, 188: June 1978, pp. 468–70; and M. Ülküsal, 'Ayaz İshaki İdilli', *Emel* (Istanbul), 106: May–June 1978, pp. 1–5. The most recent work about him, his Pan-Turk and other activities is a large volume edited by Tahir Çağatay and others, *Muhammed Ayaz İshaki hayatı ve faaliyeti, 100. doğum yılı dolayısıyla*, 1979.
91. X, 'Le Panislamisme et le Panturquisme', *RMM*, XXII: Mar. 1913, p. 194.
92. Zehra Önder, 'Panturanismus in Geschichte und Gegenwart', *Osterreichische Osthefte*, XIX (2): May 1977, p. 94.
93. See above in ch. 3.
94. 'Iyād Ishāqī, *Risāla khatīra ilā 'l-Mu'tamar al-Islāmī 'l-'āmm al-mun'aqad fī Bayt al-Maqdis yawm 27 rajab sanat 1350 Hijriyya 'an ḥālat al-Muslimīn fī 'l-Rūsiyā.* N.d. [1350]; 16 pp. In Latin characters he signed his name variously as Ayas or Ayaz Ishaki.
95. Basry Bey, *Le monde turc et l'avenir de sa mission historique*, p. 230; translation mine.
96. Leader of the Pan-Turk party *Müsavat* in Azerbayjan and active in the cause of Pan-Turkism for many years. See about his life and work Hostler, *Turkism*, pp. 215–17.
97. On this book's back-cover, one can consult a list of works by Azerbayjan émigrés, in Turkish, Persian, German, Russian, French and Polish.
98. H.M. Ahmad, *Kampf um Leere Räume: Turan — Turkestan — Tibet*, esp. pp. 44, 132–5.
99. First published in Istanbul in 1925, this was reprinted, in Latin characters, in Ankara in 1966.
100. On which see also Jäschke, in *Beiträge*, p. 471.
101. Resulzade had also been involved in the publication of the above *Kurtuluş* monthly and a shorter-lived Pan-Turk periodical (in 1923).

Yeni Kafkasya (The New Caucasus). See on his literary and journalistic activity, Ettore Rossi, 'Publicazioni di Musulmani anti-bolscevichi dell'Azerbaigian Caucasico', *OM*, IV (6): 15 June 1924, pp. 395–408.
102. *Milliyetperver ve Türkçü.*
103. Admiralty Staff — Intelligence Division, *Personalities — Turkey*, 2nd edn, Jan. 1916 (= C.B. 1148), p. 11, a copy of which is available in the India Office library.
104. Reşit Saffet is probably the same person as Réchid Safvet, who wrote, at about the same time, *Les Türk Odjaghis* — see above, note 102, ch. 2 of our study — and later, in 1952, as Reşid Safvet Atabinen, published *Les apports turcs dans le peuplement et la civilisation de l'Europe orientale* — see Ernst Werner, 'Pantürkismus und einige Tendenzen moderner Türkischer Historiographie', *Zeitschrift für Geschichtswissenschaft*, 1965, no. 8, pp. 1353–4.
105. For his Pan-Turk views, cf. the interview with him in *Altın Işık* (Istanbul), 8: 25 Sep. 1947, p. 8.
106. Saffet, *Türklük ve Türkçülük izleri*, pp. 161–8.
107. *Türklüğün kökleri ve yayılışı*, pp. 10–15.
108. Already mentioned as the author of a book on the life of Yusuf Akçura.
109. The term *Kavim* may also denote 'tribe'.
110. *Büyük Turan.*
111. *Turan Birliği.* The term birlik means both 'unity' and 'union'.
112. See Togay's booklet, esp. pp. 14 ff.
113. For whom see more at the end of the present chapter.
114. The first edition appeared in Cairo, 1939; it was subsequently published in Turkey, too.
115. Cafer Seydahmet [Kırımer], *Gaspıralı İsmail Bey.*
116. An obvious exaggeration of the ratio of the Turkish element in Iran to the total population.
117. See, e.g., *İctihat*, 176: 15 Mar. 1925; 177: 1 Apr. 1925.
118. Baltacıoğlu, *Türk'e doğru*, pp. 5–8.
119. An incomplete set of the first 93 issues, 26 Sep. 1923–15 Sep. 1927 (all published?) may be consulted at the library of the Turkish Historical Society, Ankara.
120. An incomplete set may be consulted in the library of the School of Oriental and African Studies, London.
121. An incomplete set may be consulted ibid.
122. A set may be consulted ibid.
123. Acc. to the encyclopaedia *Meydan-Larousse*, s.v. Atsız (vol. I, p. 352). Of the seventeen issues published, the first twelve may be consulted in the library of the Faculty of Political Science at the University of Ankara.
124. *Atsız Mecmua*, 2: 15 June 1931, pp. 30–3; 5: 15 Sep. 1931, pp. 103–9.
125. Ibid., 5: 15 Sep. 1931, p. 110; 6: 15 Oct. 1931, p. 133.
126. Ibid., 9: 15 Jan. 1932, pp. 228–31; 10: 15 Feb. 1932, pp. 247–50.
127. Ibid., 12: 15 Apr. 1932, pp. 290–2.

128. Ibid., nos 1–4; 15 May to 15 Aug. 1931.
129. Ibid., 1: 15 May 1931, p. 9.
130. Ibid., ibid., pp. 6–7, Atsız's 'Türkler hangi ırktandır?'
131. Ibid., 11: 15 Mar. 1932, pp. 279–81; 12: 15 Aug. 1932, pp. 290–2.
132. Orhun is a river in Central Asia, allegedly close to the birthplace of the ancient Turks, and supposedly the capital of a state in the seventh century C.E. It figures in Ziya Gökalp's famed poem *Kızıl elma* (The red apple — symbolic name for a promised land). See also Henderson in *The Asiatic Review*, XLI: Jan. 1945, p. 91.
133. Issues 1–9 will be discussed here; 10–16 are more relevant to ch. 4, below. Incomplete sets of *Orhun* may be consulted at the Beyazıd Library and Atatürk Kitaplığı, both in Istanbul.
134. *Orhun*, 5: 21 Mar. 1934, pp. 106–8.
135. Ibid., 7: 25 May 1934, pp. 136–7, review of Cafer Seydahmet's book on Gasprinsky.
136. Ibid. and 8: 23 June 1934.
137. Ibid., 4: 20 Feb. 1934.
138. 'Türkistan bizimdir!' 'Bütün Türkistan ve bütün Türkelleri bizimdir!'
139. *Orhun*, 9: 16 July 1934, esp. pp. 157–60, Atsız's article on 'Yirminci asırda Türk meselesi'.
140. See C.S. Fer, in *Gök Börü*, 1: 5 Nov. 1942, p. 3.
141. The Beyazıd Library, Istanbul, has nos 1 to 19–21 (should read: 21–22), 10 Dec. 1935–Sep. 1938 (all published?).
142. Muammer Lütfü Bahşı, 'Ulusal edebiyata doğru', *Çağlayan*, 1st series, 1: 10 Dec. 1935, p. 1.
143. A place name, related to Turan. It was also the title of one of Ziya Gökalp's famous poems (which the magazine reprinted, 1: 10 Nov. 1938, p. 3).
144. The first three may be consulted at the Beyazıd Library and at the University Library, both in Istanbul. *Ergenekon* was briefly revived as an Istanbul monthly in April 1972.
145. Cf. about him Hostler, 'Trends in Pan-Turanism', *MEA*, III (1): Jan. 1952, esp. pp. 7–8.
146. See at the end of the present chapter, pp. 96–7.
147. *Ergenekon*, cover of 1: 10 Nov. 1938: 'Her şeyin üstünde Türk ırkı!'
148. Ibid., cover of 3: 10 Jan. 1939: 'Her ırkın üstünde Türk ırkı!'
149. Ibid., pp. 1–13.
150. Ibid., pp. 4–5.
151. Ibid., 2: 10 Dec. 1938, p. 2.
152. Ibid., 3: 10 Jan. 1939, p. 24.
153. Ibid., p. 25: 'Irkçılık esası üzerine devlet kuran ilk ırk, dünyada, Türklerdir! . . . Öğrenin: Irkçılığın ilk kurucuları ve tatbikçileri, Pan-cermanistler veya Hitler değil, Türklerdir!'
154. *Kopuz* is the name of one of the oldest Turkish musical instruments.
155. The library of the Faculty of Political Science at the University of

Ankara has six issues, the last of which is dated 15 Sep. 1939; it continued to appear, however, at least up to (and including) 9: 15 Jan. 1940.

156. Miss Fevziye Abdullah Tansel, of Ankara, had in her private library the first four issues, May–Aug. 1943 (all published?).
157. On the *bozkurt* in the life and lore of the Turks, see Muzaffer Ünlü, *Türklük için dediler ki*, Adana, 1973, pp. 23–36.
158. See *Bozkurt*, May–June 1940, p. 65.
159. The Beyazıd Library, Istanbul, and the library of the Faculty of Political Science at the University of Ankara have between them an almost complete set. The last issue in the latter library is dated 2 July 1942. *Bozkurt* was revived in 1948 and then again in 1972–7, but these were different magazines and will be discussed later.
160. There was, apparently, a bitter struggle for the ownership of *Bozkurt* between Türkkan and Barıman. See C.S. Fer, in *Gök Börü*, 1: 5 Nov. 1942, pp. 3–4, 9.
161. Cf., e.g., *Bozkurt*, Aug. 1940, p. 121; 12 Mar. 1942, pp. 35–6; 26 Mar. 1942, pp. 75–6.
162. So outspokenly that several issues were seized by the authorities.
163. *Bozkurt*, May 1939, p. 18; June 1939, pp. 33–4; May–June 1940, pp. 81–3; Sep. 1940, pp. 129–30; Dec. 1940, pp. 208–13.
164. Ibid., May 1939, pp. 7–9; Sep. 1940, pp. 140–1; 12 Mar. 1942, p. 25.
165. Ibid., Sep. 1940, p. 150, 'Moda afeti'.
166. Ibid., 5 Mar. 1942, p. 6.
167. Ibid.
168. Ibid., July 1940, pp. 89–90.
169. Or: All-Turk Union.
170. A name for the Tien-Shan mountain range, home of the ancient Turks. For the symbolism of this name, 'Mountain of God', see Hostler, in *MEA*, III (1): Jan. 1952, pp. 4–5.
171. In that year, eighteen issues were published. A second series appeared, twice a month, since 5 Nov. 1950. All eighteen issues of the first series of *Tanrıdağ* and six of the second (all published?) may be consulted in the library of the Turkish Historical Society, Ankara.
172. See the end of the present chapter, p. 96.
173. Already mentioned (above, p. 2) as author of a book on Pan-Turkism.
174. *Tanrıdağ*, 2: 15 May 1942, pp. 6–7.
175. Ibid., 5: 5 June 1942, pp. 10–11.
176. Ibid., 15: 14 Aug. 1942, pp. 6–7.
177. E.g., ibid., 1: 8 May 1942, p. 3; 3: 22 May 1942, p. 15; 4: 29 May 1942, p. 8; 5: 5 June 1942, p. 9; 12: 24 July 1942, p. 15.
178. E.g., ibid., 3: 22 May 1942, pp. 4–7; 8: 26 June 1942, pp. 5–8; 16: 21 Aug. 1942, pp. 11–13; 17: 28 Aug. 1942, pp. 6–7, 11–12.
179. 'Türk, ordu ve savaş', ibid., 3: 22 May 1942, pp. 8–9.
180. 'Milliyetçiliğimiz nasıl olmalıdır?' ibid., 10: 10 Aug. 1942, pp. 9–10.
181. 'Fedakârlık seferberliği', ibid., 5: 5 June 1942, pp. 6–7.

182. 'Türk nasyonalizmi', ibid., 1: 8 May 1942, pp. 4–6.
183. Which he called *irredenta* — Italian style.
184. In Turkish, *Anadoluculuk*. There may be a somewhat pejorative nuance in the way Rıza Nur employed the term. By contrast, those in favour of this category of nationalism preferred to call it *Türkiyecilik* (Turkeyism), as did Gökalp, see above, ch. 2 of our study; or Bilgehan, in *Tanrıdağ*, 5: 5 June 1942, pp. 10–11.
185. *Irkçı Türkçülük*.
186. *Gök Börü*, 1: 5 Nov. 1942, explained on its cover that the title was synonymous with *Bozkurt*, 'wolf of the steppes'.
187. The Beyazıd Library, Istanbul, has the first twelve issues, up to 12: 6 May 1943. In all, thirteen issues appeared.
188. *Gök Börü*, 1: 5 Nov. 1942, pp. 17–18; 6: 1 Feb. 1943, pp. 6–7; 9: 25 Mar. 1943, pp. 4–6.
189. Ibid., 1: 5 Nov. 1942, p. 5.
190. Ibid., p. 2; 7: 15 Feb. 1943, pp. 13–14, 18; 8: 1 Mar. 1943, pp. 4–5; 9: 25 Mar. 1943, pp. 4–6; 12: 6 May 1943, supplement.
191. Ibid., 1: 5 Nov. 1942, pp. 8–9, 16–17; 6: 1 Feb. 1943, pp. 6–7.
192. E.g., O. Bozkurt (pseudonym?), 'Solcu sapıklara Bozkurt cevabı', ibid., 5: 1 Jan. 1943, pp. 2, 21–3.
193. In his 'Kandaş ve ülküdaşlarımıza!', ibid., 1: 5 Nov. 1942, p. 2.
194. This is, probably, what is meant by *sakat zahniyetler*.
195. *Gök Börü*, 12: 6 May 1943, supplement by Türkkan, entitled *Irka dair münakaşalar*, Istanbul, Bozkurtçu Yayını, 1943; 16 pp.
196. 'Türkçülüğe bakışlar', ibid., 1: 5 Nov. 1942, pp. 5–6.
197. Türkkan, however, changed the order, listing Pan-Turkism first.
198. 'İlerliyen Türkçülük', *Gök Börü*, 11: 22 Apr. 1943, pp. 3–4.
199. It was briefly revived in 1948.
200. A set may be consulted in the library of the School of Oriental and African Studies, London, and other libraries.
201. For whom see Gövsa, s.v., and Muhtar Tevfikoğlu, 'Orhan Seyfi Orhon', *TK*, 122: Nov. 1972, pp. 80–81.
202. See above, ch. 2 of our study, p. 10.
203. *Çınaraltı*, 1: 9 Aug. 1941, p. 3.
204. E.g., ibid., 2: 16 Aug. 1941, p. 4, 'İdeale doğru!' (Toward ideals!).
205. See below, ch. 4 of our study, p. 110.
206. 'Türkçülük ve milliyetçilik', *Çınaraltı*, 3: 23 Aug. 1941, p. 4: 'Her milliyetçi Türk Türkçüdür ve her Türkçü milliyetçidir.'
207. E.g., Kâzım İsmail's series on 'Irkın sıhhat davası', ibid., 1: 9 Aug. 1941, p. 5 and subsequent issues. Cf. a poem on this subject, ibid., 49: 29 Aug. 1942, p. 11.
208. See, e.g., ibid., 93: 3 July 1943, pp. 3, 6–7.
209. E.g., Nebil Buharalı, 'Kültürü zayıf millet ve kültürü kuvvetli millet', ibid., 5: 6 Aug. 1941, p. 6.
210. 'Millî şuur', ibid., 27: 7 Feb. 1942, p. 5.
211. 'Türkçülük programı', ibid., 26: 31 Jan. 1942 and subsequent issues.

212. 'Türk millî bütünlüğü', ibid., 83: 24 Apr. 1943, pp. 5–7, 15.

213. The library of the Grand National Assembly, Ankara, has an incomplete set of issues 1–8; July 1942–Feb. 1943 (all published?).

214. 'Yakın Türk tarihine bakışlar: Şamil', *Türk amacı*, 6: Dec. 1942, pp. 241–7.

215. 'Trakyada Türk kabileleri', ibid., 7: Jan. 1943, pp. 311–17.

216. 'Bir kaç söz', ibid., 1: 1 July 1942, pp. 1–2.

217. For others, more ephemeral ones, cf. R.P. Kondakchyan, *Vnutryennaya politika Turtsii v godi vtoroy mirovoy voyni*, ch. 5. Incidentally, this is the most detailed discussion in Russian of Pan-Turkism (pp. 164–219). For a briefer one, see R.S. Korkhmazyan, *Turyetsko-Gyermanskiye otnoshyeniya v vtoroy mirovoy voyni*, pp. 94 ff.

218. See our next chapter.

219. For a view supporting the relevance of race, cf. Celâl Nuri, 'Irk ve millet', *Edebiyat-ı Umumiye Mecmuası*, 37–38: 7 Şaban 1336/18 May 1918.

220. See above, ch. 2 of our study, pp. 37–8.

221. Karpat, *Turkey's politics*, p. 263, thinks that certain Nazi racist ideas penetrated into Turkey after 1935.

222. As we shall attempt to demonstrate at the beginning of ch. 4 of our study.

223. As mentioned above, p. 89.

224. Cf., e.g., *Gök Börü*, 7: 15 Feb. 1943.

225. Atsız, 'Yirminci asırda Türk meselesi', *Orhun*, 9: 16 July 1943, esp. pp. 157–60.

226. Türkkan, in *Bozkurt*, Dec. 1940, pp. 208–13; Akansel, in *Tanrıdağ*, 3: 22 May 1942, pp. 4–7; cf. ibid., 16: 21 Aug. 1942, pp. 11–13; 17: 28 Aug. 1942, pp. 6–7.

227. E.g. Türkkan, in *Bozkurt*, Mar. 1942, p. 6; Akansel, in *Tanrıdağ*, 17: 28 Aug. 1942, pp. 6–7.

228. Dr V.V. Akan, 'Irk hıfzısıhhası', *Bozkurt*, May–June 1940, pp. 81–3; Atsız, 'Kan ve uruk şartı', ibid., Sep. 1940, pp. 129–30; Akansel, in *Tanrıdağ*, 8: 26 June 1942, pp. 5–8; Dr Fethi Tevet, ibid., pp. 12–13.

229. Akansel, in *Tanrıdağ*, 3: 22 May 1942, pp. 4–7. Dr Z. Gögem, ibid., 16: 21 Aug. 1942, pp. 11–13 and 17; 28 Aug. 1942, pp. 11–12; A.N.Y., in *Gök Börü*, 7: 15 Feb. 1943, pp. 13–14, 18; Prof. S. Aygun, ibid., 8: 1 Mar. 1943, pp. 4–5.

230. See his *Türkün kitabı. Türk ırkı hakkında tetkikler*, Istanbul, Akbaba Yayını, 1943; 63 pp.

231. Cf. C.S. Fer, in *Gök Börü*, 1: 5 Nov. 1942, pp. 3–4, 9.

232. Henderson, in *The Asiatic Review*, XLI: 1945, p. 91.

233. *Türkistan Türk Gençliği*. See *Bozkurt*, 3: May–June 1940, p. 78. Cf. ibid., 9: Dec. 1940, p. 224, for an 'Evening of Pan-Turkists', dedicated to the memory of Ziya Gökalp.

234. FO 371/9287, N 5598/153/97, summary of *Meshed Intelligence Diary*, no. 60, for the period ending 16 Apr. 1923.

235. E.g., in the emigrants' Russian-language journal *Znamya bor'bi* (Berlin), 9–10: Feb.–Mar. 1925, pp. 14–18 (signed A.V. Validi).

236. See, besides Togan's own published works and the papers left in his private collection (esp. the 'large numbered files' 1–5), FO 371/48708, R 6848/177/44, Maurice Peterson's no. 118, confidential, to Eden, dated Ankara, 16 Apr. 1945. See also Mustafa Müftüoğlu, '60ıncı yılı münasebetiyle Prof. Zeki Velîdî Togan', *Tanrıdağ*, 2nd series, 4: 20 Dec. 1950, p. 6; *Ötüken*, 91: July 1971; Henderson, in *The Asiatic Review*, XLI: 1945, p. 88; Hostler, in *MEA*, III (1): Jan. 1952, p. 7; id., *Turkism*, index; Edward Weisband, *Turkish foreign policy 1943–1945*, pp. 241 ff; J.M. Landau, *Radical politics in modern Turkey*, pp. 197–8 and the references in the footnotes.

237. FO 371/44133, R 7775/789/44, British Ambassador H. Knatchbull-Hugessen's cyphered cable no. 771, to the Foreign Office, dated 19 May 1944.

238. *Irkçı, Türkçü ve Turancı.*

239. FO 371/44133, R 8011/789/44 and R 8021/789/44, both Knatchbull-Hugessen cables from Ankara, dated 19 May 1944.

240. See below, ch. 4.

241. See, besides Atsız's own works, the study of O.F. Sertkaya, 'Hüseyin Nihâl Atsız', in Erol Güngör et al. (eds), *Atsız armağanı*; pp. LVII–XCII list Atsız's writings. Cf. the personal biography of Altan Deliorman, *Tanıdığım Atsız*. See also *Meydan-Larouse*, s.v. (vol. I, p. 852); R.O. Türkkan, in *Bozkurt*, Sep. 1940, pp. 138–40; C.S. Fer, in *Gök Börü*, 1: 5 Nov. 1942, pp. 3–4, 9; '1944–1945 Irkçılık-Turancılık davası', *Orkun*, 3: 20 Oct. 1950 and subsequent issues; Henderson, in *The Asiatic Review*, XLI: 1945, p. 89; Hostler, in *MEA*, III (1): Jan. 1952, p. 9; id., *Turkism*, p. 183; Karpat, *Turkey's politics*, pp. 265–9; Ali Kemal Meram, *Türkçülük ve Türkçülük mücadeleleri tarihi*, 1969, pp. 225–33; Weisband, pp. 239–40; Sâdık Kemâloğlu, 'Atsız'ın ardından', *TK*, 160: Feb. 1976, pp. 245–7.

242. Ali Kemal Meram, *Türkçülük ve Türkçülük mücadeleleri tarihi*, pp. 187–9, has Rıza Nur's draft for the establishment of such a party.

243. Entitled, in Turkish, first *Türk Bilig Revüsü*, then *Türkbilik Revüsü*.

244. A set may be consulted in the library of the Turkish Historical Society, Ankara.

245. Rıza Nur has published extensively; some of his manuscripts are in the British Library, London, located under Mss. Or. 12588–12591. See, besides his own works, *Bozkurt*, Aug. 1940, p. 111; *Gök Börü*, 1: 5 Nov. 1942, p. 7; *Altın Işık*, 8: 25 Sep. 1947; H.N. Orkun, pp. 78–80; C.O. Tütengil, *Doktor Rıza Nur üzerine üç yazı — yankılar — belgeler*, Ankara, 1965. K.H. Karpat, 'Ideology in Turkey after the revolution of 1960: nationalism and socialism', *Turkish Yearbook of International Relations*, VI: 1965, esp. pp. 83–4; Hostler, *Turkism*, p. 183; A.K. Meram, pp. 183–91; Landau, *Radical politics*, pp. 193, 195.

246. See *Bozkurt*, July 1940, pp. 89–90.

247. R.O. Türkkan, *Tabutluktan gurbete*, esp. pp. 413–16.
248. Istanbul, 1940. Cf. F. Ronnenberger, 'Türkismus und Turanismus', *Volkstum im Südosten* (Vienna), Dec. 1942, pp. 197–203.
249. *Türkçülüğe giriş*, p. 116, quoted by Hostler in *MEA*, III (1): Jan. 1952, p. 8. For other works by Türkkan, see below in our selected bibliography.
250. See, besides Türkkan's own works, particularly his *Kuyruk acısı* (The grudge); C.S. Fer, in *Gök Börü*, 1: 5 Nov. 1942, pp. 3–4, 9; *Tanrıdağ*, 2nd series, 2: 20 Nov. 1950, p. 6; Henderson, in *The Asiatic Review*, XLI: 1945, pp. 88–9; Hostler, in *MEA*, III (1): Jan. 1952, pp. 7–9; id., *Turkism*, pp. 181–2; Karpat; *Turkey's politics*, pp. 265 ff, 270; Weisband, pp. 240–1.
251. R.O. Türkkan, 'The Turkish press', *MEA*, I (5): May 1950, pp. 144–5. Türkkan continued to hold on to these views even many years later, in his 1975 memoirs, *Tabutluktan gurbete*, see esp. pp. 400–12.
252. See above, in the present chapter, pp. 90–1.
253. Hostler, in *MEA*, III (1): Jan. 1952, p. 9; id., *Turkism*, p. 183; Jäschke, in *Beiträge*, pp. 478–9, 482.

4

PAN-TURKISM IN THE REPUBLIC OF TURKEY: RESURGENCE

The reassertion of Pan-Turkism during the later years of the Second World War and the two succeeding decades will be considered herein. Prior to this period, during the 'latent' stage, Pan-Turkism was meaningfully active only in the capitals of Central and Western Europe.[1] In Turkey itself it had to contend not only with conditions unfavourable for its development, but also with considerable opposition, ranging from moderately critical circles — which considered Pan-Turkism a romantic fantasy — to bitter antagonists who decried its racist and chauvinistic character, stressed the dangers inherent in foreign irredentist ventures,[2] and referred pejoratively to Pan-Turkists as 'Turanists' (*Turancı*). In response, Pan-Turkists started to call themselves Turanists with pride,[3] their propaganda emphasising a balanced realistic approach and purely nationalist objectives. They saw no reason to back down on their racist theories, which extolled the Turkish race, as these theories even appealed to certain non-Pan-Turkist circles in Turkey[4] (although they met with strong disapproval among others[5]).

Virtually from its outset, the Second World War seemed to offer Pan-Turkism a unique opportunity for reasserting itself and reaffirming its goals. At the time, Pan-Turkism was still a small, elitist movement in Turkey, although it did have increasing latent support.[6] Among its most visible promoters were Tatars from the Crimea and the Northern Caucasus, Azeris, Turkestanis, Daghestanis and other Outside Turks who were holding forth on their views at literary and artistic *soirées*.[7] These were joined increasingly by local Turks,[8] including even a few from official circles.[9] Refugees of Turkic stock who had fled from the Soviet Union, and their associates from within Pan-Turkist circles in Turkey, felt that Pan-Turkism offered the opportunity they had been waiting for. Several Pan-Turk organs printed suggestive articles about Enver Pasha's exploits in Central Asia in 1921-2,[10] while others extolled the warlike qualities of the Turkish

race. In February 1940, the French Ambassador Massigli informed
Paris: *'Dans le public, notamment dans les milieux militaires mais
pas dans ceux-là seulement, on parle de plus en plus des musulmans
du Caucase et de Bakou.'*[11]

Pan-Turk publications increased their aggressiveness following the
Nazi attack on the Soviet Union in June 1941, and its intensity rose
in direct proportion to the German victories there, together with a
marked increase in anti-Russian sentiment.[12] At this point, it seemed
that the realism of Pan-Turkism's general approach was being effectively proven. It was believed that, with the apparently impending
defeat and dismemberment of the Soviet Union, the vision of Pan-
Turkism would soon materialise. Ignoring the Turkish Government's
declared policy of neutrality, bold calls for Turkey's joining the war
(evidently against the Soviet Union) were voiced in Pan-Turk publications, not always overtly, but obviously enough — as in appealing
to President İsmet İnönü to come to the aid of the Turks in the Soviet
Union. Thus, following the German attack on the Soviet Union,[13] one
issue of *Bozkurt* not only carried a map of the Turks in Turkey and
Central Asia on its cover, but also addressed the following appeal to
İnönü to respond to the fateful course of events: 'O İnönü, selected
by history for this great day! We are ready to shed our blood for the
sacred independence of Turkdom! All Turkdom is awaiting thy sig-
nal!'[14] The call for a Pan-Turk war was clear, and was repeated in
various[15] increasingly aggressive forms, as for instance: 'The right
which is not given, should be taken. By war? — Yes, when necessary,
by war!'[16] And, it was averred, Pan-Turkists, aiming at a nation of
65 million, were ready to fight.[17]

Pan-Turkist involvement in the Second World War (particularly
in its later years) transcended mere journalistic activity, however, and
assumed a more directly practical character. Indeed, several Pan-
Turkist groups in Europe seemed to have maintained ties with Nazi
Germany or its supporters since the beginning of the war, if not earlier.
For example, the Turco-Tatars in Romania had cooperated with the
Iron Guard, a Nazi-inspired militant organisation. The crucial factor,
however, was obviously Turkey's own attitude. The facts concerning
the Turkish involvement in the war, before they joined the Allies near
its end, on 22 February 1945,[18] have not yet been fully uncovered.
The Turkish archives for that period have not so far been opened for
inspection; nevertheless, the files of the German Foreign Ministry[19]
and Public Record Office do provide sufficient data for a fairly
complete picture to be obtained.[20] Publicly and officially, the Government of Turkey maintained strict neutrality, closely watching
developments — particularly near its own borders. In practice, how-

ever, there had been confidential semi-official contacts both in Germany and in Turkey, since 1941, one facet of the relations between the two states. The Germans had directed an intensive propaganda campaign at Turkey since the early days of the war,[21] continuing it throughout[22] and allocating sizeable sums of money for this purpose.[23] Nazi Germany had displayed some interest in the Turco-Tatar groups and the areas inhabited by them in the Soviet Union, even before the Second World War.[24] During the war, scholarly and other articles were published in Germany about these Turkic groups — not a few with a Pan-Turk slant.[25] Furthermore, there was no little sympathy for Germany in Turkey at the time; in 1940, the renowned journalist Nadir Nadi, writing in the respectable *Cumhuriyet* daily, called several times on Turkey to join Germany in the war.[26] A ten-year Turco-German 'Treaty of Friendship' was signed in Ankara on 18 June 1941,[27] four days before Hitler invaded the Soviet Union. Germany apparently wanted to cover its southern flank, before attacking, while Turkey probably wanted to see Russia weakened. Certain German circles felt that Germany could tempt Turkey with territorial aggrandisement, while the Allies would not. This seemed a strong possibility, especially after the German attack on the Soviet Union, when the Nazis began to consider more seriously how Pan-Turkism could be exploited.[28]

Accordingly, during the second half of 1941 and the early months of 1942, a series of unofficial and semi-official contacts took place in Berlin and Ankara. The main participants were the German Ambassador to Ankara, Franz von Papen, and several officials of the German Foreign Office; and, on the Turkish side, General H.E. Erkilet,[29] himself of Tatar origin and a frequent contributor to Pan-Turk journals such as *Çınaraltı*;[30] another General, Ali Fuad Erdem;[31] and Nuri Pasha,[32] the brother of Enver Pasha, a romantic figure for Pan-Turkists. While Erkilet discussed military contingencies with the Germans and visited their Eastern front in 1941 (he subsequently wrote a book on these experiences, *Şark Cebhesinde gördüklerim* — What I saw on the Eastern front), Nuri offered the Germans his plans for creating independent states — allies but not satellites of Turkey — out of the Turkic populations in the Crimea, Azerbayjan, Turkestan, northwestern Iran and northern Irak. Nuri himself offered to assist with propaganda activities to this effect.[33] Several senior officials at the German Foreign Office, notably von Hentig, were enthusiastic at the possibilities of Pan-Turk propaganda in the Soviet Union[34] and even made concrete preparations for it;[35] while others toyed with the idea of using the Pan-Turks to recruit fighting units from among the Turkic prisoners-of-war in German camps,[36] then numbering about

55,000,[37] a proposal later put into practice.[38] The Turkish Government was aware — unofficially — of many of these moves,[39] but remained reticent. Gerede, Turkey's Ambassador to Berlin, while expressing interest in the Turkic groups in the Soviet Union, repeatedly declared that Turkey had no territorial ambitions.[40] Indeed, von Papen reported that he thought the Turkish Government might even be embarrassed by open Pan-Turk propaganda from Berlin,[41] intimating that Mehmet Şükrü Saraçoğlu, Turkey's Minister for Foreign Affairs (later Prime Minister), had told him that until Germany crushed the Soviet Union definitively, Turkey could not join Germany for fear of Soviet reprisals against the Turkic minorities there.[42] Perhaps the Turkish Government was also apprehensive of the Soviet Union's might. In any event, Turkey refused to be drawn in openly, although the Chief-of-Staff, Fevzi Çakmak himself, appears to have pulled some of the strings in the negotiations.[43] Even von Papen — who had made it his job to observe Turkish officialdom closely — expressed doubts as to whether the Turkish Government could really be bought with territorial inducements.[44] Various pressures also failed to budge it from its declared neutrality.[45]

At a less official level, emigrants from among the Turkic groups in the Soviet Union played a crucial role in some of these contacts and negotiations, in both Turkey and Germany. According to a secret despatch from von Papen,[46] among those working in Turkey were such well-known emigrants and Pan-Turkist activists as Ahmed Zeki Velidi Togan, Mehmet Emin Resul-Zade, Mirza-Bala, Ahmet Caferoğlu (a Crimean Turk and known Turcologist [died 1975] and a frequent contributor to Pan-Turk periodicals), Said Şamil and Ayaz İshakî,[47] already mentioned[48] for their Pan-Turk activism in the inter-war period. In Germany were Müstecib Ülküsal, a Turco-Tatar who had edited *Emel* in Romania[49] and went to Germany from Turkey in November 1941 (favouring us later with his memoirs[50]), the above-mentioned Mustafa Çokay-oğlu and, after his death on 27 December 1941,[51] another Turkestani, Veli Kajum Khan; all were apparently prime movers in organising military units of Turkestanis, Azeris, Volga-Ural and Crimean Tatars, Uzbeks, Kirghiz, Kazakhs, Karakalpaks, Tajiks, Daghestanis and others — in Turco-Tatar and Caucasian Muslim legions, as appropriate.[52] These units, comprising mainly prisoners-of-war, joined the Germans against the Soviet Union, generally fighting as guerrillas. Many of them were imbued with hopes for independence; several aspired to a Pan-Turk union. The units, which were continually regrouped and reinforced, finally numbered several hundreds of thousands of people of Turkic origins.[53]

Needless to say, the Russians have never forgotten nor forgiven this insurgency.[54]

The Turkish Government, for its part, does not seem to have harboured any serious irredentist plans. The British Ambassador to Ankara remarked, several years later:

Nor was there even the slightest justification for the notion that the Turkish Government had irredentist ambitions in regard to the Turkish populations in South Russia. The Turkish Government knew where their interests lay . . . if irresponsible individuals hinted tendentiously at the presence of populations of Turkish race outside Turkey, they received nothing but discouragement from the Turkish Government.[55]

That government, of course, had more than a fair idea of what was going on,[56] but evidently declined to commit itself until, on the one hand, the highest German echelons recognised the national independence of the Turkic areas in the Soviet Union, and on the other, the Germans had defeated the Soviet Union militarily. The Germans hesitated about the former condition, as they had their own plans for Soviet Central Asia;[57] Hitler himself wanted the Crimea and the Caucasus to be colonised by Germans.[58] However, following their decisive defeat at Stalingrad, the Germans could hardly be expected to carry out the latter stipulation.

It will remain a moot point for future students of diplomatic history to decide how seriously İnönü and his government had considered intervening in the war.[59] What is clear is that neutrality prevailed in Turkey at the time, on the assumption that discretion was the better part of valour. Pan-Turkist groups in Turkey were, to say the least, exasperated by their own government's inaction and by what they manifestly regarded as the waste of a golden opportunity for bringing Pan-Turkism to realisation; hence they themselves began taking the initiative. The Turkish Government, however, particularly during the last years of the war, had every reason to reassert its neutrality, in order to dispel any Soviet suspicions of pro-German sympathy on its part. This became even more important during 1944; after the Red Army's breakthrough in the Ukraine in January, Soviet troops approached the Polish and Romanian frontiers and subsequently advanced into the Balkans. Consequently, the Turkish authorities increased their surveillance of Pan-Turkist activities which might provoke the Russians. The Pan-Turkists, however, considered that time to be the very last possible opportunity for concentrated efforts at bringing Turkey into the war against the Soviet Union, in order to fulfil their irredentist vision. Thus the stage was set for the 1944 events.

During the war years, Pan-Turkism's propaganda campaign in Turkey could hardly be directed against its obvious rival for popularity, namely nationalism. Rather, the two ideologies were in competition, with Pan-Turkists increasingly contending for a monopoly on true patriotism. The room for manoeuvre for both Pan-Turkists and other nationalists was, however, limited due to Turkey's inactive neutrality. The two schools of thought did compete, for example, in heightening anti-minority feeling, especially after such activity was given implicit approval through the enactment of a very harsh government-inspired 'Wealth Tax', the *Varlık Vergisi* of 1942. This was especially in evidence during 1943 (as in the lecture of Mahmut Esat Bozkurt, erstwhile Minister of Justice and then Member of the Grand National Assembly for Izmir, delivered on 5 June at the People's Home of Üsküdar) and was remarked upon by foreign diplomats in Turkey.[60] However, it was more natural for Pan-Turkism to launch a frontal attack on its arch-enemy, Communism, with particular emphasis on local Communists, real or imaginary. This was even more the case when Turkish Communist sympathisers began attacking Pan-Turkists, as in a pamphlet published in 1943 by Faris Erkman, an employee of the Electricity Company, entitled *En büyük tehlike* (The greatest danger). This work was designed to unmask what Erkman termed 'the Pan-Turkist, Turanian, racialist puppets',[61] whose strings were moved by foreign hands.[62] Quoting from Pan-Turk periodicals, he roundly attacked Atsız, Rıza Nur, Erkilet and others, accusing them of war-mongering and of degrading their claims to nationalism. The Pan-Turkists responded in kind, in their own press;[63] the whole matter was even debated in the Grand National Assembly.[64] It is hardly surprising that Communism increasingly became the whipping-boy of Pan-Turkism. However, during the Second World War, and particularly in its later years, such policies were hardly welcomed by a government keen on demonstrating its neutrality.

Open conflict between Pan-Turkists and the Government was thus inevitable. On 20 February and on 21 March 1944, respectively, Atsız published two open letters to Premier Mehmet Şükrü Saraçoğlu in his monthly *Orhun*,[65] denouncing subversive activities in Turkey — chiefly those of Communists — and demanding a more active Turkist and (by inference) Pan-Turkist policy.[66] Several issues of *Orhun* were confiscated and the periodical was subsequently closed down. The Pan-Turkists then took to the streets, crossing the critical threshold between ideological propaganda and political action. On 3 May 1944, in defiance of martial law regulations, large anti-Communist demonstrations took place in both Istanbul and Ankara, to protest against what the demonstrators considered the penetration of Communism into Turkey's government bureaucracy and educational system. Pan-Turk slogans were also in evidence, probably inspired by growing anxiety over the fate of Turkic groups in the Soviet Union (the deportation of Tatars and others was then being planned and was in fact carried out a few days later). Such notable Pan-Turkists as Atsız, Türkkan and others were involved, as well as a young captain, Alparslan Türkeş, who was yet to make his mark in Turkish politics;[67] many students also joined in.[68]

The government over-reacted, perhaps in an attempt to display its neutrality *vis-à-vis* the Soviet Union.[69] Six days after the above demonstration, more than thirty leading Pan-Turkists and sympathisers were arrested,[70] including Togan, Atsız, Sançar, Türkkan, Erkilet, Peyami Safa, Türkeş, Hikmet Tanyu, M. Zeki Sofuoğlu, Nurullah Barıman, Tevetoğlu, and others. A large-scale campaign of speeches and press articles against Pan-Turkism was initiated simultaneously by the Turkish Government and circles close to the Republican People's Party, which volunteered to explain their own version of Turkish nationalism. The press accused Pan-Turkists roundly of being 'racists and Turanists', and 'enemies of the nation and of public order'.[71] The central themes were determined by İnönü himself, barely sixteen days after the Istanbul demonstration, in a speech at the Ankara Stadium. He declared that Turkey was a national and nationalist state, imbued with ideals, while Pan-Turkism (which he steadfastly termed 'Turanism') was a diseased phenomenon, liable to embroil the nation in hostilities with its neighbours. He roundly accused the Turanists (i.e. the Pan-Turkists) of forming secret societies, and consequently of harbouring sinister designs perilous for Turkey.[72] These arguments were soon echoed in many other speeches and press reports.[73]

Pan-Turkist organisations were then banned,[74] but the ensuing trials of their leaders[75] and the campaign against the movement in general served the Pan-Turkist cause admirably, giving Pan-Turkism the extensive free publicity which it had long desired. There were actually two series of trials. The first began on 11 September 1944, before the Martial Law Court in Istanbul, with considerable media coverage. Twenty-three people were charged with spreading subversive ideas (racist-Turanist propaganda) and with setting up clandestine groups to overthrow the government. Most prominent among these were Togan, Atsız, Sançar and Türkkan. Others were junior officers, reserve officers, government officials, teachers and students. On 29 March 1945, ten of the accused were sentenced to between one and ten years of hard labour, while the rest were acquitted. Togan was sentenced to ten years and Atsız to four.[76] On appeal, however, the Military Court of Cassation, in October the same year, quashed the sentences. The war was over by then and the country's relations with the Soviet Union had changed. In a very different mood and with scant media coverage, a retrial was held from August 1946 to March 1947, at which all charges against all the accused were dismissed by the Court. In effect, Pan-Turkism had been vindicated by the Courts as neither subversive nor illegal. The public had been fed a large dose of Pan-Turk ideology, emphasising its strongly nationalist character; indeed, as the accused themselves maintained,[77] a public image was being created that they were the only true nationalists. (Both Türkeş and Türkkan later recorded their experiences in jail and court.[78]) This continued to be a *Leitmotif* of Pan-Turk propaganda in Turkey during the following years, with the Pan-Turkists using the trials as a starting-point.

Encouraged by their own activities during the latter part of the Second World War as well as by the publicity of the above trials and their ultimate acquittals, Pan-Turkists in Turkey, during those years and afterwards, visibly increased their activities and intensified their propaganda. One obvious target was the Turkish Cypriots, who were displaying signs of increasing politicisation during the late 1940s in reaction to the increasing demand of the Greek Cypriots for *Enosis* (union with Greece). This became a popular issue in Turkey as Pan-Turkists encouraged the Turkish Cypriots to organise themselves, and the Turks in Turkey itself (students and others) to demonstrate and write for the cause.[79] During the 1950s, similar attention was directed towards the Turkish minority in Bulgaria.[80]

In their propaganda campaign, Turkish Pan-Turkists found wholehearted cooperation among Outside Turks, living in Turkey and abroad, who had stepped up their political organisation and had attempted to obtain support for their cause among Western and Third World countries. One example is that of the Turkestani emigrants, who had formed their own association, such as the East Turkestan Emigrants' Society (*Doğu Türkistan Göçmenler Cemiyeti*). The society's chairman, İsa Alptekin, joined others, during the 1950s and 1960s, in launching appeals and writing letters to President Lyndon B. Johnson, Chiang Kai-Shek and many others; he met 'Azzām, Secretary-General of the Arab League, as well as other personalities, and attended the Bandung and other international meetings to seek support. Moreover, these and other Outside Turks who had emigrated to Turkey tried hard to mobilise support there too — considering Turkey as the most likely ally for their cause.[81]

The renewed Pan-Turk drive found expression in books and periodicals alike, with added emphasis on both race and anti-Communism. In the former case, Pan-Turk thinking had evidently been affected by Nazi 'research' on race[82] during the 1930s and the 1940s (although Pan-Turkists denied this).[83] In the latter, anti-Communism not only fitted aptly into the basic credo of Pan-Turkism, but was also certain to cash in on some popular support. The total effect of these publications was quite impressive and sufficed to make the Soviets take note and criticise them adversely.[84]

Not a few of these works were written by such active Pan-Turkists as Türkkan, Atsız and Sançar.

Türkkan, perhaps more than the others, combined the appeals for racism and anti-Communism. His books and pamphlets bear such titles as *Irk muhite tâbi midir* (Does race depend on the environment? 1939), *Türkçülüğe giriş* (An introduction to Pan-Turkism, 1940), *4 ictimaî mesele* (Four social problems, 1941), *Irka dair münâkaşalar* (Arguments concerning race, 1943), *Solcular ve kızıllar* (Leftists and Reds, 1943), *Kızıl faaliyet!* (Red activities! 1943), *Kuyruk acısı* (The grudge, 1943), *Milliyetçilik yolunda* (On the road of nationalism, 1944) and *İleri Türkçülük ve partiler* (Progressive Pan-Turkism and the parties, 1946).[85] Of these, only *Four social problems* took no stand regarding Pan-Turkism, while the others were most emphatically supportive. For example, the pamphlet *On the road of nationalism*[86] defined Pan-Turkism as 'Turkish nationalism'.[87] Türkkan further elaborated that the basic principle of Pan-Turkism was 'a national union';[88] its objective comprised the 65 million Turks of the same blood and language, as well as the same religion, history, traditions and culture, inhabiting the wide area from Bulgaria to Altai. 'Turkish national union' was also the main way to develop and strengthen Turkey itself.[89] This was exemplified in Türkkan's tables on the figures of the world Turkish population, whose calculation became an absorbing pastime for many Pan-Turkist writers and journalists. According to Türkkan,[90] the figures were as follows in 1944:

Country	Turkic Population
Yugoslavia	500,000
Bulgaria	1,000,000
Romania	300,000
Greece and the Islands	120,000
Turkey	15,000,000
Russia	24,000,000
Afghanistan	2,000,000
China	8,000,000
Syria	40,000
Irak	500,000
Total[91]	57,460,000

Nejdet Sançar also warmly supported the concepts of 'race' and 'Turkish race'. In his *Irkımızın kahramanları* (The heroes of our race), first published in 1943 and partly based on his own articles in *Çınaraltı*, he frankly recounted the exploits of heroes of the Turkish race — not only Turks — aiming at rendering his readers proud of their race's heritage. Neither his trial (with other Pan-Turkists) nor his transfer as a teacher to Edirne in 1951 — which he alleged to be a reprisal by the authorities[92] — served to change his views, which were elaborated further in his *Türklük sevgisi* (The love of Turkism), published in 1952.[93] Militant by nature,[94] Sançar argued that there was a Turkish race,[95] which evidently included the Outside Turks,[96] although it did not *per se* comprise all born as Turks or speaking Turkish; one had to feel oneself a Turk and harbour national sentiments in order to be worthy of this name.[97] The Outside Turks, who indeed manifested such feelings, were a part of this race.[98]

Although in general Atsız supported the concept of a Turkish race, he was more interested during the years following the Second World War in employing his pen for avowedly irredentist aims. In a collection of articles — mostly from the 1940s and 1950s — entitled *Türk ülküsü* (The ideals of the Turks), which went through several editions,[99] he argued passionately for 'an ideal of greatness', maintaining that it would be inconceivable for Turkey to be the size of Nepal, Panama or Switzerland.[100] The solution for Turkey ought to be a union of all Turks, who — he estimated — numbered between 82,840,000 and 99,200,000.[101] He then pointed out that there was strength in numbers.[102] Atsız reminded his readers that many countries desired to recover their lost territories: the Germans wanted East Germany, sequestered by the Russians, the Finns Karelia, the Hungarians Transylvania, the Yugoslavs Macedonia, the Greeks North Epirus and Eastern Thrace, and the Syrians Hatay. Why should not the Turks, too, aspire towards unity and joy?[103] 'To unite means to grow, and to grow means to unite.'[104] This implied sacrifices, for which everyone should be prepared.[105] Atsız defined Pan-Turkists as 'those ready to be twentieth-century martyrs for the Turkish nation'.[106]

During and following the latter years of the Second World War, a number of books and pamphlets were written by Pan-Turkists less renowned than Türkkan, Sançar or Atsız, but enthusiastically dedicated to this cause. The authors of some of them were Outside Turks, living abroad or in Turkey. Among the former, those living in the Soviet Union produced several works praising their own history and culture, with a hint of Pan-Turkism for the *sapienti docet*; while those living in Western Europe published several journals (to be discussed below) and a number of books, many of which were written by an energetic exile from Turkestan, Dr Baymirza Hayıt, an indefatigable fighter for Pan-Turkism, especially for the liberation of Russian Turkestan and Chinese Turkestan and their union. Hayıt, who lives in Federal Germany, presented a memorandum to the Second Conference of Asian and African Countries, meeting in 1965, entitled *Soviet Russian colonialism and imperialism in Turkistan as an example of the Soviet type of colonialism of an Islamic people in Asia*; he also wrote several books and numerous articles.[107]

Among the Outside Turks living and writing in Turkey, special mention should be made of Muharrem Feyzi Togay and his 1944 *Yusuf Akçuranın hayatı* (The life of Yusuf Akçura), based on personal acquaintance and full of admiration for Akçura's indefatigable struggle, in word and deed, on behalf of the Outside Turks and the cause of Pan-Turkism. Also noteworthy are two booklets edited by Dr Aslanapa Oktay: one on Mustafa Çokayoğlu and the national movement in Turkestan[108] and another on the views of nationalist Turkestani exiles in Turkey.[109] The latter book was based on lectures presented at several public meetings of such exiles, held in Ankara and Istanbul, during 1952.[110] Oktay also edited a two-part book on Pan-Turkism and populism in Turkestan,[111] replete with enthusiasm for Turkestan's struggle for independence. Yet another Turkestani exile in Turkey, Tahir Çağatay, published a three-volume Pan-Turk-inspired attack on Soviet policies in Turkestan, entitled *Kızıl imperyalizm* (Red imperialism).[112] Other important writers were Ahmet Hazer Hızal, author of the 1961 *Kuzey Kafkasya (hürriyet ve istiklâl davası)* (The Northern Caucasus: the problems of freedom and independence); Ziyaeddin Babakurban and his 1962 *Dış Türkler ve Türkistan davası* (The Outside Turks and the cause of Turkestan);[113] or a posthumous collection of articles, written between 1931 and 1954, by the Crimean Turk leader, Cafer Seydahmet Kırımer, *Mefkûre ve Türkçülük* (Ideals and Pan-Turkism).[114] While these Outside Turks had an axe to grind on behalf of their own community, along with their more general call for Pan-Turkism, most natives of Turkey writing on the matter focused on an all-Turk union as their principal objective.

Several characteristic examples may be cited. In 1944 Hüseyin Namık Orkun[115] wrote *Yeryüzünde Türkler* (The Turks over the globe), a study of the Turks, past and present, living throughout Central Asia, Turkestan, the Volga, the Crimea, Azerbaycan, Irak, Rumelia, Dobruja, Bulgaria, Cyprus and elsewhere, presented in a Pan-Turk spirit, with considerable empathy and hope of seeing them liberated and independent (as a step towards union with Turkey). In

1947, Hikmet Tanyu, one of those tried for the demonstrations of the Pan-Turkists three years earlier, published his pamphlet *Türk gençliğin kükreyişi* (The roar of Turkish youth), in which he combined the preaching of nationalism, Pan-Turk style, with a strong attack on Communism in Turkey. Five years later, Hocaoğlu Selâhattin Ertürk, a philosophy instructor in Konya, attempted yet another probe of Pan-Turkism in his *Türkçülük nedir?* (What is Pan-Turkism?), in 1952. His argument ran as follows.[116] Syria, Jordan, Irak and Saudi Arabia are separate Arab nations, but are all of one and the same nationality. In the same way, Ertürk maintained, the people inhabiting Turkey, Azerbayjan, Kazan and Turkestan — united in language, religion, customs, arts, race and history — might be considered as naturally belonging to the Turkish nationality. Only those living in Turkey formed a nation, while the others were subjects of Russia, Iran or the Balkan countries. However, since all belonged not only to the Turkish race but also to the Turkish nationality, it was the duty of the Turks in Turkey to assist their brethren in achieving their independence, as a step towards union in a 'Great Turan'.

In a book published six years later in 1958,[117] M.E. Erişirgil attempted to prove the validity and relevance of race theories,[118] also devoting some attention to a reinterpretation of Pan-Turkism which suited the new times.[119] He opposed the French and British interpretations of nationalism, preferring the German view (probably based on racist principles). As Erişirgil saw it, Pan-Turkism was basically a political system geared to achieve happiness and prosperity for all Turks everywhere.

Kurt Tarık Öz-Han's *Hayır! Prof. H.E. Adıvar esir Türk illeri kurtarılacaktır* (No to Professor H.E. Adıvar: the captive Turkish territories will be saved!), with introductions by Dr Ahmet Temir, M. Zeki Sofuoğlu and Cemal Kutay, all active Pan-Turkists (Sofuoğlu was one of those who stood trial for Pan-Turkism in the 1940s), was published in 1960. The book condemned the above-mentioned Halide Edib (Adıvar) for having treated Pan-Turkism as a reflection of Pan-Slavism in one of her books, arguing that Pan-Slavism had been rejected in the Balkans (by Yugoslavia, for example) while Pan-Turkism had been wholeheartedly accepted by Turks.[120] Besides, Pan-Slavism had been a phenomenon of the nineteenth century, while Pan-Turkism belonged to the twentieth.[121] The author then proceeded to his own characterisation of Pan-Turkism[122] as an intellectual and organisational system aiming at enabling all peoples[123] of Turkish race to live together and form a state [of their own], and in assisting all Turkic peoples under the Soviet yoke to obtain their independence and exercise their natural rights. According to these criteria, Pan-

Slavism had been unlawful, while Pan-Turkism was absolutely law-ful.[124] Öz-Han's work was supplemented, soon afterwards, by a pamphlet by Tahsin Ünal, a contributor to Pan-Turk periodicals, entitled *Milliyet üzerine düşünceler* (Thoughts on nationality) and published in 1961. Ünal identified Turkish nationalism with Pan-Turkism and made a passionate plea for the liberation and union of all Turks abroad.

The search for a redefinition of Pan-Turkism was also reflected in the Pan-Turk press of that period, which was even more indicative of the issues considered and the solutions proffered than were the relatively few monographs issued at the same time.

There were several Pan-Turkists who contributed to various Western publications, notably those having an anti-Soviet character and concentrating on Central Asia. One example is *The East Turkic Review*, an annual published by the Institute for the Study of the Soviet Union in Munich, since 1958. Among its contributors were known Pan-Turkists, such as A. Battal-Taymas,[125] while articles in-cluded such pronouncements as 'In the past, Turkestan had been, essentially, a single entity.'[126] Other periodicals were published, generally by emigrants from Soviet Central Asia, and mostly in Federal Germany and Switzerland. The following may serve as ex-amples:

1. *United Caucasus*, edited by A. Kantemir, published in Munich since 1951 as the organ of the Committee for Caucasian Inde-pendence, involving leading Azeri emigrants.[127]

2. *Svobodniy Kavkas* (Independent Caucasus), edited by A. Av-torkhonov, a monthly, published from 1951 to 1953, as an organ for Caucasian national-democratic ideas, with Azeri participation.[128]

3. *Azerbaycan* (Azerbayjan), edited by A. Fatalıbeyli, a monthly appearing in Munich since 1952 and an organ of the Azerbayjan National Association.[129]

4. *Millij Türkistan* (National Turkestan), whose English subtitle was *Journal of the National Turkistanian Unity Committee for the struggle of national liberation of Turkestan*. Edited by V. Jurtcı, it has been published since 1950, first in Geneva and then in Düsseldorf, in Turkestanian (in both Latin and Arabic scripts), Arabic and English.[130] Most articles described conditions in Soviet Turkestan, protesting against Russian discrimination and forced assimilation.

5. *Türkeli* (Land of the Turks), whose English subtitle was *Review of the National Committee for the liberation of Turkestan*, published in Munich in 1951–2, in two languages — Turkestanian in Latin char-acters[131] and Russian,[132] calling principally for the national liberation of Turkestan.

6. *Azat Vatan* (Independent Homeland), organ of the National Committee of Tatar-Bashkirs, which began publication in 1952.[133]

7. *Caucasian Review*, published irregularly in Munich during the 1950s and 1960s, by the Institute for the Study of the Soviet Union. Unlike the preceding six publications, which were entirely devoted to their single respective causes, *Caucasian Review* comprised sections regularly earmarked for the Northern Caucasus, Georgia, Azerbayjan and Armenia.[134]

Similar separateness was generally in evidence in periodicals published by various emigrant groups in Turkey itself, which is our principal concern. Only local Turks were willing and able to propagate a more wide-embracing concept of Pan-Turkism. Thus the Azeris have published, since April 1952, in Turkish, such journals as *Azerbaycan* (Azerbayjan) — a monthly literary periodical and organ of the Azeri Cultural Society in Ankara (later, this became a quarterly, which still appears irregularly in Ankara) — [135] or *Azerbaycan yurt bilgisi* (Civics of Azerbayjan), published in Istanbul.[136] Their longest-lived periodical, at that time, seems to have been *Mücahit. Aylık. İktisadi içtimai fikir mecmuası (Mücahit:*[137] A monthly journal of economic and social ideas). This appeared in Ankara between July 1955 and November 1964,[138] in Turkish, although some of the articles were translated into English — indicating that the journal's propaganda value abroad was not underrated. Its publisher was Cengiz Gökgöl and its editor Safvet Zerdabi. Most contributors were Azeris, although some others, too, participated. *Mücahit* was almost solely interested in the Outside Turks, with a heavy emphasis on those in Azerbayjan. It was symptomatic that, even when dealing with culture — chiefly history, language and literature — the perspective was generally political, with marked Pan-Turk overtones, strongly attacking the Soviet Union and communism.

Other emigrant groups were similarly active. Tatars published *Kırım* (The Crimea), a monthly edited by Sermet Arısoy in Ankara, during 1957, in Turkish. Turkestanis in Turkey had their own periodicals during these years. One such journal was *Türkistan. İlmî, içtimaî, iktisadî ve kültürel aylık dergidir* (Turkestan: a Scholarly, Social, Economic and Cultural Monthly), edited by Mehmet Emin Buğra (1901–65) and Ziyaeddin Babakurban and published in Istanbul, during 1953, in Turkish.[139] Although this journal's avowed objectives were to acquaint readers of Turkish with Turkestan's history and culture and to advise immigrants from Turkestan on how to adapt to life in Turkey,[140] many of its articles and poems had a definite political character with Pan-Turk overtones: examples are a frontal attack on 'the crimes of the Red Imperialists',[141] an attack on China's policies in East Turkestan[142] and another on the annihilation policies of the Soviets.[143] Of special interest are *Türkistan's* letters from and articles by Turkestanis from all over the world (Turkey, Lahore, Kashmir, Cairo, Munich and Washington). *Türkistan* was succeeded by another monthly, *Türkistan Sesi. Aylık. İlmî ve kültürel dergi* (Voice of Turkestan. Monthly: a scholarly and cultural journal), edited by the same M.E. Buğra and published in Ankara, during 1956–7, in Turkish.[144] An English edition, *The Voice of Turkistan*, appeared simultaneously in Ankara as a quarterly.[145] Turkestan's history and literature were again given special treatment in *Türkistan Sesi*, although many contributions by Buğra himself and by other Pan-Turkists such as İsa Yusuf Alptekin and Arın Engin gave the journal a marked political character. Buğra's poem, 'The Fatherland is ours',[146] which appeared in the first issue, was the *Leitmotif* for all subsequent ones. The journal's 'National Credo' was full independence for the whole of Turkestan[147] — for which it displayed some readiness to cooperate with Azeris and Caucasus Tatars.[148] *Türkistan Sesi's* primary goal, however, was to enlist support from Muslims everywhere, from Indonesia[149] to the Arab states,[150] as well as from other opponents of Communism, such as Nationalist China.[151]

Since the end of the Second World War, Pan-Turk publications issued by local Turks were characterised by a more aggressive stage of *Realpolitik*, focusing on an anti-Communist (rather than a narrow racist) approach, with an attendant search for potential allies against world Communism. The high tones which characterised Pan-Turk propaganda in the latter part of the war — when adepts did not fear conflict with the forces of law and order — were no less evident in the post-war years. Once the multi-party era was ushered in, in 1946, the formerly all-powerful position of the Republican People's Party was weakened; during the 1950s, Democrat Party governments were not committed to the anti-Pan-Turkism of the Republican People's Party, and the various coalition cabinets of 1961–5 were too concerned with other matters to pay much attention to Pan-Turkist activities.

As may be expected, Pan-Turkists in Turkey also contributed to general periodicals which were not averse to their cause, such as the monthly *Türk Yurdu*, reissued in Ankara since April 1959 (under the editorship of Professor Osman Turan).[152] Its pages were open to such known Pan-Turkists as A. Battal-Taymas, Aslanapa Oktay and Nejdet Sançar. Others issued their own, generally short-lived periodicals. There were, however, several new Pan-Turk magazines to take the place of those which had ceased publication as a result of government intervention or lack of funds. Some chose new names, while others adopted those of defunct Pan-Turk organs. In 1943, a year of great excitement and many expectations among Pan-Turkists, no less than four Pan-Turk journals appeared. A brief discussion of the most active periodicals and of their themes follows.

Türk Sazı (The *saz*[153] of the Turks), published by Reşide Sançar (wife of Nejdet Sançar) with editorials by Atsız, produced its first issue on 15 May 1943[154] and included articles by Professor Togan on a well-known Central Asian Khan,[155] as well as translations of studies by noted Turcologists, such as Tadeusz Kowalski and Barthold.[156] The journal's centre of attraction, however, was probably Atsız's editorial,[157] which re-examined the essence of Pan-Turkism. He proclaimed that Pan-Turkism is a 'national ideal',[158] and set as its goal the unrestricted sovereignty of the Turkish race in all Turkish territories. Other contributors, such as Nejdet Sançar and Mustafa Hakkı Akansel, tended to write in much the same vein.

One of the journals revived in 1943 was *Kopuz*, edited in Samsun by Fethi Tevetoğlu (born in 1916), a frequent contributor to Pan-Turk publications and one of those to be committed to stand trial in the mid-1940s;[159] a dedicated anti-Communist, Tevetoğlu was, in both personality and writing, a characteristic example of a combined Pan-Turkist and anti-Communist, such as was to be found frequently in the foremost ranks of the Pan-Turkists.

Yet another journal revived in 1943, and appearing in Istanbul as a monthly, was *Çağlayan. Aylık fikir ve edebiyat dergisi*. Its publisher-editor was, again, Sıtkı Tekeli.[160] In this new series, articles clearly proclaimed a commitment to the Turkish nation, the Fatherland and Turkism.[161] From here it was only a short step to call for 'a realist Pan-Turkism',[162] arguing that Pan-Turkism was a feasible proposition, not just romantic adventurism. An article attacked Communists, particularly the book *En büyük tehlike* referred to above, in aggressively nationalist Pan-Turk terms.[163] Another discussed approvingly the concept of racialism (*ırkçılık*).[164] On the whole, however, *Çağlayan* seems to have been less aggressive than several other Pan-Turk periodicals of that time.

Another journal was *Orhun*, which had closed down with its ninth issue on 16 July 1934, and now reappeared with its tenth on 1 October 1943 as a monthly, published in Istanbul.[165] Atsız served once again as editor and main contributor, notably with his two letters to Prime Minister Saraçoğlu.[166] As Nejdet Sançar[167] and others[168] continued writing about the superiority of the Turkish race and about the Outside Turks (e.g. the 100,000 Turks living in Irak[169]), the most politically aggressive contribution may well have been Nihad Sami Banarlı's 'Great ideals and little idealists',[170] a strongly-worded article calling on Turkey to grow in order to achieve the Turanian ideal. Although under circumstances then existing, its author could hardly advocate the use of force explicitly, his message could be inferred easily by readers who were free to draw their own conclusions.

One of the first Pan-Turk periodicals after the end of the Second World War was *Toprak. Fikir-sanat-ülkü dergisi* (Earth: a journal of ideas, art and ideals). A monthly, it was published in Adana between July 1945 and December 1947.[171] Strongly nationalist and anti-Communist, it counted among its contributors such noted Pan-Turkists as M. Zeki Sofuoğlu, Arif Nihat Asya and Nejdet Sançar.

Next came *Özleyiş. Bilim-sanat-ülkü* (Yearning: Science, art and ideals), a monthly published in Ankara between October 1946 and November 1947.[172] Its editor was Himket Tanyu, then a lecturer at the Faculty of Theology in Ankara University; he had been one of the Pan-Turkist demonstrators arrested on 3 May 1944. Other well-known Pan-Turkists (several of them arrested and tried in 1944 with Tanyu) contributed, notably Atsız, Nejdet Sançar, M. Zeki Sofuoğlu, R.O. Türkkan, and Arif Nihat Asya. In addition to articles about Pan-Turkism, Turkey and the Turks, quite a number attacked Communism. One noteworthy contribution by Nejdet Sançar, 'Nationalists, unite!',[173] evidently wishing to put the inauguration of the multi-party system in Turkey to good use, pleaded, shortly before it came into force, for united political action by all sympathisers of Pan-Turkism.

A short-lived journal was *Türkeli. Aylık. Siyaset-fikir-sanat-dergisi* (Land of the Turks: a monthly journal of politics, ideas and art), published in Istanbul[174] between January and April 1947.[175] It was published by Rıza Gür and edited by Ruhi Ovalı. The contributors included Türkkan and Sofuoğlu. There was considerable emphasis on the Outside Turks and reports on 'The World of the Turks'. Some articles analysed Pan-Turkism and examined such questions as 'Why are we Turanists?'[176]

Another short-lived periodical was *Altın Işık. İlmî-edebî-syasî-dergi* (Golden Light: a scientific, literary and political journal), a monthly published in Istanbul between 15 January and 25 September 1947.[177] It was published by İhsan Koloğlu and edited by M. Fahrettin Kırzıoğlu. The contributors included Atsız, Sançar, Arif Nihat Asya and others identified with Pan-Turkism. The publisher, in an editorial in the first issue, entitled 'The way of *Altın Işık*',[178] promised to set the journal on the road to nationalism. There is no doubt, however, that Pan-Turkism was the brand of nationalism intended. Turkish history was constantly presented via a Pan-Turk prism; the Outside Turks were encouraged ('We want our Alsace-Lorraine!'[179]); and

Communists were attacked in no uncertain terms. The Republican People's Party, too, was scolded and urged to quit the Government.[180] These and other articles point to the vigorous campaign led by *Altın Işık*.

Meanwhile, the irrepressible brothers Atsız and Sançar started their own monthly periodical, *Kür Şad*. *Türkçü dergi* (*Kür Şad*:[181] A Pan-Turk Journal), which appeared in Ankara on 3 April 1947.[182] While a special issue was dedicated to the anniversary of the 3 May 1944 demonstrations,[183] with Atsız arguing that this had been the turning-point which changed the idea into a movement,[184] a major part was devoted to a campaign to combat Communism; articles by Sançar[185] and Tevetoğlu[186] as well as a whole double issue[187] dealt with this. One of the most powerful contributions, however, was by Hocaoğlu [Selâhattin Ertürk] on 'Turanism from the point of view of the ideal of humanitarianism'.[188] Its main contention was that Turanism was a righteous cause and an anti-imperialist ideology; as such, it could be an inspiration to others and would end in victory.

The monthly *Yeni Bozkurt* (The new *Bozkurt*) was a 1948 revival of the defunct *Bozkurt*, bearing its original motto upon the masthead: 'The Turkish race above any other race!' Its publisher was İlhan Eğemen Darendelioğlu, a fervent anti-Communist, and its editor was Ahmet Sözmen Mirkelâmoğlu.[189] Most of the contributions are characteristic of Pan-Turk trends and arguments. The editor attacked the Communists ('Red ones! Down with your masks!'[190]); Nejdet Sançar defended racism as a fact of life;[191] while the retired General H.E. Erkilet[192] called for the rescue of 40–50 million Turks from captivity.[193] The most important article, however, was Mirkelâmoğlu's; his first editorial, '*Yeni Bozkurt* and us',[194] demonstrated how deeply irredentism had penetrated the mainstream of Pan-Turk ideology. As he saw it, Anatolia was contained within *political* borders, while the homeland of all Turks, Ergenekon — synonymous with Turan — was characterised by *natural* ones; *Yeni Bozkurt's* objective was to remind both the Turks and their brethren, the Outside Turks, of such facts.

Another periodical, which was briefly revived, was *Çınaraltı*, which appeared weekly in Istanbul from 17 March to 26 May 1948.[195] Its publisher-editor was Yusuf Ziya Ortaç who had also been one of its editors during the Second World War. Contributors included such well-known Pan-Turkist figures as Peyami Safa, M. Emin Erişirgil and İ.H. Danişmend.

This was supplemented by *Serdengeçti* (Volunteer), which appeared irregularly (every few months) in Ankara, from 1947 to 1951.[196] Its publisher-editor was Osman Yüksel. The first editorial spoke for an ardent nationalist line — although it emphasised that *Serdengeçti* was not connected with any political party. Subsequent issues took a very determined anti-Communist line as well as a Pan-Turk one, e.g. in the journal's support for the 3 May 1944 demonstrations and for all Outside Turks — past, present and future.

Tanrıdağ was also revived once the Democrat Party came to power following the 1950 General Elections. Obviously hoping for a better official attitude towards Pan-Turk aspirations under the new government, *Tanrıdağ* started afresh on 5 November 1950, appearing twice a month.[197] In addition to interesting profiles on several leading Pan-Turkists, the journal included contributions by Hüseyin Namık Orkun writing on the Crimean Turks,[198] Abdullah Taymas (Battal) on the Caucasus Turks,[199] Arif Nihat Asya (another active Pan-Turkist[200]) on the evils of Communism,[201] and an appeal by R.O. Türkkan for all Turks to preserve the purity of their race.[202] The most aggressive contribution, however — surely a sign of the new times — was a menacing manifesto[203] by the Organisation of Turkish Youth, of which more below,[204] which threatened the Bulgarians with dire punishment if they continued to mistreat the Turks living in their country: it served notice to 'the red dogs' that a second note would be affixed in Sofia's Red Square . . .

By far the most important Pan-Turk journal of this period was *Orkun. Haftalık Türkçü dergi* (Orkun:[205] a Pan-Turk weekly), which appeared in Istanbul since 6 October 1950.[206] Its masthead proclaimed 'All Turks are one army',[207] while the cover depicted the steppe-wolf, *bozkurt*. Edited throughout by the indefatigable Atsız, this was a long-lived Pan-Turk periodical basing itself on the hoped-for liberalisation under the new government of the Democrat Party: it was also one of the most aggressively outspoken. Its campaign was two-pronged: defence and offence against detractors and re-examination and propagation of Pan-Turkism. Thus, for example, a lengthy series on the 1944 demonstrations and the trials which followed[208] emphasised the importance of these events and the groundless character of the accusations against the Pan-Turkists who were found not guilty by the Courts. Spearheaded by Sançar,[209] Togan[210] and others,[211] a concerted attack was launched on Communists in Turkey and Communism everywhere. This served as a convenient springboard for attacking the Russians and Soviets in general[212] and their policy towards the 'captive Turks' in particular.[213] The Bulgarians, too, were blamed for allegedly persecuting their minority of 250,000 Turks, especially in the field of education.[214] Furthermore, racism was defended as pride in the superiority of the Turkish race,[215] just as nationalism implied pride in one's patriotic feelings:[216] 'Being nationalist could never be identified with being fanatic'[217] (this contention recurred frequently). *Orkun* published many articles favouring the liberation of all Turks everywhere, particularly those of Asia,[218] e.g. in Azerbayjan[219] — and with special emphasis on uniting Cyprus with Turkey[220] (again, an ever more frequently recurring demand). To drive all this home, Atsız himself scolded those who maintained that the idea of uniting all the world's Turks was fantastic and adventuristic; he contended that it was indeed conceivable — just as the Jews had returned to their old land, revived their language and set up their own state[221] (this was evidently written soon after the establishment of the State of Israel).

In order to familiarise *Orkun's* readers with the principles of Pan-Turkism, Atsız opened the journal's pages to discussion of these very principles. His editorial in the first issue[222] maintained that Pan-Turkism was the name of Turkish nationalism, a synonym for 'loving the Turks': no one loves the Turks but the Turks themselves. Pan-Turkism, as an ideal, was moral food for the nation; moreover, it was an ideal superior to those of other nations. Pan-Turkism demanded unconditional rule by the Turkish race over all Turkish areas. This had already occurred in the past and could happen again, provided everyone desired it and worked for it, although it was no simple task to be a Pan-Turkist. Two weeks later, Atsız attempted to define a Pan-Turkist[223]: 'A Turk who believes in the superiority of the Turkish race, respecting its national past and ready to sacrifice himself for the ideals of Turkdom, especially in the fight against Moscow, the implacable enemy.' Sançar, however, considered[224] the main objectives of Pan-Turkism to be action on behalf of the captive Turks, brethren of Turkey's Turks in blood, language and history — millions of captives in danger of losing their Turkism and their lives. Just as the Turks in Hatay had been reunited with Turkey, those held captive in the Soviet Union could and should be freed as well. In another article,[225] Sançar argued that the banner of Pan-Turkism was that of the Turks who eventually would triumph over external enemies — Russians, Bulgarians and Italians[226] — as well as internal ones. He then defined the latter in yet another article[227] as the Reds, Freemasons, Zionists and the members of the minority races in Turkey, who (he claimed) were merely feigning to like the Turks; but only Turks could love one another and 'think Turkish' — this being the essence of Pan-Turkism. Thus Sançar evidently drew closer to Atsız's definition of Pan-Turkism. Another contributor to *Orkun*, A. Kazanoğlu, took a somewhat different approach.[228] Rejecting charges of chauvinism, he asserted that Pan-Turkism resembled many other types of nationalism in its intention to secure human rights for its compatriots and the freedom to determine their own future. None could thus question the captive Turks' determination to unite culturally, or even politically. H.S. Ertürk, an active Pan-Turkist, did indeed support this view and even carried it one step further.[229] Nationalism stood for human rights, while imperialism denied them; hence the objective of Pan-Turkism was to assist all Turks in obtaining their own independence. In another article,[230] Ertürk argued that Kemalism had lost much of its relevance under the changing circumstances of the 1950s, while Pan-Turkism had acquired genuine significance. This was, also, the essence of the message of Atsız's editorial, 'Farewell', in the last issue of *Orkun*,[231] in which he called upon all people of Turkish race to unite for their own protection.

In February 1955, *Türk Dünyası. Bölünmez bir bütündür* (The world of the Turks is an indivisible whole) made its appearance briefly in Istanbul.[232] A monthly, it was edited by Altan Deliorman. The slogan which formed part of its title indicated the general tone and tendency. With the participation of known Pan-Turkists like Hüseyin Namık Orkun writing on 'The world of the Turks',[233] Namık Zafer Alpsu on 'The sentiment of Pan-Turkism',[234] Müstecib Ülküsal, a Turco-Tatar, very active in Pan-Turk journalism, on 'The world of the Turks',[235] Tahsin Ünal, author of numerous articles with Pan-Turk tendencies, on 'The bankrupt theories of Marx',[236] or Hasan Ferit Cansever, one of those arrested at the 3 May 1944 demonstrations, on 'My proposals',[237] the general trend was unmistakable.

Much longer-lived was *Toprak. Aylık fikir-sanat-ülkü dergisi* (Earth: a monthly of ideas, art and ideals), which later changed its name to *Toprak. Aylık ülkü dergisi* (Earth: a monthly of ideals). A journal of nearly the same name had appeared in the 1940s.[238] It appeared, from December 1954, for twenty-two years,[239] making it the longest-running Pan-Turk periodical. A monthly, it was edited in Istanbul by İlhan Eğemen Darendelioğlu, author of a book on subversive movements in Turkey, a determined anti-Communist and a journalist close to Pan-Turkist circles. So it was hardly surprising that, although the anti-Communist line predominated, one notices numerous Pan-Turkists contributing articles for their own cause. Among these were Nejdet Sançar, Arif Nihat Asya, Ziyaeddin Babakurban, Hüseyin Namık Orkun and Hikmet Tanyu. Material included reports by and about Outside Turks, and articles, poems and cartoons relative to their sufferings at the hands of Communist governments. While in periodicals dedicated primarily to Pan-Turkism, Communist misdeeds were seen from a Pan-Turk perspective, in *Toprak* Pan-Turk desires were generally considered through the lens of the struggle against world Communism. Articles written solely within Pan-Turk parameters, like those supporting the Idealists (*ülkücüler*) or like Hikmet Tanyu's 'Things to do for the Captive Turkish countries',[240] were less frequent than anti-Communist ones.

Most of the above were political periodicals. Only in 1962 did a scholarly monthly with Pan-Turk tendencies start publication in Ankara. Named *Türk Kültürü* (Culture of the Turks), it carried not only studies of the Turkish and Turkic past, but also articles with a Pan-Turk content and sympathies, along with determined anti-Communist essays.[241] We shall discuss it in greater detail later.[242]

Along with their intensified propaganda campaign, Pan-Turkists also invested some serious efforts in organising. During the latent stage, in the first twenty years of the Republic of Turkey, there had been several attempts at association, often in semi-clandestine groups, as shown by the above-indicated initiatives of Togan and Türkkan.[243] The group recruited by Togan even had the following secret oath: 'We shall work, even at the cost of our lives, for the unity of thought, language and culture among the Turkestanis from North Caucasia to Chinese Turkestan, and we shall die for the cause, if necessary.'[244] Türkkan's group, *Kitap sevenler kurumu* (The Society of Book-Lovers), was banned in April 1940.[245] During the Second World War, two small Pan-Turk societies, *Gürem* (set up by Türkkan[246]) and *Gök-Börü*, had been active underground for a short time, as was a Turkish Cultural Union, established in 1942 to preserve and promote the cultural heritage of the Eastern Turks, which organised special meetings on behalf of 'all lands of Turan'.[247] Other associations, comprising emigrants from among those Outside Turks living in Turkey, were active during the Second World War, displaying Pan-Turk tendencies in varying degrees, through cultural, philanthropic and political activities. Of these, Turkestanis and Azeris were most active, arranging cultural *soirées*, underscored by political appeals.[248]

The 3 May 1944 demonstrations indicated an emphasis on organisation, with Atsız closest to becoming the leader of a small group of Pan-Turkist intellectuals (although there were other contenders for this position). The indubitable propaganda value of the demonstrations, the counter-campaign initiated by the government and the Republican People's Party, the arrests and trials of leading Pan-Turkists and the establishment of their innocence by the Courts all served to popularise Pan-Turkism among wider circles. During the war, activities were circumscribed by martial law; little could be accomplished beyond assisting Outside Turks who had fled from the Balkans and emigrated to Turkey.[249] After the war, however, wider opportunities presented themselves. Outside Turk circles in Turkey began vigorous activity, as in their protest against their compatriots

being handed over to Soviet military forces for trial.[250] In the years
that immediately followed, local Turks also began to evince a perceptibly growing sensitivity to the plight of the Outside Turks and
commensurate support for Pan-Turkism among youth and others
outside the small parameters of the earlier intellectual groups. One
of the first characteristic instances dated from December 1946 when,
following press reports about the persecution of Turks in Bulgaria,
Yugoslavia and Greece,[251] the Students' Union of Istanbul University
and the Medical Students' Association of Ankara University staged
demonstrations and sent cables to Turkey's Prime Minister.[252]

Various associations with Pan-Turk leanings were soon formed.
The first seems to have been *Türk Kültür Ocağı* (Hearths of Turkish
Culture), set up in 1946 to spread Turkish culture and defend it from
both internal and external attacks by foreign ideologies. Essentially
a nationalist grouping with Pan-Turk tendencies, it was chaired by
Bahadır Dülger.[253] Others were *Türk Gençlik Teşkilâtı* (Organisation
of Turkish Youth), *Türk Kültürü Çalışmaları Derneği* (Association
for Activities of Turkish Culture) and *Türk Kültür Derneği* (Association for Turkish Culture — this one in Ankara). All these were loosely
affiliated in a single umbrella-organisation, *Milliyetçiler Birliği
Federasyonu* (Federation of Unions of Nationalists).[254] Note that the
term 'Nationalists' (*Milliyetçiler*), rather than 'Pan-Turkists'
(*Türkçüler*), was employed, perhaps because the latter was still in
some disfavour while the former was blameless. Headed by Bekir
Berk, a lawyer close to both Pan-Turkists and orthodox Muslims in
Turkey,[255] the Federation arranged a commemorative evening in Istanbul for those Turks killed in the Korean War, which was addressed
by Arif Nihat Asya and İsmet Tümtürk, among others.[256] The meeting
soon assumed a marked Pan-Turk and anti-Communist character. The
Federation also issued a manifesto rejecting charges of racism and
reaction, laying the blame for these accusations at the door of the
Communists; it maintained, on the contrary, that the Federation was
motivated by highly moral values and was striving to assist the captive
Turks — a worthy design in and of itself.[257]

The Federation was organisationally weak, however, because of
its loosely-bound nature. Its most active element was the Organisation
of Turkish Youth which somewhat impetuously, perhaps, let its own
views be known openly. It called a public meeting in Samsun[258] and
issued a bluntly-worded warning to the Bulgarian 'puppets of
Moscow' to stop infringing the individual freedoms of the Turks
living in Bulgaria.[259] Organised countrywide on the model of a
countrywide political association (with some interest in culture and
sports as well),[260] this body convened an extraordinary general con-

gress on 9 January 1951, and one of its decisions was to merge with
the above Hearths of Turkish Culture Association.[261] At the same
time, local groups of Pan-Turkists organised in *Türkiye Milliyetçiler
Derneği* (Association of the Nationalists of Turkey) continued to
proliferate; by October 1951, there were branches in Ankara, Istanbul,
Samsun, Konya, Kayseri, Kütahya, Kars, Kirikkale, Kirikhan, Muğla,
Tire, Menemen, Gümüşhaciköy, Uzunköprü, Derik, Uşak, Hani,
Nevşehir, Çanakkale, Burhaniye, Uluborlu, Kirşehir, Diyarbakir,
Afyon, Malatya and Arpaçay[262] — that is, in the major cities and
towns and in some smaller localities as well. At its peak, when it was
closed down in January 1953, the Association had more than eighty
branches.[263] These had a varied membership, largely made up, however, of the free professions, students, clerks, and technicians, as well
as some farmers and industrial workers. Several members were active
in publishing for the cause.[264] The official regulations of this association,[265] however, were couched in terms of Turkish nationalism. Also,
not all members were committed Pan-Turkists. For instance, Nurettin
Topçu (1909–75), a prominent figure in the Hearths of Turkish Culture and in the Association of Turkish Nationalists, and for some time
a close collaborator of Atsız, held other views on nationalism. In his
posthumous book, *Milliyetçiliğimizin esasları* (Principles of our nationalism), published in 1978, Topçu maintained that unity of race or
land was insufficient for creating a nation; only in Anatolia, with a
common race, economy, language, history and religion, was a nation
viable.[266] Most others, however, were dedicated Pan-Turkists, including the organisation's leaders, who were responsible for setting the
tone.

The frequent meetings held by some of these groups and societies,
the recurring call for reestablishment of *Türk ocakları*,[267] and especially the demand for setting up a political party to support the cause
of Pan-Turkism[268] sufficed to cause concern within Democrat Party
government circles. On 22 January 1953, all branches of the Association of Turkish Nationalists were closed down,[269] and the activities
of other Pan-Turkist groups were curtailed. This situation differed,
however, from the conditions prevalent during the early days of the
Republic: Mustafa Kemal was dead, a multi-party system had replaced that of the Republican People's Party, and ideologies competing with Kemalism were actively rivalling one another. Throughout
the 1950s and early 1960s, Pan-Turkists continued busily to propagate
cultural Pan-Turkism and in setting up nationalist groups to further
this cause politically. Certain international contacts were also maintained, chiefly by emigrants from among the Outside Turks,[270] and
journalistic activity continued. Among the most active Pan-Turk peri-

odicals was *Toprak* (Earth), revived in the early 1960s, characterised by its strong support of racism and anti-Communism.[271] Opponents of Pan-Turkism responded in a no less determined style.[272] The ideological battle went on, spreading in the late 1950s and the 1960s from the partisan periodicals to the mass-circulation daily press[273] (which may have been what Pan-Turkists desired). This was particularly evident in times of national crisis, such as the escalation of the Cyprus conflict, which had been one of the pet issues of Pan-Turkists in Turkey since the end of the Second World War.[274] During the 1950s, the Association of Turkish Nationalists had indeed established contact with various groups defending the cause of the Turkish minority in Cyprus,[275] thereby injecting a Pan-Turk element into those activist groups. Once the Association of Turkish Nationalists had been closed down, various nationalist groups (several with Pan-Turk tendencies) continued to demonstrate for the Cyprus Turks; later (e.g. in 1961), they also expressed support for the Outside Turks in Kirkuk, who were being persecuted by the Iraki authorities.[276]

NOTES

1. Even there, it displayed no united front. See E. Rossi, in *OM*, XXIII (9): Sep. 1943, p. 388.
2. See examples in Arnakis's article in *Balkan Studies*, I: 1960, pp. 30–1.
3. Cf., e.g., Nejdet Sançar, *Türklük sevgisi*, pp. 60–5, the chapter 'Türkçülük düşmanları ve Turancılık' (based on an earlier article of his).
4. See the Republican People's Party booklet *C.H.P. konferansları*, no. 19, Ankara, 1940, the lectures of Agop Dilaçar and Z.F. Fındıkoğlu.
5. E.g., Muzaffer Şerif Başoğlu, *Irk psikolojisi*, Istanbul, Üniversite Kitabevi, 1943, 123 ff.
6. FO 371/33375, R 1541/810/44, 'Report on public opinion, Jan. 1942', written by Grant (British Council representative in Ankara), forwarded by British Council's Martin Blake to the Foreign Office on 2 Mar. 1942.
7. See the lively description of Saint Hervé, 'Le Panturquisme sentimental et l'autre', *Le Temps* (Paris), 18 and 21–22 June 1942.
8. Ibid.
9. Cf. FO 171/33395, R 5618/2713/44, memorandum by R.A.B. Beaumont, dated Damascus, 13 Aug. 1942, as to the views of Ahmet Umar, Turkey's Consul in Damascus.
10. See Hostler, *Turkism*, p. 156.
11. Quoted by Krecker, pp. 209–10.
12. FO 371/30069, R 10322/112/44, Consul D.H.K. Wright's no. 12, to Ambassador Knatchbull-Hugessen, dated Trebizond, 8 Nov. 1941.

13. *Bozkurt*, 11: July 1941.
14. Ibid., p. 249: 'Ey tarihin bu büyük gün seçtiği İnönü! Türklüğün mukaddes istiklâli için kanımızı hazırız! Bütün Türklük senin işareti bekliyor! BOZKURT'. The 'Turkdom', or *Türklük*, was an obvious reference to the Outside Turks.
15. Cf. ibid., 12: Dec. 1941, p. 283.
16. Ibid., 2nd series, 1: 5 Mar. 1942, p. 6: 'Hak verilmez, alınır. Savaş mı? — Evet! Gerektiği anda, savaş!'
17. Ibid.
18. On that date, a unanimous vote of all 401 Members present in the Grand National Assembly declared war on Germany and Japan as of 1 Mar. 1945.
19. In particular, the files of the 'Büro des Staatssekräters' for 1941–2. See below.
20. In addition to the above documents, one ought to refer, also, to Krecker, ch. 9 ('Turanisches Zwischenspiel').
21. Details in FO 371/25017, file R 318 (for 1940).
22. Details in FO 371/44159, file R 2883 (for 1944).
23. Further details in Zehra Önder, *Die türkische Aussenpolitik im zweiten Weltkrieg*, esp. pp. 138 ff.
24. See 'Les puissances et la politique turco-tatare', *Politique Etrangère* (Paris), III (3): June 1938, pp. 236–41.
25. For examples, cf. Johannes Benzing, 'Die Türkvölker der Sowjetunion', in H.H. Schaeder (ed.), *Der Orient in deutscher Forschung*, pp. 18–26; J. Glasneck and I. Kircheisen, *Türkei und Afghanistan — Brennpunkte der Orientpolitik im zweiten Weltkrieg*, esp. p. 102.
26. FO 371/25016, R 7638/316/44, Knatchbull-Hugessen's no. 423, to Viscount Halifax, dated Ankara, 6 Aug. 1940.
27. On Turco-German relations during the Second World War see, besides the archives of the German Foreign Office (e.g., the series 'Botschaft Ankara'), FO 371/33369. For an analysis by the British Ambassador to Ankara during the war years, cf. Hughe Knatchbull-Hugessen, *Diplomat in peace and war*, chs 11–14.
28. The British were not unaware of the inducements the Germans were offering Turkey concerning contiguous areas inhabited by Turkic groups — but could do nothing about it. See FO 371/3368, R 2363/486/44, report from Ankara dated 25 Mar. 1942.
29. Cf. the archives of the German Foreign Office, Büro des Staatssekretärs, Panturan adh. 1941, file Büro Pers. M (as photostated and catalogued after the war by the Hoover Institution, 1071/313732–313738), dated Oct.–Nov. 1941. Erkilet was received by Hitler and ranking military officers. See ibid., Büro des Staatssekretärs, Panturan 7.41–3.42 (= Hoover Institution catalogue 1047/311652), dated 31 Oct. 1941. Some of these documents have been translated into English by the Soviets, as: Ministry of Foreign Affairs of the U.S.S.R., Archives Division, *German Foreign Office documents — German policy in*

Turkey (1941–1943), Moscow, 1948. This was not available to me and I have used a Turkish translation (by Levent Konyar), entitled S.S.C.B. Dış İşleri Bakanlığı Arşiv Bölümü, *Alman dış işleri dairesi belgeleri. Türkiye'deki Alman politikası (1941–1943)*, whose documents nos 13 and 15 reproduce the Erkilet correspondence.

30. See above, ch. 3 of our study, p. 90.
31. For whose activities cf. Glasneck and Kircheisen, pp. 109–10.
32. Archives of the German Foreign Office, Büro des Staatssekretärs, Panturan 7.41–3.42 (= Hoover Institution catalogue, file 1047), passim.
33. Ibid. (= Hoover Institution catalogue, 1047/311599, 311653–4, 311667, 311670–9, 311682–6). The reports on Nuri's discussions with German officials were published in *Akten zur Deutschen Auswärtigen Politik 1918–1945, Serie D. 1937–1941*, XIII (1): 1970, pp. 386–7, dated Berlin, 10 Sep. 1941; and XIII (2): 1970, pp. 467–70, dated Berlin, 26 Sep. 1941.
34. Archives of the German Foreign Office, Büro des Staatssekretärs, Panturan adh. 1941, file Büro Pers. M (= Hoover Institution catalogue, 1047/311615, 311620, 311643–4). Cf. *Akten zur Deutschen . . . Serie D*, XIII (2): 1970, pp. 578–9, dated Berlin, 28 Oct. 1941.
35. Ibid. (= Hoover Institution catalogue, 1047/311635–8), dated 22 Dec. 1941.
36. Ibid. (= Hoover Institution catalogue, 1047/311612–4, 311627).
37. Ibid. (= Hoover Institution catalogue, 1047/311650), dated 31 Oct. 1941.
38. See below, p. 114.
39. FO 371/72543, R 1374/1374/44, report of the Foreign Office Research Department. Further details in Hostler, in *The Middle East Journal*, XII (3): Summer 1958, pp. 265 ff; id., *Turkism*, pp. 171 ff; Karpat, *Turkey's politics*, pp. 264–5.
40. *Akten zur Deutschen . . . Serie D*, XIII (1): 1970, pp. 235–6, 306–8, dated, respectively 5 and 25 Aug. 1941.
41. German Foreign Office archives, Büro des Staatssekretärs, Panturan 7.41–3.42 (= Hoover Institution catalogue, 1047/311652). Von Papen's letter is dated Ankara, 31 Oct. 1941. Franz von Papen's voluminous memoirs (entitled *Der Wahrheit einer Gasse*, Munich, Paul List Verlag, 1952; 678 pp.), although devoting several chapters (pp. 506–601) to his service in Turkey during the Second World War, make no mention of his contacts with the Pan-Turkists.
42. See von Papen's cable no. 519, very secret, to the German Foreign Office, dated Ankara, 6 Apr. 1942, reprinted in *Akten zur Deutschen Auswärtigen Politik 1918–1945, Serie E. 1941–1945*, II: 1972, pp. 197–8; von Papen's no. 524/42.g.Rs., to the German Foreign Office, dated Ankara, 27 Aug. 1942, ibid., III: 1974, pp. 411–14; cf. ibid., pp. 486–7 for the reserved reaction of the German Foreign Office (Internal Correspondence, Berlin, 12 Sep. 1942).
43. Glasneck and Kircheisen, p. 110, for details.

138 *Pan-Turkism*

44. Von Papen's no. 265/172883–6, secret, to von Ribbentrop, dated Ankara, 29 May 1941, repr. in *Akten zur Deutschen . . . Serie D*, XII (2): 1969, pp. 760–1. See also Krecker, pp. 210 ff, for these negotiations.
45. Examples in Önder, in *Österreichische Osthefte*, XIX (2): May 1977, p. 98.
46. Dated 5 Apr. 1941 — text in the archives of the German Foreign Office, Büro des Staatssekretärs, Panturan 7.41–3.42 (= Hoover Institution catalogue, 1047/311692–5). French translation in *Documents secrets du Ministère des Affaires Etrangères d'Allemagne, traduits du russe par Madeleine et Michel Eristov. Turquie*, 1946, pp. 36–41. English translation in Hostler, *Turkism*, pp. 172–4.
47. Archives of the German Foreign Office, Büro des Staatssekretärs (= Hoover Institution catalogue, 1047/311700), dated 25 July 1941. Ibid., Panturan adh. (= Hoover Institution catalogue, 1071/313734), Erkilet's letter of 10 Nov. 1941.
48. See above, ch. 3.
49. Cf. ibid., p. 82.
50. Müstecib Ülküsal, *İkinci dünya savaşında 1941–1942 Berlin hatıraları*. See pp. 8 ff, for his trip to Berlin; pp. 13 ff, 76 ff for his conversations with German officials. Ülküsal has recorded, also, several of his discussions with other Turks and Outside Turks in Germany and Romania.
51. Cf. A. Oktay (ed.), *Türkistan millî hareketi ve Mustafa Çokay*, pp. 2 ff.
52. See Önder, in *Österreichische Osthefte*, XIX (2): May 1977, p. 99; id., *Die türkische Aussenpolitik*, pp. 148–9.
53. Details in Hostler, *Turkism*, pp. 177 ff. Krecker, p. 220, estimates the number of the volunteers at 200,000; see also ibid., p. 221.
54. As attested in Shakibayev's above-mentioned 'chronicle-story', published almost thirty years after these events.
55. Knatchbull-Hugessen, *Diplomat*, p. 138.
56. It seems to have been busily negotiating throughout with both the Germans and the British. See A.C. Edwards, 'The impact of war on Turkey', *International Affairs* (London), XXII (3): July 1946, pp. 389–400. The military, also, prepared contingency-plans. See Jäschke, in *Beiträge*, p. 476, and the French diplomatic sources he quotes.
57. Cf. I. Erhorn, *Kaukasien*, which appeared in a series entitled 'Die Bücherei des Ostraumes'(!) in 1942, passim. See also Önder, in *Österreichische Osthefte*, XIX (2): May 1977, p. 99.
58. See the evidence in Krecker, pp. 218–9. For a critique of the German policy, see Glasneck and Kircheisen, pp. 99–111.
59. For a careful analysis of this issue, cf. Weisband, pp. 246–56.
60. FO 195/2480, Knatchbull-Hugessen's report to Eden, dated Ankara, 21 June 1943. M.E. Bozkurt was considered to be close to the Pan-

Turkists and articles of his appeared in *Çınaraltı*, e.g., 95: 17 July 1943, p. 15.

61. 'Pan türkist, Turancı, ırkçı Türkçü kuklalar.'
62. *En büyük tehlike*, p. 4.
63. E.g. *Çınaraltı*, 93: 3 July 1943, pp. 3, 6–7.
64. For a detailed report of the whole affair, cf. FO 371/37491, R 6829/123/44, British Press Counsellor Leigh Ashton's memorandum, dated 12 July 1943, enc. in Knatchbull-Hugessen's no. 292, to Eden, dated Ankara, 15 July 1943. See also E.R. (= Ettore Rossi), in *OM*, XXIII (8): Aug. 1943, pp. 326–7.
65. Of which more below, in the present chapter.
66. See *3 Mayıs Türkçüler antolojisi*, vol. I, 1967, pp. 4 ff. For the public excitement aroused by these two letters, as viewed by the Pan-Turkists themselves, cf. Nejdet Sançar, *Afşın'a mektuplar*, passim.
67. We shall deal with him again, in more detail, in ch. 5.
68. For the whole affair, cf. FO 371/44133, R 7715/789/44, Knatchbull-Hugessen's no. 173, confidential, to Eden, dated Ankara, 6 May 1944. See also *The Times*, 16 May 1944, and the Turkish press of the time.
69. Which, incidentally, did not placate the Russians. Starting with *Izvyestiya* of 1 June 1944, the Soviet press complained of what it considered as government inactivity toward 'a Nazi-backed Turanian movement'. Then, in an article by V. Krimskiy, 'Pantyurkisti — fashistkaya agyentyura v Turtsii', *Bol'shyevik*, 10–11: May–June 1944, pp. 79–85, the Pan-Turkists were attacked and Turkey blamed for harbouring them. The article ended as follows: 'The activity of the fascist agency in Turkey endangers, first and foremost, the internal and external security of the Turkish Republic. It is in the interests of the Turkish people and government to put an end to the provocative activity of the Pan-Turkists and liquidate these Hitlerite agents' (translation mine).
70. For the complete list, see Weisband, p. 244, n. 50.
71. See, e.g., *Ulus*, 6 May 1944, and *Cumhuriyet* (Istanbul daily), 7 and 9 May 1944.
72. FO 371/44133, R 8021/789/44, Knatchbull-Hugessen's cyphered cable no. 772, to the Foreign Office, dated Ankara, 19 May 1944. The text of the speech appeared in the Turkish press, e.g., in *Cumhuriyet*, 20 May 1944.
73. Many of these were collected soon afterwards in a volume entitled *Irkçılık-Turancılık*, Ankara, 1944. İnönü's speech appeared there, too. For the reaction of the Pan-Turkists to this campaign see, e.g., Nejdet Sançar, *Ismet Inönü ile hesaplaşma*, esp. part 2.
74. FO 371/67273, R 964/4/44, David V. Kelly's no. 20, secret, to Ernest Bevin, dated Ankara, Jan. 1947.
75. For the trials see, besides the Turkish press, a special issue of *Kürşad* (Ankara), 2: 3 May 1947; '1944–1945 Irkçılık Turancılık davası', *Orkun*, 3: 20 Oct. 1950 and subsequent issues; *Tanrıdağ*, 2nd series,

2: 20 Nov. 1950, p. 6; 3: 20 Dec. 1950, p. 6; A. Türkeş, *1944 milliyetçilik olayı*; N. Sançar, *Türklük sevgisi*, p. 4; Hostler, in *MEA*, III (1): Jan. 1952, pp. 10–11; id., in *The Middle East Journal*, XII (3): Summer 1958, pp. 267–8; id., *Turkism*, pp. 185–8; Karpat, *Turkey's politics*, pp. 267 ff.

76. FO 371/48708, R 6848/177/44, Maurice Peterson's no. 118, confidential, to Eden, dated Ankara, 16 Apr. 1945.
77. Togan's testimony indicated that Pan-Turkists had attempted, and failed, to interest government officials in the fate of the Turkic groups in the Soviet Union. See Hostler, *Turkism*, pp. 187–8.
78. Alparslan Türkeş, *1944 milliyetçilik olayı*; R.O. Türkkan, *Tabutluktan gurbete*, esp. pp. 18 ff, 168 ff.
79. CO 67/342, file 1, no. 90215/36, despatches for 1948; CO 67/352, file 2, no. 90580/3, Sir N. Charles's cyphered cable no. 576, to the Foreign Office in London; CO 537/4973, file 90215, esp. the Governor's reports for Jan., Feb., Apr., June and Oct. 1949.
80. Cf. Ernst Werner, in *Zeitschrift für Geschichtswissenschaft*, 1965, no. 8, p. 1354.
81. See İsa Alptekin, *Doğu Türkistan insanlıktan yardım istiyor*, subtitled as *East Turkistan expects help from humankind*, 1974.
82. This seems to have gone on in Germany at least until 1950. See Ilse Schwidetzky, *Turaniden-Studien*, in: Akademie der Wissenschaften und der Literatur in Mainz, *Abhandlungen der mathematisch-naturwissenschaftlichen Klasse*, IX: 1950, pp. 235–91. This is based on an anthropological study, at Breslau University, of prisoners of war from among the Turkic groups.
83. Actually, studies on race — most particularly, the Turkish one — were undertaken by non-Pan-Turkists, too, just after the Second World War, e.g., by Afetinan (= Afet İnan), *Türkiye halkının antropolojik karakterleri ve Türkiye tarihi: Türk ırkının vatanı Anadolu*, Ankara, Türk Tarih Kurumu, 1947.
84. E.g. Rafikov, in *New Times*, 37: 7 Sep. 1949, pp. 30–32, who accused Pan-Turkists of trying to rob the peoples of Central Asia of their past, and ended with the following warning: 'Do the Turkish rulers realise how fatal and dangerous is the ideology of Pan-Turkism which they support?'
85. See *Tanrıdağ*, 2nd series; 2: 20 Nov. 1950, p. 6.
86. Its full title is *Milliyetçilik yolunda: Ergenekon — Bozkurt — Gök Börü (yeni ve eski yazılar)*, N.p., Müftüoğlu Yayınevi, 1944; 136 pp.
87. Ibid., p. 5: 'Türkçülük, Türk milliyetçiliği demektir'.
88. Ibid., p. 6: 'Millî birlik'.
89. Ibid., pp. 6–7.
90. Ibid., p. 95.
91. Actually, the total should read 51,460,000. Anyway, this differs from his earlier estimate of 65,000,000. It is noteworthy that Turkey's Turks numbered about a third of the total.

92. Nejdet Sançar, *Afşın'a mektuplar*, 1963, passim.
93. This, also, is partly based on his own articles, published previously.
94. *Türklük sevgisi*, pp. 25–9: 'Türk, ordu ve savaş'.
95. Ibid., pp. 46 ff, 'Türk ırkçılığı'.
96. Ibid., pp. 37–42, 'Dış Türkler'.
97. Ibid., p. 24: 'Türk doğan, Türkçe konuşan her insan Türk adına lâyık olamaz. Türk adına lâyık olmak için Türklüğünü duymak, millî şuura sahip olmak . . . lâzımdır.'
98. Ibid., pp. 37 ff.
99. I have used the 3rd edn, Ankara, Afşın Yayınları, 1973; 120 pp.
100. *Türk ülküsü*, 3rd edn, pp. 18–20.
101. Ibid., p. 39, 'Türk birliği.'
102. Ibid., p. 41. See also Karpat, *Turkey's politics*, p. 269.
103. *Türk ülküsü*, 3rd edn, pp. 41–2.
104. Ibid., p. 20.
105. Ibid.
106. Ibid., p. 36, 'Türkçü kimdir?': 'Kısacası, Türkçüler, XX yüzyılda Türk milletinin fedâîleridir.'
107. Some of B. Hayıt's books are as follows: *Turkestan im XX. Jahrhundert*, Darmstadt, Leske Verlag, 1956; 406 pp. *Documents: Soviet Russia's anti-Islam policy in Turkestan*, Düsseldorf and Köln, 1958; 48 pp. *Turkestan und der Orient*, Düsseldorf, Forschungsdienst Osteuropa, 1960; 51 pp. — a collection of his articles, mainly in the *Basler Nachrichten. Sowjetrussische Orientpolitik am Beispiel Turkestans*, Köln and Berlin, Kiepenheuer and Witsch, 1962; 289 pp. *Some problems of modern Turkistan history*, 1963; 61 pp. *Sowjetrussischen Kolonialismus und Imperialismus in Turkestan*, Oosterhout, Anthropological Publications, 1965; 117 pp. *Turkestan zwischen Russland und China*, Amsterdam, Philo Press, 1971; xvi, 415 pp.
108. A. Oktay (ed.), *Türkistan millî hareketi ve Mustafa Çokay*, 1950.
109. İstiklâlci (pseudonym), *Türkistan'a dair bazı cereyanlar hakkında görüşlerimiz*, Istanbul, 1952, edited by A. Oktay.
110. Ibid., p. 3.
111. Y.T., *Türkistan'da Türkçülük ve halkçılık*, 2 vols, 1951–4. Edited by A. Oktay.
112. Tahir Çağatay, *Kızıl imperyalizm*, 3 vols, 1958–62–67. The first 2 vols. were edited by A. Oktay.
113. See also Landau, *Radical politics*, p. 198.
114. Edited by İbrahim Otar, 1965. For Kırımer, see Hostler, *Turkism*, esp. pp. 211–12.
115. Orkun had already published several other studies on the Outside Turks, during the 1930s (mainly on the Oghuz and Peçenegs). In 1944, he published his *Türkçülüğün tarihi*, mentioned above, in the introduction to our present study.
116. *Türkçülük nedir?* esp. pp. 5–6.
117. Erişirgil, *Türkçülük devri*.

118. Ibid., pp. 77 ff.
119. Ibid., p. 25.
120. *Hayır! Prof. H.E. Adıvar esir Türk illeri kurtarılacaktır!* pp. 10 ff.
121. Ibid., pp. 14–15.
122. Ibid., pp. 25, 30 ff.
123. Turkish *kavim*, also 'tribes' or 'nations'.
124. Pp. 62 ff of the same vol. comprise a lengthy article by M. Sadık Aran on the need to assist the Captive Brethren in Azerbayjan.
125. *The East Turkic Review*, II: 1959, pp. 80–9.
126. Ibid., I: 1958, p. 15.
127. Hostler, *Turkism*, p. 189.
128. Ibid.
129. Ibid., p. 190.
130. Several issues of the English edition may be consulted in the National Library, Jerusalem. Some of the later issues, in Turkestanian (Latin script), from 1965 to 1973, are available in the library of the School of Oriental and African Studies, London.
131. Of which one issue — II (5): May 1952 — may be consulted in the library of the Turkish Historical Society, Ankara.
132. Of which the first ten issues, 1951–2, may be consulted in the library of the School of Oriental and African Studies, London. The periodical was briefly revived, as *Türkeli*, an Izmit fortnightly, 1974.
133. Hostler, *Turkism*, p. 190.
134. Several volumes of this periodical may be consulted in the National Library, Jerusalem.
135. *Azerbaycan. Aylık kültür derigisi* was later renamed *Azerbaycan. Aylık Türk kültür derigisi*. Its first issue was dated 1 April 1952; the last known one is 231: July–Sep. 1979.
136. See *Caucasian Review* (Munich), II: 1956, p. 139. *Azerbaycan Yurt Bilgisi* had been the title of an earlier journal of the Azeri emigrants in Turkey, mentioned by us above. This was closed down in the 1930s, see Jäschke, in *Beiträge*, p. 472.
137. Approximate translation: 'Fighters in a good cause'.
138. The National Library, Ankara, has 59 issues, July 1955–Nov. 1964 (all published?).
139. The first five issues (April to August 1953) may be consulted in the library of the Turkish Historical Society, Ankara. Several issues are available in the library of the School of Oriental and African Studies, London. For Buğra, cf. obituary in *Cultura Turcica* (Ankara), II (1): 1965, pp. 110–11.
140. *Türkistan*, 1: Apr. 1953, pp. 3–4, editorial.
141. Arifhan, 'Büyük rehberimiz Münevver Karı', ibid., pp. 14–19.
142. M. Ruhi Uygur, 'Doğu Türkistan ve Çin tarihinde bir mühim nokta', ibid., 21 May 1953, pp. 25–7.
143. Timuroğlu, 'Kremlin hadisesi ve Münih müzakerelerinden alınan intibalar', ibid., 5: Aug. 1953, pp. 32–3.

144. A set may be consulted in the library of the Turkish Historical Society, Ankara.
145. Of which several copies may be consulted in the Bodleian Library, Oxford.
146. 'Vatan bizimdir', *Türkistan Sesi*, 1: July 1956, p. 2.
147. 'Millî Âmentu', ibid., 3–4: Sep.–Oct. 1956, pp. 41–2.
148. Cf. ibid., 7: Jan. 1957, pp. 4, 22–3.
149. Ibid., 8–9: Feb.–Mar. 1957, pp. 1–2, 23–4.
150. Ibid., 10–11: Apr.–May 1957, pp. 10–13.
151. Ibid., 8–9: Feb.–Mar. 1957, pp. 4–6; 10–11: Apr.–May 1957, pp. 1–4.
152. It continued to appear regularly until the end of 1965. A complete set may be consulted in the library of the School of Oriental and African Studies, London.
153. The *saz*, as already explained, is a Turkish musical instrument. *Türk sazı* also refers to the title of a book of patriotic poems by Mehmet Emin Yurdakul.
154. The first issue may be consulted in the National Library, Ankara and the Istanbul University Library. It seems that no subsequent issues were published.
155. *Türk sazı*, 1: 15 May 1943, pp. 17–19.
156. Ibid., pp. 8–9, 11–13.
157. Ibid., p. 1.
158. 'Bizim millî ülkümüz Türkçülük'tür'.
159. *Tanrıdağ*, 2nd series, 6: 20 Jan. 1951, p. 4. See, on Tevetoğlu, Gülsün Dündar, *Türkçülüğün alfabesi*, pp. 123–4.
160. The Beyazıd Library, Istanbul, has nos 23/1 to 23/8–13: May 1943 to Dec. 1943–May 1944 (apparently all published).
161. Türkan Şahinbaşkan, 'Bizim sesimiz', *Çağlayan*, 2nd series, 23/1: May 1943, p. 12.
162. Saffet Sıtkı, 'Realist Türkçülük', ibid., 23/3: July 1943, p. 9.
163. Mehmet Hikmet Öner, 'Biz ve onlar', ibid., 23/8–13: Dec. 1943–May 1944, p. 3.
164. Saffet Sıtkı, 'Zehirli zihniyet', ibid., p. 7.
165. The Beyazıd Library, Istanbul, has a set of *Orhun* up to, and including, no. 16: 1 Apr. 1944.
166. *Orhun*, 15: 1 March 1944, pp. 1–4; 16: 1 Apr. 1944, pp. 1–6. These letters caused the authorities to seize *Orhun* and close it down.
167. 'Türklerde ırk ve ırkçılık fikri', ibid., 10: 1 Oct. 1943, pp. 3–6 and subsequent issues.
168. Turan Tamar, 'Irk ve hakikat', ibid., 15: 1 Mar. 1944, p. 8.
169. Nüzhet Ulusoy, 'Irak Türkleri', ibid., 13: 1 Jan. 1944, p. 8.
170. 'Büyük ülküler ve küçük idealistler', ibid., 11: 1 Nov. 1943, pp. 2–4.
171. The National Library, Ankara, has a set of 25 issues, July 1945–Dec. 1947 (all published?).
172. The National Library, Ankara, has a set of 7 issues, Oct. 1946–Nov.

1947 (all published?). For the policies of *Özleyiş* see Türkkan's article in *MEA*, I (5): May 1950, p. 145.

173. 'Milliyetçiler birleşiniz!', *Özleyiş*, I (3): Dec. 1946, p. 13.
174. This was a different periodical from the *Türkeli* published in Munich in 1951–2, for which see above in the present chapter.
175. The first issue is wrongly dated as January 1946. The National Library in Ankara has 4 issues, Jan.–Apr. 1947 (all published).
176. *Türkeli*, 4: Apr. 1947, pp. 6–8.
177. The National Library, Ankara, has 8 issues, 14 Jan.–25 Sept. 1947 (all published?).
178. Ihsan Koloğlu, 'Altın ışık yolu', *Altın Işık*, 1: 15 Jan. 1947, p. 7.
179. Atsız, ibid., 5: 25 May 1947, pp. 3–4.
180 Ihsan Koloğlu, 'Partiler ve millet', ibid., 4: 25 Apr. 1947, p. 11.
181. Name of a hero of Turkic stock, *circa* 1300 years ago.
182. The Beyazıd Library, Istanbul, has the first 5 issues, up to and including 4–5: 3 Nov. 1947 (all published?)
183. *Kür Şad*, 2: 3 May 1947.
184. Ibid., p. 3.
185. 'Kızıl âfete karşı Kür Şadlık ruhu', ibid., 1: 3 Apr. 1947, pp. 9–14.
186. 'Bu vatan satılmaz!', ibid., p. 8.
187. Ibid., 4–5: 3 Nov. 1947.
188. 'İnsanlık ülküsü bakımından Turancılık', ibid., 2: 3 May 1947, pp. 12–13.
189. Its first seven issues (all published?), from January to July 1948, may be consulted in the Istabul University Library.
190. 'Kızıllar! maskeler aşağı!', *Yeni Bozkurt*, 1: Jan. 1948, pp. 5, 12.
191. 'Laboratuar ırkçılığı', ibid., 5: May 1948, pp. 1, 13.
192. Hüsnü Emir Erkilet, of Tatar origin, had been a member of the special group in Ankara, appointed by the Turkish Government to advise on Eastern Turkish affairs, acc. to von Papen. See Hostler, *Turkism*, p. 174.
193. 'Türkçülük yollarında birkaç hatıra', *Yeni Bozkurt*, 6: June 1948, p. 7.
194. 'Yeni Bozkurt ve biz', ibid., 1: Jan. 1948, p. 2.
195. A set of these ten issues (all published?) may be consulted in the library of the School of Oriental and African Studies, London.
196. The library of the Turkish Historical Society, Ankara, has the first 13 issues. The first is undated, but appeared in the first half of 1947; the last is from June 1951 (all published?).
197. The first six issues (all published?) may be consulted in the library of the Turkish Historical Society, Ankara.
198. 'Yeryüzünde Türkler: Kırım Türkleri', *Tanrıdağ*, 2nd series, 2: 20 Nov. 1950, pp. 2, 8.
199. 'Kafkasya Türkleri', ibid., 3: 5 Dec. 1950, p. 2.
200. For whose profile see ibid., p. 6.
201. 'Komünizm', ibid., 1: 5 Nov. 1950, p. 3.
202. 'Irkçılık kan esasına dayanmaz', ibid., 2: 20 Nov. 1950, pp. 4, 7.

203. 'Türk Gençlik Teşkilatının Bulgarlara notası', ibid., 1: 5 Nov. 1950, p. 1.
204. See below in the present chapter.
205. Orkun is the name of a river in Mongolia, a variant of Orhun — itself the title of yet another Pan-Turk journal, also edited by Atsız, previously (see above, ch. 3).
206. The last issue was 68: 18 Jan. 1952. An incomplete set may be consulted at the library of the Turkish Historical Society, Ankara.
207. 'Bütün Türkler bir ordu'.
208. '1944–1945 Irkçılık-Turancılık davası', *Orkun*, 3: 20 Oct. 1950 and subsequent issues.
209. 'Türkçülük düşmanları', ibid., 1: 6 Oct. 1950, pp. 4–5.
210. 'Komünizm plânları ve istikbalı', ibid., 14: 1 Jan. 1951, pp. 5–7.
211. E.g., İsmet Tümtürk, 'Komünizmle mücadele', ibid., 2: 13 Oct. 1950, pp. 3 ff and subsequent issues.
212. Atsız, 'Tarihin barışmaz düşmanları', ibid., 5: 3 Nov. 1950, pp. 3–4.
213. Nejdet Sançar, 'Dış Türkler', ibid., 3: 20 Oct. 1950, pp. 4–5; id., 'Türkçülük düşmanları ve Turancılık', ibid., 20: 16 Feb. 1951, pp. 3–4; Hızaloğlu Mustafa, 'Kardeş Azerbaycanın istiklâli', ibid., 35: 1 June 1951, pp. 4–5.
214. H.A. Akkoyunlu, 'Son göçler ve iskân politikamız', ibid., 5: 3 Nov. 1950, pp. 15–16; H.A. Bayrak, 'Kızıl Bulgaristandaki Türkler', ibid., 16: 19 Jan. 1951, pp. 13–14.
215. Atsız, 'Son yüzyılı örten yalan perdesi ne zaman yırtılacak?', ibid., 6: 10 Nov. 1950, pp. 3–4; cf. ibid., 24: 16 Mar. 1951, p. 5.
216. Nejdet Sançar, 'Maalesef Türkler!', ibid., 5: 3 Nov. 1950, p. 10.
217. Kazanoğlu, 'Taassup', ibid., 8: 21 Nov. 1950, p. 12.
218. E.g. Nejdet Sançar, 'Türkçülük düşmanları ve Turancılık', ibid., 20: 16 Feb. 1951, pp. 3–4.
219. E.g. Hızaloğlu Mustafa, 'Kardeş Azerbaycan'ın istiklâli', ibid., 35: 1 June 1951, pp. 4–5.
220. Namık Zeki Alpsu, 'Kıbrıs Türkiyenin olmalıdır', ibid., 18: 2 Feb. 1951, p. 5; cf. ibid., 24: 16 Mar. 1951, p. 5.
221. Ibid., 2: 13 Oct. 1950, p. 3.
222. Atsız, 'Türkçülük', ibid., 1: 6 Oct. 1950, p. 3.
223. Id., 'Türkçü kimdir', ibid., 3: 20 Oct. 1950, p. 3.
224. Sançar, 'Dış Türkler', ibid., pp. 4–5.
225. Id., 'Türkçülük bayrağı', ibid., 12: 22 Dec. 1950, p. 3.
226. Sançar has no explanation as to why the Italians, of all people.
227. Sançar, 'Türkçülük düşmanları ve Turancılık', *Orkun*, 20: 16 Feb. 1951.
228. A. Kazanoğlu, 'Türkçülük ve Türk birliği', ibid., 6: 10 Nov. 1951, pp. 6–7.
229. Hocaoğlu S. Ertürk, 'Turancılık', ibid., 7: 17 Nov. 1950, pp. 12–13.
230. 'Türkçülük ve Kemalizm', ibid., 39: 29 June 1951, pp. 3–5.
231. Atsız, 'Veda', ibid., 68: 18 Jan. 1952, pp. 1–7.

146 Pan-Turkism

232. Atatürk Kitaplığı Library, Istanbul, has nos 1: Feb. 1955 and 2: Mar. 1955 (all published?).
233. 'Türk dünyası', *Türk Dünyası*, 1: Feb. 1955, pp. 4–5.
234. 'Türklük şuuru', ibid., p. 6.
235. Ibid., 2: Mar. 1955, pp. 6–7.
236. 'Marx'ın iflâs eden nazariyeleri', ibid., pp. 12–13.
237. 'Tekliflerim', ibid., pp. 14–15.
238. See above, in the present chapter.
239. The library of the Grand National Assembly, Ankara, has a set of nos. I (1): Dec. 1954–xx (36): Dec. 1976 (all published?).
240. 'Esir Türk ülkeleri için yapılacak işler', *Toprak*, XVIII (9–10): Sept.–Oct. 1974.
241. Cf. Landau, *Radical politics*, p. 197.
242. See below, ch. 5, pp. 158–9.
243. See above, ch. 3.
244. Translation by Hostler, *Turkism*, p. 187; cf. ibid., p. 188.
245. Cf. Jäschke, in *Beiträge*, p. 480.
246. Acc. to Henderson, in *The Asiatic Review*, XLI: 1945, p. 88.
247. See Arnakis, in *Balkan Studies*, I: 1960, p. 32.
248. See Saint-Hervé, in *Le Temps*, 18 and 21–22 June 1942. Other examples in Jäschke, in *Beiträge*, pp. 480–1. For somewhat later instances of Azeri activities, cf. *TK*, 19: May 1964, pp. 91–3.
249. FO 371/48784, file R 7366, reports dated Apr.–May 1945.
250. E.g., FO 371/56714, N 3851/8/38, cable to Clement Atlee, dated 22 Mar. 1946; FO 371/56718, N 11582/8/38, cable to Atlee, dated 10 Sep. 1946.
251. Summary in FO 371/58663, R 18045/18045/67, dated Ankara, 9 Dec. 1946.
252. FO, ibid., R 18226/18045/67, dated Ankara, 16 Dec. 1946.
253. *Türkeli* (Istanbul), 1: Jan. 1947, p. 11. Cf. B. Dülger, in *Altın Işık*, 7: 25 Aug. 1947, pp. 11–12.
254. Cf. *Orkun*, 12: 12 Dec. 1950, p. 6.
255. Landau, *Radical politics*, pp. 231–2.
256. Report in *Orkun*, 12: 12 Dec. 1950, pp. 6–7.
257. 'Milliyetçiler Federasyonu'nun beyannamesi', ibid., 24: 16 Mar. 1951, p. 5.
258. *Tanrıdağ*, 2nd series, 1: 5 Nov. 1950, p. 4.
259. Ibid., p. 1.
260. Ibid., 6: 20 Jan. 1951, p. 4.
261. Cf. ibid., p. 2.
262. *Orkun*, 55: 19 Oct. 1951, p. 10. See also Karpat, 'Ideology in Turkey', p. 87.
263. Öner, pp. 45–6.
264. For instance, the *Türk Milliyetçiler Derneği* in Konya published in 1952 a booklet, *Türkçülük nedir?*, by the above H.S. Ertürk.
265. *Türk milliyetçiler derneği tüzüğü*, 1951.

266. *Milliyetçiliğimizin esasları*, pp. 43–4, 55.
267. E.g., *Yeni Bozkurt*, 6: June 1948, p. 6.
268. Expressed as early as 1946 by R.O. Türkkan in his *İleri Türkçülük ve partiler* (Progressive Pan-Turkism and the parties), p. 127; then by Mustafa Eyuboğlu, 'Türkçü bir parti kurulabilirmi?', ibid., 1: Jan. 1948, pp. 7–13; and, later, several times by Nejdet Sançar.
269. *Bayram 32. Türkçüler bayramı*, p. 44.
270. Details in Hostler, *Turkism*, p. 189.
271. K.H. Karpat (ed.), *Political and social thought in the contemporary Middle East*, pp. 361 ff. I have been unable to consult *Toprak* of the 1960s. Karpat thinks that several Pan-Turk publications were subsidised from secret state funds during the decade of Democrat Party rule.
272. E.g. A.N. Kırmacı (pseudonym?), 'Türkiyede aşırı cereyanlar: Milliyetçilik-Irkçılık-Turancılık', *Vatan* (Istanbul), 24–27 Nov. 1960, transl. in part by Karpat, *Political and social thought*, pp. 361–4.
273. Examples in Karpat, ibid., pp. 361–71. There had been indications of this as early as the 1940s, cf. Jäschke, in *Beiträge*, p. 481.
274. See Details in Frank Tachau, 'The face of Turkish nationalism as reflected in the Cyprus dispute', *The Middle East Journal*, XIII (3): Summer 1959, pp. 262–72.
275. İ.E. Darendelioğlu, *Türkiyede milliyetçilik hareketleri*, pp. 215 ff.
276. Cf. ibid., pp. 302–3. Their partisans in Turkey organised a 'Kirkuk evening' of solidarity with them on 7 Sep. 1963, in Ankara. See *TK*, 12: Oct. 1963, p. 57.

5

PAN-TURKISM IN THE REPUBLIC
OF TURKEY: BACK INTO
THE MAINSTREAM

During the period following the Second World War, Pan-Turkists in Turkey and elsewhere faced a tragically difficult situation: the large majority of Outside Turks, in the Soviet Union, the Balkans and Mainland China, were living under Communist regimes which, by all indications, were there to stay. Increasingly, Outside Turks were referred to as 'Captive Turks'. Although Turkey had courageously resisted Stalin's territorial demands, it could hardly expect to wrest the Turkic peoples from the rule of a Superpower or its allies. In consequence, most Pan-Turkists — particularly those concerned with convincing others that their approach was realistic — continued to talk and write about the Communist-dominated Outside Turks and the hope of liberating them and uniting them with Turkey at some future date, perhaps following a war between the Superpowers (assuming that the patterns of the First and Second World Wars would be repeated in an eventual third one). For the time being, post-war Pan-Turkists increasingly turned toward the Outside Turks living in Cyprus, Greece, Iran, Irak and Syria, on the one hand, while strenuously mounting an anti-Communist propaganda campaign on the other.

Conditions prevailing in Turkey during the 1960s brought about the introduction of a new element on the political scene. Relatively liberal attitudes were adopted towards press censorship and party activity following the 1960–1 military intervention, but rapidly spiralling inflation adversely affected the personal finances of many Turkish individuals and families. The inflation encouraged the rise of extremist groups promising economic (as well as political) redress, while the former offered a framework for the establishment of new, legitimate (or quasi-legitimate) radical political forces, some of which were leftist[1] and others Islamist in character.[2] Pan-Turkists were

148

prepared to combat the leftists, but maintained a certain ambivalence towards Islamists, as their own sympathisers included some who were committed to a secular type of Pan-Turkism and others who had inscribed on village walls such slogans as *Rehber Kuran — Hedef Turan* (Our guide is the Koran; our aim is Turan).

One way for Pan-Turkists to fight Communism and increase their own political clout was once again to organise. In the late 1940s and the 1950s, Pan-Turkists were much concerned with organisational aspects;[3] during the 1960s, especially in their latter years, organised activity was emphasised once again, in the new conditions prevailing. Most outstanding among these activities was undoubtedly the 1965 takeover of the conservative Republican Peasants and Nation Party (later renamed the Nationalist Action Party) by a group whose leaders included several acknowledged Pan-Turkists. Pan-Turkism was subsequently adopted as one of the party's official tenets, thereby enabling it to re-enter legitimately the mainstream of politics in Turkey.

This 1965 takeover was preceded by several other organisational moves. Throughout the 1950s and 1960s, Pan-Turkists were active in the anti-Communist groups which had proliferated at the time, such as *Türkiye Komünizmle Mücadele Derneği* (Association for fighting Communism in Turkey). Branches of this and other similar organisations sprang up throughout Turkey; one was headed by Nejdet Sançar, while another included such noted Pan-Turkists as Peyami Safa and Z.V. Togan. These societies were not exclusively Pan-Turkist in character however, enjoying support from Islamist and other circles; as such, they are outside the scope of this study and will not be examined in detail.[4] Their primary significance in this context is the support tendered to the aforementioned political party since 1965.

Pan-Turkist organisation may be best evaluated through a study of the activities of Outside Turk emigrés and other Turks in Turkey. The former carried on their previous activities, continually regrouping, either in order to conform to Turkish legal specifications or as a result of personal rivalries. Among these Outside Turks there were several veteran activists: Ayaz İshakî, for example, a Volga Tatar, already mentioned for his memorandum to the General Islamic Congress in Jerusalem,[5] and then for his connections with the Germans during the Second World War,[6] visited the American and British embassies in Ankara, in August 1945,[7] where he presented memoranda on the conditions of the Tatars in the Soviet Union, offering to mobilise his compatriots in the event of a Third World War![8]

Pan-Turkist societies of, and for, the Outside Turks proliferated. A list of these in 1964, on the eve of the period under discussion, comprised the following: the Federation of the Refugee and Immigrant Associations of Turkey, Western Turkestan Cultural Association, National Centre for the Liberation of Eastern Turkestan, Eastern Turkestan's Refugees Association, Azerbayjani Cultural Society, Azerbayjani Youth Association, Idel-Ural Cultural Society (all in Istanbul), Association for Culture and Assistance of the Crimean Turks, Refugees Association of Northern Caucasus (both in Ankara), National Turkestani Unity Committee (Düsseldorf, West Germany), Turkestanian American Association Inc. (Collingdale, Pennsylvania), Azerbayjanian Society of America (Newark, New Jersey), and American Association of Crimean Turks (New York City).[9]

There were also some relatively new groupings, such as the Society for the Culture and Assistance of the Iraki Turks (*Irak Türkleri Kültür ve Yardımlaşma Cemiyeti*). The Crimean Turco-Tatars had set up a National Centre in Istanbul, the *Kırım Türk-Tatarları Millî Merkezi*. Subsequently, they organised in the above Association for Culture and Assistance of the Crimean Turks (*Kırım Türkleri Kültür ve Yardımlaşma Derneği*) which reportedly had about 3,000 members in the late 1970s. Of these, some 600 were in Istanbul, the rest in branches in Bursa, Ankara, Eskişehir and Adana and another 2,000 abroad, mostly in New York, Detroit and Chicago.[10] Azeris in Turkey were active too,[11] and the Turkestanis seemingly even more so. The latter continued to strive for recruiting worldwide support for their cause, particularly among Muslims. For instance, İsa Yusuf Alptekin,[12] 'former Secretary-General of the Eastern Turkistan Government and President of the National Centre of Eastern Turkistan', prepared a special memorandum, presented in 1962 to Muslim World Conferences convened in Karachi and Mecca; to the Muslim World League, meeting in Mecca in 1963; and to the 1964 General Islamic Congress, also held in Mecca.[13] The memorandum, written in Turkish, Arabic and English, was entitled *A memorandum concerning Great Turkistan which we offer to the governments and heads of state of all Muslem and peace-loving countries about the resolutions passed, but not put into practice by the Muslem Conferences.*[14] Several years later, a Tatar, Said Şamil, lectured and wrote in the Muslim countries on the Outside Turks and their Pan-Turk sentiments (the lectures and articles were published in one volume in 1971[15]).

While the activities of Outside Turks in Turkey were hardly an innovation, the *élan* of organised groups of local Pan-Turkists during the 1960s and 1970s merits special consideration. After the Association of Turkish Nationalists had been closed down,[16] Pan-Turkists who had belonged to this and other groups continued their activities with varying degrees of intensity. Soon after the 1960–1 military intervention and the ensuing liberalisation, many groups had organised, with varying platforms.[17] Pan-Turkists were among those who exploited these new conditions. A number of Pan-Turkists met in Istanbul on 16 September 1962 in order to establish the *Türkçüler Derneği* (Association of Pan-Turkists). The overt use of the term *Türkçü* (Pan-Turkist) was an evident result of the above-indicated liberalisation. The association's averred goals were: (1) to strengthen Pan-Turk sentiments amongst the Turks; (2) to train exemplary Pan-Turkists — loving God, Turkism and the Fatherland, people committed to the history, historic homeland, language, culture, race and sacred values of the Turks; (3) to strive for furthering justice, morality, knowledge, freedom and discipline within the Turkish nation; (4) to combat ideas harmful to Turkish unity and in opposition to the Fatherland, morals and national traditions; and (5) to support all nationalist attitudes within the Homeland.[18] The slogan of this association was 'God, protect the Turks!' (*Tanrı Türkü korusun*), in which the choice of *Tanrı*, a non-Islamic term for God, rather than *Allah*, was hardly accidental and had already been frequently employed by Pan-Turkists.

On 22 February 1963, an additional 'hearth' of this association was inaugurated in Ankara, and the association's centre was transferred there on 26 April 1964. A general congress, meeting in Ankara on 30 August 1964, changed the association's name to *Türkiye Milliyetçiler Birliği* (Union of the Nationalists of Turkey), probably because the new name was likely to have wider appeal. That its aims remained unchanged was evident from the association's first manifesto, issued in 1964,[19] which reasserted its support for Turkism in Turkey and abroad and its commitment to the Outside Turks.[20] Branches were soon opened, not only in Ankara and Istanbul but in Kayseri, Adana, Mersin, Tarsus, Polatli, Boğazlayan, Antalya, Izmir and Yeşilhisar. The association's Central Board (*Genel Merkez*) branched into hearths (*ocaklar*) and the smaller chambers (*odalar*) and tents (*obalar*). In 1967, the association comprised sixteen hearths, two chambers and two tents. Its first president was Hüseyin Nihal Atsız, followed by Nejdet Sançar, then İsmail Hakkı Yılanlıoğlu; the Vice-President was Hikmet Tanyu, a lecturer at the Faculty of Theology at Ankara University. The association convened meetings, held lectures and published and distributed Pan-Turk writings.[21]

Pan-Turkists, like other political groups in Turkey and elsewhere, have been beset by competing personalities and contending factions. A rival congress of nationalists, whose leaders included İbrahim Kafesoğlu, a distinguished professor of Seljuk history at the University of Istanbul, first assembled in 1967, and decided to convene a seminar on nationalism (*milliyetçilik*) at their second congress, scheduled to meet in Istanbul in May 1969. The proceedings of this seminar,[22] running to 216 pages, are highly informative regarding the views, interests and activities of Pan-Turkists at that time. Communications presented to the Seminar's five sections expressed concern about separatist underground movements in Turkey (a reference to the Kurds?), sounded a warning against the penetration of self-confessed leftists into the country's largest teachers' union, and discussed the Outside Turks (estimated at 69,500,000). Relatively new topics introduced were the emphasis on Turkey's economic and developmental problems (which had attracted considerable public attention at that time) and the relationship between nationalism and religion. The latter had apparently become the most hotly-debated issue among Pan-Turkists in Turkey: some considered Islam a rival ideology, not essentially nationalist or Pan-Turkist; others realised its emotional impact on the masses, still effective after almost fifty years of secularisation, and consequently were reluctant to alienate the Believers. The 1969 seminar adopted a clear stand, stating that Islamism (*Müslümanlık*) was, and should remain, an integral component of nationalism.

During the 1970s, nationalist groups proliferated, most frequently those with Pan-Turk tendencies. These generally called themselves *ülkücü* (idealist);[23] most group names included the term *ülkü* (ideal) or *ülkücü*, for example *Genç Ülkücüler Teşkilâtı* (Organisation of Young Idealists),[24] *Türk Ülkücüler Teşkilâtı* (Organisation of Turkish Idealists), *Büyük Ülkü Derneği* (Association for a Great Ideal), *Ülkü Ocakları Birliği* (Union of the Hearths of Ideals), *Ülkü Ocakları Derneği* (Association of the Hearths of Ideals), *Ülkü Gençliği Derneği* (Association of Idealist Youth), *Ülkücü Öğretim Üyeleri ve Öğretmen Derneği* (Association of Idealist Teachers), *Ülkücü Köylüler Derneği* (Association of Idealist Villagers), *Ülkücü Esnaflar Derneği* (Association of Idealist Artisans), *Ülkücü Memurlar Derneği* (Association of Idealist Clerks),[25] *Ülkücü Maliyeciler ve İktısatçılar Derneği* (Association of Idealist Financiers and Economists),[26] and *Ülkücü Gazeteciler Cemiyeti* (Society of Idealist Journalists).[27] Of these, the Hearths of Ideals was the most important. Set up in 1969 as an anti-Communist group, it later assumed Pan-Turk views.[28] It soon became the largest group, allegedly numbering about 100,000 members in the late 1970s, mostly youths, in some 1,500 hearths, busily participating in nationalist seminars and avidly reading patriotic publications.[29] The left, perceiving the potential of the Hearths of Ideals, immediately labelled them 'Fascists', which the group's sympathisers angrily rebutted.[30]

Not all these groups were active concurrently. Several of them had supplanted those which closed down voluntarily or were banned. For instance, when the Association of Hearths of Ideals was disbanded by the authorities early in 1979, an Association of Idealist Youth was set up to take its place, with virtually the same leadership.[31] Groups may have varied in the intensity of their zeal, but the very fact of their proliferation is itself significant. It was partly a response to the activity of a growing number of extreme leftist groups and partly the result of recruiting support for a central nationalist Pan-Turkist element that had appeared on Turkey's internal political scene — the Nationalist Action Party.

Although we are concerned primarily with the Pan-Turk element of the Nationalist Action Party and its connections with Pan-Turkists in Turkey, further explanation is required in order to evaluate properly its special place in contemporary Turkish politics.[32] The party's leader, Alparslan Türkeş,[33] was born in Nicosia, Cyprus, in 1917, and moved to Istanbul when he was fifteen years old. He chose a military career, and rose to the rank of colonel. As indicated above,[34] he participated in the 1944 anti-Communist demonstrations which brought about his arrest and trial — which led to the final dismissal of charges against him and the other demonstrators. The 1944 events marked a watershed in Türkeş's life: detractors have frequently mentioned it as a sign of his extremism, while supporters have brought it up no less often as proof of his dedication to nationalism and Pan-Turkism. Deeply involved in the military intervention of 1960–1, Türkeş and a minority group among the officers who had seized power were expelled from Turkey by the majority of that group for alleged authoritarianism.[35] This appears to have been the second crisis in Türkeş's career. However, he returned to Turkey in 1963, resigned his commission and entered politics. By the end of July 1965, he had succeeded in taking over the leadership of a medium-sized conservative party, the Republican Peasants and Nation Party, whose name was changed in 1969 to the more suitable Nationalist Action Party or the Nationalist Movement Party (*Milliyetçi Hareket Partisi*). The party's electoral fortunes varied from eleven seats in the 450-member National Assembly in 1965, to only one in 1969 (Türkeş himself), three in 1973 and sixteen in 1977.[36] Considered by many as a part of the extreme Right, it has never succeeded in becoming a mass party, as it was unable to move the liberal, moderately right-of-centre Justice Party from this position. Nonetheless, the nature of Coalition-Cabinet politics in Turkey since 1973 has been such that the party was a partner in coalition cabinets from early 1975 to mid-1977, with Türkeş serving as Vice-Premier.

Considering Türkeş's own past and the Nationalist Action Party's claim to a monopoly on nationalism, it was hardly surprising that a strong element of Pan-Turkism was evident in both the symbols and the ideology of this party. Türkeş's common title within the party has been *başbuğ* (leader), a term borrowed from the lore of the Central Asian Turks, and favoured by Enver Pasha as well during his Pan-Turkist days.[37] The *bozkurt*, one of the party's emblems, has even been considered as the party symbol — Türkeş himself liked to be photographed with it;[38] an organ of the party carried this name, and its youth groups were called *bozkurtlar*[39] (plural of *bozkurt*). Furthermore, Türkeş frequently ended his speeches with the invocation of 'God, protect the Turks!' (*Tanri Türkü korusun*), a phrase favoured by Pan-Turk organs, which had been the slogan of the Organisation of Turkish Youth[40] in the 1950s and of the Union of Nationalists of Turkey[41] in the 1960s.

Türkeş's own writings and speeches are the best indication of the Nationalist Action Party's ideology, as it was he who determined the basic lines of its ideology and policy throughout. Nationalism was the central theme, although Pan-Turkism recurred within it frequently and emphatically. Türkeş had already contributed to the Pan-Turk press as a young man, signing his articles 'Alparslan'. He later defended his own participation in the 1944 demonstrations and his standing trial in a semi-autobiographical book, entitled *1944 milliyetçilik olayı* (A case of nationalism, 1944), also a defence of Pan-Turkism. Türkeş recorded that he had told his judges: 'Turan, that is the union of the Turks, means the union of not only the Asiatic Turks, but of all the Turks — a union in spirit, traditions, culture and religion . . . that is, according to my understanding, Turan applies to the Turks in Greece, Bulgaria and every other place.'[42]

This and other works by Türkeş were all published during the latter half of the 1960s, as he was making his *début* in party politics, to provide written guidance for the party he had been leading since 1965. The most important and most frequently reprinted and quoted of Türkeş's works was the booklet *Dokuz ışık* (Nine lights), first published in 1965, which was to serve as the party's vademecum. Although chiefly concerned with Turkey's own problems, the booklet's first two chapters insisted that nationalism implied assistance to all the Turks and that idealism meant striving to enable Turks living outside Turkey to determine their own fate (without drawing Turkey into risky ventures). The term employed for idealism, one of the party's nine principles, was, not coincidentally, *ülkücülük*, also in use by many Pan-Turkist groups.

Türkeş discussed the Outside Turks in greater detail in another booklet, based on his 17 December 1965 lecture to the *Kıbrıs Türk*

Kültür Derneği (Association for the culture of the Cypriot Turks), a Pan-Turkist group. In this 1966 booklet, entitled *Dış politikamız ve Kıbrıs* (Our foreign policies and Cyprus), he surveyed the concept and movements for a Greater Turkey, past and present, focusing upon the issue of Cyprus,[43] which he considered to be as Turkish as Anatolia, Western Thrace and Salonica. As the last two had become parts of Greece since the end of the First World War, this (along with his militant attitude on Cyprus) indicates an anti-Greek Pan-Turk thrust. A 1969 collection of papers, bearing the name of the first article, *Türkiye'nin meseleleri* (The problems of Turkey), was largely devoted to Turkey's own problems, although it did express strong views against Communism and Communists, along with emphatic support for close relations with the Outside Turks, in Cyprus and elsewhere,[44] as a part of Türkeş's vision of a Greater Turkey of 80–100 million Turks.[45]

During the 1970s, there was an apparent slowdown in the frequency, though not the intensity, of Türkeş's pronouncements of Pan-Turk sentiments for the Outside Turks. This may be explained by several factors. First, Pan-Turkism was not then the most immediate concern of many Turks in Turkey, who were becoming increasingly interested in their own socio-economic issues, to which Türkeş and his party, in consequence, had to devote more attention. Secondly, Pan-Turkist support for the Nationalist Action Party was essentially assured; hence the party attempted to recruit the support of other circles as well. And thirdly, when the party participated in coalition cabinets, the responsibilities of government necessitated a cautious approach to such delicate issues as those of the Outside Turks, to which the Soviet Union, in particular, displayed evident sensitivity. Nevertheless, the party did participate in the 1976 public campaign in Turkey following the death in a Soviet jail of Mustafa Cemiloğlu, a leader of the Crimean Tatars. The party could not but demonstrate its sympathy for 'the liberation of the brethren suffering under a foreign yoke'.[46] The Nationalist Action Party has also continued to incorporate Pan-Turk elements in its verbal propaganda activities among Turkish workers in Federal Germany and other Western European countries.

Most party propaganda, however, consists of published works, such as the 1975 collection of articles, old and new, by Türkeş and others repudiating accusations of racism and Turanism.[47] The central argument was that Turkish racism differed from other forms in its not being directed against anyone; rather, it created a common feeling among all Turks, both inside and outside Turkey.[48] The party press also regularly printed contributions with marked Pan-Turk tenden-

cies;[49] one of Türkeş's closest collaborators, Dündar Taşer,[50] asserted
that the unity of the world's 150 million Turks (*sic!*) was crucial for
Turkey's own future. He openly referred to those in the Soviet Union,
in particular.[51]

Türkeş himself later returned to these same issues in two collec-
tions of his own articles, published in 1979. The first was entitled
Gönül seferberliğine (For a mobilisation of the heart) and included
his 'Türkçülük ve Türk birliği' (Pan-Turkism and the union of the
Turks[52]), first published on 10 November 1950,[53] shortly after the
advent of the Democrat Party to power. The reprinting of this article
seems to indicate that the author continued to subscribe to the same
views. 'Pan-Turkism and the union of the Turks'[54] showed Türkeş
to be committed to Pan-Turkism: having rejected charges of fascism
and adventurism, he defined Pan-Turkism essentially as the ideal of
achieving a powerful all-Turkish Union. Claiming that such union
was no utopia, he called for assistance to be given to the Captive
Turks by cultural and diplomatic means, helping their emigrants with
all available resources and preparing for the day when each Turkic
land would achieve its own independence. Such sentiments were as
legitimate for Pan-Turkism as they would be for any other Pan
movement, even if at some future date they led to war with the Soviets
for 'Independence or Death'.[55] Another (undated) article by Türkeş
in the same volume, 'Dış Türkler meselesi' (The problem of the
Outside Turks),[56] bore the imprint of a more mature Türkeş with
greater political responsibility as party leader. He refrained from
proclaiming a Holy War against the Soviet Union for the sake of the
Outside Turks. Rather, he began by emphasising that no step ought
to be taken which would endager the existence of Turkey, which was
a pre-condition for assisting the Outside Turks. Türkeş then asserted
that to strive for the sake of the Outside Turks was not imperialistic
but merely an effort to ensure their freedom, an attitude essentially
approved by the United Nations. Consequently, Turkey ought to
demand freedom for the Turks living in Greece and in the Communist
countries and strive to strengthen its cultural ties with the Outside
Turks. In yet another volume, published in 1979 and entitled *Temel
görüşler* (Basic views), Türkeş returned to Pan-Turkism and Turkish
unity,[57] employing an even more cautious style. He maintained that
the days of Turanism were over, as the concept was fit only to be
buried in scholarly books. Pan-Turkism, on the other hand, was a
living ideal, to be handled by Turkey's foreign policymakers with all
due caution, based on experience acquired in the First World War
and subsequently.

Relations between the Pan-Turkists in Turkey and the political party headed by Türkeş were rather complex. Although the latter's avowed Pan-Turk sympathies were never seriously in doubt (even when toned down for *raisons d'état*), not all Pan-Turkists found a common language with this party, for a variety of reasons. First, there was a manifest difference in order of priorities; while Pan-Turkism was everything for its devotees, it was only one component (albeit a significant one) of Nationalist Action Party ideology. Secondly, while the original platform of the Republican Peasants and Nation Party drawn up by Türkeş spoke of a secular state, the 1969 electoral campaign of the party (renamed the Nationalist Action Party) displayed a definite opening towards Islam, probably geared to vote-getting.[58] This brought about a rift in the party and some of its adherents (including several close collaborators of Türkeş) eventually left it. Among these, there were a number of Pan-Turkists who had associated with Türkeş since the 1940s and had joined his political party,[59] such as İsmail Hakkı Yılanlıoğlu, third President of the Union of the Nationalists of Turkey, who was a Nationalist Action Party member of the National Assembly from 1965 to 1969.[60] The party's choice of the Three Crescents — rather than the *bozkurt* — as its official emblem at its 1969 third general congress in Adana was yet another sign of veering towards Islamism which, for some party members at least, meant moving away from Pan-Turkism. Thirdly, the efforts of Atsız and other leading Pan-Turkists to dominate the party from within failed,[61] as they were out-manoeuvred by Türkeş. Thus, although some Pan-Turkists continued to support the Nationalist Action Party — even continuing their membership in it — others have left it, working outside the party for what they considered the true interests of Pan-Turkism. Among those who broke all contacts with the party was Atsız, who resumed writing in his forceful, aggressive style and was condemned in 1973 to a fifteen-month prison term; he was pardoned by Turkey's President in January 1974.[62]

The Nationalist Action Party itself, on the one hand, has maintained strong ties with such organisations which support Pan-Turkism as the Association of Hearths of Ideals and later with its successor, the Association of Idealist Youth — probably one of the largest such groups in Turkey in the 1970s (apparently owing to its connections with the party); this link has never been acknowledged officially, although people closely associated with these movements often alluded to it.[63] On the other hand, the party has repeatedly attempted to discourage the activities of rival Pan-Turkist groups which could compete with its own interests.[64]

Political organisation and activity notwithstanding, many —

probably most — of the Pan-Turkist efforts were invested after 1965, as formerly, in the publication of both books and periodicals.

Books and pamphlets continued to discuss the nature and merits of Pan-Turkism. Among the more characteristic is Professor Şükrü Elçin's *Türkçülük ve milliyetçilik* (Pan-Turkism and nationalism), published in 1978; based on a lecture to a women's group, the author, who was President of *Türk Kültürünü Araştırma Enstitüsü*, identified Pan-Turkism with nationalism, maintaining that this ideology ought to seek ways of increasing both the material and moral happiness of the World of the Turks. A somewhat different view was taken by Gülsün Dündar, in *Türkçülüğün alfabesi* (The alphabet of Pan-Turkism), published a year later. An ardent partisan of Pan-Turkism, perceived as the sole true Turkish nationalism, the author considered it as both traditional and revolutionary, in the widest sense. A dedicated sympathiser of Türkeş and the Nationalist Action Party, this book reveals Gülsün Dündar as an exponent of Pan-Turkism close to the Nationalist Action Party. A somewhat different example is provided by an earlier work, İzettin Mete's 1965 *Türklük en yüce gayemizdir* (Turkism is our supreme objective). While essentially an exposé of patriotism and its merits in the Turkish case, it also provided a proud look back at the days when Turks and Huns were cooperating in conquests and government (i.e. a presentation in the Kemalist tradition). Other works, however, followed more closely than İzettin Mete the Pan-Turk line, as in the 1966 collection of essays by Atsız, entitled *Türk tarihinde meseleler* (Problems in the history of the Turks). Articles were largely selected from his earlier publications such as *Türk ülküsü*[65] as well as from several Pan-Turk journals published between 1941 and 1966. Atsız's most relevant comment was that Turkish history ought to be considered as a single entity; while the histories of many peoples were those of their respective Fatherlands, Turkish history related to one nation, divided into two mutually complementary aspects: the history of the Turks in their homeland and that of the Turks in foreign countries,[66] evidently a basic Pan-Turk approach.

In his 1966 *Türklük meseleleri* (Problems of Turkism), İsmail Hami Danişmend, a researcher of Ottoman and Turkish history, argued strongly that, although Turkism is based on language, race and culture,[67] race is the most important element; the Turks are a race by themselves.[68] Turning to Cyprus, Danişmend emphasised that the Turks there were of the same race as those in Turkey and that in any event Cyprus was physically and spiritually an integral part of Anatolia.[69] In another work, *Türk ırkı niçin Müslüman olmuştur* (Why did the Turkish race become Muslim?),[70] Danişmend returned even more forcefully to his pet theory of the supremacy of the Turkish race — in which he included, as a matter of course, the Oghuz, Turkmens and other Outside Turks — 'demonstrating its superiority over the Arab race.[71] Somewhat similar views were held by Arın Engin, in his 1968 *Türklük düşmanları sosyalist ve osmanlıcı geçinenlere karşı Atatürkçülük 'Manifesto'su* (A Kemalist Manifesto against the Socialist and Ottomanist partisans, the enemies of Turkism). Although claiming to be a Kemalist, the author was a known contributor to Pan-Turk periodicals; his approach in this book is definitely more Pan-Turk than Kemalist. He appealed to Turkish youth to fight 'the Red Pan-Slavists' and defend Pan-Turkism, Turkish unity[72] and the Turkish race.[73] Engin went on to praise Turkish racism which, unlike Pan-Slavism, did not aspire to subjugate and torture others, but rather to nurture national pride.[74] He then argued that if Pan-Turkism was justified in the case of the Outside Turks in Hatay and Cyprus, it was similarly justified on behalf of those in Turkestan and other Communist-governed countries.[75] Engin's racist approach did not prevent him from asserting that the Kurds, Lazes and Circassians were in reality Turks.[76] This argument actually suited the objectives of Turkists and Pan-Turkists alike, to prove that all Turkey's inhabitants were originally Turks with special characteristics applying to the Kurds[77] and others in Eastern Anatolia.[78]

In recent years, many other Pan-Turk publications in Turkey have given less attention to race issues and more to those of the Outside Turks. For instance, the 1971 booklet *Türk dünyasında Irak Türkleri* (The Iraki Turks in the world of the Turks) featured a map on its cover, indicating the Turkish area of Irak to the environs of Baghdad. Several articles, most of them written specially for this publication, argued in strong language that the Turks in Irak, numbering at least 720,000, were being held prisoner, deprived of their individual freedoms, and having their lives and possessions endangered under a discriminatory government. Indeed, their problems were presented as representative of those of all Captive Turks. In 1976, Enver Yakuboğlu returned to this theme in his *Irak Türkleri* (The Turks of Irak), a collection of articles and some poems about the situation of these Outside Turks — pulsating with affection for them. In a similar vein, Ünal Türkeş published *Unutulmuş Türkler: Batı Trakya'da 4 yıl* (The forgotten Turks: four years in Western Thrace). Printed in 1971, this is a record of what the author witnessed or heard, during his visits to the 100,000 Turks in Western Thrace, once an Ottoman possession. He claimed that they were suffering from discrimination in education, cultural activities and land sales, and that their situation had worsened since the Cyprus problem had become more acute. Implied is an appeal for Turks in Turkey to come to their assistance.[79] The same approach pervades another volume, written by M. Celâlettin Yücel and also published the same year. Repeating some of the author's arguments in another, 1971 book, *Bütün dünya Türkleri* (The Turks of the entire world), the new one, entitled *Dış Türkler* (The Outside Turks)[80] is primarily an account, past and present, of the Outside Turks in Siberia, Central Asia, the Volga, the Crimea, Azerbayjan, Iran, Syria, Irak, Lebanon, Egypt, Bulgaria, Yugoslavia, Romania, Cyprus, Greece and Afghanistan, as well as Japan and Finland. A clear Pan-Turk perception may be noted in the long chapter dealing with 'the Turkish world and Russian imperialism',[81] which offers an interpretation of history based on the constant conflict between these two rivals. According to the author, Soviet imperialism against the Turkish world is merely a continuation of Czarist policies.

A similar but considerably more extensive work, *Türklük kavgası* (The struggle of Turkdom), was published in 1977; it was a collection of short articles by Ergun Göze, mostly written during the 1970s, of which a large section[82] was devoted to the struggle of the Captive Turks.[83] Göze called attention to the Turks captive in the Crimea, the Volga-Ural region, the Northern Caucasus, Turkestan and Azerbayjan, arguing that even their languages were imprisoned, as they all had to speak 'a Marxist language'. He then called for establishment of an 'Independent Eastern Turkestan Government' and vehemently attacked discrimination against local Turks by the Ba'th regime in Irak; here a specific complaint was that the October 1970 population-census had queried people only as to whether they were Arabs or Kurds. Göze blamed the political parties in Turkey for ignoring the Captive Turks and appealed to them to struggle for the individual freedoms and cultural rights of their brethren.[84] This book is complemented by a later one, by Erkin Alptekin (reportedly, the son of İsa Alptekin, Pan-Turk activist and author of works on Turkestan),[85] *Uygur Türkleri* (The Uygur Turks), published in 1978. This research into the history, culture and economics of the Uygurs — whom Alptekin treats as Turks — is marked by bursts of anti-Communism, in which the author reproaches bitterly both Communist China[86] and the Soviet Union[87] for their unfair treatment of the Uygurs. These reproaches and others have recurred frequently in Pan-Turk publications, e.g. in a book by Necmettin Hacıeminoğlu, a university professor closely involved with Pan-Turkist circles. Entitled *Milliyetçilik, ülkücülük, aydınlar* (Nationalism, idealism and the intellectuals), it went through several printings in the 1970s.[88] In a chapter on Pan-Turkism,[89] Hacıeminoğlu pinpoints its enemies: those keeping the

Outside Turks captive, those assisting the jailers, and the indifferent, ignorant and cowardly in Turkey itself.[90] For him unity of 'the Turkish world' was an axiom, as it was for another university professor close to the Pan-Turk ideology, Mehmet Eröz. In his 1977 book, *Türk kültürü araştırmaları* (Studies of the culture of the Turks), Eröz returned to the cultural premise of Pan-Turkism, that 'there is one single culture from Turkestan to Cyprus.'[91]

A considerable amount of Pan-Turk writing had been produced by the 1970s and several anthologies of poetry and prose were published. For example, Yaman Arıkan's 1976 *Türklük gurûr ve şuûru* (The pride and sentiments of Turkism) was a collection of views on Turkism and Pan-Turkism by the editor and others. Arıkan himself supplied the connecting prose for a fairly large number of poems, by various poets, praising the ancient common heritage of all Turks. The first poem began: 'Who are we? We are men coming from Altai',[92] and ended with an appeal to idealist youths to unite and lead the way.[93] A collection of poems by İsmailoğlu Mustafa Yılmaz, entitled *Turanda çakan şimşek. Şiirler* (A lightning flashing in Turan. Poems), was published in 1977. Several of these poems expressed longing for Turan and Ergenekon. A typical poem, entitled 'We are Turks',[94] concluded:[95] 'Let us stop the world for the sake of Turan/Let us extinguish with faith the fire coming at us.'[96] Also in 1977, Faruk Çil, an active Pan-Turkist,[97] edited another anthology, entitled *Kavgamız — Türkçülük kavgası* (Our struggle is the struggle of Pan-Turkism), comprising both prose and poetry, including several articles by Atsız. The book called primarily for energetic action on behalf of the Outside Turks.

Various Pan-Turkist societies (or groups with Pan-Turk leanings) had also published volumes to propagate their views. One example is the 1967 publication by the Union of the Nationalists of Turkey of a *3 Mayıs Türkçüler günü antolojisi* (An anthology of 3 May, the day of the Pan-Turkists), commemorating the 3 May 1944 demonstrations. Atsız's two famous letters to Premier Saraçoğlu were reprinted, as well as several speeches by his colleagues — Nejdet Sançar, Alparslan Türkeş, Hikmet Tanyu, Zeki Velidi Togan, Fethi Tevetoğlu, Zeki Sofuoğlu, and others — delivered at the trials or while in exile. No less interesting is a 1978 booklet by Akkan Suver, *Ülkücüye notlar* (Notes for the idealist). This is a sort of vademecum for the Idealist Turk (*Ülkücü Türk*) — referring to the various Idealist groups, mentioned above, and most particularly to the youth among them. While this work purported to interpret Turkish nationalism on a general level, it openly identified with the Nine Lights ideology of the Nationalist Action Party.[98] It also took a definite stand favourable to

Pan-Turkism, reminding its readers of the days of glory when the
Turks had founded a great empire and a lasting civilisation extending
from Vienna to Turkestan, from the Crimea to the Arabian Peninsula
and from India to Gibraltar.[99] More to the point, perhaps, it also
elaborated on the duties of the Idealist *vis-à-vis* the Outside Turks,[100]
describing the suffering of 'the captive member of our race'[101] in
some detail and with numerous statistics, roundly attacking Communism and calling on Turkey's Turks to become more involved in
the fate of the Outside Turks as a step towards an all-Turk union.
Special attention was devoted to the discrimination against the Outside Turks in Irak, with an appeal that they be allowed to maintain
and develop their own cultural life and institutions.[102]

From 1965 onwards, the pro-Pan-Turk press continued with much
the same characteristics noted above. Outside Turkey, the Hungarian-
language *Turan* continued to be published in Stuttgart, in mimeographed form,[103] while the *Millij Türkistan*[104] appeared more or less
regularly. In Turkey, *Türk Kültürü*[105] has been published by the *Türk
Kültürünü Araştırma Enstitüsü* (The Institute for Research of the
Culture of the Turks) in Ankara, a Turkist and nationalist body, set
up in 1961 with a number of Pan-Turkists in key positions. The
Institute has numerous publications having a bearing on Pan-Turkism,
its *magnum opus* being a large tome entitled *Türk dünyası el kitabı*
(Handbook of the World of the Turks). This is a collection of research
papers by various scholars on geography, culture and history — but
the most revealing part is 'The contemporary world of the Turks',[106]
a solid block of articles amounting to 400 pages, committed to the
proposition of the essential unity of the world of the Turks. *Türk
Kültürü* itself has been continuously published from November 1962
up to the present. It is not only one of the longest-lived of all the
periodicals under consideration, but probably the best example of a
combination of moderate Pan-Turkism and scholarship. Its masthead,
'The Journal of the World of the Turks',[107] indicates its scope and
objectives. A monthly which insisted on a low price (for a long time,
no more than one Turkish pound per issue) in order to boost sales,
Türk Kültürü was fortunate in enlisting the participation of many
Turkish (and some foreign) historians, linguists and literary critics.
Its aims were clearly stated in its first editorial, signed by the institute.
Entitled 'Our objective and our way',[108] it asserted that the institute
had been established for scholarly research on the Turkish world in
all its aspects, as one entity,[109] covering such wide-apart fields as
history, ethnography, language, art, social problems, philosophy,
geography and economics, while the principle was to improve
knowledge of all Turks, in order to strengthen the Turkish nation and

its nationalist ideals. In other words, the wide parameters were those of Turkish culture, past and present, with a definite Pan-Turk viewpoint.

Doubtlessly, the political commitment of the journal influenced the choice of topics and contributors, although its scholarly standards were generally maintained. As most contributors probably agreed with the irredentist *dictum* that 'wherever there are Turks, there is a Turkey',[110] history was examined to provide examples for development of the idea of a Great Turkey (*Büyük Türkiye*) in past ages.[111] Professor İbrahim Kafesoğlu and others re-examined Turkish nationalism,[112] in its Pan-Turk context, usually opting for a cultural rather than a racial bond. According to Kafesoğlu, Pan-Turkism, which he termed *Bütün Türklük*,[113] was not a mere romantic fantasy, but a matter of vital importance for Turkey itself. Notwithstanding such approaches, cultural studies predominated in the journal, including articles on the need for national (i.e. nationalist) education in Turkey,[114] purified of Communist infiltration (needless to say, *Türk Kültürü* assumed a committed anti-Communist stand).[115] Some of the articles in *Türk Kültürü* and others found their way into two other periodicals of the same Institute, *Türk Kültürü Araştırmaları* and *Cultura Turcica* (the latter in English, French or German).

Evidently, much discussion centered on the Outside Turks,[116] their culture[117] and history as well as their political and economic situation. Many of their personalities were studied, particularly those whose contributions to Pan-Turkism were considered worthwhile.[118] Along with an appeal to strengthen culture among all Outside Turks,[119] due attention was given to those in the Crimea,[120] the Caucasus,[121] Turkestan,[122] Azerbayjan,[123] Kazakhstan,[124] Turkmenistan,[125] Siberia,[126] Afghanistan,[127] Iran,[128] Irak,[129] Syria,[130] Bulgaria,[131] Yugoslavia,[132] Western Thrace[133] and Cyprus.[134]

Several new journals also appeared, as well as a number of anthologies of earlier articles collected by their authors, of which we will discuss two important volumes. The first, Atsız's *Türk ülküsü*,[135] was revised in 1973 to include additional articles written for *Ötüken*, an active Pan-Turk periodical. Always politically-minded, Atsız called on all Pan-Turkists — in an article entitled 'Pan-Turkism and politics'[136] — to unite in a single party with Pan-Turkism written into its platform. In 'National policies',[137] he declared aggressively that 'concern with the Outside Turks did not mean "imperialism"; even if it did, this was a sacred imperialism',[138] just as de Gaulle had encouraged the French in Canada to unite with France (this was Atsız's interpretation), or as the Republic of Ireland wished Ulster to unite with it. A second collection of articles was Nejdet Sançar's

Türkçülük üzerine makaleler (Articles about Pan-Turkism), published posthumously in 1976, which reaffirmed his well-known Pan-Turk credo and accused the governments of the Republican People's Party — especially İsmet İnönü himself — of neglecting the Outside Turks.[139] Other articles discussed the Turks in Irak[140] and Cyprus,[141] appealing to the Turkish Government to assist them.

One of the longest-lived Pan-Turk periodicals among those which began publication after 1965 was the monthly *Türk Birliği* (Union of the Turks or Unity of the Turks), founded and published in Ankara by Kerim Alhan (Yaycılı), from April 1966 to October 1971.[142] The first issue's masthead read: 'Organ of the Turkdom of Anatolia, the Caucasus and Azerbayjan. Monthly. A nationalist journal for culture and art';[143] from the second issue on, however, it read: 'A Monthly striving for Turkdom. A nationalist journal for culture and art'.[144] One way or the other, *Türk Birliği* was pronouncedly Pan-Turk throughout and, not surprisingly, vehemently anti-Communist.[145] The general objectives of this periodical found expression in many articles, stories, poems and plays about the history, language and current events of the Outside Turks, particularly those in Azerbayjan[146] and Turkestan, with special emphasis on nationalism[147] and on aspirations for the independence of the Outside Turks and their joining with Turkey. It was argued that this was particularly relevant, as African tribes of 40–50,000 people were obtaining their independence, while 60–70 million Turks were held captive and could not be freed.[148] Soviet Imperialism was principally blamed for this situation;[149] a series of articles by Arın Engin on 'The wars of Muscovitism and Turkism'[150] (later published in book form) appeared not merely to describe the past, but also to hint at the future.

Another long-lived Pan-Turk periodical was *Emel. İki Aylık kültur dergisi* (Hope: a cultural bi-monthly), published since November 1960 in Istanbul.[151] A revival of *Emel Medjmuası* (which had appeared in Pazarcık between 1930 and 1941[152]), it was issued by the National Centre of the Crimean Turco-Tatars.[153] The life and soul of this periodical was Müstecib Ülküsal, a Tatar who had studied and practised law in Romania, where he had been the publisher-editor of *Emel Medjmuası* (under his former name of Müstecib H. Fazıl) and involved in Pan-Turkist circles, before moving to Turkey; there he became chairman of the Association for Culture and Assistance of the Crimean Turks.[154] By 1979 he had reportedly succeeded in increasing the distribution of *Emel* to about 6,000 copies, including subscribers overseas.[155] Ülküsal is also the author of several books with Pan-Turk content, such as *Dobruca ve Türkler* (Dobruja and the Turks); the latest is *Kırım Türk-Tatarları* (The Turco-Tatars of the

Crimea), published in 1980. Some of the articles in *Emel* were in English, indicating the readership it desired to reach. Its aims were asserted to be Pan-Turkism (*Türkçülük*) and Crimeanism (*Kırımcılık*), by which was understood Crimean independence.[156] *Emel* published not only patriotic and Pan-Turk poems, historical articles — e.g. on Cafer Seydahmet Kırımer (1889–1960)[157] or on İsmail Gasprinsky[158] — and chapters from the past and present of the Crimeans and other Captive Turks in history, literature and language, but also surveys of world affairs with a strong anti-Soviet flavour in almost every issue. The periodical's Pan-Turk tendencies were evident throughout, even in dealing with less frequently discussed issues, such as the Cyprus conflict.[159] Hope for the future was based not only on the Western powers, but also on the Islamic states[160] and on all conferences propounding human rights.[161]

Ötüken. Fikir ve ülkü dergisi (Ötüken:[162] a Journal of ideas and ideals) was Atsız's last periodical. A monthly, it appeared in Istanbul under his editorship from January 1964 to September 1975,[163] i.e. shortly before his death. Its slogan, like that of some of its predecessors, was '*Bütün Türkler bir ordu*' (All the Turks are one army) — taken from Ziya Gökalp. The editorial in the first issue, by Atsız himself, was entitled 'Pan-Turkism'.[164] It ended by proclaiming: 'The first duty of Pan-Turkists is to carry out their task with a heart full of conviction.' This *Ötüken* set to bring about. It frequently reported on *Türkçüler Derneği*, which Atsız chaired for a while, and on other Pan-Turkist groups. Numerous articles with Pan-Turk content appeared; Atsız and Sançar contributed to many of them, but so did a number of younger contributors. Articles were against the Soviet Union, but for its Turks (many issues devoted the first page to 'The situation of the Outside Turks'); and they called for strengthening Turkey's armed forces, praised the *Komünizmle Mücadele Derneği*, called on the Turks to rely on themselves, appealed for an increase in nationalist organised groups in Turkey, spoke up in favour of the Turks in Iran and in Irak, and attacked the leftists in Turkey (such as the writer and journalist Çetin Altan). Increasingly, the political aspect became preponderant: even cultural presentations or economic analyses were frequently presented through a political prism, with Pan-Turkism being the criterion for what was approved, or disapproved; and all those rejecting the idea of a 'Great Turkey' were considered as enemies.[165] In a parallel manner, a serious effort was made to prove that Pan-Turkism was a practical, feasible proposition.[166]

Adsız. Türkçü siyaset ve kültür dergisi (Adsız: a Pan-Turk journal of politics and culture) was a monthly, which started to appear in Istanbul in October 1972.[167] Its publisher was Abdülhalûk M. Çay

and its editor Orhan Tuncer. Atsız was a contributor, and indeed wrote
the editorial in the first issue,[168] in which he promised that the journal
would focus on Pan-Turkism — with special emphasis on the Outside
Turks — but also attempt to spread the knowledge of Turkism and
Turkish culture. These, he asserted, had been the objectives of Pan-
Turk periodicals throughout. However, he argued, Pan-Turk publications ought to concentrate, not only on culture and education, but also
on politics and economics. So alongside poems on 'My captive
Azerbayjan'[169] or articles on the Oghuz epics,[170] Ziya Gökalp,[171] and
the Turkish character of Anatolia,[172] one finds political and economic
interpretations of Pan-Turkism in the contemporary Turkish and international system. One example is an editorial[173] proclaiming that
Pan-Turkists are not rightists, but merely Pan-Turkists. Others
criticised the politics of the coalition cabinets in Turkey[174] or discussed public opinion and foreign policies.[175] Another maintained
that the ideals of Pan-Turkism give support to the positive sciences,
Western technology, and industrialisation.[176] Similarly, Tonyukuk, a
chemical engineer, wrote on industrialisation and technology, based
on A. Türkeş's *Nine Lights*.[177] Nevertheless, this, like other Pan-Turk
journals, hardly offered any cogent economic interpretations and
proposals connected with Pan-Turkism.

A more recent periodical is *Türk'e çağrı. Türkçü siyaset ve kültürü
dergisi* (An appeal to the Turk: a Pan-Turk journal of politics and
culture). Edited by A. Feridun Azeri, it started to appear in Istanbul
in May 1979, in mimeographed form.[178] An editorial in the first issue
declared that the journal would struggle for the Pan-Turk idea and to
organise the Pan-Turkists.[179] Among the objectives this periodical set
itself were the following: to discuss the problems of Turkey and the
Turkish nation from a Pan-Turk vantage-point, to be involved in
protecting the Outside Turks, to reveal to Turkish public opinion the
trends hostile to Pan-Turkism, to be tied to no party — but to try and
convince all the parties to see matters in a Pan-Turk way. These aims
Türk'e çağrı strove to achieve by means of aggressive propaganda.
In addition to reprinting such Pan-Turk classics as Atsız's 1944 letters
to Saraçoğlu,[180] it reported on the Outside Turks in Iran,[181] the Soviet
Union,[182] Eastern Turkestan,[183] Western Thrace,[184] and others,[185] attacked the leftists in the Turkish universities,[186] published historical
articles from a Pan-Turk perspective, discussed the ideas of Pan-
Turkism,[187] wrote on Atsız, Rıza Nur, Ziya Gökalp, Mehmet Emin
Yurdakul, Arif Nihat Asya, Nejdet Sançar and other personalities
who had contributed to Pan-Turkism, and published patriotic poems
with a Pan-Turk content.[188]

Yet another relatively new Pan-Turk journal is *Turan. Aylık Türkçü siyasi dergi* (Turan: a political Pan-Turk monthly), which later changed its name to *Turan Kavgamız* (Our struggle is Turan), published monthly in Istanbul since August 1976,[189] for several years. Edited by Faruk Çil, this has been a pronouncedly aggressive Pan-Turk journal. The first issue quoted on its first page sayings on Pan-Turkism by Atsız and Türkeş and since it started publication only a few months after Atsız's death and was full of reprints of his quotations and articles, one may assume that Çil wished to continue in the same general line. Çil himself asserted his pride in Pan-Turkism, which he called *Turancılık* (Turanism), and appealed to all Pan-Turkists to run together towards victory.[190] The periodical strove to convince all nationalists, Pan-Turkists and ideologically close groups to unite for political action.[191] The feasibility of Pan-Turkism was not doubted; after all, the Jews, without a homeland, succeeded after 2,000 years in making a dream come true.[192] A great deal was written against 'the Reds' and the Soviet Union and considerable interest was shown in the Outside Turks everywhere,[193] while other articles appeared regularly on Ziya Gökalp, Ömer Seyfeddin, Enver Pasha (whose body *Turan* demanded should be returned to Turkey)[194] and others.

The Outside Turks were the central issue for *Hür Türkistan için. İstiklâlci gazete* (For a Free Turkestan: an independent magazine), published in Istanbul irregularly in 1975–6, and for another recent Pan-Turk periodical, *Dilde, Fikirde, İşde Birlik. Aylık dış politika dergisi* (Unity in language, thought and action: A monthly of foreign politics), a monthly published in Ankara since February 1977,[195] and edited by Necip Abdülhamitoğlu, a Crimean Tatar. Committed to Gasprinsky's slogan (adopted as the title of the journal), this was an outspoken Pan-Turk organ, striving for the Union (*Birlik*) of all Turks.[196] Besides articles about the Outside Turks everywhere, the periodical called for a new strategy on their behalf in Turkey's foreign policy, adapted to the conditions of each community of Outside Turks — that towards the Soviet Union, for instance, differing from that towards Greece. With this in view, the periodical, and in particular Dr Ahmet Kıpçak (who contributed a series of articles on this topic), proposed to enlist the support of all states and organisations concerned with human rights, and all those having a common denominator with the Captive Turks (like the Islamic countries) — everything to be carried out with well-coordinated propaganda. This broad view and comprehensive approach differed perceptibly from that of some other Pan-Turk periodicals, such as *Batı Trakya Türkünün Sesi. Siyasi, kültürel ve Türkçü dergi* (The voice of the Turk of Western Thrace: a political, cultural and Pan-Turk journal), a mimeographed monthly appearing in Istanbul and interested almost solely in the Turkish minority in Greece, chiefly in Western Thrace.[197]

More sporadic were such periodicals as *Ülkü Ocakları Derneği Genel Merkezi Bülteni* (The Bulletin of the Central Committee of the Association of Hearths of Ideals), a one-sheet irregular publication appearing in Ankara since 1974.[198] Dedicated to nationalism (*milliyetçilik*) in the Pan-Turk spirit, this periodical aimed to inform the members of the association about the views of its committee on self-reliance, friendship to all Turks, support for the Outside Turks, Cyprus, anti-Communism and anti-leftism, the importance of propaganda, and the relevance of industrialisation. This bulletin was supplemented, since 15 December 1976, by *Ülkücü Kadro* (The idealist cadres), an Istanbul fortnightly published by Ahmet B. Karabacak and edited by Hasan Külünk.[199] Outspokenly nationalist and close to the Nationalist Action Party, *Türkiye Ülkücü Gençlik Dergisi* (The journal of the idealist youth of Turkey), a monthly published in Istanbul since 1970, openly supported the cause of the Outside Turks in a Pan-Turk spirit. Articles appeared on such topics as the current cultural problems of Yugoslavia's Turks[200] or Turkey's concern in the Captive Turks.[201] These themes were taken up later by *Ülkücü Kadro*,[202] and since 1979 by *Ülkü Ocağı* (The hearth of the idealist, or: The hearths of the idealists), edited in Ankara during 1979 by Orhan Alpaslan as the organ of an Idealists' group with obvious commitment to the Nationalist Action Party. Similar characteristics were exhibited by *Genç Arkadaş* (Young companion), appearing in Istanbul and then in Ankara, between 1975 and 1979, first as a fortnightly and later as a weekly.[203] Strongly nationalist and close to the circles of the Idealists in outlook, this periodical published a number of articles and discussions expressing views to which Pan-Turkists would have subscribed, e.g. about Enver Pasha, Ziya Gökalp and the Outside Turks. The same applied to *Gençliğe hedef* (The objective for youth), a 1977 Istanbul monthly with the slogan *Dünya Türklüğün ve ezilen milletlerin kurtuluşu* (The liberation of world Turkdom and of oppressed nations).

As for the press close to the Nationalist Action Party itself, this took from the start a positive attitude towards Pan-Turkism, writing aggressively about the Outside Turks. Thus *Millî Hareket* (National action or National movement), a monthly published in Istanbul from October 1966 to August 1971; and *Devlet* (State), which began publication as a weekly on 7 April 1969 in Ankara, later moving to Konya and then becoming a fortnightly and eventually a monthly until it was discontinued in 1979.[204] These and other organs supporting the party were decidedly well-disposed towards Pan-Turkism. For example, inflated statistics were used to demonstrate the impressive number of Outside Turks: 70 million in the Soviet Union, 30 million in China, 12 million in Iran, 3 million in Irak, 2 million in the Balkans[205] and hundreds of thousands in Western Thrace.[206] A concerted drive was undertaken for the revival of past glories in 'a Turkey of 100 million people',[207] with the minimalists writing about Cyprus, the Aegean Islands and Western Thrace[208] becoming parts of Turkey and the maximalists dreaming of 'Tomorrow's Turanian state'.[209] These themes were taken up, repeated and elaborated further by other journals connected with the Nationalist Action Party, such as *Bozkurt* and *Töre*.

Bozkurt was revived in October 1972 and published in Ankara and then in Konya for about five years, entitled *Bozkurt. Aylık ülkü dergisi* (Bozkurt: a monthly of ideals).[210] Its slogan was 'Everything for, according to, and by the Turks'.[211] The editor was Osman Oktay, well-known in Pan-Turkist circles. Closely connected with, and supportive of, the above organisations of Idealists, *Bozkurt* took a determined stand in many matters dear to the heart of Pan-Turkists. Its very first issue comprised an editorial by Sami Somuncuoğlu, one of the leaders of the Nationalist Action Party, entitled 'Nationalism, Pan-Turkism and Idealism',[212] arguing that for Turks Pan-Turkism was the only category of nationalism. Furthermore, almost every issue included articles about the Outside Turks, later renamed the Captive Turks — their past, present and future — and expressing hopes for their eventual liberation and union. An article on 'Fearing Pan-Turkism'[213] appealed for pride in Pan-Turkism and for fearlessness in using the term. Another considered the Captive Turks in the framework of all captive nations and called for total solidarity with them.[214] Other articles attacked Communism,[215] frequently with Pan-Turk overtones. Poems were published, praising the idea of Turan and of Pan-Turkism in enthusiastic terms.[216]

Töre has appeared much more regularly and for a longer period than *Bozkurt*. It was a monthly coming out in Ankara since 1971.[217] Its publisher-editor was Emine İşinsu, a writer with several successful novels to her credit. This was an outspoken periodical, supporting both the Nationalist Action Party and Pan-Turkism. Alparslan Türkeş had some articles in it, as did numerous Pan-Turkist activists or sympathisers, e.g. Arif Nihat Asya, Necmettin Hacıeminoğlu, A. Ergenekon, Mustafa Kapalı, Ahmet Cebeci, Baymirza Hayıt, Reha Oğuz Türkkan and others. The subjects comprised the Captive Turks and the proper ways for Turkey to approach their problems;[218] analyses of Pan-Turk literature[219] and ideology,[220] including discussions on 'Racism and nationalism'[221] and others on 'the union of the Turks'.[222]

It may indeed be said that since 1965 the Nationalist Action Party, through its organisation and propaganda, has succeeded in introducing Pan-Turkism into the mainstream of Turkish politics. By its virtual monopolising of Pan-Turkism, together with those groups of Idealists close to the party, the Nationalist Action Party may have given Pan-Turkism a narrower meaning, focusing almost exclusively on propaganda for the Outside Turks, and even playing this theme down when political considerations seemed to warrant it. The Nationalist Action Party has thus to some extent pre-empted the Pan-Turkist activities of other groups in Turkey, which must now reckon with the former in all moves they undertake. In any event, Pan-Turkist activity has now come full circle. At the end of the nineteenth century, it was carried on mainly abroad, with only a few manifestations in Turkey. One hundred years later, there are only scattered and sporadic signs of Pan-Turkism abroad, while in Turkey it carries on a sustained cultural and political campaign. While it has failed to become a popular ideology or a mass movement in the Republic of Turkey, it has nonetheless achieved enough importance in recent years to bring about a vehement public condemnation (along with revived Islamism) by the State President in 1976.[223] However, the closing down of all political parties and associations, following the military intervention of 12 September 1980, raised doubts about the continuation of publicly organised activity by Pan-Turkists. These doubts were dispelled during the decade following the return to civilian rule in 1983. Pan-Turkism survived, but assumed a somewhat different character, as we shall see below.

NOTES

1. Details in Landau, *Radical politics*, chs 3 and 4.
2. Id., 'Political involvement of religious groups in modern Turkey: some observations', *Proceedings of the VIth Congress of Arabic and Islamic Studies, 1972*, Stockholm, Almqvist and Wiksell, 1975, pp. 64–74, and the sources in the footnotes.
3. See above, pp. 132 ff.
4. Details in Darendelioğlu, pp. 222–4, 286–9, 353–60; K.H. Karpat, 'Ideology in Turkey after the revolution of 1960: nationalism and socialism', *Turkish Yearbook of International Relations*, VI: 1965, pp. 87–8; Landau, *Radical politics*, pp. 203–4.
5. See above, ch. 3 of our study, p. 81.
6. Ibid., ch. 4, p. 111.
7. He called himself then the Head (or President) of the Volga-Ural Turco-Tatars, living in the Far East (*Uzak Şark'ta yaşayan Türk-Tatarların reisi*).

8. FO 195/2488, file 671, İshakî's letter and memorandum, dated 27 Aug. 1945.
9. As listed on the back-cover of Arın Engin's *The voice of Turkism behind the Iron Curtain on the occasion of the centenary anniversary of the Russian invasion of Turkestan.*
10. Based on my interview with Müstecib Ülküsal, the chairman of this association, in Istanbul, on 26 Sep. 1979.
11. Cf. *TK*, 19: May 1964, pp. 91–3 and passim.
12. See above, ch. 4 of our study.
13. Landau, *Radical politics*, p. 203.
14. Istanbul, 1967.
15. Said Şamil, *Dış Türkler ve sosyalizm.*
16. See above, the end of ch. 4 of our study.
17. Details in A.N. Yücekök, *Türkiyede örgütlenmiş dinin ve sosyo-ekonomik tabanı*, Ankara Üniversitesi Siyasal Bilgiler Fakültesi Yayınları, 1971. However, Yücekök was not interested in Pan-Turkist groups.
18. See *Ötüken*, 1: 15 Jan. 1964, pp. 4–7. Fuller details in Deliorman, pp. 308 ff, 348 ff.
19. *Türkiye Milliyetçiler Birliği'nin görüşü. İlk bildiri.*
20. For which cf. ibid., esp. p. 9.
21. Such as *Türkiye milliyetçiler birliği'nin görüşü*, 1964; *3 mayıs Türkçüler günü antolojisi*, vol. I, 1967. See also Gülsün Dündar, *Türkçülüğün alfabesi*, pp. 83–4; Darendelioğlu, pp. 351–2; M. Toker, *Solda ve sağda vuruşanlar*, p. 159; Landau, *Radical politics*, pp. 201–2.
22. *Milliyetçi Türkiye doğru. 10–11 mayıs 1969da yapılan milliyetçiler ilmî seminerinde varılan neticeler*, 1969. See also Landau, *Radical politics*, pp. 202–3.
23. For *ülkücü* ideologies and organisations, see Öner, pp. 49 ff.
24. For the 1970 convention of this organisation, see *Ötüken*, 82: Oct. 1970, pp. 14–15.
25. Whose Secretary-General, Kemalettin Cam, was shot and wounded in Ankara, in Sep. 1979 — presumably for his contacts with the Nationalist Action Party. See *Milliyet* (Istanbul daily), 19 Sep. 1979, p. 12.
26. For which see ÜMİD-BİR Ülkücü Maliyeci ve İktisatçılar Birliği Derneği Genel Merkezi, *1. Türk Milli İktisat kurultayı — Kurultay teblileri* (sic!), N.p., Kent Matbaa, 1979; 192 pp.
27. *Bayram 32. Türkçüler bayramı*, p. 46.
28. See Xavier Jacob, 'Phénomènes de scission interne en Turquie', *L'Afrique et l'Asie Modernes*, 121: 1979, p. 48.
29. Acc. to my interviews with several of their leaders in Ankara during August 1979.
30. E.g. Galip Erdem, *Suçlamalar. I. Sağcılık. Faşizm*, esp. pp. 126–42.
31. Information collected in Ankara and Istanbul, during August–September 1979.

172   *Pan-Turkism*

32. Little has been printed about this party, outside the party's own publications, which are evidently a mine of information. See however Landau, *Radical politics*, pp. 205–42; cf. id., 'The militant right in Turkish politics', in Landau, *Middle Eastern themes: papers in history and politics*, 1973, pp. 277–89; id., 'The Nationalist Action Party', *Journal of Contemporary History*, xvii (4): Oct. 1982, pp. 587–606.
33. In addition to Türkeş's own writings and speeches, several works have been published about him, notably, M. Özdağ, *Alparslan Türkeş*, Ankara, 1965; Fuat Uluç, *İşte liderler*, Ankara, 1965, esp. pp. 13 ff; Bekir Berk and N.M. Polat, *Islamî hareket ve Türkeş*, N.p. [Istanbul], 1969; Cemâl Anadol, *Türklük gurûr ve şuûru, Islâm ahlâk ve fazileti, haksızlığa, yolsuzluğa, Siyonizme, Komünizme ve her türlü emperyalizme karşı Türkeş*, Istanbul, n.d. [prob. 1976].
34. Cf. ch. 4 of our study, p. 117.
35. See W.F. Weiker, *The Turkish revolution of 1960–61: aspects of military politics*, Washington, D.C., 1963, esp. pp. 125–7; E. Özbudun, *The role of the military in recent Turkish politics*, Cambridge, Mass., 1966; Landau, *Radical politics*, pp. 12, 206–8.
36. Cf. Landau, in *The World Today* (London), xxvi (4): Apr. 1970, pp. 156–66; and ibid., xxx (4): April 1974, pp. 170–80.
37. Cf. Harry Luke, p. 158. The party's opponents, however, claimed that *Başbuğ* could also well be the equivalent of *Duce* and *Führer*.
38. See Tahsin Ünal, *Türklüğün sembolü Bozkurt*, Konya, Millî Ülkü Yayınları, 1977, the photograph facing p. 72.
39. Landau, *Radical politics*, pp. 215 ff for details.
40. See ch. 4 of our study.
41. See above, in the present chapter of our study.
42. *1944 milliyetçilik olayı*, p. 75. Translation mine.
43. See also, for Türkeş's views on Cyprus, Cemâl Anadol, *Türklük gurûr*, pp. 43–66, 118–19.
44. *Türkiye'nin meseleleri*, esp. pp. 23, 36 ff.
45. Ibid., pp. 17–18, 59, 97.
46. Cf. 'Unruhe und Unordnung in der Türkei', *Neue Zürcher Zeitung*, 6 Mar. 1976.
47. Galip Erdem (ed.), *Suçlamalar*, vol. II, 1975.
48. Ibid., pp. 262–3.
49. Several examples will be listed below, near the end of the present chapter.
50. For whom see Erol Güngör, *Türk kültürü ve milliyetçilik*, 2nd printing, Istanbul, Ötüken Yayınevi, 1976, pp. 135–49.
51. L.N., *Dündar Taşer'in Büyük Türkiye'si*, 4th edn, 1979, esp. pp. 165–6.
52. Or: Pan-Turkism and the unity of the Turks.
53. *Gönül seferberliğine*, 4th edn, p. 23.
54. Ibid., pp. 17–23.
55. Ibid., p. 23: *Ya istiklâl, ya ölüm*.
56. Ibid., pp. 263–5.

57. *Temel görüşler*, pp. 19–20.
58. Details in Landau, *Radical politics*, pp. 231–2, 277–8.
59. Cf. ibid., pp. 214, 218.
60. Kâzım Öztürk, *Türkiye Büyük Millet Meclisi albümü, 1920–1973*, Ankara, 1973, p. 456.
61. Interview in Istanbul, on 19 Sep. 1979, with Professor Erol Güngör, of Istanbul University, who was at the time close to Türkeş and other leaders of the Nationalist Action Party.
62. *The Times* (London), 23 Jan. 1974.
63. See, e.g., Cemâl Anadol, *Türklük gurûr*, pp. 211–13. Cf. Sami Cohen, 'Student violence threatens Turkish democracy', *The Observer Foreign News Service*, no. 35662, 27 Jan. 1977.
64. Such as the group headed by Faruk Çil, editor of the Istanbul monthly *Kavgamız Turan* (Turan is our struggle) and his associates — acc. to my interview with him, in Istanbul, on 18 Sep. 1979.
65. See above, ch. 4 of our study, p. 120.
66. Atsız, *Türk tarihinde meseleler*, pp. 5–12.
67. *Türklük meseleleri*, p. 147 and passim.
68. Ibid., pp. 42 ff; cf. pp. 93–5.
69. Ibid., p. 224; cf. ibid., p. 233.
70. 2nd edn, 1978.
71. *Türk ırkı niçin Müslüman olmuştur*, esp. pp. 44–5, 51–9, 129–59.
72. Or: a Turkish union.
73. *Türklük düşmanları sosyalist ve osmanlıcı geçinenlere karşı Atatürkçülük 'Manifesto' su*, p. 25.
74. Ibid., pp. 32–3.
75. Ibid., pp. 67–71.
76. Ibid., pp. 33–4.
77. See, e.g., Mahmut Çapar, *Doğu illerimizde aşiretlerin Türklüğü*, Istanbul, Akın Yayınları, 1972; 77 pp.
78. Necati Ökse, *Van Gölü ve Fırat Nehri çevresinde yaşayan Türkler*, 1976.
79. For a similar appeal, five years later, cf. the anonymous *West Thrace Turks*, n.d. [1976].
80. The publisher's name, Hun Yayınları, means 'Hun Publications'.
81. *Dış Türkler*, pp. 142–68.
82. *Türklük kavgası*, pp. 133–60.
83. 'Esir Türk kavgası'.
84. Some of the arguments are repeated in İsmail Kaybalı and Cemender Arslanoğlu, *Ortaasya Türklüğünün tarihi ve bugünkü durumu*, Ankara, Köymen, 1978.
85. Whose most recent work appeared in 1975, entitled *Doğu Türkistan dâvâsı* (the first edition is from 1973).
86. *Uygur Türkleri*, pp. 131 ff.
87. Ibid., pp. 169–74.
88. The third edition appeared in 1978.

89. *Milliyetçilik ülkücülük aydınlar,* pp. 179–217.
90. Ibid., 180 ff.
91. *Türk kültürü araştırmaları,* pp. 201–11.
92. *Türklük gurûr,* p. 9.
93. Ibid., pp. 226–30.
94. *Biz Türküz.*
95. *Turanda çakan şimşek. Şiirler,* p. 13.
96. 'Turan ülküsü için dünyayı durdururuz
    Karşı gelen ateşi imanla söndürürüz.'
97. Already mentioned above, in the present chapter.
98. *Ülkücüye notlar,* pp. 38–9.
99. Ibid., pp. 16–17.
100. Ibid., pp. 44–5.
101. Ibid., p. 44: *esir ırkdaşlarımız.*
102. Ibid., pp. 56–7.
103. Incomplete set in the library of the Turkish Historical Society, Ankara.
104. See above, ch. 4 of our study, p. 123.
105. Cf. ibid., p. 132.
106. *Türk dünyası el kitabı,* pp. 1039–1428.
107. *Türk dünyasına dergisidir.*
108. 'Amacımız ve yolumuz', *TK,* 1: Nov. 1962, pp. 5–13.
109. Ibid., p. 5: 'Enstitümüz Turk dünyasını bir bütün olarak ve her yönden
    araştırmak gayesiyle kurulmuştur. Fakat . . . tamamiyle ilmî olacaktır.'
110. 'Nerede Türk varsa orada Türkiye vardır', the title of an article by
    Tekin Erer, reprinted in *TK,* 166: Aug. 1976, pp. 606–7.
111. As Emel Esin did, ibid., 43: May 1966, pp. 607–13.
112. İbrahim Kafesoğlu, 'Türk milliyetçiliği', ibid., 2: Dec. 1962, pp. 1–5;
    and 5: Mar. 1963, pp. 1–5.
113. For this neologism, cf. ibid., 8: June 1963, p. 8.
114. Ibid., most of the issue no. 18: Apr. 1964. See also Necmettin
    Hacıeminoğlu, ibid., 44: 1966, pp. 669–72.
115. Fethi Tevetoğlu, 'Millî eğitimde kızıl faaliyet', ibid., 40: Feb. 1966,
    pp. 333–43. Cf. 54: Apr. 1967, pp. 434–45; Ercümend Kuran,
    'Dünyada ve Türkiyede sosyalizm ve Komünizm', 58: Aug. 1967, pp.
    766–72; İsmet Binark, 'Türkiye'de komünizm tehlikesi ve komünist
    faâliyetler', 84: Oct. 1969, pp. 907–14; R.O. Türkkan, 'Türkiyede
    solculuğun başlangıcı', 184: Feb. 1978, pp. 209–13.
116. A special issue of *TK,* 21: July 1964, was devoted to Captive Nations
    (*Esir milletler*), with obvious emphasis on the Captive Turks.
117. E.g., Ahmet Caferoğlu, 'Dış Türkler kültürünün korunması meselesi
    üzerine', ibid., 7: May 1963, pp. 12–16.
118. One example, out of many, is Tebrizli Ali, an Azeri. See Ağçaköylü,
    'Bilinmeyen büyük bir Türkçü ve Türkçeci', ibid., 1 Nov. 1962, pp.
    41–5.
119. E.g., İsmet Parmaksızoğlu, 'Türkiye ve Dış Türkler', ibid., 65: Mar.
    1968, pp. 305–7.

120. Kemal Ortaylı, 'Kırım Türklerinin millî efsanelerinden', ibid., 1: Nov. 1962, pp. 46–7; 'Kırım Türklerinin başına gelenler', 80: June 1969, pp. 559–67; T.K., 'Kırım Türklerinin yurtlarına dönüşü hikâyesi ve gerçekler', 156: Oct. 1975, pp. 331–6; Nâdir Devlet, 'Kırım Türklerinin Kremlin'e çağrıları', 192: Oct. 1978, pp. 743–5.
121. Cemal Gökçe, 'Kafkasya istiklâl savaşları üzerine notlar', ibid., 23: Sep. 1964, pp. 44–6; Ahmet Caferoğlu, 'Kafkasya Türkleri', 38: Dec. 1965, pp. 172–8; Tarık Kutlu, 'Şimalî Kafkasya'da Çeçenler', 113: Mar. 1972, pp. 295–302.
122. İbrahim Yarkın, 'Türkistan'ın hürriyet şairi Çolpan', ibid., 5: Mar. 1963, pp. 37–41; Ahmet Ardel, 'Doğu Türkistan', 8: June 1963, pp. 26–33; Abdülkadir İnan, 'Türkistanda 1916 yılındaki ayaklama', 12: Oct. 1963, pp. 26–30; Ahmet Caferoğlu, 'Doğu Türkistan Türklüğü', 30: Apr. 1965, pp. 372–6; İbrahim Yarkın, 'Türkistanın cedidçi devri', 58: Aug. 1967, pp. 773–7; J.A., 'Türkistanda Sovyet merkezinin kontrol vasıtaları', 108: Oct. 1971, pp. 941–4; K.İ. Cengiz, 'Büyük Türkistan'a bakış', 158: Dec. 1975, pp. 106–11.
123. Ahmet Caferoğlu, 'Azerbaycan mizah şairi Ali Ekber', ibid., 3: Jan. 1963, pp. 8–13; Sadık Aran, 'Azerbaycan', 8: June 1963, pp. 34–9; most of no. 19: May 1964; Ahmet Caferoğlu, 'Azerbaycan'ın öztürkçeliği', 48: Oct. 1966, pp. 1101–3; Hüseyin Baykara, 'Azerbaycan istiklâli dramı', 79: May 1969, pp. 481–93.
124. Hızır Bek Gayretullah, 'Kazak Türklerinde kışı adları', ibid., 10: Aug. 1963, pp. 13–17; M.K. Özergin, 'Türkiye'deki Kazak Türkleri', ibid., pp. 55–6; Ahmet Caferoğlu, 'Kazak Türkleri', 29: Mar. 1965, pp. 302–6; Hasan Oraltay, 'Kazak Türklerinin çadırları', 192: Oct. 1978, pp. 746–7.
125. Ahmet Caferoğlu, 'Türkmenler', ibid., 20: June 1964, pp. 23–8; Ahmet Ardel, 'Türkmenistan', ibid., pp. 29–32.
126. Ahmet Caferoğlu, 'Sibirya Türkleri', ibid., 24: Oct. 1964, pp. 44–8.
127. Ahmet Ateş, 'Kardeş Afganistan'da bir yıl dönümü', ibid., 3 Jan. 1963, pp. 17–22; and 7: May 1963, pp. 31–6; Erdoğan Merçil, 'Afganistan' daki Özbekler', 39: Jan. 1966, pp. 269–71; Mehmet Eröz, 'Afganistan'da Türk aşiretleri', 83: Sep. 1969, pp. 846–50.
128. Yusuf Azmun, 'İran'da yaşayan Türkmenler hakkında küçük bir not', ibid., 28: Feb. 1965, pp. 245–6; id., 'İran'da yaşayan Türkmenler', 33: July 1965, pp. 583–8; Ahmet Caferoğlu, 'İran Türkleri', 50: Dec. 1966, pp. 125–33; Faruk Sümer, 'İran'da yaşayan Türk oymakları', 120: Oct. 1972, pp. 1238–41.
129. Necmettin Esin, 'Irak Türkleri', ibid., 1: Nov. 1962, pp. 48–9 and subsequent issues; İzettin Kirkük, 'Iraklı bir Türk kadın şairi', 4: Feb. 1963, pp. 49–52; Sönmez Ateş (pseudonym?), 'Irak Türkleri Hakkında', 5: Mar. 1963, pp. 42–5; Osman Mazlum, 'Canım Kerkük' (a poem), 64: Feb. 1968, pp. 234–5; Erşet Hürmüzlü, 'Irak Türkleri edebiyatında Erbil', 71: Sep. 1968, pp. 844–51; Necmettin Esin, 'Irak

Türkleri edebiyatından yaprakları', 125: Mar. 1973, pp. 303–4; Ümit Akkoyunlu, 'Irak Türklüğünün meseleleri', 165: July 1976, pp. 551–9.

130. Ali Sevim, 'Suriye'de ilk Türkler', ibid., 32: June 1965, pp. 548–9.

131. A.C. Eren, 'Pomaklara dair', ibid., 4: Feb. 1963, pp. 37–41; B. Sakarbalkan, 'Bulgaristan Türk okullarıyla ilgili istatistikler', 32: June 1965, pp. 521–8; Atilâ Cengiz, 'Bulgaristan'da Türk dili', 59: Sep. 1967, pp. 847–52; D. Piroğlu, 'Bulgaristan'da yaşayan Türk kardeşlerimiz', 75: Jan. 1969, pp. 234–43; Edward Tryjarski, 'Dobruca'dan birkaç türkü', 123: Jan. 1973, pp. 167–76; Zeliha Yeşilyurt, 'Bulgaristan Türk çocuklarının fâcıası', 153–5: July–Sep. 1975, pp. 288–92.

132. M.K. Özergin, 'Yugoslavya'da yaşayan Türkler', ibid., 11: Sep. 1963, pp. 14–19; Hasan Kaleşi, 'Yugoslavya'da ilk Türk kütüphaneleri', 38: Dec. 1965, pp. 168–71.

133. Cengiz Orhonlu, 'Batı Trakya Türkleri', ibid., 17: Mar. 1964, pp. 5–8; M. Toroslu, 'Batı Trakya Türklerine baskı yapılıyor', 31: May 1965, pp. 436–41; Tahsin Ünal, 'Batı Trakya Türkleri', 76: Feb. 1969, pp. 279–87; special issue no. 159: Jan. 1976.

134. H.F. Alasya, 'Kıbrısta Türk kültürü hareketleri', ibid., 2: Dec. 1962, pp. 49–50; id., 'Kıbrıs'ta belediyeler konusu', 5: Mar. 1963, pp. 52–3; F.A. Armaoğlu, 'Kıbrıs'ta Türk hakları', 14: Dec. 1963, pp. 7–11; most of no. 16: Feb. 1964; Tebrizli Ali, 'Kıbrıs için' (a poem), 26: Dec. 1964, pp. 109–10; B.R. Özoran, 'Enosis oyunu', 32: June 1965, pp. 515–20; id., 'Kıbrıs'ta Uygur Türklerinin izleri', 88: Feb. 1970, pp. 240–3; id., 'Kıbrıs Türkü ve Rum tahrikleri', 89: Mar. 1970, pp. 332–41; H.F. Alasya, 'Kıbrıs'ta Türk nüfusu ve nüfusun dağılışı', 94: Aug. 1970, pp. 663–9; B.R. Özoran, 'Kıbrıs'ta Cumhuriyet bayramları', 120: Oct. 1972, pp. 1225–30; special issue no. 139–41: May–July 1974.

135. See above, ch. 4 of our study, p. 120.

136. 'Türkçülük ve siyaset', first published in *Ötüken* in 1970, then reprinted in Atsız's *Türk ülküsü*, 3rd edn, pp. 116–20.

137. 'Millî siyaset', first published in *Ötüken* in 1972, then reprinted in *Türk ülküsü*, as above, pp. 111–15.

138. Ibid., p. 114: 'Dış Türklerle ilgilenmek emperyalizm değildir. Emperyalizm ise mukaddes bir emperyalizmdir.'

139. *Türkçülük üzerine makaleler*, pp. 76–9, 97–105. Sançar attacked İnönü in yet another volume, entitled *Ismet Inönü ile hesaplaşma*, 1973.

140. *Türkçülük üzerine makaleler*, pp. 80–1.

141. Ibid., pp. 82–7.

142. The National Library, Ankara, has issues 1: Apr. 1966 to 67: Sep.–Oct. 1971 (all published?). *Türk Birliği* was briefly revived, as an Istanbul monthly, in March 1978.

143. *Anadolu, Kafkas, Azerbaycan Türklüğünün sesi. Aylık. Milliyetçi Kültür ve Sanat Dergisi*.

144. *Türklük için çalışır. Aylık. Milliyetçi, Kültür ve Sanat Dergisi*.

145. See also Landau, *Radical politics*, p. 197.

146. E.g., Ahmet Caferoğlu's 'Azerbaycan'ın öztürkçeciliği', *Türk Birliği*, 10–11: Jan.–Feb. 1967, pp. 23–5.
147. E.g., Süleyman Tekiner, 'Türkistanda milliyetçi hareketleri', 9: Dec. 1966, pp. 7–15.
148. Tekin Erer, 'Türkleri nasıl parçaladılar', ibid., 4: July 1966, pp. 38–9.
149. E.g., ibid., 2: May 1966, p. 40.
150. Arın Engin, 'Moskofluk-Türklük savaşları', ibid., 1: Apr. 1966 and subsequent issues.
151. The National Library, Ankara, has a complete set.
152. See above, ch. 3 of our study, p. 82.
153. See above, in the present chapter, p. 150.
154. Ibid.
155. Based on my interview with Müstecib Ülküsal in Istanbul, on 26 Sep. 1979.
156. Editorial in *Emel*, 1: Nov. 1960, esp. p. 15.
157. By İbrahim Otar, ibid., pp. 18–26.
158. By M. Ülküsal, ibid., 24: Sep.–Oct. 1964, pp. 7–12.
159. E.g., M. Ülküsal, 'Türkiye'nin Kıbrıstaki barış harekâtı', ibid., 84: Sep.–Oct. 1974, pp. 1–12.
160. E.g., M. Ülküsal, '7. İslam Konferansı', ibid., 95: July–Aug. 1976, pp. 1–2; or an unsigned article on 'Onuncu İslam konferansı', ibid., 112: May–June 1979, pp. 38–40.
161. M. Ülküsal, 'Belgrad Konferansı ve insan hakları', ibid., 101: July–Aug. 1977, pp. 1–3.
162. Name of a mountain range in Central Asia.
163. The National Library, Ankara, has 141 issues, Jan. 1964–Sep. 1975 (all published?). *Ötüken* was revived, in December 1979, as a supplement to the monthly *Turan* (Istanbul).
164. 'Türkçülük', *Ötüken*, 1: 15 Jan. 1964, p. 1.
165. E.g., G.Y. Yücel, 'Türklük bir bütündür', ibid., 56: Aug. 1968, pp. 10–11.
166. Atsız, 'Turancılık romantik bir hayal değildir', ibid., 51: Mar. 1968, pp. 3–4.
167. The National Library in Ankara has the first seven issues, Oct. 1972 to Mar.–Apr. 1973.
168. *Adsız*, 1: Oct. 1972, pp. 3–4.
169. Elmas Yıldırım, 'Esir Azerbaycan'ım', ibid., p. 7.
170. Gündoğu Saruhanlıoğlu, 'Oğuzlama', 2: Nov. 1972, pp. 45–6.
171. Ibid., 3–4: Jan. 1973, pp. 19–22.
172. Tansu Say, 'Anadolunun Türklüğü üzerine', ibid., 5: Feb. 1973, pp. 17–24.
173. Ibid., 3–4: Jan. 1973, pp. 3–4.
174. Yıldırım Orkun, 'Dünden bugüne doğru kısa bir bakış', ibid., pp. 11–18.
175. M.F. Yücesoy, 'Kamuoyu ve dış politika', ibid., 5: Feb. 1973, pp. 50–4.
176. Ertuğrul Afşın, 'Türkçülük ülküsü', ibid., 1: Oct. 1972, pp. 13–18.

177. 'Endüstricilik ve teknikçilik', ibid., 2: Nov. 1972, pp. 22–6, and 3–4 Jan. 1973, pp. 27–30.

178. The National Library, Ankara, has the first 10 issues, May 1979–Feb. 1980; further issues have appeared, however, at least up to 14: June 1980.

179. *Türk'e çağrı*, 1: May 1979, p. 2.

180. Ibid., pp. 18–27.

181. Ibid., pp. 28–30.

182. Ibid., 2: June 1979, p. 5.

183. Ibid., 7: Nov. 1979, pp. 16–18.

184. Ibid., 10: Feb. 1980, pp. 7–10.

185. Ibid., 6: Oct. 1979, pp. 11–13.

186. Ibid., 5: Sep. 1979, pp. 29–31.

187. Ibid., 10: Feb. 1980, pp. 3–6.

188. Ibid., 7: Nov. 1979, p. 30; 8: Dec. 1979, p. 24.

189. The Beyazıd Library, Istanbul, has the first year of this periodical.

190. Faruk Çil, 'Turancı hareket', *Turan*, 1: Aug. 1976, p. 5.

191. Id., 'Açıklama', ibid., 2: Sep. 1976, p. 2.

192. A. Ergenekon, 'Hezeyanlar ve gerçekler', ibid., pp. 3–8.

193. E.g., *Kavgamız* (Supplement to *Turan*), 1: 1977, pp. 12–14.

194. *Turan*, 8: Mar. 1977, pp. 1 ff.

195. The library of the Türk Kültürünü Araştırma Enstitüsü, Ankara, has the first twelve issues, Feb. 1977–Jan. 1978 (all published?).

196. From the very first issue, see its editorial, 'Birlik'e davet', *Dilde, Fikirde, İşde Birlik*, 1: Feb. 1977, p. 1.

197. *Batı Trakya Türkünün Sesi* is a periodical of long duration; I have been able, however, to consult only issues 149–153: 15 Sep. 1979–15 Jan. 1980, available in the library of Türk Kültürünü Araştırma Enstitüsü, Ankara.

198. The Beyazıd Library, Istanbul, has several issues, between 5 July 1974 and 1 Oct. 1976.

199. My private collection has nos 1–17: 15 Dec. 1976–1 Nov. 1977 (all published?).

200. Necati Zekeriya, 'Yugoslavya'da Türk dil davâsı ve anayurdun yakın ilgisi', *Türkiye Ülkücü Gençlik Dergisi*, 11: July 1971, pp. 19–20.

201. Ahmet Aydınlı, 'Esir Türkler ve biz', ibid., 12: Aug. 1971, pp. 6–7.

202. Examples in *Ülkücü Kadro*, 5: 15 Feb. 1977, pp. 13–14; 9: 15 Apr. 1977, p. 12.

203. The Library of the University of Istanbul has an incomplete set, 1975–9, according to which the following may be deduced. Issues 1–24: 15 Jan. 1975–15 Mar. 1976, Istanbul fortnightly; 1–13: 15 Dec. 1976–3 Mar. 1978, Ankara fortnightly; 18 Dec. 1978–15 Jan. 1979, Ankara weekly.

204. More details in Landau, *Radical politics*, pp. 232–9; id., *Middle Eastern themes*, p. 285.

205. *Millî Hareket*, 1: n.d. [Oct. 1966]; ibid., 7: 1 Feb. 1967, Aran's article.

206. Ibid., Güngör Aslan, in 26: Sep. 1968.
207. 'Yüz milyonluk Türkiye', *Devlet* (for dates, cf. Landau, *Radical politics*, p. 235, n. 122).
208. Gökçeoğlu, in *Millî Hareket*, 18: Jan. 1968.
209. 'Yarınki Turan devleti', ibid., 20: Mar. 1968.
210. In my own library there are nos 1–76: Oct. 1972–July 1977 (all published?).
211. 'Herşey Türk için Türk'e göre Türk tarafından'.
212. 'Milliyetçilik Türkçülük ülkücülük', *Bozkurt* (2nd series), 1: Oct. 1972, pp. 3, 13.
213. Elif Bilge, 'Turancılık korkusu', 2: Nov. 1972, p. 6.
214. Galip Erdem, 'Esir milletler ve Türk dünyası', 10: July 1973, pp. 8–9.
215. E.g., Nejdet Sançar, 'Komünizmin Türkiye'deki başarısı', 44: 15 Feb. 1976, pp. 8–9.
216. E.g., M. Veli Bilici, 'Arzum', 65–66: 1–15 Jan. 1977, p. 12.
217. In my own library there are nos 4–110: Sep. 1971–July 1980. An earlier series of thirty-one issues of this monthly appeared in Ankara between 1969 and 1971.
218. Hasan Oraltay, 'Türkiye esir Türklere yanlış tanıtılıyor', *Töre*, 15: Aug. 1972, pp. 42–6; Mustafa Kaflı, 'Azerbaycan ve Azeri Türkleri', 16: Sep. 1972; S. Yılmaz Kuşkay, 'Sovyet Türklüğünde kültüre ve nüfusa bağlı eğilimler', 26: July 1973, pp. 18–33; and many others.
219. Haydar Ali Diriöz, ' "Bozkurtların destanı" hakkında', ibid., 21: Feb. 1973, pp. 35–9; Orhan Türkdoğan, 'Gökalp sosyolojisinde kültür tekâmülü teorisi', 61: June 1976, pp. 19–21.
220. Necmettin Hacıeminoğlu, 'Ülkücülük ve ülkücüler', ibid., 28: Sep. 1973, pp. 3–7; id., 'Ziya Gökalp'de Turancılık ülküsü', 63: Aug. 1976, pp. 15–23 and 65: Oct. 1976, pp. 42–4.
221. M. Emin Ziya, 'Irkçılık ve milliyetçilik', ibid., 71: Apr. 1977, pp. 5–8.
222. Hasan Oraltay, 'Türk birliği üzerine', ibid., 72: May 1977, pp. 25–6.
223. See X. Jacob in *L'Afrique et l'Asie Modernes*, 121: 1979, pp. 33–4.

6

PAN-TURKISM AS AN
IRREDENTIST PHENOMENON

The best way to understand irredentist Pan-Turkism in Turkey might well be to attempt an analysis of its typology in relation to other Pan-ideologies and movements, both in the Middle East and elsewhere.

On the one hand, one may learn something about Pan-Turkism from the extensive literature on nationalism in general. The numerous works of Hans Kohn[1] — probably the first to attempt a scholarly study of nationalism in the Middle East[2] — are still relevant, although much has been added to them by the works of Benjamin Akzin,[3] Elie Kedourie[4] and Anthony D. Smith,[5] to mention only a few of the most outstanding authors in English. On the other hand, some of the studies on Pan ideologies and movements (to be mentioned later) serve a useful purpose by providing a basis for comparison, although no comprehensive comparative work on this subject, or for that matter on irredentism, has been published to date.

Pan ideologies and movements generally aim (more intensely than merely nationalist movements) at promoting the solidarity or union of groups physically in different states, but bound to each other by a 'common or kindred language, race or tradition or by some other postulated tie, such as geographical proximity'.[6] On the other hand, great distances (or practical considerations, for that matter), have never dampened the ardour of Pan ideologies.[7] While there is more than a grain of truth in the statement that 'the environments out of which they arose, their aims, forms of organisation, methods and ideologies have been so diverse as to make valid generalisations about the Pan movements almost impossible',[8] there are actually more similarities than meet the eye.

In order to compare the various Pan ideologies and movements and assess the role of Pan-Turkism in this context, one ought first to differentiate between schools of thought which merely aim at a common policy and those which are essentially of a militantly nationalist

180

NATIONALISMS — IRREDENTIST, PAN AND DIASPORA

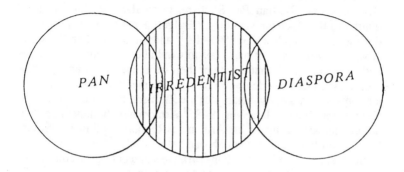

character aiming at political union. Among the former, Pan-Americanism is a striking example of a movement that has regarded its goal as cooperation in preserving and furthering common hemispheric interests, virtually devoid of any politically formulated ideology. Even Pan-Africanism, although claiming a cogent Pan ideology, has hardly taken any practical steps toward achievement of overall political union. Pan-Africanism originally aimed more at 'Africa for the Africans'[9] than at African unity; this has largely continued to be true, as 'Pan-African' in Africa today apparently denotes overall solidarity and concerted action rather than total union.

The latter category, that of nationalist ideologies and movements aiming at political union, is of more immediate concern to us, since Pan-Turkism should be classified among them. Two sub-categories can be perceived: the first is the ideology or movement aiming at a union of independent states with common traditions or interests. Examples are Pan-Arabism, particularly since the establishment of the Arab League in 1944;[10] Pan-Europeanism, as founded in The Hague in 1948; and Pan-Islamism in the 1960s and the 1970s, when a growing number of Muslim states strove for rapprochement and concerted action through international congresses and specially constituted bodies.[11] The second sub-category is the irredentist type — explicit or implicit — of Pan ideology or movement. An extension of nationalism, this is characterised by the desire of a state, whose political frontiers do not comprise all the members of the same (broadly-conceived) cultural or ethnic group, to redeem the minorities (and territories) having a common tie with the 'mother-country'. This category of movement could start and develop either within the state or abroad (sometimes even without the state's assent). Examples are Pan-Italianism in the nineteenth century and the no less irredentist activity of d'Annunzio in Fiume in 1919; the Pan-Germanism of the Bismarck era; Russian Pan-Slavism, particularly during the third quarter of the nineteenth century;[12] Bulgarian nationalism, especially during the Balkan Wars of 1912–13;[13] and, of course, Pan-Turkism. A variant of this type of nationalism would be 'Diaspora' ideologies and movements, without a state of their own, hoping for an ingathering of exiles and a redemption of what seemed to them the ancient land, real or imaginary. Examples are Zionism, before the establishment of the State of Israel in 1948;[14] Armenian nationalism abroad, before the setting up of an Armenian Republic within the Soviet Union; and Irish nationalism abroad before 1921.

   Several characteristics of Pan-Turkism stand out against this background of other Pan ideologies and movements.

1. *Its inception and early development* were typical of many Pan ideologies. While it is true that an attempt to establish the paternity of any Pan ideology is an arduous task, one may assert that Pan-Turkism began as Diaspora nationalism in Czarist Russia, late in the nineteenth century — although there was some variance of opinion as to precisely which land its exponents wished to redeem. As to the time factor, virtually all Pan ideologies, in Europe and in the Middle East alike, were products of that century, even though their origins may have been of earlier date. This is true no less of Pan-Slavism, Pan-Italianism and Pan-Germanism than of Pan-Turkism, Zionism, Pan-Arabism and Pan-Islamism. In all cases, a period of ideological gestation preceded the political organisation into movements. The convening of the first Pan-Slav Congress at Prague in 1848 was preceded by more than half a century of debate, as were the First Zionist Congress at Basel in 1897 and the meetings of the Pan-Turkist leaders in Czarist Russia early in the twentieth century. With regard to place, the search for new common symbols which people of Turkic origin were conducting in order to find common ground for a collective identity (which had existed only nebulously beforehand) was carried out in exile — in this case in Russia, probably for two main reasons: the large number of Turkic peoples in that country and the impact of Pan-Slavism. When this diaspora type of Pan ideology was joined by Turks in the Ottoman Empire, early in the twentieth century, Pan-Turkism became a two-pronged movement. Its adoption by intellectual, and subsequently by official circles was an indication of the Empire's difficulties with its own non-Turk minorities, on the one hand, and its isolation in its immediate area as well as in its international relations, on the other hand. An identical situation prompted

Hungary, for example, to seek Hungarians in Central Asia and Western Siberia.[15] Since this isolation has remained more or less a constant factor, the Pan-Turk ideology and movement have displayed remarkable persistence over an entire century.

2. *The nature of Pan-Turk ideology* is likewise characteristic of that of several other Pan schools — albeit with certain variations. It has been simultaneously romantic in the vast scope of its ambitions and its strong sense of destiny, resembling Pan-Germanism, Pan-Slavism, Pan-Arabism and Zionism, and radically clear-cut in its black-and-white *Weltanschauung*, which allowed only for the 'very good' and the 'positively evil'. Despite variation in intensity, there was no doubt about the dedicated earnestness of Pan-Turkist spokesmen. In common with other Pan ideologies — indeed, with many nationalist ones — Pan-Turkism aimed at the revival of an ancient culture, as part of its search for common roots and a return to the most appealing among them. While the totality of the ancient culture, as one single entity, was brought up as proof of a joint heritage different from and at least equal to those of other cultures, prominence was accorded to language, history and literature (apparently in this order of importance) in Pan-Turkism, no less than in Turkish nationalism, as the three interconnected pivots of intellectual discourse. This has also been true of, respectively, Slavonic research, studies in Arabic language and literature and the revival of Hebrew as a spoken language, no less than in the efforts dedicated to Turkish and Turkic studies, examined above.[16] While exponents of Pan-Turkism had much in common with the spokesmen for Turkish nationalism regarding the trend towards purifying the Turkish language, the former laid greater emphasis on finding or evolving a language common to all Turkic groups, minimising differences and maximising similarities. In this respect, they worked on lines similar both to Pan-Slavists, who were attempting to incorporate many languages and dialects into the Slavonic group, and to Pan-Germanists who were arguing that Dutch was clearly a Germanic language. Indeed, the very 'Turkification' of the non-Turkish elements in the Ottoman Empire by the Young Turks is somewhat reminiscent of the German campaign to 'Germanise' Alsace-Lorraine after 1871.

3. *Language, culture, race and territory.* For many Pan-Turkists, the existence of a 'common language' served as sufficient proof that all its speakers were members of one and the same nation. In addition to language, Pan-Turkists perceived several other cultural characteristics in history, literature, culture and mythology. Adopting a 'historicist' approach (in the 'German sense') — i.e. focusing almost exclusively on those issues of linguistic, historical and literary re-

search which bolstered their case and linked them with all available
fellow-nationals — they sought (and allegedly found) proof of ancient
persisting bonds with these fellow-nationals. As in similar cases
relating to other Pan ideologies, this aided Pan-Turkists in the redis-
covery and reassertion of their own culture, which was suitable for
creating a nation of all the fellow-nationals and differentiating them
from others. Next came the matter of common origins which, although
still controversial from a scholarly point of view, was *subjectively*
credible enough to be convincing to themselves. Emphasis on the
ethnic bond, on the other hand, has been less pronounced in Pan-
Turkism than in Turanism (where it was the central element), or in
the Pan-Germanism of the Hitler era. Nevertheless, it had been
brought up by Ziya Gökalp and others in the late Ottoman Empire,
who lauded all people of common Turkish-Turkic ethnic origins —
without, however, denigrating others. This trend reached exaggerated
proportions in the racist writings of Türkkan and others in the 1930s,
which consistently stressed the superiority of the Turkish race, possibly under Nazi influence; and included the often-heard claims of
common physical attributes and their influence on mental abilities.
Many Pan-Turkists highlighted and extolled group sentiments and
loyalties at that time, particularly if these were considered to be
racially based. Geographical contiguity was indicated (as in most Pan
ideologies), sometimes ignoring, on the one hand, the vast empty
spaces and, on the other, the presence of other people between the
kindred groups. In Pan-Turk doctrine, language, culture, race and
territory are indeed infrequently interwoven as inseparable elements
of an ideology aspiring to cultural unity and, consequently, to political
union.

4. *Economic Arguments*. Two essential elements of Pan ideologies,
the economic and religious arguments, play only small roles in Pan-
Turkism. Economic arguments are much more in evidence in the
ambitions of Pan-Germanism in the nineteenth and early twentieth
centuries and the systematic plans laid down to achieve them;[17]
Pan-Asianism, as interpreted to serve Japan's interests in East Asia
during the 1930s, particularly as expressed in the doctrine of 'The
Greater Asia Co-Prosperity Sphere';[18] or Pan-Arabism, which would
ultimately enable the poorer nations to share the wealth of the oil-
producers. Pan-Turkists, however, are generally much less concerned
with economic considerations. Their journals and other publications
occasionally mention the wealth and economic advantages of Azerbayjan but the overall impression is that such arguments may not
have been considered in good taste and were frowned upon. Also,
Pan-Turkists were well aware of Turkey's own grave economic

problems and hardly felt in a position to preach economics to the Diaspora. In any event, economics factors were subordinate to the cultural, ethnic and political considerations in their arguments.

5. *The attitude of Pan-Turkism to religion* is more complex. As mentioned previously, Pan-Turk nationalism was frowned upon in Czarist Russia[19] and was in direct competition with Pan-Islam in the late Ottoman Empire.[20] Early exponents of Pan-Turkism, like Akçura and Ağaoğlu, had doubts about the place of religion in Pan-Turkism.[21] It has also been explained that the leading members of the Committee of Union and Progress, who ruled the Ottoman Empire, continued during the Empire's last decade to use Pan-Islam (albeit in a downgraded version) along with the Pan-Turkism they were championing.[22] Indeed, they employed such a typically Pan-Islamic organization as *Anjuman-ı Khuddam-ı Kaaba*, made up of Indian Muslims, in order to bolster Pan-Turkism.[23] The rivalry went deeper than this, of course, as Pan-Turkism was, in more ways than one, a political version of religion, in the sense that it was a type of nationalism substituting its own criteria for political action for those of the religious establishment. Its ideals were largely a throwback to the Turks of the pre-Islamic times. Careful not to antagonise Muslim sentiment, Pan-Turkists perceived that only a secular movement might avoid taking sides in the Sunnite-Shiite rivalry within the Turkic groups. In this respect, religion had — and still has — an inferior standing in Pan-Turkism than, say, in Pan-Slavism, some of the major exponents of which linked its ideology with the Russian Orthodox Church;[24] or in Zionism, where it was closely associated with its inception and organisational development (along with a strong atheistic socialist component) and still plays a substantial role in political considerations for many; or in Pan-Arabism, in which Islam has been brought up even more frequently as a potent factor in policy-making for union (conveniently disregarding the existence of a sizeable Christian population).[25] In other words, 'Many Jews have replaced Judaism with Zionism, whereas most Arabs still remain loyal to Islam'[26] and, one might add, 'in their approach to nationalism and Arabism'. One recent major exception in the Arab case has been the Ba'th movement, particularly the Syrian version, where Pan-Arabism bears a markedly secular character. Pan-Turkists, for their part, have generally adopted a secular stance, preferring — for both doctrinaire and tactical reasons — to keep religion out of their ideological formulations.

6. *Attitudes to other nationalisms.* An understanding of Pan-Turkism is helped by a consideration of its attitude towards other nationalisms. There was apparently more than a passing relationship among several

of the Pan ideologies and movements. Pan-Arabism may well have begun as a consequence of the forced Turkification introduced by the Pan-Turk leadership of the Ottoman Empire,[27] continuing as an important facet of opposition to European colonialism during the Inter-War period; Pan-Turkism itself was initially, to some extent, a reaction to Pan-Slavism and forced Russification. In other words, nearly every Pan ideology and movement has, in addition to its own commitments, a 'villain image' as well, to be negated and fought against. Pan-Islam, in its early stages, attacked imperialism; Pan-Africanism — colonialism; Pan-Slavism — the German menace; Pan-Arabism — the State of Israel. Pan-Turkism itself had started largely as a counter-movement to Pan-Slavism and later provided the Ottoman Empire with a weapon against its old enemy, Czarist Russia, just as Russians had earlier employed Pan-Slavism against the Ottoman Empire and Austria-Hungary.[28] Since the end of the First World War, the Soviet Union and Communism have assumed the role of Pan-Turk bogeys, along with (to a slightly smaller degree) Pan-Hellenism and its *Megale* concept. This attitude converged, of course, with sentiments for the Outside Turks, most of whom live under Communist-governed regimes.

7. *Irredentism* merits special consideration as a vital component of Pan-Turkism, and has undoubtedly been the main element differentiating it from Turkish nationalism. Conflict between the views espoused by a Pan nationalism — particularly of an irredentist category — and those of a local, patriotic type is often unavoidable. This has been true of Pan-Slavism too and strong sentiments of local nationalism constitute a major factor preventing both Pan-Arabism and Pan-Africanism in their respective ways from achieving union. Pan-Germanism has generally succeeded in preventing this conflict, as has Zionism; but then the latter has been as concerned with bringing all Jews to their ancestral home as with molding them into a new nation and state — thus largely obviating this conflict. In the Republic of Turkey, however, the clash of ideologies was virtually inevitable. Kemalism had not only displaced Pan-Turkism as the official state ideology; it also focused on the nation-state's narrower interests, renouncing the overriding concern for the Outside Turks, which had been — and remained — the core of Pan-Turkism. No less relevantly, Kemalism was polycentric in character, while Pan-Turkism was an essentially ethnocentric ideology and movement.[29] Under Mustafa Kemal's firm guidance, the new Turkey, although possessing its own brand of nationalism, sought to join other nations on an equal footing in the mainstream of world civilisation. Pan-Turkists, on the other hand, have consistently emphasised the special attributes of all Turks,

past and present, with a view to uniting them, demonstrating much less concern for modernisation or world civilisation and the place of Turkey in those elements. As a tactical move, Pan-Turkists explained repeatedly that there was no real conflict between these two approaches to nationalism; and that on the contrary their own policies were bound to serve the interests of the nation-state admirably. The Kemalists were not convinced and remained wary of the Pan-Turkists and their activities. From 1923 to 1950, the Kemalists alone governed the state, bearing down on the Pan-Turkists with particular firmness in 1944.[30]

Once again, the principal different dimension was the irredentism adopted and preached by Pan-Turkists. This was less pronounced in the earlier stages, when Pan-Turkism still largely retained the character of a diaspora nationalism, fostered among politically aware minorities abroad.[31] Later, however, Pan-Turk ideology, as it evolved in the late Ottoman Empire and then in the Republic of Turkey, increasingly assumed an irredentist character, as manifested in the writings of Atsız, Sançar, Türkkan and others during the 1930s and then in Pan-Turkist activities from the 1940s on. At first, the irredentist element was only implicit, displaying mere sympathy and concern. As Pan-Turk ideology developed, however, it became ever more explicitly irredentist, first indicating the need for protecting the Turkic groups abroad, then seeking to assist in their liberation, and in their union — first among themselves and afterwards with Turkey. Avowedly or not, this union was also to include the territories they inhabited. Pan-Turkists frequently spoke and wrote of a 'Great Turkey', stretching from the Mediterranean nearly to the Pacific — a powerful and affluent state, with its ancient glories restored and old customs revived. Maximalism has always been one of the hallmarks of irredentist Pan movements. Thus the Pan-Slav vision, as expressed by the poet Tyuchyev, was to extend the Russian realm from the Neva to the Nile, the Elbe to Cathay, the Volga to the Euphrates, and the Danube to the Ganges.[32] The extreme Pan-Turkists held that Turkey's frontiers should reach all Turk habitations.[33] In any event, the contiguity with Turkey's own borders of territories desired by Pan-Turkists lent some additional credence to Pan-Turk propaganda which, combined with the historical and other arguments adduced and the call for redress of an injustice and rectification of a situation unbearable to national pride, supplied an aura of messianism to Pan-Turk preaching.[34]

Some Pan ideologies and movements may not be irredentist at all — as, for example, Pan-Africanism. Others may be only partly so, such as the Ba'th movement in Syria and Irak, or the Revisionist

Party (later, *Herut*) in Israel. Pan-Turkism, however, no less than
Bulgarian nationalism, represents an extreme case of political irredentism. An example of this was shown in the 1933 clashes between
Pan-Turkist groups and Bulgarian authorities in Bulgarian Thrace.[35]
Although not specifically preaching violence, Pan-Turk irredentism
has generally been careful not to abjure it.[36] Since the 1930s,
moreover, Pan-Turkists have more than once hinted that the use of
force ought not to be discounted for the liberation of Outside Turks
and territories. Thus, even if irredentism has not always been equally
evident and intense on both sides of the border,[37] it has usually had
an impact on Pan-Turkist thought and deed. In other words, although
Pan-Turk ideology has evolved over the years and become increasingly politicised, it has remained throughout a cultural, racial (although not always necessarily racist), political and territorial type of
Pan nationalism, marked by strong irredentism.

8. *Composition and organisation*. The socio-economic character of
Pan-Turkism is very difficult to ascertain with any degree of accuracy.
Empirical research has not been carried out in this area so far and
would be impossible to accomplish nowadays. Spokesmen of Pan-
Turkist organisations are either unaware of the movement's socio-
economic nature or loath to discuss it in any detail, offering the stock
reply, 'It is supported by all classes.' However, the impression created
in examining what Pan-Turkists have written, said and done is that
it has consistently been a small, elitist movement, led by intellectuals
and supported by students and some middle-class townspeople —
indeed rather typical of all Pan movements. Its size has been modest,
probably at most times several hundred to a few thousand members,
except during the First World War and then in the 1970s, when it
may have increased somewhat and diversified its socio-economic
representation to some extent. But then this has been the case for
most Pan movements, with the exception of the Pan-German League,
which reached its peak in 1901, during the Boer War, with 21,924
members,[38] and the World Zionist Organization. Both these organisations, however, were nationalist as well as Pan movements; the
former, in fact, had more of an economic colonialist outlook than a
Pan-German one.[39]

Like most other Pan movements (the Pan-German League excepted), Pan-Turkism was plagued by an ineffective organisation and
bickering among the various groups; arguments were not motivated
by difference of approach as to final goals so much as by personal
rivalries and varying preferences concerning strategy and tactics.
Furthermore, due to their special character and small number, Pan-
Turkists (just like other Pan movements) utilised mostly written

propaganda — i.e. pamphlets and a good many journals;[40] the latter were however ephemeral and (with few exceptions) lasted for only a few weeks or at most several months at a time. Published material was supplemented by cultural and artistic gatherings, featuring lectures, music and performances. Neither these nor the congresses convened and demonstrations organised (as in 1944) enabled Pan-Turkists to establish the significant mass movement to which they aspired.

9. *The course of Pan-Turkism.* Human affairs seldom move smoothly toward fulfilment. This is particularly true of Pan movements, especially irredentist ones. Overt aspirations for a change in frontiers — to be accomplished if necessary by military force — inevitably clash with the *status quo* which most states wish to maintain as a guarantee of continuing peace and their self-preservation within it. Hence one often notes a zig-zag in the fortunes of many, perhaps most Pan movements. Pan-Islam, active before the First World War, was latent during the inter-war period[41] (at that time the Muslim Brotherhood was more fundamentalist than Pan-Islamist) and obtained a new lease on life during the 1960s and 1970s. Russian Pan-Slavism was latent from about 1880 until it revived just before the First World War, and again became latent until renewed by Stalin in 1941 shortly after the German attack on the Soviet Union. Similarly, Pan-Turkism enjoyed an era of flourishing and great hopes from its inception to the end of the First World War, encouraged by the state leadership during the Young Turk rule. This was followed by a latent period in the Kemalist-led Republic until some time during the Second World War, which again fanned Pan-Turkist hopes everywhere. This resurgence reached its peak during the 1944 demonstrations and subsequent trials, then continued more moderately in seminars and other ideological and organisational efforts. Since 1965 Pan-Turkism has re-entered the mainstream of politics, having been adopted as an ideological component of the Republican Peasants and Nation Party, later renamed the Nationalist Action Party.

These zig-zags have been anything but fortuitous. Pan movements increase their activities visibly during a war — more particularly, a world war — as this provides a genuine opportunity (generally, the sole opportunity) for a possible change in political borders to suit irredentist hopes. Thus, for example it is not surprising that a small, strongly anti-Soviet Pan-Iranian Party was constituted at the end of the Second World War. Of course, much depends on obtaining the support of a victorious Great Power. The Zionist movement received significant British and subsequently international support for its in-gathering of exiles in a national home in Palestine under the terms of the Balfour Declaration of November 1917. The Arab League was formed, again with British support, towards the end of the Second World War. Pan-Turkism seemed to come nearest to actual achievement during both the world wars. However, during the First World War it was allied to a Great Power which was defeated; during the Second, the Turkish Government had no obvious commitment to Pan-Turkism and remained neutral, joining the victors too late for any spoils of war of the sort Pan-Turkists desired.

It is noteworthy that the zig-zag evolution of Pan-Turkism was paralleled by a see-saw relationship in Pan-Turkist activity between Turkey and the diaspora. At first, such activity was mostly evident in the latter, chiefly in Czarist Russia. Approximately from 1908, with the return of the Czar to absolutist rule, leading Pan-Turkists left Russia and moved to the Ottoman Empire, where Hamidian despotism had ended, displaced by what had initially appeared to be a more liberal government. The sympathy expressed by a part of the Young Turk leadership further encouraged Pan-Turkist activity in the Ottoman Empire, especially after some of them had joined influential circles within the Committee of Union and Progress. Conversely, during the first two decades of the Republic of Turkey, Pan-Turkism again displayed greater activity abroad — though not in the Soviet Union, of course, where it was very risky, but rather in Thrace and Cyprus.[42] Since the end of the Second World War, when an overwhelming majority of Outside Turks were living under various Communist regimes — which evidently banned Pan-Turkist activity — such activity has again demonstrated a definite resurgence in Turkey itself, where the multi-party period (since 1946) and the relative liberalisation of censorship (since 1961) have afforded Pan-Turkism new opportunities for relatively unhampered political activity.

Finally, an explanation should be offered for the failure of Pan-Turkism to achieve its goals, at least up till the time of writing. One wonders why, despite its cultural impact, it has registered no definite political success. A part of the answer lies, as has been suggested, in the movement's not having obtained any significant political support among governments and states. No Pan movement as such was successful unless, in the absence of Great Power support, it had at least obtained state commitments. The Italians set up an Italian kingdom largely thanks to the active leadership of King Victor Emmanuel of Sardinia; and it was Bismarck's Prussia that was instrumental in creating a union of German states. The success of these two ventures may well have kindled the hopes of others. Later, Japan's success with Pan-Asianism during the 1920s and 1930s was due to state intervention: but the support which this ideology obtained in Burma,

Indonesia and Indochina (and, to some extent, in Malaya and India[43]) during the Second World War proved ephemeral, disappearing completely after Japan's defeat in this war. The same was true of the Pan-German thrust of the Third Reich. On the other hand, the Pan-German League failed,[44] as did Pan-Slav circles, because of the absence of committed support by the German and Russian governments, respectively, over any length of time; the re-adoption of Pan-Slavism by the Soviet Union in 1941 was too short-lived to be effective. If Pan-Arabism and Pan-Africanism have made some progress, that has been entirely thanks to the respective states which agreed to meet and approve the desirability and feasibility of union. The second thoughts of certain Arab leaders, in the former case, have led an Arab commentator to consider Pan-Arabism to be approaching death.[45] In the case of Pan-Africanism, observers have opined that the force of particularism, clash of interests and diversity of language provide almost insurmountable obstacles to its progress.[46] Zionism seems to be an exception, but then, as has already been said, it is both a Pan movement and a local nationalist one; it may therefore have been nationalism which prevailed. Nationalism has a better chance of success than Pan movements in the political arena — as history has often demonstrated — thanks to its ability to generate stronger sentiments and deeper loyalties. Pan-Turkism has indeed not only failed to obtain state support, except during the First World War (when it did appear to be near achievement), but has also never had quite the same appeal, in the Republic of Turkey, as the nationalism sponsored by Mustafa Kemal. Additional causes for the failure of irredentist Pan-Turkism were its very limited support outside a small number of intellectuals (among whom leftist ideologies have also been competing); its inability to put across a programme which could easily be grasped by a partly illiterate population; and its almost total disregard for Turkey's socio-economic problems, currently considered by most Turks to be the major issues affecting their lives.[47] Pan-Turkism's situation has changed perceptibly, however, since the late 1980s.

NOTES

1. Such as *The idea of nationalism: a study in its origins and background*, 1961.
2. See his *Geschichte der nationalen Bewegung im Orient*, 1928. For the irredentist element in Middle Eastern nationalism, cf. J.M. Landau, 'Irredentism and minorities in the Middle East', *Immigrants and Minorities*, ix (3): Nov. 1990, pp. 242–8.

3. *State and Nation*, 1964.
4. *Nationalism*, 1960. Kedourie has also edited *Nationalism in Asia and Africa*, 1970, to which he contributed a very useful introduction.
5. Especially his *Theories of nationalism*, 1971, and his *Nationalism in the twentieth century*, 1979.
6. As defined by Hans Kohn, 'Pan-Movements', *Encyclopaedia of Social Sciences*, XI: 1933, p. 544.
7. Cf. Karl Haushofer, *Geopolitik der Pan-Ideen*, pp. 66 ff.
8. F. Kazemzadeh, 'Pan movements', *International Encyclopaedia of Social Sciences*, XI: 1968, p. 366.
9. Cf. Colin Legum, *Pan-Africanism: a short political guide*, 1962, pp. 22–3.
10. See Michel Laissy, *Du Panarabisme à la Ligue Arabe*, 1948.
11. See Shaukat Ali, *Pan-movements in the Third World: Pan-Arabism, Pan-Africanism, Pan-Islamism*, pp. 227 ff.
12. M.B. Petrovich, *The emergence of Russian Panslavism 1856–1870*, 1956; Hans Kohn, *Pan-Slavism its history and ideology*, 2nd edn, 1960.
13. Cf. Myron Weiner, op. cit.
14. See, among other works, David Vital, *The origins of Zionism*, 1975; and W.Z. Laqueur, *A history of Zionism*, 1972.
15. We have already discussed the Turanist movement in Hungary. See further examples in P.F. Sugar and I.J. Lederer (eds), *Nationalism in Eastern Europe*, 1969.
16. See chs 1–2, above.
17. R.G. Usher, *Pan-Germanism*, 1914.
18. Cf. C.C. Wang, 'The Pan-Asiatic doctrine of Japan', *Foreign Affairs*, XIII (1): Oct. 1934, pp. 59–67; and M. Krása, 'The idea of Pan-Asianism and the nationalist movement in India', *Archiv Orientální* (Prague), XL: 1972, pp. 238–60.
19. See above, ch. 1.
20. Ibid., ch. 2.
21. Cf. details in Dumont, in *Cahiers du Monde Russe et Soviétique*, XV (3–4): July–Dec. 1974, pp. 328–9.
22. See above, ch. 2.
23. Cf. ibid. and FO 882/15, V. Vivian's memorandum, dated 30 July 1917, in the files of the [British] Arab Bureau, Egypt.
24. Kohn, *Pan-Slavism its history and ideology*.
25. For some secular advocates of Pan-Arabism, see S.G. Haim (ed.), *Arab nationalism*, 2nd edn, 1964, introduction, pp. 27–30.
26. A.D. Smith, 'Nationalism and religion: the role of religious reform in the genesis of Arab and Jewish nationalism', *Archives de Sociologie des Religions*, XXXV: 1972, p. 28. See also Haim, op. cit. and A.H. Hourani, *Arab thought in the Liberal age, 1798–1939*, 1967.
27. For this stage of Pan-Arabism, see Shaukat Ali, pp. 34 ff.
28. How seriously the Ottoman rulers regarded Pan-Slav propaganda in their domains is attested to by the Ottoman Ambassador to Berlin, M.

Moukhtar Pacha, *La Turquie l'Allemagne et l'Europe depuis le traité de Berlin jusqu'à la guerre mondiale*, 1924, p. xv.
29. See A.D. Smith, *Theories of nationalism*, pp. 158 ff.
30. See above, ch. 4.
31. Cf. R.D. McLaurin (ed.), *The political role of minority groups in the Middle East*, 1979.
32. Petrovich, p. 241.
33. X. Jacob, in *L'Afrique et l'Asie Modernes*, 121: 1979, p. 35.
34. Similar arguments appear in other irredentist ideologies, see A.D. Smith, *Theories of nationalism*, p. 222. Cf. Akzin, pp. 168–9.
35. See above, ch. 3. For the Greek case, cf. Th.G. Tatsios, 'The Megali idea and the Greek-Turkish war of 1897: The impact of the Cretan problem on Greek irredentism, 1866–1897', unpublished Ph.D. thesis, Columbia University, New York, 1973.
36. Already noticed by Toynbee, as early as 1917, in his *Turkey: a past and a future*, p. 33.
37. See Chirol, in the *Quarterly Review*, CCXXIX: Apr. 1918, esp. pp. 508–9.
38. Others had less. See the dates and estimates in W.J. Argyle, 'Size and scale as factors in the development of nationalist movements', in A.D. Smith (ed.), *Nationalist movements*, 1976, pp. 31–53.
39. M.S. Wertheimer, *The Pan-German League, 1890–1914*, pp. 95 ff.
40. For a preliminary list see below, Select bibliography, 2; additional titles in Öner, pp. 46–7.
41. Cf. George Young, 'Pan-Islamism', *Encyclopaedia of Social Sciences*, s.v.
42. See above, ch. 3.
43. C.P. Fitzgerald, 'Pan-Asianism', in Guy Wint (ed.), *Asia: a handbook*, 1965, pp. 367–403.
44. Wertheimer, op. cit.
45. Fouad Ajami, 'The end of Pan-Arabism', *Foreign Affairs*, LVII (2): Winter 1978–9, pp. 355–73.
46. Legum, pp. 55–80; Immanuel Geiss, *Panafrikanismus: zur Geschichte der Dekolonisation*, 1968, pp. 9 ff; Vincent Bakpetu Thompson, *Africa and unity: the evolution of Pan-Africanism*, 1969, pp. 293–313.
47. See also J.M. Landau, 'The fortunes and misfortunes of Pan-Turkism', *Central Asian Survey*, VII (1): 1988, pp. 1–5.

7

FROM IRREDENTISM TO SOLIDARITY

As an irredentist phenomenon Pan-Turkism has failed to achieve its political goals;[1] but few, if any, irredentist movements have had greater success, for a variety of reasons discussed in earlier chapters. Like other Pan-ideologies, such as political Pan-Islam,[2] Pan-Turkism has recently been moving steadily away from its earlier aggressive stand, towards the more moderate objective of Pan-Turk rapprochement, aiming at greater solidarity and cooperation among the components of Turkish-Turkic populations. The changing circumstances of the 1980s and early 1990s have been consistently conducive to this trend.[3]

Many of the Turkic communities in the Soviet Union, China, the Balkans, Iran and Irak have been prevented, in varying degrees, from expressing their political views and hopes, making it difficult for outsiders to gauge their Pan-Turkic sentiments. A rare exception, in the Soviet Union, was an historical novel by Mamadali Mahmudov, an Uzbek writer, published in 1981. This author suggests that had Central Asian Turks been more united in the nineteenth century, they could have opposed the Russian conquerors.[4] In Turkey itself, where there are no such restrictions on publishing, individuals and small groups have continued to invoke irredentist solutions for the 'Outside Turks'. Their final objective was summed up in the reinvented slogan 'From the Adriatic to China' (or 'From the Adriatic to the Chinese wall'), used in the dwindling Pan-Turkist press and reaching other newspapers when feasible.[5] This is also the title of a typical collection of essays on the subject by Nezih Uzel, written between 1987 and 1992 and published in book form in 1993.[6]

This propaganda, however, has remained far from the centre of public debate. The large parties were not interested, while radical circles in the 1960s and 1970s concentrated most of their political arguments and activities on the three-sided conflict between the extreme left, chauvinist nationalism, and politically-involved Islam. The peripheral position of irredentist Pan-Turkism in Turkey itself during those two decades can be estimated in retrospect by the fact that the

194

third military intervention of September 1980 did not bring about the arrest and trial of any known Pan-Turkists, but only of leftists, radical nationalists and Muslim extremists. Alparslan Türkeş, the only politician conspicuous for his Pan-Turk attitudes, was charged with other offences, chiefly subversive activities. His Nationalist Action Party was banned, together with all other political parties[7] — another setback for Pan-Turkism.

While the feasibility of an irredentist change of borders became less persuasive to Turkish public opinion, this should not be taken to mean that the Turks, as a people, and their leaders were indifferent to what was going on among Turkish-Turkic populations in other countries. On the contrary, discrimination against such groups brought about waves of popular support in Turkey, usually in the shape of emotional outpourings, expressed by mass demonstrations. The most visible sign of this reaction was the national excitement which contributed to urging the military intervention of the Turkish government in Cyprus in 1974, in a situation which seemed to endanger the lives of the Turkish minority there. Even then, however, there was little if any irredentist demand in Turkey to annex the Cypriot Turks and their lands to Turkey; at all events, Turkish government circles never considered such an option seriously, if it was brought up at all. The Cypriot Turks, besides, never came out strongly for such a solution, but rather continued trying during the 1980s to enlist the support of both Turks and Muslims, worldwide, for their cause.[8] During the two decades that have passed since this intervention, Turkish public opinion has repeatedly identified with the Outside Turks in Cyprus and elsewhere, the best-known example being the wave of public protests in the late 1980s against the harsh treatment and subsequent expulsion of the local Turkish minority by Bulgaria.[9] In these matters, while most of the Turkish press was emotionally involved, the strongest reactions appeared in the Pan-Turkist periodicals that had survived over the years (chiefly those published by the émigrés to Turkey), as well as several new ones. An example of the latter is *Türk Dünyası Tarih Dergisi* (Journal of the History of the Turkish World), which has appeared monthly in Istanbul since 1986; it attacked both the Bulgarian and the Iraki persecution of their Turkish minorities and called for Turkey's intervention.[10] Otherwise, there seems to be little substance to the claims of Turkey's critics in the Balkans, who accuse it of 'Neo-Ottomanism', implying that it aims at setting up a Pan-Turk empire there.

However, the general political situation has been changing radically during the late 1980s and early 1990s, most obviously in the disintegration and then the dissolution of the Soviet bloc. This in itself did not visibly affect the Cyprus problem, for instance, and Turkish public opinion continued to identify closely with the Turkish community there. However, the situation of the Turks in Bulgaria improved, and they were allowed to participate, apparently unhindered, in the October 1991 elections there.[11] More far-reaching, of course, was the political and economic breakup of the Soviet Union, which revived and strengthened ethnic and cultural particularism, resulting in 1991 in the political independence of several of its components. Among these was a Turkic Muslim republic in the Caucasus, Azerbayjan; and five others in Central Asia — Kazakhstan, Uzbekistan, Kirghizstan, Turkmenistan and Tajikistan (the latter with a Turkic *minority*, albeit a substantial one). All six proclaimed their sovereignty between June and October 1990 and their independence between August and December 1991.[12]

In addition, there are smaller units, inhabited by little Turkic groups such as the Tatars on the Volga, with their own nationalist aspirations for statehood, or the Chechens and Ingush in the Caucasus, eager for autonomy,[13] or the Gagauz in Moldavia.[14] All their hopes of secession were met by the determined opposition of larger political units (e.g. Russia and the Ukraine in the case of the Volga Tatars,[15] and Moldavia in the case of its own minorities). This meant that the government of Turkey had to be cautious in expressing its Pan-Turk sympathies for these smaller groups, in order not to antagonise their host states. The six independent Muslim republics, however, were now free to determine the pattern of their relations with Turkey, while the smaller Turkic entities were attempting to do the same. Turkey itself, sensing a great historic opportunity, had to reassess its strategic thinking, so as to adapt to these new circumstances[16] while extending its own foreign policy options.[17] As one observer, Peri Pamir, phrased it, 'Central Asia currently constitutes the richest reservoir of opportunity from Turkey's viewpoint.'[18]

To enable us to make a better evaluation of these new relationships, we should briefly consider some data concerning each of these new republics, on the geopolitical, ethnic, economic, religious and linguistic levels.[19] The military factor, though of some importance, is still of limited relevance because all six republics have only small armies, equipped with weapons of restricted technological significance. (An exception is Kazakhstan, which was left with a nuclear arsenal following the breakup of the Soviet Union; however, at the time of writing it apparently lacks the full capacity to put it to efficient use.)[20] Moreover, all these republics are connected with Russia and with most of the former components of the Soviet Union in the Commonwealth of Independent States (CIS). The latter was set up on 8 December 1991 and the Central Asian republics and Azerbayjan joined in on 21 December 1991. In CIS meetings convened during 1992 the five Central Asian Muslim republics agreed to maintain merely symbolic military units of their own and to let Russia serve as a defence shield for them all. In this and some other respects, each of the six Muslim republics seems to be a state in the process of shaping a nation.

– *Azerbayjan* has a territory of 86,600 sq. km. and a population of 7,000,000, of whom 78 per cent are Azeris, 8 per cent Armenians, 8 per cent Russians and the other 6 per cent Tatars and Daghestanis. This republic is geographically closest to Turkey and the only one to have a common frontier with it, in the Nakhichevan autonomous province. It has, however, a considerably longer frontier with Iran, on the other side of which live another 8–10 million Azeris, a fact which has nourished a vocal irredentist movement aimed at shaping a united Azerbayjan. Since February 1988 the new state has been engaged in a protracted war with its neighbour, Armenia, which wishes to annex Nagorno Karabach, a mountainous enclave largely populated by Armenians. The state has extensive natural gas and oil reserves, exploited at its capital, Baku, a port on the Caspian Sea. Azerbayjan has close ties with Iran, since both belong to the Shiite branch of Islam, in addition to the ethnic affinity with Iran's Azeri minority; but also with Turkey, whose language Azeri closely resembles (more so than do the Turkic languages of Central Asia). Azerbayjan was the first of the new republics to adopt the Latin script. It is fiercely independent and strongly nationalist, with a Pan-Azeri tendency for unity with the Azeris in Iran, perhaps a Pan-Turk one as well. Indeed, Pan-Azerism seems to wish to use Pan-Turkism against Iran in order to achieve a union north and south of the Iranian border. All this is expressed in the 'Declaration on restoring the state independence of the Azerbaijan Republic', dated 30 August 1991. Further, of the six Muslim republics that joined the CIS, Azerbayjan was the only one to have reservations about doing so. Indeed, on 7 October 1992, its Parliament voted to leave the CIS, but it is not known whether this decision was fully implemented.[21]

– *Kazakhstan*, whose capital is Alma Ata, is the largest of the new Muslim republics. Covering a territory of 2.7 million sq. km., it has a population of less than 17 million, of whom only 40 per cent are Kazakhs, others being Russians (38 per cent), Germans (6 per cent), Ukrainians (5 per cent), Uzbeks and Tatars (each 2 per cent) and some smaller groups. Thus Kazakhstan is a republic of minorities, and the only one without a clear ethnic majority. Its longest border is with Russia, with which it maintains extensive economic ties, selling it sizeable amounts of its large cotton and coal production, as well as other materials. Culturally, the Kazakhs have a strong affinity with Turkey, in both religion (Sunni Islam) and language kinship. These considerations, as well as its varied ethnic composition, seem to dictate a cautious balancing act between Russia and Turkey. Its nuclear arsenal, however, enables Kazakhstan to negotiate with other states from a position of strength (with the United States, for instance, from which it is demanding economic and technological aid in exchange for non-proliferation, and indeed at a higher level in return for a possible undertaking to destroy this arsenal in due course). Although it naturally supports Pan-Turk cooperation, the attitude of its leadership is somewhat ambivalent. Kazakhstan accepts Turkey's assistance, but hankers more for Western economic investment. Further, it seems inclined to promote a policy of Pan-Kazakhism — encouraging Kazakhs outside Kazakhstan to return to it so as to alter the demographic balance — rather than of Pan-Turkism.[22]

– *Uzbekistan*, with an area of 447,000 sq. km., is the most populous of the Muslim republics, counting 20,300,000 inhabitants. These are heterogeneous groupings: Uzbeks (71 per cent), Russians (8 per cent), Tajiks (5 per cent officially, but probably more), and others. The capital, Tashkent, is an ancient city, rebuilt after the 1966 earthquake, where about 900,000 Uzbeks and 700,000 Russians live. The Uzbeks were the third largest ethnic group in the Soviet Union (after the Russians and the Ukrainians), with about 16,700,000, of whom some 85 per cent live in Uzbekistan itself, and others in Tajikistan, Kirghizstan, Afghanistan and China. While the economy is largely based on cotton growing, Uzbekistan produces large amounts of natural gas. In November 1991 the government seized control of the republic's goldmining enterprises. At odds with the other ethnic groups (as violent riots in the Ferghana Valley have demonstrated), the Uzbeks, more than other groups in Central Asia, gravitate towards Turkey, with which they feel kinship on religious (Sunni) and linguistic grounds. Moreover, an informal but lively movement in Uzbekistan, *Birlik* (union or unity), favours the future creation of a Turkestani federation or confederation of the five Central Asian states, based on economic cooperation. Some local observers surmise that this union could also curb the spread of Islamic fundamentalism, which causes apprehension among certain Uzbek élites.[23]

– *Kirghizstan* has a population of 4,250,000 in a territory of about 200,000 sq. km., among whom the Kirghiz form a majority of 52 per cent, followed by the Russians (21.5 per cent) and Uzbeks (13 per cent); smaller groups comprise Ukrainians, Germans and others. The capital, Bishkek, is inhabited by a majority of Russians and a minority of Kirghiz. Hundreds of thousands of Kirghiz live in Uzbekistan, Tajikistan, China and Afghanistan. Although more democratically inclined than other Central Asian republics (it is the only one whose President, Askar Akayev, was not a member of the Soviet Communist bureaucracy), inter-ethnic tension has several times resulted in violent clashes. Such rioting occurred in 1990 between Kirghiz and Uzbeks, and several hundred people were killed. Some ethnic minority members consequently emigrated, so that the population percentages noted above are liable to change rapidly. Kirghizstan is the poorest of the six Muslim republics, with an economy based on agriculture, which is difficult to sustain in this rugged mountainous country. As in the other Central Asian republics, the commonality with Turkey is based on religion (Sunni) and linguistic kinship. A language law passed in 1989 symbolically gave preference to Kirghiz (over Russian) names for towns, squares and shops, and Kirghiz-language periodicals increased in number and the size of their print-runs. This was more than a sign of patriotism, and had Pan-Turk implications too.[24]

– *Turkmenistan*, with an area of 488,000 sq. km., is second in size only to Kazakhstan among the Muslim republics. But it is sparsely populated, with about 3,600,000 inhabitants, of whom the Turkmens are in the majority (almost 72 per cent), followed by the Russians (9.5 per cent), the Uzbeks (9 per cent), and several smaller groups. The capital, Ashkabad, has only 400,000 inhabitants. A long frontier with Iran has conditioned Turkmenistan's relations with it — chiefly the economic ones. Another factor is that about 1 million Turkmens live in Iran and another million or more in Afghanistan, close to Turkmenistan's borders. While 80 per cent of its surface is covered by desert, it grows cotton and has some mineral resources, mostly natural gas, sulphur and oil. Without renouncing its economic cooperation with Iran, Turkmenistan is interested in close ties with Turkey as well, based on a common religion (Sunni) and linguistic affinity. Recent intensive debate publicly supports Turkmenisation in publishing and higher education, at the expense of Russian. That all this could affect Pan-Turkism may be learned from the establishment in late 1990 of the *Vatan* (Fatherland) Association, to focus on the Turkmens in Iran and Afghanistan; while in May 1991 a first international Conference of World Turkmens met in Ashkabad, attended by people from Afghanistan, Iran, Turkey, Syria, Britain and Germany. One of the movement's main objectives has been to promote ties with Turkmens living abroad, in a spirit of Pan-Turkmenism rather than Pan-Turkism.[25]

– *Tajikistan* is the smallest of the Muslim republics, comprising 143,000 sq. km. Its population of around 5,200,000 is divided among

Tajiks (62 per cent), Uzbeks (23.5 per cent), Russians (8 per cent) and others. Its recognition by the Soviets in the 1920s as a republic with Iranian cultural affinities, distinct from Uzbekistan, was primarily intended to break up Pan-Turk hopes for a united Turkestan.[26] Continuing tension between Tajiks and Uzbeks exploded in 1992 into a civil war, which claimed about 20,000 victims. Tajikistan has long borders with Afghanistan and China, but is separated from Iran, with which it has a strong cultural affinity, by Uzbekistan and Turkmenistan. Its capital is Dushanbe. The economy is mostly agricultural — food products and cotton — but there is also some mining (of uranium *inter alia*). Part of its commerce is with Iran, whose language has a close relation to Tajik. Indeed, this is the only Central Asian republic in which the minority language, Uzbek, rather than the majority one, Tajik, is close to Turkish. Yet another affinity to Turkey is in religion, Sunni, although there are several small Shiite pockets. However, since Turkey is known as a secular state, Iran seems to carry considerable weight in its religious impact on Tajikistan, and the public display of photographs of Khomeyni is reported. Tajik élites may turn to Iran and the Persian world not only for economic reasons, but probably out of fear of being submerged by the Turkic environment in Muslim Central Asia.[27]

Except for their Islamic background,[28] the shared experience of seventy-four years of Communism, and near-universal literacy in Russian, the six Muslim republics differ from one another in several ways, such as their economic situation and the levels of modernisation they have achieved.[29] They are all ethnically and linguistically mixed, a result of the Soviet political engineering of borders and cultures, which was intended to prevent or at least delay the development of monolithic popularly-supported local nationalism, as well as Pan-Turkism. Not unexpectedly, Soviet nationality policies[30] not only hindered the establishment of a unified Pan-Turk movement, but also brought about several persistent conflicts relating to sovereignty, territoriality and the minorities. Of these, the last is at present the most serious, resulting in strong ethnocentricity and ethnophobia, the latter increasingly directed at the numerous Russian and Ukrainian inhabitants (and in some instances at Germans),[31] but also at other local minority groups. This is an ethnic time-bomb.[32] With the disappearance of the Pax Sovietica, latent ethnic, nationalist and religious conflicts have been coming to the surface with growing violence in the six Muslim republics.

Although many and perhaps most people in these republics abhor Marxism and what it stands for, Marxist ways of thinking and Soviet ways of governing have largely persisted. The republics were governed in an authoritarian style by a centralised party, the bureaucracy and the KGB. Except for Kirghizstan's President Akayev, most of the political leaders in the early 1990s came to power as Communists championing socialist internationalism and they have found it somewhat difficult wholeheartedly to foster ethno-nationalism after having condemned it only a few years ago. Economically, the republics were underdeveloped, treated as Russia's own kind of 'Third World' destined to produce merely what might be needed for the larger Soviet Union.[33] In practice, this meant chiefly agriculture, in particular cotton monoculture: the Central Asian Muslim republics, just before the disintegration of the Soviet Union, were responsible for over 90 per cent of Soviet cotton production but only 7 per cent of cotton processing, reflecting the lack of industrialisation in these republics and their subsequent difficulties in achieving economic independence.

As has already been noted, all six Muslim republics proclaimed their sovereignty in 1990 and their independence in 1991. It must have been evident to all of them that they could not base their plans for development on Russia alone, both in view of past experience and because of the acute problems, political and economic, with which Russia itself was struggling. However, they maintained some of their economic connections with Russia, the natural market for many of their products, and with which five of them (Azerbayjan excepted) signed an economic agreement on 18 October 1991. Moreover, many higher officials in all six Muslim republics had been Communist bureaucrats in the Soviet Union and were still strongly attached to Russia and its methods of governing. Other politicians in these republics, however, sought models elsewhere for their political regimes, economic development and technological advance, all within a market economy. Since the West, probably regarded as an ideal model by some of these leaders, was so remote, they turned their attention towards Turkey or Iran, or both, for help in their search for a new identity — national or religious[34] — and in their efforts to solve pressing problems.

It seems that the choice between these two states depended on a variety of factors.[35] First, *proximity*: Turkey has a tiny frontier with Azerbayjan alone, while Iran borders on Azerbayjan, Uzbekistan and Turkmenistan; this, as already mentioned, has encouraged Turkmenistan to turn partly to Iran. Secondly, there are *cultural tradition* and *language affinity*, accounting for Tajikistan's special relationship with Iran, and for the five other republics' increasing connections with Turkey. Thirdly, *political considerations* possibly prompted some leaders in Azerbayjan to forge ties with Turkey, since they correctly perceived Iran as strongly opposing on all-Azeri union. Fourthly, there are *religious inclinations*: Azerbayjan is 70 per cent Shiite (like Iran), while the five Central Asian republics are preponderantly Sunni (like Turkey). This implies a choice between Iran's fundamentalist Islam (although not all shades of Islam in the new republics are attracted to the Iranian model) and Turkey's secular posture (which nonetheless has freely permitted religious practice). Fifthly, there is the need for substantial *economic investment*, which is less available from Turkey than from Iran, although Iran, too is financially hampered by its immense outlay on advanced weaponry. Sixthly, when it came to building an economic and political bridge to *the West* — for those who wished it — Turkey was naturally better suited; indeed, Turkey attempted (but failed) to persuade the United States to grant 'Marshall Aid' to the six republics.[36] While the political regimes in the six Muslim republics were still in part authoritarian and centralised, Turkey could well serve as a model for a more pluralistic, democratic society and polity.[37] Lastly, the activity of *the diasporas* which each of these peoples — as well as several others, like the Tatars — have in Turkey and (to a lesser extent, except in the case of Azerbayjan and Tajikistan) in Iran is important. These diasporas act as natural bridges, striving to create closer ties between their home and their host country. They were throughout — and have remained — the most ardent protagonists of Pan-Turk rapprochement and solidarity.[38]

Much depends, of course, on those in power in each of the Muslim republics — Communists, Islamists or nationalists. The *Glasnost*' or openness prevailing in speech and writing since 1987 enables one to understand better the unresolved 'nationalities problem' and the over-riding factor of nationalism,[39] both in late Czarist Russia and during the Soviet era.[40] In the newly independent Muslim republics, with their heterogeneous make-up, it was usually the nationalist élites which opted for a rapprochement in a Pan-Turk spirit of cooperation with Turkey, which in its turn responded in kind, stretching its limited means to the maximum. We shall attempt to describe and analyse the Pan-Turk trend towards increased solidarity, chiefly in the first two years of the Muslim republics independence, that is from late 1991 to late 1993. In so doing, we shall look at a number of relevant facts and attempt to make some sense of their juxtaposition.

Turkey's own reasons for cooperation and solidarity with the Turkic populations in the Muslim republics are obvious. Turkey's own modernising élites, which consider themselves European, have felt frustrated and humiliated at the reluctance of the European Community (EC) to accept Turkey as a full and equal member. While ceaselessly continuing their efforts to obtain full EC membership, they have nevertheless been looking around for options to integrate Turkey into other sub-systems as well. This seemed particularly necessary after the break-up of the Soviet Union, when it appeared that its role in NATO had become less crucial than before. True, this regression in Turkey's standing was corrected when President Turgut Özal permitted the United States to use its airfields in the 1991 Gulf War, but this move also incurred Iraki hostility. Hence Turkey's increased interest in lessening its dependence on the Arab world by getting oil as well as natural gas from the new Muslim republics, for its own use and for transit to Europe.

Thus, while pursuing its efforts at closer collaboration with the United States and Western Europe, the Turkish government also continued to look for other options nearer home. An Islamic policy was never a real alternative for secular Turkey, wary of fundamentalist Islam's political advance in Iran, Afghanistan, Pakistan and several Arab states; nonetheless, cooperation with single Islamic states was pursued with considerable determination. In the post-Soviet period, the Turkish government seems to have adopted two mutually complementary policies of rapprochement and cooperation, one with several of its neighbouring states and the other with the six new Muslim republics.[41]

It was Turkey which, in the main, planned and carried through the project for the Black Sea Economic Cooperation Region (BSECR). Apparently first proposed by Şükrü Elekdağ, Turkish Ambassador to the United States, early in 1990, it was adopted by President Özal at the end of that year. The details were worked out at joint meetings by the interested parties in Ankara, Bucharest, Sofia and Moscow, between December 1990 and July 1991. With the break-up of the Soviet Union, the number of contracting parties increased, ultimately to include Turkey, Romania, Bulgaria, Greece and Albania, as well as Azerbayjan, Armenia, Georgia, Moldavia, Russia and the Ukraine. This was more than an agreement among Black Sea states, for it encompassed the Balkans and the Caucasus as well. On 25 June 1992 the BSECR Agreement was signed in Istanbul by all eleven parties. It declared their support for the values of democracy, individual rights and basic freedoms, as well as prosperity via economic freedom, social justice and security; it also contained an awareness of environmental issues and of their significance for economic development. In the main, however, this Agreement emphasised economic cooperation — in industry, science, technology, transport, communications, energy, agriculture, medicine and pharmaceutics.[42]

The BSECR Agreement officially aimed at a future unimpeded

flow of people and merchandise, resembling the European Economic Community and complementing rather than competing with it. As Turkey perceived it, it was intended to improve its overall economic and political relations with the neighbouring states, including those with which it had longstanding conflicts, such as Greece and Bulgaria. If one of the goals was to demonstrate an interest in Turkish-Turkic groups abroad, this would have been only peripheral; at all events, nothing specific is spelled out in the matter (although the reference to individual rights and basic liberties probably had this issue in view). However, it seems as if the government of Turkey, aware of widespread popular sympathy for the Turkish minorities in Greece and Bulgaria, was attempting to insure itself against becoming involved unnecessarily in protecting them by force of arms.[43]

A much clearer case is that of Turkey's relations with all six Muslim republics, where all parties have been very keen on fostering mutual ties. This applies much less to bilateral connections among the republics themselves, where old and new rivalries seem to condition interstate relations. After all, the centralised Soviet system had oriented the republics towards Moscow and away from each other.

We now turn to Turkey's political, economic and cultural relations with all six Muslim republics in recent years, on both the multilateral and the bilateral levels. On the former, one of the most visible results is Turkey's decisively embarking, from January 1992 onwards, on a campaign to promote the republics' adherence to the United Nations; the European Security and Cooperation Conference; the Economic Cooperation Organization (ECO), which Turkey, Iran and Pakistan revived in 1985; the BSECR; the Organization of the Islamic Conference;[44] and NATO.[45] Except for the last, Turkey has succeeded remarkably well.

Independence brought the six Muslim republics a plethora of massive problems, as well as new perspectives, with most of which they were inadequately equipped to deal. These included deciding on their respective political regimes; launching themselves on a market economy; exploiting their largely untapped natural wealth; establishing ties with other states; reorganising society and education; and acquiring advanced technologies — to mention but a few. These more or less common goals should not conceal the fact that each of these republics is itself hardly homogeneous and that, when seen as a whole their heterogeneity increases. These factors have reinforced their difficulties in cooperating with each other. Azerbayjan is somewhat remote, but in Central Asia the potentially rich Kazakhstan and Uzbekistan are reluctant to share their wealth with the poorer republics, while the latter fear the possible hegemony of the former. Nonetheless, the presidents of all five Central Asian republics started negotiations for an economic union as early as August 1990. However, when the five, meeting at Bishkek in April 1992, were close to approving a single investment bank adopting a joint policy and coordinating plans for economic development, a hitch occurred: not only did Tajikistan's President, Rahman Nabiyev, refuse to attend (sending his deputy instead with observer status only),[46] but President Saparmurad Niyazov of Turkmenistan refused to sign the protocol, thus postponing the advent of economic Pan-Turkism in the region for some time. A month later, at the ECO meeting in Ashkabad, attended by the Prime Ministers of Turkey, Iran, Pakistan and the five Central Asian Muslim republics, to discuss multilateral economic cooperation, Kazakhstan's President, Nursultan Nazarbayev, claimed observer status and refrained from signing;[47] perhaps he was hoping for a better deal at the CIS meeting in Tashkent a few days later.[48]

Destabilisation of Central Asia, leading to a power vacuum,[49] has been a definite possibility, causing anxiety to Russia (10 million Russians live in the five Central Asian Muslim republics alone), to China (which has a large Muslim Turkic population of its own to the east of this area, which shows signs of Pan-Turk identity), and to Pakistan (which is interested in promoting Pan-Islamic political solidarity). Further, Iran has been exporting its own brand of Shiite Islamic fundamentalism to this area (although most Muslims in Central Asia are Sunni), combined with economic inducements, such as projects to lay pipelines and railway tracks from Turkmenistan to Iran.[50] In February 1993 Iran's Foreign Minister, Ali Akbar Velayati, toured the Central Asian capitals. These Iranian moves brought about an increasing Saudi Arabian counter-involvement, involving substantial investment by Saudi Arabian companies in Kazakhstan and Uzbekistan, construction of mosques, the granting of scholarships, and the sending of large quantities of Korans and educational materials (Sunni, as part of the campaign to undercut its Shiite competitor, Iran).[51] In February 1992, only a few weeks after Uzbekistan, Turkmenistan and Tajikistan had become independent, the Foreign Minister of Saudi Arabia visited them, discussing the possible establishment of an Organisation for Economic Cooperation.[52] The involvement of Pakistan and Afghanistan (the latter mainly in the planning stage) has seemed to be minor by comparison with that of Turkey, Iran and Saudi Arabia.[53]

However, it is Turkey's activities in the new Muslim republics, based on and promoting Pan-Turk elements, with which we are chiefly concerned here. Naturally, some of these were undertaken in response to the activities of other states in the region, such as Iran.

On the symbolic level, the Presidents of the six Muslim republics were invited to Ankara and received there with great honour; President Özal and Prime Minister Süleyman Demirel returned the visits, and were greeted with equal pomp. All sides repeatedly referred to Pan-Turkism as a common bond among the 'Brethren'. That this was no more than a ritual exercise can be deduced from numerous plans, projecting the image of a 'Turkish-Turkic Common Market' with the participation of Turkish government agencies and investment by Turkish private enterprises (Tajikistan, however, has accepted hardly any Turkish offers to date, perhaps because of economic inducements from Iran; this also reflects the non-Turkic character of the ruling Tajik élite). One of the most important suggestions made by Turkey was the setting up of a development bank for Muslim Central Asia, based in Ankara. Since the investments by Turkish private business in the new republics, though substantial, were insufficient for their needs, the Turkish government made considerable efforts to persuade German businessmen to share in these investments, a proposition which Chancellor Helmut Kohl was reported to have supported.[54]

Turkey's grand policy has been to strive to institutionalise its relations with the 'Turkic Brethren', both in conjunction with other states and on a Turkish-Turkic basis. Its greater success in the former approach reflects the attitudes of some of the Muslim republics. In addition to the invitation to Azerbayjan to join the BSECR Agreement, in February 1992 Turkey successfully proposed to coopt all six into the ECO; in the same month it convinced the Organisation for European Security and Cooperation to offer them membership;[55] and lobbied for their acceptance by the United Nations (they were officially voted in on 2 March 1992).

Countering these successful moves, however, unexpected difficulties arose when Turkey attempted to set up a joint forum consisting of itself and five of the Muslim republics (Tajikistan was not included). On 30–31 October 1992, a summit meeting of the Presidents of the five Turkic republics and of Turkey convened in Ankara, following the invitation extended by Prime Minister Süleyman Demirel when he visited the republics in April–May of the same year. A wide range of topics concerning the Outside Turks were sympathetically discussed, but it was not a simple matter to arrive at common decisions. Despite the cordiality of the gathering, or possibly because of it, Nazarbayev and Niyazov, Presidents of Kazakhstan and Turkmenistan respectively, suspected Turkey (not unreasonably, perhaps) of planning to establish a common market with the Turkic republics. The four Presidents of the Central Asian republics had met the Russian ambassador earlier in Ankara, and he apparently warned them of this possibility. Thus Nazarbayev, with some support from Niyazov, declared that cooperation could not be based solely on shared religion or ethnicity, and pointed out the importance of the economic ties with Russia that already existed as well as the presence of substantial Russian populations in each of the Turkic republics. Here one sees a repetition of earlier Russian — and Soviet — opposition to political Pan-Turkism, this time expressed mostly in economic terms. Turkey was disappointed in its hopes of quickly obtaining deliveries of oil and natural gas, which would cross Turkey to the Mediterranean, from Kazakhstan and Turkmenistan (both of which were simultaneously negotiating such deliveries with Iran, to reach the Gulf). Perhaps the main significance of the forum remained in the fact that it was held at all, and in the decision to set up committees to deal with further technical and cultural matters before the next annual meeting of the forum was due to take place in Baku.

One gets the impression that the government of Turkey, which was at the same time busily establishing relations on various levels with each of the new Muslim republics, perceived that this latter approach was conducive to better and speedier results than the attempts to foster all-round Pan-Turk projects. After all, despite declarations of brotherly sentiments among the Muslim republics, frequent conflict between them was in evidence, due to economic competition and frontier misunderstandings — such as there was between Uzbekistan and Kirghizstan.[56] Since 1992, then, more effort has been invested in bilateral contacts, while high-level negotiations for common moves continue. Not coincidentally, this runs parallel to Russia's relations with the other members of the Commonwealth of Independent States (CIS). Since the CIS rules of procedure allow every member to adhere only to the decisions it accepts, Russia too has perceived advantage in circumventing lengthy multilateral negotiations by signing many bilateral treaties within the CIS.[57] Turkey seems to have followed this lead. While in the early days of the CIS Turkey's ambassador to Moscow, Vulkan Vural, served as a sort of 'super ambassador' to the other CIS capitals as well,[58] quite soon special envoys, diplomatic or otherwise, were appointed to the Muslim republics directly. In the economic domain the ECO states, meeting at Quetta (Pakistan) in February 1993, resolved to encourage bilateral relations between the member states; Turkey, Iran and Pakistan agreed to start matters off by setting up an ECO fund of $300,000 for that purpose. Further progress was made at the second, expanded ECO summit in Istanbul on 6–7 July 1993. This was attended by the

Presidents or Prime Ministers of Turkey, Iran, Pakistan, Azerbayjan, Kazakhstan, Uzbekistan, Kirghizstan, Turkmenistan, Tajikistan and Afghanistan.

Bilateral relations between Turkey and the new republics may be divided into several main domains which seem to have received the greatest attention. These are economics, administration, communications, culture and education. For these purposes, in January 1992 the Turkish government allocated an initial sum for that year of 400,000 million Turkish liras[59] (about $80 million at the time).

In economics a heavy legacy of dependence carried over from the Soviet period weighs on the CIS states. The Soviet policies of industrial integration (e.g. in the supply of energy) and centralised financial control created serious obstacles to the transition to a market economy. All six Muslim republics are dependent on one another as well as on Russia, none having reached complete control of its own economy;[60] at the time of writing they are only starting to consider seriously the adoption of a market economy, implying political decentralisation along with economic depoliticisation and debureaucratisation — measures which are not easily acceptable by the current Communist-trained leadership and the rather narrow élites which may have a say in these matters. Moreover, these republics badly need foreign investment and industrial development. Since little capital is forthcoming from either the West or the East, several of them have taken Turkey as their economic model,[61] and found it ready and willing to play the game. Aware that Russia, Iran and others were rushing in with various inducements, Turkey's assistance was at first concerned with immediate needs, such as providing Turkish, United States and European food and medicines to the republics (in Turkish and American planes). This has been going on since February 1992.[62] Turkey then also turned to medium-range and long-range projects, such as flights by Turkish Airlines, with plans for setting up local air companies, and the construction of an oil pipeline running through Turkey, which would get the transit fees (an agreement with Azerbayjan was signed in March 1993).

Private businessmen in Turkey, while acknowledging the economic potential of the Muslim republics, were understandably wary about risking their investments there. The authorities had to intervene and encourage private investment, protected by the Exim Bank's guarantees. This encouragement first took the form of sending about seventy businessmen (together with three cabinet ministers) on a mission to Alma Ata on 12 April 1992; later, President Turgut Özal invited about 100 Turkish businessmen to accompany him on an official visit to the Muslim republics. Among the projects negotiated (and apparently carried through) were a leather factory in Tashkent, a four-star hotel in Samarkand, a sugar factory in both Uzbekistan and Tajikistan,[63] telephones and computers.[64] Other deals followed. According to the statistics of the Turkish Foreign Ministry, about sixty Turkish banks and businesses bought into factories or set up offices in the Muslim republics during 1992, and another 150 have established trading links.[65] As a result of government and private initiative, Turkey's import and export trade grew by the month, chiefly with Azerbayjan but also with Kazakhstan, Uzbekistan and Turkmenistan, though less so with distant Kirghizstan and Tajikis-tan.[66] To give one example, the Turkish Engineering Company signed a protocol on 13 July 1992 undertaking to provide Kazakhstan with $11,700 million worth of energy services, operate four oil fields there, rehabilitate a fifth and explore a sixth, and build a power plant in Aktyubinsk (in the country's northwest) as well as a pipeline to bring in Kazakh natural gas to fuel it.

In administration, the new republics were badly in need of trained people, particularly in the upper echelons of the bureaucracy, which had formerly been managed directly from Moscow or by local Rus-sians. Turkey's basic approach was to assist them in building state institutions and encourage non-governmental bodies to take part in these efforts.[67] As a more experienced state, it offered civil service training, including diplomacy (at the Ankara Faculty of Political Science and other universities); army command (either in Turkey or on the spot — the latter method was applied in Azerbayjan[68] and planned for Uzbekistan[69]); health services (on 15 July 1992, a con-gress of the health ministers of all six republics and Turkey convened to this effect[70]); agricultural expertise (in the same month, Uzbekistan sent its specialists to Adana, in southern Turkey, to study improved methods of growing cotton[71]); statistics and technical skills (in an agreement with Azerbayjan, signed in November 1992).

In communications all six Muslim republics needed immediate help, because soon after they had proclaimed their independence Moscow cut off (in January 1992) all their telephone connections with the outside world. Foreseeing this, Turkey's Bureau of Posts, Telephones and Telegraphs had already installed the necessary 'Central Office' in Azerbayjan and had set out to help the other Muslim republics, starting with Kazakhstan in telecommunication technology and providing the personnel to operate it.[72] In early December 1992 Turkey inaugurated its network with the five Central Asian republics, first supplying a public exchange with a 2,500-line capacity to each of the five, linked by satellite to the Turkish gateway exchange and the rest of the world. This involved a Turkish donation of $25 million.[73] It was part of the communications infrastructure which Turkey is planning to install in all six republics, focusing on telephones, computers and television, and prompting private communications companies to use bank credits and invest in electronics and telecommunications.[74] Protocols in communications were signed between Turkey and the new republics in July 1993.

While several Turkish newspapers have set up offices in the Muslim republics, Turkey's television service seems to have had the most immediate impact. Since April 1992 more than 50 million people in all six republics can receive (without the help of cables, for the Turks rapidly installed relay stations in each republic) Turkish-language television broadcasts from Ankara, eleven hours each day and fourteen on Saturday and Sunday. These include newscasts four times a day, as well as documentaries, general information, music and children's programmes. All these are in Turkish, and about a third are in an easily understood simplified language. Subtitles are meant to encourage and facilitate the use of the Latin alphabet (as opposed to the Russian Cyrillic alphabet) in local languages as well.[75]

Spreading culture and education is less expensive than economic investment — an important consideration, although the difficulties are obvious. For many years Soviet policymakers aimed at reorganising cultural and educational institutions — no less than political, social, and economic ones — in a way that would facilitate the development of the Soviet man and woman into competent, internationalist-minded and loyal Communists. This was one of the reasons for the migration of skilled Russians into other republics. However, for the Muslim parts of the Soviet Union, the result was that the local population had less than sufficient opportunity to play a part in the professional classes. To have a chance to join the élites knowledge of Russian was imperative, often at the expense of the national language and culture. The disincentives imposed on those were intended to discourage nationalist (as well as Pan-Turkish or Pan-Iranian) sentiments, which were perceived as divisive and thus dangerous. Russian, on the other hand, was seen as essential for creating a homogeneous Soviet society, and its use was strongly encouraged at school and in the bureaucracy. Dissociation from the national culture — and, Soviet policymakers hoped, from earlier tradition and religion — was reinforced by replacing the Arabic script with the Latin, then the Cyrillic, which effectively cut off the entire younger generation from whatever works of literature, history etc. that might still have been available. Of course, this dependence on Russian could not immediately disappear when the Muslim republics became independent,[76] but each of them declared the language of its

·majority its official language and worked to promote it, in varying degrees, at the expense of Russian.

Thus Turkey was faced by a complex situation in attempting to export its cultural, educational and linguistic values to the new Muslim republics. Non-governmental moves were made, particularly in airmailing Turkish newspapers. Early in 1992, a few weeks after the Muslim republics had proclaimed their independence, three dailies — the Turkish Islamist *Zaman*, the strongly nationalist *Türkiye* and the liberal *Milliyet* — were airmailing thousands of copies to Azerbayjan and Kazakhstan.[77] However, insofar as official Turkish assistance was concerned, it found itself on rather fragile ground. In all cultural services Turkey had to beware of seeming to patronise or to be seeking to instill its own culture at the expense of the local one. Nonetheless, culture was the best common ground between Turkey and the new Muslim republics (Tajikistan excepted) — so much so that one feels that all parties have been driving at some sort of cultural Pan-Turkism, with a high degree of mutual cooperation.[78] At the third meeting of the Culture Ministers of the Turkic-speaking nations, held in Alma Ata in July 1993 and attended by representatives from Turkey, Kazakhstan, Azerbayjan, Uzbekistan, Kirghizstan and Turkmenistan, important decisions were taken. The main one was an agreement jointly to promote and preserve Turkish-Turkic culture in the Middle East, the Caucasus, the Balkans, Central Asia, China and the Mediterranean area. The Joint Administration for Turkish Culture and Arts was seen as resembling UNESCO in its objectives and methods; there were suggestions that a TURESCO — Turkish Republics Education, Scientific and Cultural Organisation — be set up on the model of UNESCO,[79] but this has not yet come about. A short while earlier, on 8–9 June 1993, a congress of writers from Turkey and the new Muslim republics, Turkmenistan excepted, met in Ankara, sponsored by the Turkish Ministry of Culture. It unanimously resolved to strengthen relations among Turkish-Turkic writers in adopting a common alphabet, in publishing and in printing. The proceedings were reported in the June 1993 issue of the quarterly *Türk Dunyası* (The World of the Turks), published by the Ministry of Culture.

In matters of language, we have already described how television is attempting to promote the Turkish of Turkey in the six Muslim republics. On a scholarly level, a new dictionary of the main Turkic languages is being prepared at the University of Ankara, intended to facilitate communication.[80] A first volume, comprising about 1,200 pages, was published in 1991 by the Ministry of Culture; printed in Latin characters in the alphabetical sequence of the Turkish of Turkey, it lists Turkish and its equivalents in Azeri, Başkurt, Kazakh, Kirghiz, Uzbek, Tatar, Turkmen, Uygur, and Russian.[81] Another book, prepared by A.B. Ercilasun, editor of the above-mentioned monthly *Türk Kültürü* and President of the state-sponsored Turkish Language Society, deals with the various alphabets of Turkish and the Turkic languages, in Latin, Arabic and Cyrillic characters.[82]

Again, Turkey has had to act circumspectly, for each of the new republics prizes its own language highly. Thus, in mid 1991 the Kazakhs proclaimed Kazakh as the official language of Kazakhstan,[83] even though less than half the population was fluent in it, while in July 1992 the Parliament of the Volga Tatars, in their 'Tatarstan', voted both Russian and Tatar as official languages.[84] Hence, Turkey is promoting Turkish as a kind of additional language, a *lingua franca* for the area, while some of its linguists are debating the possibility and advisability of creating a new language with elements common to Turkish and the main Turkic languages (reminiscent of Gasprinsky's attempt at the end of the nineteenth century[85]). Similarly, Turkey officially offered to help with the hoped-for transition from the Cyrillic to the Latin alphabet — which five of the new republics seem to favour (Tajikistan is again the exception) — by freely providing appropriate textbooks, typewriters and printing machines, as well as offering the training necessary for using them. A round table conference, held at Marmara University in Istanbul on 18–20 November 1991, adopted a 34-letter common alphabet. At meetings in Istanbul between 19 and 21 March 1992 and in Ankara between 8 and 10 March 1993 the five republics decided in principle gradually to adopt the Latin alphabet; this was a marked success for Turkey and the West. While Tajikistan, due to its cultural and linguistic affinities with Iran, opted for the Arabic alphabet,[86] the others grasped that the Latin alphabet was one component of the 'Turkish way', as well as a bridge to the West. Nevertheless, they continue to hesitate, partly because of pressures and inducements from Iran and Saudi Arabia to persuade them to prefer the Arabic alphabet.[87] Further, Kazakhstan, with almost half its population consisting of Russians and Ukrainians, still considers the Cyrillic alphabet to be a bridge between Russia and the Muslims.[88] Pan-Turkists in Turkey, on the contrary, have ardently endorsed the notion of a common alphabet and some have proposed the Latin alphabet used in Turkey, with several added symbols for the Turkic languages, as a common denominator.[89] As several Pan-Turkists have phrased it, they perceive the final goal as the creation of a literary language common to all Turkic peoples.[90] The Turkish authorities, for their part, have enthusiastically supported the idea, e.g. in organising as early as 4–5 May 1992 a

'Continuing Congress of the Turkish Language' in Ankara, attended by Turks and twenty-five guests from the Muslim republics. Its goals, formulated by the sponsor, Turkey's Minister of Culture D.F. Sağlar, were to discuss and offer suggestions for a common language to all Turkish-Turkic peoples. The debates and resolutions were published in the Ministry's official monthly, *Milli Kültür*, of June 1992.

In education, too, some important steps have been taken. Universities in Turkey, despite continuous pressure from local students wishing to register, opened their doors to students from the six Muslim republics (1,000 to 2,000 a year from each). The Permanent Conference of Turkic World University Rectors met in Ankara in July 1993, to institutionalise these arrangements. Turkey, Azerbayjan, Kazakhstan, Uzbekistan, Kirghizstan, and the Turkish Republic of Northern Cyprus attended. Apart from this, plans were drawn up to establish schools to teach standard Turkish. Further, private institutions, such as the Türk Dünyası Araştırma Vakfı, a think-tank set up in 1980 to do research on the Turkish world, disbursed grants to Turkic students from abroad to study Turkish in Turkey, and also established a college in Azerbayjan and another in Turkmenistan,[91] as well as secondary schools in Kazakhstan, Uzbekistan and Kirghizstan.[92] Complementing such moves were grants for trainees to participate in courses in banking, management, language, diplomacy and other subjects, held in Turkey.[93]

In addition to Turkey's activities in all the new Muslim republics, let us now consider its specific bilateral relations with each of them separately.

Azerbayjan. Azerbayjan society has been marked by earlier Turkish and Iranian domination as well as later Russian and Soviet rule. All three elements are involved in its attempts to determine its own identity. Turkey, however, has had very special relations with this neighbouring society,[94] whose language is closest to Turkish. Numerous articles about the affinities between Turks and Azeris have been published in the Turkish press in recent years, even in such staid publications as the Ankara-based monthly *Yeni Forum*.[95] Not surprisingly, Turkey was the first member of the international community to recognise Azerbayjan's independence, on 9 November 1991; Azerbayjan was also the first new Muslim republic with which it signed a Friendship and Cooperation Treaty, on 24 January 1992. On the other hand, as the only Muslim republic which is not a full CIS member, Azerbayjan can expect only limited support from Russia, which indeed it still reproaches for a brutal one-sided intervention in Baku as late as January 1990. Moreover, it suspects the Russians of arming its arch-enemies, the Armenians.[96] This is the Azeri leaders' explanation for the series of military victories the Armenians scored in 1993, when they succeeded in gaining territory and establishing a land corridor between their own state and the Armenian enclave of Nagorno Karabach.[97] Although we do not know the exact Kremlin strategy in the matter, it is difficult to see why Russia should passively accept the departure of Azerbayjan, with its large oil reserves, from the CIS as well as its negotiations with British Petroleum and United States, French and Italian companies for sea shore exploitation; not to mention that, in Russia's perception, Azerbayjan could provide a dangerous precedent for other CIS member-states. Hence Russia's probable readiness to arm the Armenians with weapons superior to the Azeri ones.

All this has pushed a part of the Azerbayjan élite closer to Turkey. The latter has cooperated with Azerbayjan on various levels, but it could not easily intervene militarily in the Armenian-Azeri war. True, Özal, during his visit to Central Asia in early April 1993 warned the Armenians against the fantasy of a Great Armenia,[98] by which he meant Armenian irredentism bent on annexing some of Turkey's border areas. Such warnings aside, Turkey finds it difficult to act militarily against Armenia, whose permission it needs for transiting to Azerbayjan and Central Asia. Indeed, Turkey has maintained good relations with Armenia since the latter's independence,[99] e.g. by sending it much-needed wheat in October 1992; however, it has repeatedly emphasised that maintaining such relations depended on Armenia's making peace with Azerbayjan.[100] A second reason against military intervention is the wish not to antagonise Western public opinion, which remains sensitive to repeated Armenian reminders of the Turco-Armenian conflict during the First World War.[101] A third reason is the consideration that Iran might also intervene to safeguard its interests in the area, as well as Russia, which has continued to worry about what it perceives as the growing powers of Pan-Turkism and Pan-Islam, and has warned Turkey against renewing 'Ottoman aggression in southern Russia'.[102]

Reportedly sending some 150 officers to train the Azerbayjan army was practically all the military help given to the Azeris by Turkey — except for medical supplies. Turkey refused to enter into a defence pact with would have spelled out an obligation to guarantee Azerbayjan's security. This, notwithstanding public opinion in Turkey during 1992 and 1993 which put pressure on the government to intervene militarily in favour of Azerbayjan;[103] as did public opinion in Azerbayjan itself.[104] Turkey, however, has continually preferred recommending mediation, both to avoid being drawn into the war and to upstage Iran, which was also attempting to mediate.[105] To achieve these two goals Turkey was prepared to work together with Russia, as transpired from the Foreign Minister Hikmet Çetin's talks with his Russian colleague, Andrey Koziryev.

Meanwhile, military defeat weakened the position of Azerbayjan's elected State President, Abulfez Elçibey, a strongly pro-Turk (and Pan-Turk) intellectual and liberal nationalist, who fled from Baku on 18 June 1993. Some of his rivals — Gaydar Aliyev, First Secretary of the Azerbayjani Communist Party since 1969,[106] and General Suret Huseynov, an avowed Communist[107] — took over the government, the former becoming Speaker of the Parliament and Acting President, the latter Prime Minister. This was a bad blow to Turkey's foreign policy, based personally on Elçibey as well as on reciprocal Pan-Turk sentiments.[108] As commentators pointed out afterwards, Elçibey's fall could mean serious difficulties for the chances of the Turkish model being accepted in the new Muslim republics.[109] Still, Turkey did not intervene either on this occasion or in the Azeri-Armenian war, although in early September 1993 the new Turkish Prime Minister, Çiller Tansu, warned Armenia in no uncertain terms not to attack the Azeri autonomous province of Nakhichevan, on Turkey's border. Meanwhile, non-intervention eroded some of Turkey's popularity in Azerbayjan.

Since 1990 Turkey has signed a number of agreements with Azerbayjan, particularly the following: — cultural and scientific exchange (in higher and technical education, library science, teacher training, art, music, opera, theatre, cinema, radio, television, folklore and sport); — economics and commerce (cooperation in industry, oil production, petrochemical enterprises, mining, telecommunications, agriculture, and examining the setting up of a common market); — health (improving the public health system, grants for young doctors and students of medicine at the Universities of Ankara and Istanbul); — setting up air, rail, sea, and river transportation; — improving radio and postal links; — examining the joint exploitation of energy and natural resources (chiefly electricity and oil); — training in statistical research.[110]

Kazakhstan, the largest of the new Muslim republics and possibly the richest (though still suffering from the Soviet-imposed concentration on cotton monoculture), was considered by Turkey a prime object for close Turkish-Turkic relations. Kazakhstan's President, Nursultan Nazarbayev, while paying fervent lip-service to this rapprochement, was in practice less committed. His wariness derived both from personal motives and from *raisons d'état*, as he perceived them. First Secretary of the Kazakhstan Communist Party since 1989 and state President since 1990, Nazarbayev was well aware that Kazakhstan was the only one of the new Muslim republics in which his own ethnic group, the Kazakhs, were in a minority (of about 40 per cent) of the total population; that the Russians made up almost the same ratio, with strong majorities in the towns; and that the economy was tightly linked to Russia, as was the small army. Nazarbayev's centralised rule was generally supported, as was his moderate economic platform — to introduce private property and a free market, but also to delay turning over agriculture exclusively to private enterprise.

A Gorbachev man, Nazarbayev set out to mend his own fences with Boris Yeltsin, taking great care to maintain overall good relations with Russia. Thus, although he felt compelled by public opinion at home to define his own republic as the home of the Kazakhs, he also described it, severally, as a hybrid of Kazakhs and Russians. Consequently, although Kazakh was proclaimed the official language, Russian remained the language of communication; further, although Kazakhstan, at an official convention in Ankara, undertook to switch to the Latin script, it continued to use the Cyrillic. Similarly, although he demanded full control of natural resources, Nazarbayev settled, in June 1991, for joint control with Russia of the mines and mineral wealth.

In foreign affairs, Nazarbayev has attempted to put Kazakhstan's relations with the other Central Asian Muslim republics, as well as with Azerbayjan, on a preferential level by promoting economic and scientific coordination. However, he has remained very cautious in his treatment of Islam, although a more secular posture may have ensured better understanding with Turkey. On 5 December 1990, Turkey and Kazakhstan signed a cultural agreement in Alma Ata, according to which Turkey would see to the restoration of certain Kazakh architectural monuments, provide annual training in Turkey in the science of restoration, and assist too in the development of Kazakh artisanship. Later, in March 1991, Özal made a state visit to Kazakhstan and in September the same year Nazarbayev responded with a state visit to Turkey, during which several bilateral agreements on economic and scientific cooperation were signed (as listed below). In April 1992 Demirel visited Kazakhstan, offering it $200 million in export credits, to be repaid in oil. Later, in September 1992, a security agreement was signed between the two states on cooperation against smuggling and terrorism.[111]

Among the agreements signed between Turkey and Kazakhstan in 1990–2, the following deserve special mention: — a protocol of intention to cooperate in the field of education, science, printing, publications, tourism, radio, television, economics and commerce; —

cultural cooperation in festivals and exhibitions, arts, music, theatre, literature, printing, publishing, bibliography, photography, archaeology and monument restoration; — public health services, pharmaceutical information, and medical education; — promoting political, economic, commercial, scientific, technical, and ecological cooperation; — developing air, rail, road, and waterway communications, telecommunications, commercial credits, exporting Kazakhstan's natural gas to Turkey, and developing the former's oil wells; — exchange of students and experts; — promoting joint Kazakh-Turkish ventures and Turkish investments in Kazakhstan (and the protection of such investments); — cooperation in television and radio.[112]

In *Uzbekistan* the President, Islam Karimov, has repeatedly emphasised his commitment to the 'Turkish model', and indeed a special relationship exists between the two states. Some of this at least results from the Uzbeks' resentment at their country having been consistently treated by the Soviet regime as a source of raw materials, based almost entirely on cotton monoculture, with disastrous ecological effects. The climate of hostility has not prevented Uzbekistan from joining the CIS, chiefly for economic reasons, as it is still a net importer of food and numerous other essentials, and consequently runs an immense budget deficit.

However, its relations with Moscow did not prevent a rapprochement of its élites with Turkey after independence. Soon after this event, Karimov was officially invited to Ankara in December 1991, when the two states signed agreements for cooperation in culture and science, economics and commerce, development and communications. Demirel visited Uzbekistan as part of his Central Asian tour, and signed yet another agreement, offering Uzbekistan $500 million, the largest Turkish offer to any Central Asian republic to date. Less publicised was an agreement by which Turkey undertook to have its officers assist in establishing the Uzbek army. Further, in the first six months of 1992, the Turkish Red Crescent donated $37 million worth of medicines and food (chiefly wheat), while in July the same year Turkey exported to Uzbekistan 2 million tons of grain and, in August, 250,000 tons of sugar.[113] All this competes with Iran, and has helped Uzbekistan to turn Tashkent into a crossroads of Central Asia.[114]

The more important agreements signed between Turkey and Uzbekistan in 1990–2 are: — public health services, medical education in Turkey, and pharmacological information; — rail, road and air travel, modernisation of Uzbekistan's communications system, cooperation in economic, commercial and industrial matters (textiles, mining) as well as in educational and technical ones; — joint economic and commercial ventures (in cotton, leather, furs, jewellery, prospecting for minerals and tourism); — student exchange, promotion of the arts, music, theatre, sport and monument restoration; — cooperation in basic and other sciences; — financing bilateral trade by providing credits, chiefly via Turkey's Exim Bank, and planning to set up a new bank, the Turkish-Central Asian Bank; — protecting investments; — cooperation in radio and television; — promoting tourism.[115]

Kirghizstan found itself at independence in as sorry an economic situation as the other Central Asian republics, probably even a worse one — with low productivity, high inflation and a steep increase in prices. Its President, Askar Akayev, emphasised his nationalist sentiments — Kirghiz was proclaimed the official language — but most of his attention and that of his government had perforce to be concentrated on economics. He had to maintain economic relations with Russia and neighbouring China, but he also set out on a course of rapprochement with Turkey, where he found a ready response. He first visited it in December 1991, when he thanked Demirel for Turkey having been the first state to recognise the independence of Kirghizstan, and praised it as the model for his own country development. On a return visit to Kirghizstan in April 1992, Demirel offered his hosts $75 million in export credits as well as loans to fund sales of Turkish wheat and sugar. In addition, Turkish companies made offers to Kirghizstan for mining gold and coal.[116]

More specifically, the following agreements ought to be mentioned: — cooperation in economics (chiefly in agriculture, mining, furs, wool and cotton, bottling mineral water, bricks, ceramics, porcelain, glass products, various light industries, searching for oil, tourism, telecommunications) as well as cultural affairs (joint preparation of dictionaries, festivals, and cooperation in music, art, museology, folklore, and monument restoration), radio and television; — cooperation in economics, commerce and industry as well as in communications, development, sport, education, and technology; — introduction of the Latin alphabet, with the assistance of Turkey; — theatre, music, opera, ballet, cinema and other arts; — scientific and medical education for Kirghiz students in Turkey; — promotion and protection of investments; — road transportation and air services; — encouraging tourism.[117]

Turkmenistan society, largely nomadic or cotton-growing, is still largely traditional, and the strong-handed regime of President Saparmurad Niyazov, formerly head of the Turkmen Communist Party, has done little to change this. Independent since October 1991, it has assumed a moderate nationalist stance, for instance in proclaiming Turkmen the official language and ordering all persons in public administration or holding any kind of managerial jobs to have a command of the language by 1995. For the time being, the impact of Islam is only marginal, which explains the involvement of Iran and Saudi Arabic in propagating respectively Shiism and Sunnism. A small part of the population lives close to the poverty line but the state seems to have enough means to feed and clothe them. However, Turkmenistan has large mineral resources, chiefly oil and natural gas, which have yet to be developed. When Niyazov went to Turkey on an official visit in early December 1991, soon after independence, he declared that Turkmenistan and Turkey ought to use his country's rich resources jointly.

In February 1992, Turkey's Foreign Minister, Hikmet Çetin, visited the capital, Ashkabad, and signed agreements concerning education and language. The main provisions were for Turkey to supply a printing press in Latin characters, send teachers to Ashkabad and provide grants for Turkmen students in Turkey. Later, in January 1993, an international university, offering instruction in Turkish, was inaugurated in Turkmenistan, with Turkish, Turkmen and Kazakh support.

When Demirel visited Turkmenistan, accompanied by many Turkish businessmen, he offered his hosts assistance in changing from the Cyrillic to the Latin alphabet, as well as credits and various agreements of which the most important was a pipeline project to bring natural gas from Turkmenistan to Europe via Turkey. This last was partly intended to rival Iran's offer of a joint pipeline. Later, a United States-Turkish consortium signed an agreement with the government of Turkmenistan, paving the way for this group to build a natural gas pipeline to Europe. Private Turkish businessmen also made some deals, but they were hampered by Turkmenistan's lack of ready cash and its wish to conclude barter deals only. In August 1992 the Turkish government promised credits worth $75 million to mitigate these difficulties for Turkish firms. As a result, between May 1992 and April 1993 Turkish companies invested between $700 and $800 million in textile plants, hotels, flour and baby food factories in Turkmenistan. The Turkish Alarko Group of Companies joined with the British John Laing Company to complete the construction of a modern airport in Ashkabad.[118]

The following agreements with Turkey seem particularly relevant: — economic cooperation (encouraging investments and protecting them); — civil aviation; — promotion of tourism; — cooperation in the natural gas, oil, and chemical industries, communications (including a telephone network), agriculture, health services, and grants for students, technicians, and engineers; — pharmaceutical information;

— monument restoration and joint cultural events (including film festivals); — encouraging private firms to invest in industry and commerce; — assisting Turkmenistan in banking and cooperating with it in tourism, sport, cultural and technological projects, and musical and folklore events; — cooperating in education via grants for higher education and for spreading the Turkish of Turkey (including the Latin alphabet); — jointly fighting terrorism and increasing internal security; — increasing bilateral trade and road transport.[119]

Tajikistan, rather poor, traditional, and tending to rely on Russian military help against incursions from Afghanistan which became frequent from July 1993 onwards, is a special case, from Turkey's point of view. The only one of the new Muslim republics with a Turkic minority, Tajikistan has apparently been anxious about the much-discussed option of a Turkic federation, in which the Tajiks would be reduced to a minority.[120] Certain Tajik élites are openly apprehensive of Pan-Turkism.[121] Moreover, Tajikistan is probably considered by Turkey as a somewhat less likely partner — even though serious effort has nonetheless been invested in cooperation. The formal instruments for promoting this have been an Agreement on Cultural Cooperation signed on 1 March 1992 (concerning education, science and technology, music, arts, cinema, radio, television, sport and tourism);[122] and a Friendship and Cooperation Agreement, signed between the two states in Istanbul on 8 July 1993, for developing political, economic, cultural, scientific and technological relations.

At all events, Turkey seems to have had less success in its relations with Tajikistan than with the other new Muslim republics, since Tajikistan is visibly influenced by Iran and Afghanistan (both of which maintain strong religious, cultural and linguistic ties with it), as well as by Pakistan and China. Actually, Tajikistan's current political leadership seem worried by the growing importance of Islamic fundamentalism within the newly-independent state and on its borders.[123] Hence its cautious moves, for instance switching from Cyrillic to the Arabic system rather than the Latin alphabet; another sign of caution is the lower number of state visits between Turkey and Tajikistan, compared to those of the other Muslim republics. Still, Turkey has attempted to present various cultural and economic projects to Tajikistan, few of which were taken up; it has also sent at least two airborne shipments of food and medicines to the capital, Dushanbe, as humanitarian aid (the last in March 1993).[124] However, as long as Tajikistan needs the presence and support of Russian troops to protect it from military incursions by Islamic fundamentalists from Afghanistan, Turkey's impact must necessarily be limited.

In conclusion, the breakup of the Soviet Union has been an historical watershed in more ways than one. For the Turkish-Turkic peoples it has reopened the Pan-Turk ideological debate and initiated new moves. It has increased the immediate importance of Pan-Turkism, which was latent for a while, although both in Turkey and in the new Muslim republics it has been only one of several issues competing for public concern — such as local nationalism, Islamic identity and tribal/clan allegiance. Nonetheless, Pan-Turkism has continued to worry leading circles in Russia — although apparently less than the dangers they perceive in Islam and Pan-Islam. Greeks, such as the Foreign Ministry Counsellor Paul Hidiroglou, have accused Turkey of continuing irredentism, concluding his book *Thrace in the Light of the National Ideal of the Turks, 1985–1991* by criticising 'the inadmissible orientations of Turkish nationalism, which . . . undeniably involves erosive and secessionist plans and the advancing of inadmissible claims'.[125] Similarly, Professor Konstantinos Skhinás, in an article published in the Athens periodical *Tetrádia* in 1992,[126] expresses suspicions of Turkey's activities in Central Asia. Similar accusations have also occasionally appeared in Kurdish publications, such as the Paris-based Arabic-language *Dirāsāt Kurdiyya*.[127]

The matter is, of course, more complex. Turkey with its 58 million inhabitants is approximately equal in population to the six Muslim republics combined, and as the more developed is necessarily the initiator in their newly-established relations. However Turkey, itself burdened with high inflation and serious unemployment, simply does not have the unlimited means required to assist the new republics; nor is its government able to carry out even all the feasible projects, since it must watch its relations with its Western allies and friends. It must equally remain on good terms with Russia, which naturally wishes to preserve some measure of its former hegemony in the Caucasus and Central Asia. Both Turkey and the Muslim republics have been unwilling to take political and military risks. The result has been a multi-directional attempt by Turkey to continue striving for full EC membership, to set up the BSECR in the region, to promote the ECO for relations with certain Islamic states, and to work for close cooperation with the new republics without alienating Russia.[128] As for the last of these, Turkey's dilemma is that Russia's continuing influence in the Muslim republics conditions their relations with Turkey.

In these republics, which are at grips with so many problems, Pan-Turkism as a political ideology may be more deeply embedded than it is in Turkey,[129] due to its having been persecuted under the Soviet Union, and, further, may be associated in some minds there with Pan-Islam.[130] Accepting a full vision of Turan implies obliterating the Russian and Soviet past, no easy matter. Thus Karimov, Akayev, Nazarbayev and other leaders in these republics have occasionally pleaded for 'a union of Turkic peoples',[131] but it is difficult to determine whether these have been more than ritual proclamations. In June 1990, at a meeting of the heads of all five Central Asian Muslim republics in Alma Ata a cooperative agreement was signed, and reaffirmed at a later gathering in August 1991. However, it remains Turkey's role to promote Pan-Turk cooperation. Özal, on his part, merely expressed the hope that the 'twenty-first century will be the century of the Turks',[132] while Demirel flatly denied that Turkey wished to head a major power based on a Turkish-Turkic federated state;[133] he asserted that Turkey only intended to assist the republics to stand on their own feet.[134] He elaborated on this later, in 1992 (when Demirel, who succeeded Özal as President, was Prime Minister), and his words deserve quoting: 'It would be a great mistake to evaluate Turkey's assistance to these states as the pursuit of a policy of Pan-Turkism or a bid to extend regional influence. It should be borne in mind that Turkey is a cultural centre and an historic magnet to many of the newly independent states in the Caucasus and in Central Asia. Turkey is not seeking a monopolistic hegemony over relations with these states. On the contrary, its aim is to increase their ties with the outside world. In short, Turkey believes that it can help these republics in their long overdue attempt to integrate with the world, and at the same time help them stand on their own two feet . . . .'[135]

Political Pan-Turkism remains, indeed, the goal of some ultranationalist circles in Turkey,[136] but these are peripheral. Many, probably most, consist of groups of Azeri, Tatar and other Turkic immigrants into Turkey, who continue to publish their organs, such as *Azerbaycan*, which appears in Ankara every two months, as well as some new publications, like *Kerkük*, issued there twice a year by Iraki Turks. But official Turkey, which aspires to pass from relative marginally to centrality,[137] wishes to become at most a regional power, thanks to its special relations with the new Turkic peoples. As it perceives the situation, this should be achieved not via political irredentism — or, one might say, irredentist politics — but rather via economic and cultural cooperation.

Of course, economic and cultural moves serve to emphasise political and ethnic difficulties in the Soviet Union's successor states as well,[138] so that cooperation intended to resolve the former may also assist in mitigating the latter. This approach is attractive to the new Muslim republics, as their long-frustrated expressions of nationalism seem to be more locally than regionally oriented, with some emphasis on their own pan-ideology (Pan-Azeri, Pan-Kazakh, Pan-Uzbek or Pan-Turkmen); and are perhaps no less Islamically-minded than Pan-Turkist.[139] As pointed out by G.E. Fuller, independence offers these states an opportunity for promoting a common culture and history, but too speedy a drive towards a common cause, *a fortiori* towards unity, would be condemned by Russia as the economic and military power in the region.[140] As we have said, Turkey's foreign policy-makers are generally cautious not to antagonise Russia and have consequently been criticised by spokesmen of both Pan-Turkist and Islamist circles as preservers of the *status quo*.[141] Again, some of the official declarations on all sides of hopes for a grand Pan-Turk entity sound ritually repetitive.[142]

While the views of non-governmental circles are naturally much less often reported than those of public figures, one may get an idea about non-official Pan-Turkist opinion from a recent convention of Pan-Turkism's supporters, which took place near Antalya (south-western Turkey), between 21 and 23 March 1993.[143] This Convention for Friendship, Brotherhood and Cooperation among the Turkish States and Societies was attended by more than 1,000 delegates from Turkey, the new Muslim republics, the Federated Turkish Republic of Cyprus and various other Turkish or Turkic groupings (Tatars, Chechens, Ingush and others). Political parties were represented and among those attending were a few public figures (like President Rauf Denktaş of Cyprus), ambassadors, poets and some Russians. This was a meeting of Turkish-Turkic peoples or, as the organisers perceived it, of the Turkish-Turkic World. Pan-Turk issues were debated in committees (language, culture, education and science, economics and technology, politics and law) and summed up in decisions adopted by the convention. The final declaration proclaimed the convention's support for the new world order, multiparty democracy and individual rights under the rule of law. In this context, the convention decided to support the concepts of national, democratic and secular states within the Turkish-Turkic world. A High Council of the Turkish-Turkic republics and an inter-parliamentary grouping would act to increase good relations and cooperation. On the political level, al-though the unity of the Turkish-Turkic world was naturally proclaimed, most of the practical resolutions adopted were to assist peoples in trouble in various ways — chiefly in Cyprus, Azerbayjan and Bosnia (some regard the Bosnians as descendants of the Turks). The proviso that future Pan-Turk unity ought to be achieved in peace speaks for itself, as does the fact that most of the commissions (four out of five) discussed cultural and economic matters. This, again, was

224 Pan-Turkism

very different from the irredentist style of earlier years, mostly in the 1940s, when Pan-Turkists sought political and military solutions.

On a parallel level Dr Ata Erim, former chairman of the Federation of Turkish American Associations in New York, established in May 1992 a Council of the World's Turks, with branches in the United States, Canada, Germany, Switzerland, Sweden, Belgium, France and Austria. Its main aim is to lobby for the interests of Turks everywhere. The Antalya convention, this new council and other similar moves are merely drops in a bucket. Insofar as expectations still exist in some circles of achieving some Pan-Turk entity, these are generally relegated to a remote future (even when they speak of the twenty-first century).[144] All that has been carried out to date has indeed focused on the economic-administrative and cultural-educational levels, emphasising the immediate needs of the new Muslim republics versus the competitive relations among them. Turkey and the new Muslim republics may form, at some future time, an official or unofficial voting bloc in regional or Pan-Islamic organisations, or at the United Nations. However, considering the persistent problems and antagonisms in the entire region, a Pan-Turk common market (say, in an economic Turkish-Turkic league) still seems a distant goal, as is a culturally and linguistically united Turkestan. It is premature to predict their chances, but economic and cultural Pan-Turkists will certainly continue to pursue their activities towards Turkish-Turkic solidarity and cooperation.

NOTES

1. J.M. Landau, 'The fortunes and misfortunes of Pan-Turkism', *Central Asian Survey*, VII (1): 1988, pp. 1–5.
2. J.M. Landau, *The politics of Pan-Islam: ideology and organization*, 1990, ch. 6.
3. See the series 'Tarihin, Türklüğün, Türkiyenin meseleleri', written by E.Z. Ökte in *Belgelerle Türk Tarihi Dergisi*, New Series, nos 2–85: Apr. 1985–Mar. 1992.
4. See William Fierman (ed.), *Soviet Central Asia: the failed transformation*, 1991, p. 296.
5. E.g. Yaşar Kaplan, 'Adriatik Çin'e Türk varlığı', *Yorunge* (Islamist, Istanbul weekly), III (146): 10 Oct. 1993, p. 15.
6. Nezih Uzel, *Adryatik'ten Çin'e Türk dünyası*, 1993.
7. J.M. Landau, 'The Nationalist Action Party in Turkey', *Journal of Contemporary History*, XVII (4): Oct. 1982, esp. p. 602.
8. See, e.g., the proclamation of the Turkish-Muslim Association of Cyprus, in its monthly, *Selâm*, published in Lefkoşe (Nicosia), I (35): Feb. 1988, pp. 1, 6.

9. On which cf. Ahmet Tacemen, *Bulgaristan Türkleri 1878–1990*, 1991. Murat Yetkin, *Ateş hattında aktif politika*, 1992, pp. 186–94. For other reactions to the problems Turks were having in the Balkan countries, see the volume titled *Balkanlar*, 1993.

10. 'Büyü yapılmış hayvanlar', *Türk Dünyası Tarih Derigis*, 81: Sep. 1993, pp. 49–51. Tuğrul Keskingören, 'Unutulan Türkler ve Irak'ta demokrasi', ibid., 41–8. Ziyad Köprülü, *İnsan hakları açısından İrak Türkleri*, 1992.

11. *Cumhuriyet*, 15 Oct. 1991, p. 10.

12. For details, Bilal Şimşir, 'Turkey's relations with Central Asian Turkish republics (1989–1992)', *Turkish Review Quarterly Digest*, VI (28): Summer 1992, esp. pp. 13–5.

13. 'Rusya'dan geri adım', *Cumhuriyet*, 12 Nov. 1991, p. 8.

14. 'Kerim Türklerine Ankara yardımı', ibid., 14 Feb. 1992, p. 9.

15. For some recent works on Tatar nationalism, see A.A. Rorlich, *The Volga Tatars*, esp. ch. 12. Peter Reddaway, 'The Crimean Tatar drive for repatriation', in Edward Allworth (ed.), *Tatars of the Crimea*, pp. 194–201. Uwe Halbach, 'Akutelle Entwicklungen in der nationalen Bewegung der Krimtataren', *Berichte des Bundesinstituts für Ost-wissenschaftliche und Internationale Studien*, 11: 1988, pp. 1–28. J.M. Landau, 'An early appeal by Russia's Muslims for international support', *Journal Institute of Muslim Minority Affairs*, XI (2): July 1990, pp. 366–9. 'Rusya'nın gözü Kırım'da', *Cumhuriyet*, 25 Jan. 1992, p. 8. The Crimea Tatars are not yet thinking of independence, but rather of returning to their homes, cf. Füreya Ersoy, 'Evimizi geri verin', *Nokta* (weekly), 22–28 Nov. 1992, pp. 46–7.

16. D.B. Sezer, 'Turkey's grand strategy facing a dilemma', *The International Spectator*, esp. pp. 21 ff.

17. For these options, see Udo Steinbach, 'Perspektiven der türkischen Aussen und Sicherheitspolitik', *Europa-Archiv*, XXIII (14): 1978, pp. 439–40. For the new situation since 1990, cf. Hans Krech, 'Die Türkei auf dem Weg zur Regionalmacht im Nahen Osten und in Mittelasien', *Zeitschrift für Türkeistudien*, V (2): 1992, pp. 248–54.

18. Peri Pamir, 'Turkey, the Transcaucasus and Central Asia', *Security Dialogue*, XXIV (1): Mar. 1993, p. 49.

19. There is a large amount of material about these republics prior to 1991, some of which will be mentioned later. Not a little, however, has been published since, mostly referring to each republic separately; see following footnotes. For all six of them, cf. Roland Götz and Uwe Halbach, *Politisches Lexikon GUS*, 1993. Karl Grobe-Hagel, *Russlands 'Dritte Welt': Nationalitätenkonflikte und das Ende der Sowjetunion*, 1992. For more data, see *A bibliography of Turks and of Turkey*, vols i–ii, 1992.

20. On the military factor, Bernd Weber, 'Das explosive Erbe der Sowjetunion, *Osteuropa*, XLII (8): Aug. 1992, esp. pp. 657–68.

21. See Alexandre Benningsen and S.E. Wimbush, *Muslims of the Soviet*

Empire: a guide, 1985, pp. 133–46. Shirin Akiner, *Islamic peoples of the Soviet Union*, 1983, pp. 105–22. Erhard Stölting, *Eine Weltmacht zerbricht: Nationalitäten und Religionen in der UdSSR*, 1990, pp. 260–78. Graham Smith (ed.), *The nationalities question in the Soviet Union*, 1990, pp. 163–79. C.F. Furtado Jr. and Andrea Chandler (eds), *Perestroika in the Soviet republics: documents on the national question*, 1992, pp. 447–66. Raoul Motika, 'Glasnost in der Sowjetrepublik Aserbaidschan am Beispiel der Zeitschrift *Azerbaycan*', *Orient* (Hamburg), XXXII (4): Dec. 1991, pp. 573–90. E.M. Auch, 'Aserbaidshan — Wirtschaftsprobleme, soziale Verwerfungen, politischer Nationalismus', *Vierteljahresberichte: Problems of International Cooperation*, 129: Sep. 1992, pp. 255–64. W.W. Maggs, 'Armenia and Azerbaijan: looking toward the Middle East, *Current History*, XCII (508): Jan. 1993, pp. 6–11. Stéphane Yérasimos, *Questions d'Orient: frontières et minorités des Balkans au Caucase*, 1993, pp. 191–247. Sh. T. Hunter, 'Azerbaijan: search for industry and new partners', in Ian Bremmer and Ray Taras (eds), *Nation and politics in the Soviet successor states*, 1993, pp. 225–60.

22. Akiner, op. cit., pp. 286–302. E.R. Bacon, *Central Asians under Russian rule: a study in cultural change*, pp. 29–47, 92–103. Benningsen and Wimbush, op. cit., pp. 67–73. Stölting, op. cit., pp. 193–202. G. Smith (ed.), op. cit., pp. 199–213. Götz and Halbach, op. cit., pp. 111–37. M.B. Olcott, *The Kazakhs*, 1987. Furtado and Chandler (eds), op. cit., pp. 471–92.

23. Benningsen and Wimbush, op. cit., pp. 93–106. Götz and Halbach, op. cit., pp. 284–308. Akiner, op. cit., pp. 366–86. E.A. Allworth, *The modern Uzbeks from the fourteenth century to the present: a cultural history*. Stölting, op. cit., pp. 172–181. G. Smith (ed.), op. cit., pp. 214–27. William Fierman (ed.), *Soviet Central Asia*. Furtado and Chandler (eds), op. cit., pp. 493–524. Gregory Gleason, 'Uzbekistan: from statehood to nationhood?' in Bremmer and Taras (eds), op. cit., pp. 331–60.

24. Akiner, op. cit., pp. 227–38. Benningsen and Wimbush, op. cit., pp. 73–85. Stölting, op. cit., pp. 202–4. G. Smith (ed.), op. cit., pp. 246–58. Götz and Halbach, op. cit., pp. 138–56. Furtado and Chandler (eds), op. cit., pp. 525–42. Gene Huskey, 'Kyrgyzstan: the politics of demographic and economic frustration', in Bremmer and Taras (eds), op. cit., pp. 398–418.

25. Mehmet Saray, *The Turkmens in the age of imperialism: a study of the Turkmen people and their incorporation into the Russian empire*, 1989. Götz and Halbach, op. cit., pp. 233–49. David Nissman, 'Turkmenistan; searching for a national identity', in Bremmer and Taras (eds), op. cit., pp. 384–97.

26. Akiner, op. cit., pp. 313–27. Stölting, op. cit., pp. 186–91. G. Smith (ed.), op. cit., pp. 228–45. Furtado and Chandler (eds), op. cit., pp. 559–81.

27. Teresa Rakowska-Harmstone, *Russia and Nationalism in Central Asia: the case of Tadzhikistan*, 1970, esp. pp. 70–1, 232. Akiner, op. cit., pp. 302–13. Benningsen and Wimbush, op. cit., pp. 85–95. Stölting, op. cit., pp. 181–5. G. Smith (ed.), op. cit., pp. 259–73. Götz and Halbach, op. cit., pp. 214–32. Furtado and Chandler (eds), op. cit., pp. 543–57. Muriel Atkin, 'Tajikistan: ancient heritage, new politics', in Bremmer and Taras (eds), op. cit., pp. 361–83.

28. Cf. Yaacov Ro'i, 'The Islamic influence on nationalism in Soviet Central Asia', *Problems of Communism*, XXXIX (4): July–Aug. 1990, pp. 49–64.

29. C.E. Black *et al.*, *The modernization of Inner Asia*, 1991, esp. pp. 326–7.

30. Two recent books on this subject are H.R. Huttenbach (ed.), *Soviet nationalities policies: ruling ethnic groups in the USSR*, 1990; and A.J. Motyl (ed.), *The post-Soviet nations: perspectives in the demise of the USSR*, 1992.

31. For the ensuing national conflicts, Nikolaj Nowikow, 'Nationalitätenkonflikte im Kaukasus und in Mittelasien', *Aus Politik und Zeitgeschichte*, 52–3: 20 Dec. 1991, pp. 24–34.

32. J.P. Dawydow and D.W. Trenin, 'Ethnische Konflikte auf dem Gebiet der ehemaligen Sowjetunion', *Europa-Archiv*, XLVIII (7): 10 Apr. 1993, pp. 179 ff.

33. M.N. Shahrani, 'Muslim Central Asia: Soviet development legacies and future challenges', *Iranian Journal of International Affairs*, IV (2): Summer 1992, pp. 331–42.

34. Yuri Bregel, E.M. Subtelny and Shahrbanou Tajbakhsh, 'Rethinking nationality in Central Asia', *Iranian Journal of International Affairs*, V (1): Spring 1993, pp. 95–106, 110–11. Muriel Atkin, 'Religious, national, and other identities in Central Asia', in Jo-Ann Gross (ed.), *Muslims in Central Asia: expressions of identity and change*, 1992, pp. 46–72.

35. For some of these, see Anthony Hyman, 'Suddenly, everybody's interested', *The Middle East*, 208: Feb. 1992, pp. 14–5. Udo Steinbach, 'Kemalismus oder Fundamentalismus', *Blätter für Deutsche und Internationale Politik*, 7: July 1992, pp. 822–9. Shahram Chubin, 'The geopolitics of the southern republics of the CIS', *Iranian Journal of International Affairs*, IV (2): Summer 1992, pp. 316–18.

36. Cf. Peter Feuilherade, 'Searching for economic synergy', *The Middle East*, 209: Mar. 1992, pp. 33–5; and Turkish press, 27 January to 5 February 1992.

37. Faruk Şen, 'Auf der Suche nach einem Entwicklungsmodell für Mittelasien', 1992, pp. 1–7. G.H. Altenmüller, 'Eine Brücke nach Westeuropa', *Frankfurter Allgemeine Zeitung*, 21 Apr. 1993, p. 14. Erol Manisalı, 'Turkey and the new Turkic republics', *Turkish Review Quarterly Digest*, VI (29): Autumn 1992, pp. 57–9.

38. G.E. Fuller, 'The emergence of Central Asia', *Foreign Policy*, 78: Spring 1990, p. 51.

39. See, for the non-Russians, Uwe Halbach, 'Ethnische Beziehungen in der Sowjetunion und rationale Bewusstseinprozesse bei Nichtrussen', *Berichte des Bundesinstituts für Ostwissenschaftliche und Internationale Studien*, 8: 1989, pp. 1–88.

40. Tadeusz Swietochowski, 'Islam and nationality in Tsarist Russia and the Soviet Union', in H.R. Huttenbach (ed.), *Soviet nationality policies*, 1990, pp. 221–34.

41. Haluk Geray, 'Türkilerle yeni dönem', *Cumhuriyet*, 7 May 1992, p. 8. Erol Manisalı, 'Gelişmeler ve Türkiye', ibid., 17 Mar. 1993, p. 8.

42. Faruk Şen, 'Schwarzmeer — Wirtschaftskooperationsregion als eine mögliche Ergänzung für die Europäische Gemeinschaft?', 1992. Tansuǧ Bleda, 'Black Sea Economic Cooperation Region', *Turkish Review Quarterly Digest*, v (23): Spring 1991, pp. 17–22. Seyfi Taşhan, 'Black Sea cooperation: a framework for hope', ibid., vi (28): Summer 1992, pp. 5–6. Nihat Gökyiǧit, 'Success of the Black Sea Economic Cooperation Zone and the role of Turkey', ibid., pp. 7–10. Murat Yetkin, op. cit., pp. 305–12.

43. Cf. Sezer, op. cit., pp. 26–7.

44. On which cf. Landau, *The politics of Pan-Islam*, op. cit., pp. 287–95.

45. 'Ankara'dan aktif diplomasi', *Cumhuriyet*, 15 Jan. 1992, p. 8.

46. Details in 'Türkilerden işbirliǧi adımı', *Cumhuriyet*, 23 Apr. 1992, p. 9.

47. Turkish press of 10 May 1992.

48. Cf. *Cumhuriyet*, 16 May 1992, p. 8.

49. See B.Z. Rumer, 'The gathering storm in Central Asia', *Orbis: A Journal of World Affairs*, xxxvii (1): Winter 1973, esp. p. 90.

50. For the competition between Turkey and Iran, see Kenneth Mackenzie, 'Azerbaijan and the neighbours', *The World Today*, xlviii (1): Jan. 1992, pp. 1–2.

51. W.G. Lerch, 'Pantürkismus oder Europa', *Frankfurter Allgemeine Zeitung*, 27 Apr. 1992, p. 14.

52. Arnold Hottinger, 'Zukunftfrage für Zentralasien', *Europa-Archiv*, xlvii (14): 25 July 1992, esp. p. 400. Further details in M.B. Olcott's 'Central Asia's post-empire politics', *Orbis: A Journal of World Affairs*, xxxvi (2): Spring 1992, esp. p. 267.

53. Canan Atılgan, 'Die mittelasiatischen Republiken und Aserbaidschan im Zuge der Unabhängigkeit', pp. 43–4.

54. Hugo Müller-Vogg, 'Kohl bringt Türken und Deutsche einander wieder nahe', *Frankfurter Allgemeine Zeitung*, 24 May 1993, p. 3.

55. Werner Adam, 'Asiatisches Debüt auf Europas Bühne', *Frankfurter Allgemeine Zeitung*, 6 Feb. 1992, p. 12.

56. For details, *Frankfurter Allgemeine Zeitung*, 18 May 1993, p. 6.

57. See Andrei Zagorski, 'Die Gemeinschaft Unabhängiger Staaten:

Entwicklungen und Perspektiven', *Berichte des Bundesinstituts für Ostwissenchaftliche und Internationale Studien*, 50: 1992, pp. 43–5.

58. *Cumhuriyet*, 24 Dec. 1991, p. 9.

59. F.M. Yılmaz, 'Türki cumhuriyetlere devlet dersi', ibid., 10 Jan. 1992, p. 9.

60. M.B. Olcott, 'Central Asia's catapult to independence', *Foreign Affairs*, LXXI (3): Summer 1992, pp. 109 ff.

61. Semih İdiz, 'Ankara, Türki cumhuriyetler için kaygılı', *Cumhuriyet*, 8 Feb. 1992, p. 9.

62. See, e.g., ibid., 10 Feb. 1992, p. 9.

63. Abdurrahman Yıldırım, 'Orta Asya'ya yatırım akıyor', ibid., 20 Apr. 1992, p. 7.

64. Haluk Geray, 'Orta Asya'da iletişim atağı', ibid., 1 May 1992, p. 8. For other investments, *Türkei Wirtschaftsnachrichten* (Bonn), 5: May 1993, pp. 8–9.

65. Reported by Hugh Pope, 'Bright horizon in the East beckons Ankara', *The Independent*, 1 June 1993.

66. Data in Faruk Şen, 'Die neue Rolle der Türkei und die europäische Sicherheit', p. 10.

67. Cf. Atila Artam, *Türk Cumhuriyetlerinin sosyo-ekonomik analizleri ve Türkiye ilişkileri*, 1993, esp. pp. 152–7.

68. A treaty was signed between Turkey and Azerbayjan, in April 1993, on military training. See *Cumhuriyet*, 22 Apr. 1993, p. 9.

69. 'Özbek ordusunu Türk subayları kuracak', ibid., 29 Apr. 1993, p. 8.

70. Ibid., 14 July 1992, p. 17. Can Karakaş, 'Artık iş zamanı', *Nokta*, 10 May 1992, pp. 22–3.

71. *Cumhuriyet*, 14 July 1992, p. 8.

72. Tayfun Gönüllü, 'Türki cumhuriyetler sağır', ibid., 21 Jan. 1993, p. 18.

73. J.M. Brown, 'Turkey gets Central Asia on the phone', *Financial Times*, 4 Dec. 1992.

74. Haluk Geray, 'Orta Asya'da iletişim atağı', op. cit.

75. Rudolph Chimelli, 'Der Traum von Turan per Satellit', *Süddeutsche Zeitung*, 6 May 1992, p. 3.

76. M.M. Shorish, 'Planning by decree: the Soviet language policy in Central Asia', *Language Problems and Language Planning*, VIII (1): Spring 1984, pp. 35–49. R.E. Weiner, 'Languages equal and free?', *Arizona Journal of International and Comparative Law*, VI: 1987, pp. 73–87. Jacques Maurais, 'Les Lois linguistiques soviétiques de 1989 et 1990', *Revista de Llengua I Dret*, 15: June 1991, pp. 75–90.

77. 'Führunganspruch der Türkel in Zentralasien', *Neue Zürcher Zeitung*, 30 Jan. 1992.

78. See, e.g., *Nokta*, 9 Feb. 1992, p. 71.

79. Hasan Duman, *Türk Cumhuriyetleriyle kültürel işbirliği*, 1993, p. 54.

80. Chimelli, op. cit.

81. *Karşılaştırmalı Türk lehceleri sözlüğü (kılavuz kitap)*, vol. I, Ankara, Kültür Bakanlığı, 1991; xiii, 1183 pp.
82. Ahmet B. Ercilasun, *Örneklerle bugünkü Türk alfabeleri*. Ankara, Kültür Bakanlığı, 1993; xv, 283 pp.
83. Kerem Çalışkan, 'Orta Asya'da milli uyanış', *Cumhuriyet*, 9 June 1991, p. 18.
84. *Cumhuriyet*, 10 July 1992, p. 8.
85. See above, ch. 2
86. *Der Spiegel* (Hamburg), 7: 10 Feb. 1992, p. 137.
87. Hans Krech, 'Die Türkei im Aufwind', *Europäische Sicherheit*, XLII (2): Feb. 1993, p. 81. Haluk Geray, 'Orta Asya'da alfabe savaşı', *Cumhuriyet*, 28 Mar. 1993, pp. 1, 17.
88. Cf. Olivier Roy, 'Ethnies et politique en Asie Centrale', *Revue du Monde Musulman et de la Méditerranée*, LIX–LX (1–2): 1991, esp. p. 31.
89. E.g., Timur Kocaoğlu, 'Türkiye ve Türk Cumhuriyetleri arasındaki münasebetlerde ortak alfabe ve imlâ birliğinin önemi', *Türk Dünyası Tarih Dergisi*, 76: Apr. 1993, pp. 17–19.
90. A.B. Ercilasun, 'Turk dilinin dünü bugünü geleceği', *Türk Kültürü*, XXXI (362): June 1993, p. 332.
91. 'Orta Asya'da Türk üniversitesi', *Cumhuriyet*, 31 Oct. 1992, p. 9.
92. Mete Çubukçu, 'Turancı diyen ahmaktır!', *Nokta*, 7 June 1992, pp. 26–7.
93. For the texts of these and other agreements in education and related areas, see T.E. Şahin *et al.* (eds), *Türkiye ile Türk Cumhuriyetleri ve Türk toplulukları arasında yapılan anlaşmalar ilişkiler ve faaliyetler*, 1993, vols ii–iii.
94. For which see Rainer Freitag, 'Aserbaidschan und die Türkei', *Orient*, XXXI (4): Dec. 1990, pp. 525–66.
95. Cf., e.g., an entire issue on 'The World of the Turks', *Yeni Forum*, XII (260): Jan. 1991.
96. As mentioned in the Russian press, quoted in *Cumhuriyet*, 7 Apr. 1993, p. 9.
97. For this conflict, see A.L. Altstadt, 'Dağlık Karabağ-Azerbaycan SSC'deki "Kavga Odağı" ', *Türk Dünyası Araştırmaları*, 74: Oct. 1991, pp. 47–62.
98. *Cumhuriyet*, 8 Apr. 1993, pp. 1, 14.
99. F.M. Yılmaz, 'Türkiye tartışması', ibid., 4 Aug. 1991, p. 9. Cf. 'Erivan'a tanıma ve uyarı', ibid., 26 Dec. 1991, p. 9. Still, some Armenians blamed Turkey for what they perceived as its 'continuing anti-Armenian policies', see, e.g., Raffi Kantian, of the German-Armenian Society of Frankfurt, in *Frankfurter Allgemeine Zeitung*, 30 June 1993, p. 8.
100. Prime Minister Demirel in June 1992, and Deputy Prime Minister Erdal İnönü in December 1992. See Elizabeth Fuller, 'The thorny path to an Armenian-Turkish rapprochement', *RFE/RL Research Report*, II (12): 19 Mar. 1993, p. 2.

101. Daniel Pipes and Patrick Clawson, 'Ambitious Iran, troubled neighbours', *Foreign Affairs*, LXXII (1): 1993, esp. pp. 135–6.

102. Ergun Balcı, 'Türkiye, Rusya ve İran: ince oyun', *Cumhuriyet*, 12 Apr. 1993, p. 9. See also 'Rafsancani'den Ermenilere uyarı', ibid., 13 Apr. 1993, p. 9. Nur Batur, 'Rusya, Pan-Türkizm'den rahatsız', *Milliyet*, 14 Apr. 1993, p. 15, based on an interview to this daily by Albert Chernishyev, Russian ambassador to Ankara. Hasan Akay, 'Türkiye'ye ağır suçlama', *Cumhuriyet*, 29 Apr. 1993, based on an interview with Russian Defense Minister, Pavel Grechkov, in *Krasnaya Zvyozda*. Another attack on Turkey's alleged intention to establish a unified Turan was published in the Russian *Moskovskiy Komsomolyets*, reported in *Cumhuriyet*, 24 July 1992, p. 9.

103. Hugh Pope, 'Turkey weighs involvement in the conflict in Azerbaijan', *The Wall Street Journal*, 13–14 Mar. 1992. Andrew Mango, 'Azerbaijan as seen from Turkey', *Zeitschrift für Türkeistudien*, V (2): 1992, esp. pp. 227–32.

104. Cf. an on-the-spot report by Kerem Çalışkan, 'Kafkasya'da barışın anahtarı Ankara'da', *Cumhuriyet*, 18 Sep. 1991, p. 11. For demonstrations in Ankara, in Azerbayjan's favour, see, e.g., ibid., 7 Mar. 1992, p. 5.

105. Elizabeth Fuller, 'Konflikte im Transkaukasus: Wer könnte vermitteln?', *Europa-Archiv*, XLVIII (7): 10 Apr. 1993, pp. 193–201. See also Semih İdiz, 'Kafkasya için işbirliği', *Cumhuriyet*, 23 Jan. 1992, p. 9.

106. For whose career see A.L. Altstadt, *The Azerbaijani Turks: power and identity under Russian rule*, 1992, ch. 11.

107. For his career, see Wolfgang Pehnt, 'Militär und Kaufmann', *Frankfurter Allgemeine Zeitung*, 7 July 1993, p. 10.

108. 'Der aserbaidschanische Präsident Elçibey appeliert an die Weltöffentlichkeit', ibid., 23 June 1993, p. 4. W.G. Lerch, 'Wirren in der "Stadt der Winde" ', ibid., 22 June 1993, p. 12. Saadettin Gömeç, 'Tarihte ve günümüzde Azerbaycan', *Yeni Forum*, XIV (291): Aug. 1993, pp. 30–42.

109. Gün Kut, 'Elçibey'in sonu, Türkiye modelinin sonudur', *Cumhuriyet*, 24 June 1993, p. 2.

110. Texts in Mehmet Saray, *Azerbaycan Türkleri tarihi*, 1993, pp. 69–150. Mehmet Şahin *et al.* (eds), op. cit., vol. I, pp. 13–162.

111. G.E. Fuller, *Central Asia: the new geopolitics*, 1992, pp. 41–62. Chantal Lemercier-Quelquejay, 'Le monde musulman soviétique d'Asie Centrale après Alma-Ata', *Cahiers du Monde Russe et Soviétique*, XXXII (1): 1991, pp. 117–22. M.B. Olcott, '*Perestroyka* in Kazakhstan', *Problems of Communism*, XXXIX (4): July–Aug. 1990, pp. 65–77. Id., 'Kazakhstan's global impact', *Iranian Journal of International Affairs*, IV (2): Summer 1992, pp. 369–82. 'Kazakistan'la sıcak ilişkiler', *Cumhuriyet*, 26 Sep. 1991, p. 10. 'Kazakistan'la kapsamlı işbirliği', ibid., 27 Sep. 1991, p. 10. W.G. Lerch, 'Für den Apfelvater sind schwere

Zeiten angebrochen', *Frankfurter Allgemeine Zeitung*, 12 June 1993, p. 6. Sadettin Gömeç, 'Tarihte ve günümüzde Kazakistan', *Yeni Forum*, XIV (288): May 1993, pp. 9–15.

112. See documents in Mehmet Saray, *Kazak Türkleri tarihi: 'Kazakların uyanışı'*, 1993, pp. 133–79. Şahin *et al.* (eds), op. cit., vol. I, pp. 175–232.

113. Fuller, *Central Asia*, op. cit., pp. 13–26. James Critchlow, *Nationalism in Uzbekistan*, 1991, esp. ch. 11. D.S. Carlisle, 'Uzbekistan and the Uzbeks', *Problems of Communism*, XL (5): Sep.–Oct. 1991, pp. 23–44. 'Özbekistan'ı tanıyoruz', *Cumhuriyet*, 17 Dec. 1991, pp. 1, 17. 'Kerimov memnun ayrıldı', ibid., 20 Dec. 1991, p. 9. 'Özbek ordusunu Türk subayları kuracak', ibid., 29 Apr. 1992, p. 8. Werner Gumpel, 'Die wirtschaftliche und soziale Lage in den Türkrepubliken Mittelasiens', *Zeitschrift für Türkeistudien*, V (1): 1992, pp. 44–5. Sadettin Gömeç, 'Tarihte ve günümüzde Özbekistan', *Yeni Forum*, XIV (287): Apr. 1993, pp. 9–14.

114. R.L. Canfield, 'Restructuring in Greater Central Asia', *Asian Survey*, XXXII (10): Oct. 1992, p. 883.

115. For the documents, see Mehmet Saray, *Özbek Türkleri tarihi*, 1993, pp. 88–133. Şahin *et al.* (eds), op. cit., vol. I, pp. 311–42.

116. Fuller, *Central Asia*, op. cit., pp. 27–40. 'Akayev: Türkiye bizim için yıldız', *Cumhuriyet*, 24 Dec. 1991, p. 8. 'Kirgizstan "fırsat ülkesi"', ibid., 29 July 1992, p. 7. W.G. Lerch, 'Schwierige Verhältnisse am Fusse des Tien Schan', *Frankfurter Allgemeine Zeitung*, 9 June 1993, p. 8. Gumpel, op. cit., pp. 43–4.

117. For the documents, Mehmet Saray, *Kırgız Türkleri tarihi*, pp. 93–143. Şahin *et al.* (eds), op. cit., vol. I, pp. 241–83.

118. Fuller, *Central Asia*, op. cit., pp. 67–76. 'Zengiliklerimizi birlikte kullanalım', *Cumhuriyet*, 3 Dec. 1991, p. 10. Jane Kokan, 'Mullahs tussle for Soviet hearts', *The Sunday Times*, 1 Mar. 1992. Steve Levine, 'Bartering for the riches of cash-starved Turkmenistan', *Financial Times*, 8 July 1992. Sami Kohen, 'Türkmenistan'da Türk olmak', *Milliyet*, 15 Apr. 1993. 'Türkmenistan'da Türk firmaları yatırim lideri', *Dünya*, 28 Apr.–4 May 1993, p. 2. 'Vom Zauber Turkmenistans', *Frankfurter Allgemeine Zeitung*, 13 May 1993, p. 8. Gumpel, op. cit., p. 46. Sadettin Gömeç, 'Tarihte we günümüzde Türkmenistan', *Yeni Forum*, XIV (286): Mar. 1993, pp. 49–51.

119. For the documents, Mehmet Saray, *Türkmen tarihi*, 1993, pp. 84–5. Şahin *et al.* (eds), op. cit., vol. I, pp. 354–436.

120. Rahim Masov and Farhod Džumaev, 'Vers une fédération de l'Asie Centrale?', *Revue du Monde Musulman et de la Méditerranée*, LIX–LX (1–2): 1991, pp. 158–62.

121. Muriel Atkin, op. cit., esp. pp. 50–3.

122. For the documents, Şahin *et al.* (eds), op. cit., vol. I, pp. 444–6.

123. Cf. Sabri Türkmen, 'Tacikistan ve Rus ittifakı karşısında mücahidlerin direnişi', *Değişim*, 7: Sep. 1993, pp. 53–5.

124. Fuller, *Central Asia*, op. cit., pp. 63–6. Werner Adam, 'Zwischen Kommunismus und Islam', *Frankfurter Allgemeine Zeitung*, 2 Oct. 1991, p. 14. 'Ankara'dan Orta Asya'ya yakın takip', *Cumhuriyet*, 14 Feb. 1992, p. 9. Aziz Niazi, 'Tajikistan in transition', *The Iranian Journal of International Affairs*, IV (2): Summer 1992, pp. 364–8. Gumpel, op. cit., p. 45.

125. Paul Hidiroglou, *Thrace in the light of the national ideal of the Turks, 1985–1991*, 1991, p. 103.

126. Konstantinos Skhinás, 'Ee Tourkiki thieísthisi ston geopolitikó chóro tis Kentrikis Asías' (Greek — 'The Turkish penetration into the geopolitical area of Central Asia'), *Tetrádia*, Winter-Spring 1992, pp. 107–16.

127. Cf., e.g., Hamīd Bozarslan, 'Hawl "al-uṭrūha al-Turkiyya fī 'l-ta'rīkh" ', *Dirāsāt Kurdiyya*, III (7): Jan. 1993, pp. 31–46.

128. See also Almuth Baron, 'Neuorientierung am Bosporus', *Frankfurter Allgemeine Zeitung*, 3 Apr. 1992, p. 14. W.G. Lerch, 'Moskau ist an Ordnung und Berechenbarkeit interessiert', ibid., 22 July 1993, p. 3.

129. Cf., for Uzbekistan, Anthony Hyman, 'The outlook for Central Asia', *International Affairs* (London), LXIX (2): April 1993, esp. p. 297.

130. Bassam Tibi, 'Pantürkismus als Menschenrecht', *Frankfurter Allgemeine Zeitung*, 19 Mar. 1992, p. 14.

131. 'Pantürkizm tehlike değil', *Cumhuriyet*, 17 Dec. 1991, p. 13. 'Nasarbayew plädiert für Union der Türkvölker', *Die Welt* (Hamburg), 11 Feb. 1992, p. 5.

132. Krech, 'Die Türkei im Aufwind', op. cit., p. 79. Cf. 'Die Vision "Turkestan" verblast', *Die Welt*, 10 Apr. 1993.

133. 'Stern des Orients', *Der Spiegel*, 7: 10 Feb. 1992, p. 138.

134. Chimelli, 'Der Traum von Turan per Satellit', op. cit., p. 2.

135. Süleyman Demirel, 'Newly-emerging centre', *Turkish Review Quarterly Digest*, VI (30): Winter 1992, p. 13.

136. Hyman, 'Suddenly, everybody's interested', op. cit., pp. 14–15. Cf. *Nokta*, 17 May 1992, p. 8. See also the interesting arguments in G.M. Winrow's 'Turkey and former Soviet Central Asia: national and ethnic identity', *Central Asian Survey*, XI (3): 1992, pp. 101–11.

137. See Seyfi Taşhan, 'Turkey from marginality to centrality', *Turkish Review Quarterly Digest*, VI (27): Spring 1992, pp. 47–56.

138. Cf. T.J. Colton and Robert Legvold (eds), *After the Soviet Union: from empire to nations*, 1992, conclusion, esp. pp. 182–3.

139. Yaacov Ro'i, 'The Soviet and Russian context of the development of nationalism in Soviet Central Asia', *Cahiers du Monde Russe et Soviétique*, XXXII (1): 1991, esp. pp. 137–9.

140. Fuller, *Central Asia*, op. cit., pp. 7–8.

141. E.g., Mustafa Özcan, 'Türkiyenin imaji ağır yara aldı', *Altınoluk*, 92: Oct. 1993, pp. 41–2.

142. See, e.g., 'Türklere tek devlet', *Cumhuriyet*, 21 Jan. 1992, p. 9. Another

is an English-language pamphlet, issued in Vienna, in 1992, by the Federation of Turkish Intellectuals in Europe, entitled *The XXI century — the century of Turkey*.

143. For a detailed report, *Türk Kültürü*, xxxi (360): Apr. 1993, pp. 193–215.

144. W.G. Lerch, 'Die Türkei als regionale Grossmacht', *Aus Politik und Zeitgeschichte*, 38–9: 17 Sep. 1993, pp. 3–9. Cf. however Bassam Tibi, 'The likelihood of an Islamic Central Asia', *German Comments*, 30: Apr. 1993, pp. 72–8.

SELECT BIBLIOGRAPHY

This comprises items frequently referred to above. For others, one should consult the footnotes.

The definite articles 'The', 'Le', etc. have not been considered in the alphabetical sequence.

Manuscript Sources

Archives of the German Ministry for Foreign Affairs, Bonn (chiefly, for the Second World War).

India Office, London (chiefly the L/P&S series).

Public Record Office, London (chiefly FO and CO series).

Pan-Turk periodicals (or with Pan-Turk leanings)

Adsız. Türkçü siyaset ve kültür dergisi. Istanbul, 1972–3.

Altın Işık. İlmî-edebî-siyasî dergi. Ankara, 1947.

Atsız Mecmua. Aylık fikir mecmuası. Istanbul, 1931–2.

Azerbaycan. Munich, 1952.

Azerbaycan. Aylık kültür dergisi, later *Azerbaycan, Aylık Türk dergisi.* Ankara and Istanbul, 1952–79.

Azerbaycan Yurt Bilgisi. Istanbul, 1932–4.

Batı Trakya Türkünün Sesi. Siyasî, kültürel ve Türkçü dergi. Istanbul, 1979–80. Mimeographed.

Bozkurt (Ist series). Istanbul, 1939–42.

Bozkurt (2nd series). Ankara, then Konya, 1972–7.

Büyük Duygu. Istanbul, 1329/1913.

Caucasian Review. Munich, 1955–60.

Cultura Turcica. Ankara, 1964–73.

Çağlayan. Aylık fikir ve edebiyat dergisi (Ist series). Antalya, 1935–8.

Çağlayan. Aylık fikir ve edebiyat dergisi (2nd series). Istanbul, 1943–4.

Çınaraltı. Türkçü fikir ve sanat mecmuası (Ist series). Istanbul, 1941–4.

Çınaraltı (2nd series). Istanbul, 1948.

Devlet. Ankara, then Konya, 1969–79.

Dilde, Fikirde, İşde Birlik. Aylık dış politika dergisi. Ankara, 1977–8.

The East Turkic Review. Munich, 1958–9.

Emel. İki aylık kültür dergisi. Istanbul, 1960–94.

Emel Medjmuası (sic). Pazarcık (Romania), 1930–41.

Ergenekon. Gençlik ve fikir dergisi. İlmî edebî-içtimaî. Ankara, 1938–9.

Genç arkadaş. Istanbul, then Ankara, 1975–9.

Gençliğe hedef. Istanbul, 1977.

236 Select Bibliography

Gök Börü. Türkçü dergi. Istanbul, 1942–3.
Halka Doğru. Istanbul, 1913–4.
Hür Türkistan için. İstiklâlci gazete. Istanbul, 1975–6.
Kırım. Aylık ilmî, siyasî ve kültürel mecmua. Ankara, 1957.
Kopuz. Aylık. Millî sanat ve fikir mecmuası. Samsun, 1939–40.
Kopuz. Aylık. Türkçü dergi. Samsun, 1943.
Kurtuluş. Azerbaycan Millî Kurtuluş Hareketinin organı. Berlin, 1934–9.
Kür Şad. Ankara, 1947.
Millî Hareket. Istanbul, 1966–71.
Millij Türkistan (National Turkistan). Journal of the Turkistanian Unity Committee for the struggle of national liberation of Turkistan. Geneva, 1950–2, then Dusseldorf, 1965–73.
Mücahit. Aylık. İktisadi içtimai fikir mecmuası. Ankara, 1955–64.
Odlu Yurt. Millî Azerbaycan fikriyatını terviç eden aylık mecmua. Istanbul, 1929–31.
Orhun. Aylık mecmua. Istanbul, 1933–4, 1943–4.
Orkun. Haftalık Türkçü dergi. Istanbul, 1950–2.
Ötüken. Fikir ve ülkü dergisi. Istanbul, 1964–75.
Ötüken. Aylık Türkçü dergi. Istanbul, 1979.
Özleyiş. Bilim-sanat-ülkü. Ankara, 1946–7.
Prométhée: Organe de défense nationale des peuples du Caucase et de l'Ukraine (later: *Prométhée: Organe de défense nationale des peuples opprimés de l'U.R.S.S.*). Paris, 1926–38.
România. Cotidian independent. Pazarcık, 1921–36.
Serdengeçti. Ankara, 1947–51.
Şimalî Kafkasya—Syevyerniy Kavkaz—Le Caucase du Nord—North Caucasus. Warsaw, 1934–9.
Tanrıdağ. İlmî, edebî, Türkçü. Bu Türklerin dergisidir (1st series). Istanbul, 1942.
Tanrıdağ. İlmî, Türkçü. Bu Türklerin dergisidir (2nd series). Istanbul, 1950–1.
Toprak. Fikir-sanat-ülkü dergisi. Adana, 1945–7.
Toprak. Aylık fikir-sanat-ülkü dergisi, later, *Toprak, Aylık ülkü dergisi.* Istanbul, 1954–1976.
Töre. Ankara, 1971–80.
Turan. Aylık Türkçü siyasi dergi, later *Turan Kavgamız.* Istanbul, 1976–80.
Turan Mecmuası. Budapest, 1913–1970.
Turkestan. Revue Nouvelle. Organe de défense nationale de Turkestan. Paris, 1934–5.
Turkey: a Monthly Organ of the Turkish Congress at Lausanne. Lausanne, 1921–2.
Türk amacı. Türk kültürü birliği mürevvicidir, later renamed *Türk amacı. Türk kültürü birliği dergisidir.* N.p. [Istanbul], 1942–3.
Türk Birliği. Ankara, 1966–71.
Türk Derneği. Istanbul, 1327.

Türk Dünyası. Bölünmez bir bütündür. Istanbul, 1955.
Türk Kültürü. Türk dünyasının dergisidir. Ankara, 1962–94.
Türk Kültürü Araştırmaları. Ankara, 1964–78.
Türk Sazı. Istanbul, 1943.
Türk Sözü. Istanbul, 1330 (1914).
Türk Yurdu. Istanbul, 1911–18.
Türk'e çağrı. Türkçü siyaset ve kültür dergisi. Istanbul, 1979–80.
Türkeli. Aylık. Siyaset-fikir-sanat-dergisi. Istanbul, 1947.
Türkeli. Munich, 1951–2.
Turkistan. İlmî, ictimâî, iktisadî ve kültürel aylık dergidir. Istanbul, 1953.
Türkistan Sesi. Aylık. İlmî ve kültürel dergi. Ankara, 1956–7 (English edition:
   The Voice of Turkestan, Ankara, 1956–7),
Türkiye Ülkücü Gençlik Dergisi. Istanbul, 1970–1.
Ülkü Ocağı. Ankara, 1979.
Ülkü Ocakları Derneği Genel Merkezi Bülteni. Ankara, 1974–6.
Ülkücü Kadro. Istanbul, 1976–7.
Yaş Türkistan. Türkistan millî istiklâl mefküresini mürevvici aylık mecmua.
   Berlin, 1931–9.
Yeni Bozkurt. Istanbul, 1948.
Yeni Kafkasya, Edebî içtimaî ve siyasî milliyetperver mecmua. Istanbul,
   1923–7.
Yeni Turan. Tampere, later Helsinki, 1931–3.
Yeni Türkistan. Istanbul, 1927–31.

Books and articles in Turkish

Ağaoğlu, Samet, *Babamdan hatıralar.* Ankara, Zerbamat Basımevi, 1940;
   213 pp.
——, *Babamın arkadaşları.* 3rd edn. Istanbul, Baha Matbaası, 1969; vi, 215
   pp.
Akansel, Mustafa Hakkı, *Türkün kitabı. Türk ırkı hakkında tetkikler.* Istan-
   bul, Kenan Matbaası, 1943; 63 pp. (= Akbaba Yayını, 8).
Akay, Hasan, 'Rus gazetesinden Türkiye ağır suçlama', *Cumhuriyet,* 29 Apr.
   1993, p. 9.
Akçura, Yusuf (ed.), *Türk yılı.* Istanbul, Yeni Matbaa, 1928; 655 pp.
——, *Türkçülük. 'Türkçülüğün tarihi gelişimi'.* Istanbul, Türk Kültür Yayını,
   1978; 253 pp. (= Akçura's chapter on this subject in *Türk yılı,* edited and
   annotated by Sâkin Öner).
Alp, Tekin (pseud. of Moïse Cohen), *Turan.* Istanbul, Türk Yurdu
   Kitaphanesi, 1330/1914; 143 pp.
——, *Türkler bu muharebede ne kazanabilirler.* Istanbul, Kader Matbaası,
   1330; 62 pp.
Alptekin, Erkin, *Uygur Türkleri.* Istanbul, Boğaziçi Yayınevi, 1978; 174 pp.
Alptekin, İsa, *Doğu Türkistan dâvâsı.* 2nd edn. Otağ Yayınları, 1975; 318 pp.
——, *Doğu Türkistan insanlıktan yardım istiyor.* N.p. [Istanbul], Otağ, 1974;
   213 pp.

Altstadt, A.L., 'Dağlık Karabağ-Azerbaycan SSC'deki "Kavga Odağı" ', *Türk Dünyası Araştırmaları* (Istanbul), 74: Oct. 1991, pp. 47–62.

Arıkan, Yaman, *Türklük gurûr ve şuûru.* Istanbul, Uyanış Yayınları, 1976; 235 pp.

Artam, Atila, *Türk Cumhuriyetlerinin sosyo-ekonomik analizleri ve Türkiye ilişkileri.* Istanbul, Sabrı Artam Vakfı, 1993; xv, 205 pp.

Atsız [Nihal Hüseyin], *Türk tarihi üzerinde toplamalar.* Istanbul, 1935; x, 140 pp.

——, *Türk tarihinde meseleler.* Ankara, Afşın Yayınları, 1966, 160 pp.

——, *Türk ülküsü.* Istanbul, Burhan Yayınevi, 1956; 146 pp. 3rd edn, Ankara, Afşın Yayınları, 1973; 120 pp.

Aydemir, Şevket Süreyya, *Makedonya'dan Ortaasya'ya Enver Paşa.* 2nd edn, 3 vols, Istanbul, Remzi Kitabevi, 1972.

Azer, San'an (pseud. of M. Sadık Aran), *İran Türkleri.* Istanbul, Cumhuriyet Matbaası, 1942; 44 pp., 2 maps.

Babakurban, Ziyaeddin, *Dış Türkler ve Türkistan dâvası.* Istanbul, Doğan Güneş Yayınevi, 1962; 30 pp.

Balcı, Ergun, 'Türkiye, Rusya ve İran: ince oyun', *Cumhuriyet,* 12 Apr. 1993, p. 9.

Balkanlar. Istanbul, Ortadoğu ve Balkan İncelemeleri Vakfı Yayınları, 1993; 299 pp.

Baltacıoğlu, İsmayil Hakkı, *Türke doğru.* Istanbul, Kültür Basımevi, 1943; 186 pp.

Battal-Taymas, Abdullah, *Kazan Türkleri, Türk tarihinin hazin yaprakları.* 2nd edn, Ankara, Türk Kültürünü Araştırma Enstitüsü, 1966; 239 pp. (1st edn, Istanbul, 1925).

Batur, Nur, 'Rusya, Pan-Türkizm'den rahatsız', *Milliyet,* 14 Apr. 1993, p. 15.

Baykara, Hüseyin, *Azerbaycan istiklâl tarihi.* Istanbul, Azerbaycan Halk Yayınları, 1975; 331 pp.

Bayram 32. Türkçüler bayramı armağandır: 3 mayıs 1976. Istanbul, 1976; 63 pp..

Baysun, Abdullah Receb, *Türkistan millî hareketleri.* Istanbul, 1943; 202 pp.

Bayur, Hikmet Yusuf, *Türk inkilâbı tarihi.* Vols I–II, 2nd edn, Ankara, Türk Tarih Kurumu, 1963–4.

Bilgehan, Şerif, 'Türkiyede (Türkçülüğün) geçirmiş olduğu merhaleler', *Tanrıdağ* (Istanbul), 1st series, 5: 5 June 1942, pp. 10–1.

Binark, İsmet, and Sefercioğlu, Nejat, *Doğumunun 95. yıldönümü münasebetiyle Ziya Gökalp bibliyografyası: kitap, makale.* Ankara, Türk Kültürünü Araştırma Enstitüsü, 1971; xxviii, 200 pp.

Caferoğlu, A., *Azerbaycan.* Istanbul, Cumhuriyet Matbaası, 1940; 47 pp.

Cami (pseudonym?), *Osmanlı ülkesinde Hristiyan Türkler.* Istanbul, 1338; 120 pp.

Candar, A. Avni Ali, *Türklüğün kökleri ve yayılışı.* Istanbul, Necmi İstikbal Matbaası, 1934; 64 pp. (= Türk Sosiologi Tetkikleri, 1).

C.H.P., *Konferanslar serisi*, vol. xix, Ankara, 1940; 80 pp.

Çağatay, Tahir, *Kızıl imperyalizm*, vols ı-ıı, Istanbul, 1958–62; vol. ııı, Ankara, 1967.

—— *et al.* (eds), *Muhammed Ayaz İshaki hayatı ve faaliyeti, 100. doğum yılı dolayısıyla*. Ankara, Ayyıldız Matbaası, 1979; xxiv, 351 pp.

Çalışkan, Kerem, 'Kafkasya'da barışın anahtarı Ankara'da', *Cumhuriyet*, 18 Sep. 1991, p. 11.

——, 'Orta Asya'da "milli uyanış" ', *Cumhuriyet*, 9 June 1991, p. 18.

Çapar, Mahmut, *Doğu illerimizdeki aşiretlerin Türklüğü*. Istanbul, Akın Yayınları, 1972; 77 pp.

Çil, Faruk (ed.), *Kavgamız—Türkçülük kavgası*. Istanbul, Turan Dergisi Yayını, 1977; 76 pp.

Çubukçu, Mete, 'Turancı diyen ahmaktır!', *Nokta*, 7 June 1992, pp. 26–7.

Danişmend, İsmail Hâmi, *Türk ırkı niçin Müslüman olmuştur (Türklük ve Müslümanlık)*. 2nd edn, Konya, Millî Ülkü Yayınevi, 1978; 287 pp.

——, *Türklük meseleleri*. Istanbul, Istanbul Kitabevi, 1966; 234 pp.

Darendelioğlu, İ.E., *Türkiyede milliyetçilik hareketleri. Toplantılar, mitingler, nümayışler, bildiriler, cemiyetler, basın*. N.p., Toker Yayınları, 1968; 377 pp.

Deliorman, Altan, *Tanıdığım Atsız*. Istanbul, Boğaziçi Yayınları, 1978; 375 pp.

Devlet, Nâdir, *İsmail Bey (Gaspıralı)*. Ankara, Kültür ve Turizm Bakanlığı, 1988; vi, 138 pp. (= Türk Büyükleri Dizisi, 99).

Duman, Hasan, *Türk Cumhuriyetleriyle kültürel işbirliği*. Ankara, Enformasyon ve Dokümantasyon Hizmetleri, 1993; vi, 58 pp.

Dündar, Gülsun, *Türkçülüğün alfabesi*. Istanbul, Su Yayınları, 1979; 127 pp.

Edib, Halide, *Yeni Turan*. Istanbul, Türk Yurdu Kitapları—Tanin Matbaası, 1329; 188 pp. 2nd edn, Istanbul, 1924; 168 pp.

Elçin, Şükrü, *Türkçülük ve milliyetçilik*. Ankara, Ayyıldız Matbaası, 1978; 23 pp.

Engin, A., *Atatürkçülük ve Moskofluk-Türklük savaşları*. Istanbul, 1953; xii, 376 pp.

——, *'Sosyalist' geçinenlere karşı Atatürkçülük savaşı. Kızıl elma*. Istanbul, Atatürkçülük Yayınları, n.d.; 128 pp.

——, *Türklük düşmanları sosyalist ve osmanlıcı geçinenlere karşı Atatürkçülük 'Manifesto'su*. Istanbul, Atatürkçülük Kültür Yayınları, n.d. [1968]; viii, 107 pp.

Enginün, İnci, *Halide Edib Adıvar'ın eserlerinde doğu ve batı meselesi*. Istanbul, Istanbul Üniversitest Edebiyat Fakültesi, 1978; 583 pp.

Ercilasun, Ahmet B., *Örneklerle bugünkü Türk alfabeleri*. Ankara, Kültür Bakanlığı, 1993; xv, 283 pp.

——, 'Türk dilinin dünü bugünü geleceği', *TK*, xxxı (362): June 1993, pp. 321–32.

Erdem, Galip (ed.), *Suçlamalar*. Vols ı-ıı, Ankara, Töre-Devlet Yayınevi, 1974–5.

Erer, Tekin, *Enver Paşa'nın Türkistan Kurtuluş savaşı*. İstanbul, Mayataş Yayınları, n.d. [1972?]; 144 pp.

Erişirgil, M. Emin, *Türkçülük devri milliyetçilik devri, insanlık devri*. Ankara, Maarif Yayınevleri, 1958; 148 pp.

Erkilet, H.E., *Şark cebhesinde gördüklerim*. İstanbul, Hilmi Kitavbevi, 1943; 248 pp., maps, photographs.

Erkman, F., *En büyük tehlike: Millî Türk davasına aykırı bir cereyanın içyüzü*. İstanbul, Ak-Ün Matbaası, 1943; 36 pp.

Eroz, Mehmet, *Türk kültürü araştırmaları*. İstanbul, Kutluğ Yayınları, 1977; 379 pp.

Ersoy, Füreyya, 'Evimizi geri verin,' *Nokta*, 22–28 Nov. 1992, pp. 46–7.

Ertürk, Hocaoğlu Selâhattin, *Türkçülük nedir?* Konya, Türk Milliyetçiler Derneği—Konya Şubesi Yayınları, 1952; 18 pp.

Fer, C. Savaş, 'Hesap veriyoruz!' *Gök Börü* (İstanbul), 1: 5 Nov. 1942, pp. 3–4, 9.

Genç, H. Mustafa, *İslâmî açıdan Ziya Gökalp ve Türkçüler*. İstanbul, Tek Yol Yayınları, n.d. [1978]; 183 pp.

Geray, Haluk, 'Orta Asya'da alfabe savaşı', *Cumhuriyet*, 28 Mar. 1993, pp. 1, 17.

——, 'Orta Asya'da iletişim atağı', *Cumhuriyet*, 1 May 1992, p. 8.

——, 'Türkilerle yeni dönem', *Cumhuriyet*, 7 May 1992, p. 8.

Gökalp, Ziya, *Türkçülüğün esasları*. Ankara, 1923; 174 pp. Reprinted frequently since.

Gökbilgin, M. Tayyib, 'Ziya Gökalp'e göre Halkçılık, Milliyetçilik, Türkçülük', *İslam Tetkikleri Enstitüsü Dergisi* (İstanbul), VI (3–4): 1976, pp. 197–211.

Gömeç, Saadettin, 'Tarihte ve günümüzde Azerbaycan', *Yeni Forum* (Ankara), XIV (292): Aug. 1993, pp. 30–42.

——, 'Tarihte ve günümüzde Kazakistan', *Yeni Forum*, XIV (288): May 1993, pp. 9–15.

——, 'Tarihte ve günümüzde Özbekistan', *Yeni Forum*, XIV (287): Apr. 1993, pp. 9–14.

——, 'Tarihte ve günümüzde Türkmenistan', *Yeni Forum*, XIV (286): Mar. 1993, pp. 49–51.

Gönüllü, Tayfun, 'Türki cumhuriyetler sağır', *Cumhuriyet*, 26 Jan. 1992, p. 18.

Gövsa, İbrahim Alâettin, *Türk meşhurların ansiklopedisi*, N.p., n.d. [prob. 1947]; iii, 420 pp.

Göze, Ergun, *Türklük kavgası*. İstanbul, Yağmur Yayınevi, 1977; 271 pp.

Güngör, Erol *et al.* (eds), *Atsız armağanı*. İstanbul, Ötüken Yayınevi, 1976; 445 pp.

Hacieminoğlu, Necmettin, *Milliyetçilik, ülkücülük, aydınlar*. 3rd edn, İstanbul-Ankara, Töre-Devlet Yayinevi, 1978; 397 pp.

Hızal, Ahmet Hazır, *Kuzey Kafkasya (hurriyet ve istiklal davası)*. Orkun Basımevi, 1961; 163 pp.

İdiz, Semih, 'Ankara, Türki cumhuriyetler için kaygılı', *Cumhuriyet*, 8 Feb. 1992, p. 9.
——, 'Kafkasya için işbirliği', *Cumhuriyet*, 23 Jan. 1992, p. 9.
Irkçılık-Turancılık. Ankara, Türk İnkilâp Tarihi Enstitüsü, 1944; vii, 236 pp.
Kaplan, Mehmet, *Edebiyatimizin içinde.* Istanbul, Dergâh Yayınları, 1978; 313 pp.
——, 'Gaspıralı İsmail'in Avrupa medeniyet, sosyalizm ve İslâmiyet hakkındaki eseri', *TK*, 180: Oct. 1977, pp. 716–31.
Kaplan, Yaşar, 'Adriyatik Çin'e Türk varlığı', *Yorunge* (Istanbul), III (146): 10 Oct. 1993, p. 15.
Karakaş, Can, 'Artık iş zamanı', *Nokta*, 10 May 1992, pp. 20–4.
Karal, Enver Ziya, *Osmanlı tarihi.* Vol. VIII, Ankara, Türk Tarih Kurumu, 1962; xvi, 631 pp.
Karşılaştırmalı Türk lehceleri sözlüğü (kılavuz kitap). Vol. I, Ankara, Kültür Başkanlığı, 1991; xiii, 1183 pp.
Keskingören, Tuğrul, 'Unutulan Türkler ve İrak'ta demokrasi', *Türk Dünyası Tarih Dergisi* (Istanbul), 81: Sep. 1993, pp. 41–8.
Kırımer, Cafer Seydahmet, *Gaspıralı İsmail Bey.* Istanbul, Matbaacılık ve Neşriyat Anonim Şirketi, 1934; 251 pp.
——, *Mefkûre ve Türkçülük.* Ed. by İbrahim Otar, Istanbul, 1965; viii, 76 pp.
Kocaoğlu, Timur, 'Türkiye ile Türk Cumhuriyetleri arasındaki münasebetlerde ortak alfabe ve imlâ birliğinin önemi', *Türk Dünyası Tarih Dergisi*, 76: Apr. 1993, pp. 17–19.
Kohen, Sami, 'Türkmenistan'da Türk olmak', *Milliyet*, 15 Apr. 1993.
Köprülü, Ziyad, *İnsan hakları açısından İrak Turkleri.* Ankara, İrak Türkleri Kültür ve Yardımlaşma Derneği, 1992; 77 pp.
Kuran, Ercümend, 'Atatürk ve Ziya Gökalp', *TK*, 13: Nov. 1963, pp. 9–12.
——, 'Türk milliyetçiliğinin gelişmesi ve Yusuf Akçuraoğlu', *TK*, 42: Apr. 1966, pp. 529–30.
Kutay, Cemal, *Enver Paşa Lenin'e karşı.* Istanbul, Ekicigil Matbaası, 1955; 119 pp.
L.N., *Dündar Taşer'in Büyük Türkiye'si.* 4th edn, Istanbul, Ocak Yayınevi, 1979; 216 pp.
Levend, Agâh Sırrı, 'Türk ocaklarından Halkevlerine, *Ulus* (Ankara), 17 Jan. 1951, p. 2.
Manisalı, Erol, 'Gelişmeler ve Türkiye', *Cumhuriyet*, 17 Mar. 1993, p. 8.
3 Mayıs Türkçüler günü antolojisi. Vol. I, Ankara, Türkiye Milliyetçiler Birliği Ankara Ocağı Yayınları, 1967; 128 pp.
Meram, Ali Kemal, *Türkçülük ve Türkçülük mücadeleleri tarihi.* Istanbul, Kültür Kitabevi, 1969; 265 pp.
Milliyetçi Türkiyeye doğru. 10–11 Mayıs 1969da yapılan milliyetçiler ilmî seminerinde varılan neticeler. Istanbul, 216 pp.
Mirza-Bala, Mehmedzade, *Azerbaycan Misak-ı Millî.* Istanbul, Necmi İstikbal Matbaası, 1927; 54 pp.
——, *Millî Azerbaycan hareketi. Millî Az. 'Müsavat ilk Halk Firkası tarihi.* N.p. [Berlin-Charlottenburg], Fırka divani, 1938; 337 pp.

Nejad, Edhem, *Türklük ne dir ve terbiye yolları*. İstanbul, Çiftçi Kitabhanesi, n.d. [1914?]; 52 pp.

Oktay, A., *Türkistan millî hareketi ve Mustafa Çokay*. İstanbul, 1950; 55 pp.

—— (ed.), *Türkistan'a dair bazı cereyanlar hakkında görüşlerimiz*. İstanbul, 1952; 28 pp.

Orkun, Hüseyin Namık, *Türkçülüğün tarihi*. İstanbul, Berkalp Kitabevi, 1944; 102 pp.

——, *Yeryüzünde Türkler*. İstanbul, Kenan Matbaası, 1944; 112 pp.

Ökse, Necati, *Van Gölü ve Fırat Nehri çevresinde yaşayan Türkler*. Ankara, 1976; v, 101 pp.

[Ökte, Ertuğrul Zekaî], 'Tarihin, Türklüğün, Türkiyenin meseleleri', *Belgelerle Türk Tarihi Dergisi* (İstanbul), New Series, 2–85: Apr. 1985–Mar. 1992.

Öner, Sâkin, *Ülkücü hareketinin meseleleri*. İstanbul, Toker Yayınları, 1977; 158 pp.

Özcan, Mustafa, 'Türkiye'nin imaji, ağır yara aldı', *Altınoluk* (İstanbul), 92: Oct. 1993, pp. 41–2.

Öz-Han, Kurt Tarık, *Hayir! Prof. H.E. Adıvar esir Türk illeri kurtarılacaktir*. Ankara, Orkun Basımevi, 1960; 116 pp.

Rásonyi, László, *Tarihte Türklük*. Ankara, Türk Kültürünü Araştırma Enstitüsü, 1971; 420 pp.

Resulzade, Mehmet Emin, *Azerbaycan Cumhuriyeti, Kayfiyet-i teşekkülü ve şimdiki vaziyeti*. İstanbul, 1339/1341 [1923]; 167 pp.

——, *İstiklâl mefkûresi ve gençlik. Esbab-ı hezimetimize bir mütâlaa*. İstanbul, 1341/1925; 29 pp.

S.S.C.B. Dış İşleri Bakanlığı Arşiv Bölümü, *Alman dış işleri belgeleri. Türkiye'deki Alman politikası (1941–1943)*. İstanbul, Havass Yayınları, 1977; 97 pp., photostats.

Sadiq, Mohammad, 'Türkçülük cereyanı—Türk milliyetçiliğinin eşiğinde (1908–1918)', *Türk Kültürü Araştırmaları* (Ankara), III–VI: 1966–9, pp. 5–18.

Saffet, Reşit, *Türklük ve türkçülük izleri*. Ankara, Türk Ocakları ilim ve san'at heyeti neşriyatı, 1930; 188 pp. (= Türkiyat Serisi, 2).

Sançar, Nejdet, *Afşın'a mektuplar*. Ankara, Afşın Yayınları, 1963; 64 pp.

——, *Irkımızın kahramanları*. Ankara, Aylı Kurt Yayınları, 1943; 102 pp.

——, *İsmet İnönü ile hesaplaşma*. Ankara, Afşın Yayınları, 1973; 360 pp.

——, *Türkçülük üzerine makaleler*. Ankara, Töre-Devlet Yayınevi, 1976; 232 pp.

——, *Türklük sevgisi*. N.p., Tanrıdağ Yayınları, n.d. [1952]; 95 pp.

Saray, Mehmet, *Azerbaycan Türkleri tarihi*. İstanbul, 1993; 150, iv pp.

——, *Kazak Türkleri tarihi: 'Kazakların uyanışı'*. İstanbul, 1993; 189, iv pp.

——, *Kırgız Türkleri tarihi*. İstanbul, 1993; 143, iv pp.

——, *Özbek Türkleri tarihi*. İstanbul, 1993; 133, iv pp.

——, *Türkmen tarihi*. İstanbul, 1993; 183 pp.

Seyfeddin, Ömer, *Millî tecrübelerden çıkartılmış amelî siyaset*. Ed. by Sâkin Öner, Istanbul, Göktüğ, 1971; 111 pp.

Suver, Akkan, *Ülkücüye notlar*. N.p., Su Yayınları, 1978; 80 pp.

Şahin, Tahir Erdoğan *et al.* (eds), *Türkiye ile Türk Cumhuriyetleri ve Türk toplulukları arasında yapılan anlaşmalar, ilişkiler ve faaliyetler*. Vols I–II–III, Ankara, Millî Eğitim Bakanlığı, 1993.

Şamil, Said, *Dış Türkler ve sosyalizm*. Istanbul, Hilâl Yayınları, 1971; 111 pp.

Şükrü, Fuat, *Turan ve Türkler. Şiir*. Istanbul, Resimli Ay Matbaası, 1931; 78 pp.

Tacemen, Ahmet, *Bulgaristan Türkleri 1878–1990*. Adana, Türk Ocağı Yayınları, 1991; iii, 219 pp.

Tanyu, Hikmet, *Türk gençliğin kükreyişi*. Ankara, Altınışık Yayını, 1947; 24 pp.

Togan, Ahmed Zeki Velidi, *Bugünkü Türkistan ve yakın mazisi*. Cairo, 1939; 704 pp. (subsequently published in Turkey, too).

——, *Hâtıralar: Türkistan ve diğer Müslüman Doğu Türklerinin millî varlık ve kültür mücadeleleri*. Istanbul, Hikmet Gazetecilik, 1969; vii, 643 pp.

——, *1929–1940 seneleri arasında Türkistanın vaziyeti*. Istanbul, Türkiye Basımevi, 1940; 43 pp.

——, *Türklüğün mukadderatı üzerine*. 2nd edn, Istanbul, Yağmur Yayınevi, 1977; 319 pp.

Togay, Muharrem Feyzi, *Turanî kavimler ve siyasî tarihlerinin esas hatları*. N.p., Osmanbey Matbaası, 1938; 30 pp. (= Türkistan Türk Gençler Birliği Yayını, 6).

——, *Yusuf Akçura'nın hayatı*. Istanbul, Hüsnütabiat Basımevi, 1944; 141 pp.

Toker, Metin, *Solda ve sağda vuruşanlar. Türkiyede iki yönlü ihtilâl ortamının anatomisi*. Ankara, Akis Yayınları, 1971; viii, 177 pp.

Topçu, Nurettin, *Milliyetçiliğimizin esasları*. Istanbul, Dergâh Yayınları, 1978; iv, 279 pp.

Tunaya, Tarık Zafer, *Türkiyede siyasî partiler, 1859–1952*. Istanbul, 1952; xi, 799 pp.

Turan, A. Şekür, 'Doğu Türkistan millî mücadelesinde Yaş Türkistan dergisinin hizmetleri', *TK*, 177: July 1977, pp. 581–3.

Türk dünyası el kitabı. Ankara, Türk Kültürünü Araştırma Enstitüsü, 1976; viii, 1452 pp.

Türk dünyasında Irak Türkleri. N.p., Irak Türkleri Kültür ve Yardımlaşma Cemiyeti Yayınları, 1971; 48 pp.

Türkeş, Alparslan, *Dış politikamız ve Kıbrıs*. Istanbul, Kutluğ Yayınları, n.d. [1966]; 391 pp.

——, *Dokuz ışık*. Istanbul, Dokuz Işık Yayınları, 1965; 16 pp. (and later editions).

——, *Gönül seferberliğine*. Ankara, Hareket Yayınları, 1979; 320 pp.

——, *1944 milliyetçilik olayı*. Istanbul, Yaylacık Matbaası, 1968; 162 pp.

——, *Temel görüşler.* Istanbul, Dergâh Yayınları, 1975; 406 pp. 2nd edn, Istanbul, Orkun Yayınevi, 1979; 368 pp.

——, *Türkiyenin meseleleri.* 1st and 2nd edns, Istanbul, Sıralar Basımevi, 1969; 232 pp.

Türkeş, Ünal, *Unutulmuş Türkler. Batı Trakya'da 4 yıl.* N.p., 1971; 104 pp.

Türkiye Milliyetçiler Birliği'nin görüşü. İlk bildiri. Istanbul, Türkiye Milliyetçiler Birliği Yayınları, 1964; 15 pp.

Türkkan, R. Oğuz, *Irka dair munakaşalar.* Istanbul, Bozkurtçu Yayını, 1943; 16 pp. (= Suppl. to no. 12 of *Gök Börü*).

——, *Irklar ve Türkleri Balmumu Sanan. Ismail Hami Danişmende cevap. Irk muhite tâbi midir?* Istanbul, Ekonomi-Reklam Matbaası, 1939; 24 pp.

——, *İleri Türkçülük ve partiler.* Ankara, Rafet Zaimlar, 1945; 128 pp.

——, *Kızıl faaliyet!* Istanbul, Bozkurtçu Yayını, n.d. [1943]; 66 pp.

——, *Kuyruk acısı.* Istanbul, Bozkurtçu Yayını, 1943; 207 pp.

——, *Milliyetçilik yolunda. Ergenekon—Bozkurt—Gök Börü (Yeni ve eski yazılar).* N.p., Müftüoğlu Yayınevi, 1944; 136 pp.

——, *Solcular ve kızıllar.* Istanbul, Bozkurtçu Yayını, 1943; 26 pp.

——, *Tabutluktan gurbete.* Istanbul, Boğaziçi Yayınevi, 1975; 499 pp.

——, *Türkçülüğe giriş.* Istanbul, Arkadaş Basımevi, 1940; 237 pp.

——, 'Türkiye'de solculuğun başlangıcı ve azınlıkları rolü', *TK*, 174: Feb. 1978, pp. 209–13.

Türkmen, Sabri, 'Tacikistan ve Rus ittifakı karşısında mücahidlerin direnişi', *Değişim* (Istanbul), 7: Sep. 1993, pp. 53–5.

Uzel, Nezih, *Adriatik'ten Çin'e Türk dünyası.* Istanbul, İrfan Yayımcılık, 1993; 248 pp.

Ülken, Hilmi Ziya, *Türkiyede çağdaş düşünce tarihi,* 2 vols, Konya, Selçuk Yayınları, 1966. 2nd edn, N.p., Ülken Yayınları, 1979; 496 pp.

Ülküsal, Müstecib, *Dobruca ve Türkler.* Ankara, Türk Kültürünü Araştırma Enstitüsü, 1966; 256 pp., maps.

——, *İkinci dünya savaşında 1941–1942 Berlin hatıraları.* Istanbul, Emel Yayını, 1976; 152 pp.

Ün, N.M., 'Ekmek, zurafanın midesinde', *Nokta,* 19 Apr. 1992, pp. 22–6.

Ünal, Tahsin, *Milliyet üzerine düşünceler.* Ankara, Rekor Matbaası, 1961; 52 pp.

Y.T., *Türkistan'da Türkçülük ve halkçılık.* Ed. by A. Oktay, 2 vols, Istanbul, 1951–4.

Yakuboğlu, Enver, *Irak Türkleri.* Istanbul, Boğaziçi Basım ve Yayınevi, 1976; 206 pp.

Yaylalıgıl, A. Münir Haymana, *Hali hazırın Türk toplulukları ve Pan-Türklüğe dair.* Istanbul, Arkadaş Basımevi, 1937; vi, 25 pp.

——, *Turkçüleri unutmıyalim! Çünkü: onlar, buna lâyıkdır.* Istanbul, Arsebük Basımevi, 1942; 4 pp.

Yetkin, Murat, *Ateş hattında aktif politika: Balkanlar, Kafkasya ve Ortadoğu üçgeninde Türkiye.* Istanbul, Alan Yayıncılık, 1992; 367 pp.

Yılmaz, F.M., 'Türki Cumhuriyetlere devlet dersi', *Cumhuriyet,* 10 Jan. 1992, p. 9.

——, 'Türkiye tartışması', *Cumhuriyet,* 4 Aug. 1991, p. 9.

Yılmaz, Fatih, 'Orta Asya uyanıyor', *Cumhuriyet,* 15–21 Dec. 1991.

Yılmaz, İsmailoğlu Mustafa, *Turanda çakan şimşek. Şiirler.* Adana, 1977; 102 pp.

Yurdakul, Mehmet Emin, *Turan'a doğru. Ey Türk uyan!* Istanbul, Ergenekon Yayınevi, 1973; 110 pp. (original edn, Istanbul, 1334).

Yücel, M. Celâlettin, *Bütün dünya Türkleri.* Ankara, Kardeş Matbaası, 1971; viii, 298 pp.

——, *Dış Türkler.* Istanbul, Hun Yayınları, 1976; 175 pp.

Books and articles in other languages

A memorandum concerning Great Turkistan. Istanbul, Şehir Matbaası, 1967, x, 27 pp.

A bibliography of Turks out of Turkey. Vols I–II, Ankara, Devlet Arşivleri Genel Müdürlüğü, 1992.

Adam, Werner, 'Asiatische Debüt auf Europas Bühne', *Frankfurter Allgemeine Zeitung,* 6 Feb. 1992, p. 12.

——, 'Zwischen Kommunismus und Islam', *Frankfurter Allgemeine Zeitung,* 2 Oct. 1991, p. 14.

Admiralty Staff, Intelligence Division, *Personalities in Turkey,* 2nd edn, 1916; 51 pp. (= C.B. 1148).

Ahmad, Feroz, *The Young Turks: the Committee of Union and Progress in Turkish politics, 1908–1914.* Oxford, Clarendon Press, 1969; viii, 205 pp.

Ahmad, H. Mazooruddin, *Kampf um leere Räume: Turan—Turkestan— Tibet.* Leipzig, Wilhelm Goldmann, 1940; 154 pp.

Ahmedzeki, Validi (i.e., Ahmed Zeki Velidi Togan), *Die gegenwärtige Lage der Mohammedaner Russlands.* Budapest, 1930; 19 pp.

Akiner, Shirin, *Islamic peoples of the Soviet Union.* London, Kegan Paul, 1993; xiii, 462 pp.

Alder, Lory and Richard Dalby, *The dervish of Windsor Castle: the life of Arminius Vambery.* London, Bachman and Turner, 1979; 512 pp.

Ali, Patria R., 'Enver Pasha: his status in modern Turkish history', *Egyptian Historical Review* (Cairo), XXII: 1975, pp. 3–36.

Ali, Shaukat, *Pan-movements in the Third World.* Lahore, Publishers United Ltd., n.d. [1976], viii, 398 pp.

Alishan, M., 'Berlin to India: can the Germans and their Turkish ally make use of Pan-Turanianism to build an Eastern Empire?', *Asia: Journal of the American Asiatic Association* (N.Y.), XVIII (5): May 1918, pp. 359–68.

Allworth, E.A., *The modern Uzbeks from the sixteenth century to the present: a cultural history.* Stanford, CA, Hoover Institution Press, 1990; xiv, 410 pp.

—— (ed.), *Tatars of the Crimea: their struggle for survival.* Durham, NC, Duke University Press, 1988; xv, 396 pp.

Alp, Tekin (pseudonym of Moïse Cohen), *Türkismus und Pantürkismus.*

Weimar, Kiepenheuer, 1915; xi, 112 pp. (a mimeographed English translation was prepared as *The Turkish and Pan-Turkish idea*, London, 1917).

Altenmüller, G.M., 'Eine Brücke nach Westeuropa', *Frankfurter Allgemeine Zeitung*, 21 Apr. 1993, p. 14.

Altstadt, A.L., *The Azerbaijani Turks: power and identity under Russian rule*. Stanford, CA, Hoover Institution Press, 1992; xxvi, 333 pp.

Arai, Masami, 'Between state and nation: a new light on the journal *Türk Yurdu*', *Turcica* (Paris), XXIV: 1992, pp. 277–95.

——, *Turkish nationalism in the Young Turk era*. Leiden, Brill, 1992; xii, 168 pp.

Arnakis, G.G., 'Turanism: an aspect of Turkish nationalism?', *Balkan Studies* (Salonica), I: 1960, pp. 19–32.

'Der aserbaidschanische Präsident Elçibey appeliert an die Weltöffentlichkeit', *Frankfurter Allgemeine Zeitung*, 23 June 1993, p. 4.

'Les aspirations politiques du monde musulman de Russie après la révolution de 1905', *RMM*, LVI: Dec. 1923, pp. 136–48.

Atılgan, Canan, 'Die mittelasiatische Republiken und Aserbaidschan im Zuge der Unabhängigkeit', Essen, Zentrum für Türkeistudien, Jan. 1993 (= Working Paper, 10).

Atkin, Muriel, 'Religious, national and other identities in Central Asia, in Jo-Ann Gross (ed.), *Muslims in Central Asia: expressions of identity and change*. Durham, NC, Duke University Press, 1992, pp. 46–72.

——, 'Tajikistan: ancient heritage, new politics', in Ian Bremmer and Ray Taras (eds), *Nation and politics in the Soviet successor states*. Cambridge University Press, 1993, pp. 361–83.

Auch, Eva-Maria, 'Aserbaidschan—Wirtschaftsprobleme, soziale Verwerfungen, politischer Nationalismus', *Vierteljahresberichte: Problems of International Cooperation* (Bonn), 129: Sep. 1992, pp. 255–64.

——, '"Ewiges Feuer" in Aserbaidschan: Ein Land zwischen Perestrojka, Bürgerkrieg und Unabhängigkeit', *Berichte des Bundesinstituts für Ostwissenschaftliche Studien* (Köln), 8: 1992, pp. 1–53.

Bacqué-Grammont, J.L., 'Turan: une description du Khanat de Khokand vers 1832 d'après un document ottoman', *Cahiers du Monde Russe et Soviétique* (Paris), XIII (2): 1972, pp. 192–231.

Baha, Lal, 'Activities of Turkish agents in Khyber during World War I', *Journal of the Asiatic Society of Pakistan* (Dacca), XIV (2): Aug. 1979, pp. 185–92.

Baron, Almuth, 'Neuorientierung am Bosporous', *Frankfurter Allgemeine Zeitung*, 3 Apr. 1992, p. 14.

'The Basmachis: the Central Asian resistance movement, 1918–24', *Central Asian Review* (London), VII (3): 1959, pp. 236–50.

Basry Bey, *Le monde turc et l'avenir de sa mission historique (l'illusion muscovite et la realité turque)*. Geneva, Editions du Foyer Turc, 1932; 236 pp.

Bennigsen, Alexandre and Chantal Lemercier-Quelquejay, *La presse et le mouvement national chez les Musulmans de Russie avant 1920*. Paris and The Hague, Mouton, 1964; 387 pp.

—— and Chantal Lemercier-Quelquejay, *Les mouvements nationaux chez les Musulmans de Russie: Le 'Sultangalievisme' au Tatarstan.* Paris and The Hague, Mouton, 1960; 265 pp.

—— and S. Enders Wimbush, *Muslim national communism in the Soviet Union: a revolutionary strategy for the colonial world.* University of Chicago Press, 1979; xxii, 267 pp.

—— and S. Enders Wimbush, *Muslims of the Soviet empire: a guide.* London, C. Hurst, 1985; xvi, 294 pp.

Benzing, Johannes, 'Die Türkvölker der Sowjetunion', in H.H. Schaeder (ed.), *Der Orient in deutscher Forschung: Vorträge der Berliner Orientalistentagung, Herbst 1942.* Leipzig, Harrassowitz, 1944, pp. 18–26.

Bérard, Victor, *Le problème turc.* Paris, E. Leroux, 1917; xiii, 272 pp.

Berkes, Niyazi, *Turkish nationalism and Western civilization: selected essays of Ziya Gökalp.* New York, Columbia University Press, 1959; 336 pp.

Black, C.E. *et al., The modernization of Inner Asia.* Armonk, NY, East Gate Book, 1991; xiii, 405 pp.

Bleda, Tansuğ, 'Black Sea Economic Cooperation Region', *Turkish Review Quarterly Digest* (Ankara), v (23): Spring 1991, pp. 17–23.

Bobrovnikoff, Sophy, 'Moslems in Russia', *The Moslem World* (London), I (1): Jan. 1911, pp. 5–31.

Bozarslan, Hamīd, 'Ḥawl "al-uṭrūha al-Turkiyya fi 'l-ta'rīkh" ', *Dirāsāt Kurdiyya* (Paris), III (7): Jan. 1993, pp. 31–46.

Bregel, Yuri, E.M. Subtelny and Shahrbanou Tadjibakhsh, 'Rethinking nationality in Central Asia', *Iranian Journal of International Affairs* (Teheran), v (1): Spring 1993, pp. 99–122.

Bremmer, Ian and Ray Taras (eds), *Nation and politics in the Soviet successor states.* Cambridge University Press, 1993; xxvii, 577 pp.

Brockelmann, Carl, *Das Nationalgefühl der Türken im Licht der Geschichte.* Halle/S., Max Niemeyer, 1918; 22 pp.

Brown, J.M., 'Turkey gets Central Asia on the phone', *Financial Times*, 4 Dec. 1992.

Canfield, R.L., 'Restructuring in Greater Central Asia: changing political configurations', *Asian Survey* (Berkeley, CA), XXXII (10): Oct. 1992, pp. 875–7.

Carlisle, D.S., 'Uzbekistan and the Uzbeks', *Problems of Communism* (Washington, DC), XL (5): Sep.–Oct. 1991, pp. 23–44.

Caroe, Olaf, *Soviet Empire: the Turks of Central Asia and Stalinism.* 2nd edn, New York, St. Martin's Press, 1967; xxxv, 308 pp.

Carretto, G.E., 'Polemiche fra kemalismo, fascismo, comunismo, negli anni '30', *Storia Contemporanea* (Rome), VIII (3): Sep. 1977, pp. 489–530.

Castagné, Joseph, *Les Basmatchis: Le Mouvement national des indigènes de l'Asie Centrale depuis la révolution d'Octobre 1917 jusqu'au Octobre 1924.* Paris, E. Leroux, 1925; viii, 88 pp.

——, 'Les organisations soviétiques de la Russie musulmane', *RMM*, LI: Oct. 1922, pp. 1–254.

——, 'Le Turkestan depuis la révolution russe (1917–1921)', *RMM*, L: June 1922, pp. 28–73.

Chatelier, A. Le, 'Les Musulmans russes', *RMM*, 1 (2): Dec. 1906, pp. 145–68.

Chimelli, Rudolph, 'Der Traum von Turan per Satellit', *Süddeutsche Zeitung* (Munich), 6 May 1992, p. 3.

Chirol, Valentine, 'Islam and the war', *Quarterly Review* (London), CCXXIX (455): Apr. 1918, pp. 489–515.

Chokaieff, Moustapha, *Chez les Soviets en Asie Centrale*. Paris, Messageries Hachette, 1928; 64 pp.

Chokayev, Mustafa, 'Turkestan and the Soviet regime', *Journal of the Royal Central Asian Society* (London), XVIII (3): 1931, pp. 403–20.

Chokay-ogli, Mustafa, *Tyurkyestan pod vlast'yu Sovyetov*. Paris, Yaş Turkestan, 1935; xx, 127 pp.

Chubin, Shahram, 'The geopolitics of the Southern Republics of the CIS', *Iranian Journal of International Affairs*, IV (2): Summer 1992, pp. 313–21.

Colton, T.J. and Robert Legvold (eds), *After the Soviet Union: from empire to nations*. New York and London, W.W. Norton, 1992; 208 pp.

Critchlow, James, *Nationalism in Uzbekistan: a Soviet republic's road to sovereignty*. Boulder, CO, Westview Press, 1991; xix, 231 pp.

Czaplicka, M.A., *The Turks of Central Asia in history and at the present day: an ethnological enquiry into the Pan-Turanian problem, and bibliographical material relating to the early Turks and the present Turks of Central Asia*. First publ. 1918, new impression London, Curzon Press, and New York, Harper and Row, 1973; 242 pp.

Dawydow, J.P. and D.W. Trenin, 'Ethnische Konflikte auf dem Gebiet der ehemaligen Sowjetunion', *Europa-Archiv* (Bonn), XLVIII (7): 10 Apr. 1993, pp. 179–92.

Demirel, Süleyman, 'Newly-emerging centre', *Turkish Review Quarterly Digest*, VI (30): Winter 1992, pp. 5–16.

Dény, J., 'Zia Goek Alp', *RMM*, LXI (3): 1925, pp. 1–41.

Djemal Pasha, *Memories of a Turkish statesman 1913–1919*. London, Hutchinson, n.d. [1992]; 302 pp.

Documents secrets du Ministère des Affaires Etrangères d'Allemagne, traduits du russe par Madeleine et Michel Eristov: Turquie. Paris, Paul Dupont, 1946; 131 pp.

Dumont, Paul, 'La revue *Türk Yurdu* et les Musulmans de l'Empire Russe 1911–1914', *Cahiers du Monde Russe et Soviétique*, XV (3–4): July–Dec. 1974, pp. 315–31.

Dzhyeltyakov, A.D., 'Pantyurkizm i Ömer Seyfeddin', *Vostokovyedyeniye* (Leningrad), VII: 1980, pp. 180–8.

Edib, Halide, *Conflict of East and West in Turkey*. Delhi, Jamla Press, n.d. [1935]; xi, 248 pp.

——, *Memoirs of Halide Edib*. London, John Murray, 1926; viii, 472 pp.

——, *Das neue Turan: ein türkisches Frauenschicksal.* Transl. by Friedrich Schrader, Weimar, Kiepenheuer, 1916; xi, 94 pp.

Edwards, A.C., 'The impact of the war in Turkey', *International Affairs* (London), XXII (3): July 1946, pp. 389–400.

d'Encausse, Hélène Carrère, *Réforme et révolution chez les Musulmans de l'empire russe: Bukhara 1867–1927.* Paris, Armand Colin, 1966; 313 pp. (= Cahiers de la Fondation Nationale des Sciences Politiques, 141).

Engin, Arın (ed.), *The voice of Turkism from behind the Iron Curtain on the occasion of the Russian invasion of Turkestan.* Istanbul, Kutulmuş Press, 1964; 49 pp.

Ergil, Doğu, 'A reassessment: the Young Turks, their politics and anti-colonial struggle', *Balkan Studies* (Salonica), XVI (2): 1975, pp. 26–72.

Erhorn, I., *Kaukasien.* Berlin, Die Bücherei des Ostraumes, 1942; 82 pp.

'Le fanatisme Panturc', *L'Asie Française* (Paris), XVII (169): Apr.–June 1917, pp. 72–4.

Federation of the Turkish Intellectuals in Europe, *The XXI century—the century of Turkey.* Vienna, 1992.

Feuilherade, Peter, 'Searching for economic synergy', *The Middle East*, 209: Mar. 1992, pp. 33–5.

Fierman, William (ed.), *Soviet Central Asia: the failed transformation.* Boulder, CO, Westview Press, 1991; xxi, 328 pp.

Fisher, Alan, *The Crimean Turks.* Stanford, CA, Hoover Institution Press, 1978; xiii, 264 pp.

Freitag, Rainer, 'Aserbaidschan und die Türkei', *Orient* (Hamburg), XXXI (4): Dec. 1990, pp. 525–66.

Fuller, Elizabeth, 'Konflikte im Transkaukasus: wer könnte vermitteln?', *Europa-Archiv*, XLVIII (7): 10 Apr. 1993, pp. 193–201.

——, 'The thorny path to an Armenian-Turkish rapprochement', *RFE/RL Research Report*, II (12): 19 Mar. 1993, pp. 1–15.

Fuller, G.E., *Central Asia: the new geopolitics.* Santa Monica, CA, Rand, 1992; xvi, 86 pp.

——, 'The emergence of Central Asia', *Foreign Policy*, 78: Spring 1990, pp. 49–67.

Furtado, C.F., Jr. and Andrea Chandler, *Perestroika in the Soviet republics: documents on the national question.* Boulder, CO, Westview Press, 1992; xxvi, 646 pp.

Georgeon, François, *Aux origines du nationalisme turc: Yusuf Akçura (1876–1935).* Paris, Editions ADPF, 1980; 156 pp.

——, 'Un voyageur tatar en Extrême-Orient', *Cahiers du Monde Russe et Sovietique*, XXXII (1): 1991, pp. 47–59.

Georges-Gaulis, Berthe, *La nouvelle Turquie.* Paris, Armand Colin, 1924; 283 pp.

Germanus, Julius, 'Türk Darnay', *Keleti Szemle* (Budapest), X: 1909, pp. 341–4.

Gigineishvili, Otar, *Turkizmi da osmaletis sagareo politika.* Tiflis, Tsodna, 1963; 212 pp.

Glasneck, Johannes and Inge Kircheisen, *Türkei und Afghanistan—Brennpunkte der Orientpolitik im zweiten Weltkrieg*. Berlin, VEB Deutscher Verlag der Wissenschaften, 1968; 306 pp.

Gleason, Gregory, 'Uzbekistan: from statehood to nationhood?', in Ian Bremmer and Ray Taras (eds), *Nation and politics in the Soviet successor states*. Cambridge University Press, 1993, pp. 331–60.

Gökalp, Ziya, *The principles of Turkism*. Transl. by Robert Devereux. Leiden, Brill, 1968; xiii, 141 pp.

Gökyiğit, Nihat, 'Success of the Black Sea Economic Cooperation Zone and the role of Turkey', *Turkish Review Quarterly Digest*, VI (28): Summer 1992, pp. 7–10.

Götz, Roland and Uwe Halbach, *Politisches Lexikon GUS*. 2nd edn, Munich, Verlag C.H. Beck, 1993; 311 pp.

Grobe-Hagel, Karl, *Russlands 'Dritte Welt': Nationalitätenkonflikte und das End der Sowjetunion*. Frankfurt a/M, ISP-Verlag, 1992; 295 pp.

Gross, Jo-Ann (ed.), *Muslims in Central Asia: expressions of identity and change*. Durham and London, Duke University Press, 1992; xiv, 224 pp.

Gumpel, Werner, 'Die wirtschaftliche und soziale Lage in den Türkenrepubliken Mittelasiens', *Zeitschrift für Türkeistudien* (Essen), V (1): 1992, pp. 33–48.

Haddad, W.W. and W. Ochsenwald (eds), *Nationalism in a non-national state: the dissolution of the Ottoman Empire*. Columbus, Ohio State University Press, 1977; x, 297 pp.

Halbach, Uwe, 'Ethnische Beziehungen in der Sowjetunion und nationale Bewusstseinsprozesse bei Nichtrussen', *Berichte des Bundesinstituts für Ostwissenschaftliche und Internationale Studien*, 8: 1989, pp. 1–88.

Hartmann, Richard, 'Ziya Gök Alp's Grundlagen der türkischen Nationalismus', *Orientalistische Literaturzeitung*, XXVIII: 1925, pp. 578–610.

Haushofer, Karl, *Geopolitik der Pan-Ideen*. Berlin, Zentral Verlag, 1931; 95 pp. (= Weltpolitische Bücherei, 21).

Hayit, Baymirza, *Some problems of modern Turkistan history*. Düsseldorf, East European Research Institute, 1963; 61 pp.

——, *Soviet Russian colonialism and imperialism in Turkistan as an example of the Soviet type of colonialism of an Islamic people in Asia*. N.p., n.d. [1965]; 123 pp.

Henderson, Alexander, 'The Pan-Turanian myth in Turkey today', *Asiatic Review*, XLI (145): Jan. 1945, pp. 88–92.

Heyd, Uriel, *Foundations of Turkish nationalism: the life and teachings of Ziya Gökalp*. London, Luzac, 1950; 174 pp.

Hidiroglou, Paul, *Thrace in the light of the national ideal of the Turks, 1985–1991*. Athens, Hellenic University Press, 1991; 103 pp.

Historical Section of the Foreign Office, *The rise of Islam and the Caliphate. The Pan-Islamic movement*. [London], Jan. 1919; 72 pp. (= Handbook 96 b).

——, *The rise of the Turks. The Pan-Turanian movement*. [London], 1919; 49 pp. (= Handbook 96 c and d).

Holdsworth, Mary, *Turkestan in the nineteenth century: a brief history of the khanates of Bukhara, Kokand and Khiva*. Oxford, St Antony's College, 1959; v, 83 pp. Mimeographed.

Hostler, C.W., 'Trends in Pan-Turanism', *MEA*, III (1): Jan. 1952, pp. 3–13.

——, *Turkism and the Soviets: the Turks of the world and their political objectives*. London, Geo. Allen and Unwin, 1957; xiv, 244 pp.

——, 'The Turks and Soviet Central Asia', *Middle East Journal* (Washington, DC), XII (3): Summer 1958, pp. 261–9.

Hottinger, Arnold, 'Zukunftsfragen für Zentralasien: Neubeginn in den Staaten am Südrand der ehemaligen Sowjetunion', *Europa-Archiv*, XLVII (14): 25 July 1992, pp. 397–402.

Hunter, Sh. T., 'Azerbaijan: search for industry and new partners', in Ian Bremmer and Ray Taras (eds), *Nation and politics in the Soviet successor states*. Cambridge University Press, 1993, pp. 225–60.

Huskey, Gene, 'Kirghizstan: the politics of demographic and economic frustration', ibid., pp. 398–418.

Huttenbach, H.R. (ed.), *Soviet nationality policies: ruling ethnic groups in the USSR*. London, Mansell, 1990; xvi, 302 pp.

Hyman, Anthony, 'The outlook for Central Asia', *International Affairs* (London), LXIX (2): Apr. 1993, pp. 289–304.

——, 'Suddenly, everybody's interested', *The Middle East*, 208: Feb. 1992, pp. 14–15.

Imhoff, D., 'Die Entstehung und der Zweck des Comités für Einheit und Fortschritt', *Die Welt des Islams* (Berlin), I (3–4): 1913, pp. 167–77.

Ishāqī, 'Iyād, *Risāla khatīra ilà 'l-mu'tamar al-Islāmī 'l-'āmm al-mun'aqad fī Bayt al-Maqdis yawm 27 Rajab sanat 1350 Hijriyya 'an 'Iyāḍ Isḥāqī*. Jerusalem, n.d. [1931]; 16 pp.

Jacob, Xavier, 'Phénomènes de scission interne en Turquie', *L'Afrique et l'Asie Modernes*, 121: 1979, pp. 23–55.

'Jadidism—current Soviet assessment', *Central Asian Review*, XII (1): 1964, pp. 30–9.

Jäschke, Gotthard, 'Der Turanismus der Jungtürken: zur osmanische Aussenpolitik im Weltkriege', *Die Welt des Islams*, XXIII: 1941, pp. 1–53.

——, 'Der Turanismus und die kemalistische Türkei', in R. Hartmann and H. Schell (eds), *Beiträge zur Arabistik, Semitistik und Islamwissenschft*. Leipzig, Harrassowitz, 1944, pp. 468–83.

Jansky, Herbert, 'Die "Türkische Revolution" und der russische Islam', *Der Islam* (Berlin and Leipzig), XVIII: 1929, pp. 158–67.

Karpat, K.H., 'Ideology in Turkey after the revolution of 1960: nationalism and socialism', *Turkish Yearbook of International Relations* (Ankara), VI: 1965, pp. 68–118.

——, *Turkey's politics: the transition to a multi-party system*. Princeton University Press, 1959; xiv, 522 pp.

—— (ed.), *Political and social thought in the contemporary Middle East*. New York, Praeger, 1968; xiii, 397 pp.

Kayaloff, Jacques, 'From the Transcaucasian past: two documents about

Turkish resistance in 1918', *Journal of Asian History* (Wiesbaden), VI (2): 1972, pp. 123–32.

Kazemzadeh, F., 'Pan movements', *International Encyclopaedia of Social Sciences*, XI: 1968, pp. 365–70.

Kirimal, Edige, *Der nationale Kampf der Krimtürken mit besonderer Berücksichtigung der Jahr 1917–1918*. Emsdetten, Verlag Lechte, 1952; xxxix, 374 pp.

Knatchbull-Hugessen, Hughe, *Diplomat in peace and war*. London, John Murray, 1949; x, 270 pp.

Kokan, Jane, 'Mullahs tussle for Soviet hearts', *Sunday Times*, 1 Mar. 1992.

Kolarz, Walter, *The peoples of the Soviet Far East*. New York, Praeger, 1954; xii, 194 pp.

——, *Russia and her colonies*. New York, Praeger, 1952; xiv, 335 pp.

Kordakchyan, R.P., *Vnyutryennaya politika Turtsii v godi vtoroy mirovoy voyni*. Erevan, Akademiya Nauk Armyanskoy SSR, 1978; 244 pp.

Korkhmazyan, R.S., *Turyetsko-Gyermanskiye otnoshyeniya v vtoroy mirovoy voyni*. Erevan, Akademiya Nauk Armyanskoy SSR, 1977; 188 pp.

Krech, Hans, 'Die Türkei auf dem Weg zur Regionalmacht im Nahen Osten und in Mittelasien', *Zeitschrift für Türkeistudien*, V (2): 1992, pp. 239–54.

——, 'Die Türkei im Aufwind', *Europäische Sicherheit* (Herford), XLII (2): Feb. 1993, pp. 79–81.

Krecker, Lothar, *Deutschland und die Türkei im zweiten Weltkrieg*. Frankfurt am Main, Klostermann, 1964; 293 pp.

Krimskiy, V., 'Pantyurkisti—fashistskaya agyentyura v Turtsii', *Bol'shyevik* (Moscow), 10–11: May–June 1944, pp. 79–85.

Kushner, David, *The rise of Turkish nationalism, 1876–1908*. London, Cass, 1977; x, 126 pp.

Landau, J.M., 'An early appeal by Russia's Muslims for international support', *Journal Institute of Muslim Minority Affairs* (London), XI (2): July 1990, pp. 366–9.

——, 'The fortunes and misfortunes of Pan-Turkism', *Central Asian Survey* (Oxford), VII (1): 1988, pp. 1–5.

——, 'Irredentism and minorities in the Middle East', *Immigrants and Minorities* (London), ix (3): Nov. 1990, pp. 242–8.

——, *Middle Eastern themes: papers in history and politics*. London, Cass, 1973; vii, 309 pp.

——, 'The Nationalist Action Party in Turkey', *Journal of Contemporary History*, XVII (4): Oct. 1982, pp. 587–606.

——, *The politics of Pan-Islam: ideology and organization*. Oxford, Clarendon Press, 1990; viii, 438 pp.

——, *Radical politics in modern Turkey*. Leiden, Brill, 1974; xii, 315 pp.

——, 'Some considerations on Panturkist ideology', in *Atti della Settimana Internazionale di Studi Mediterranei Medioevali e Moderni*. Instituto di Studi Africani e Orientali, Università di Cagliari—Milan, Giuffrè, 1980, pp. 113–22.

—— (ed.), *Atatürk and the modernization of modern Turkey*. Boulder, CO, Westview Press and Leiden, E.J. Brill, 1984.

Larcher, M., *La guerre turque dans la guerre mondiale*. Paris, Chiron and Berger-Levrault, 1925; 681 pp.

Lee, D.E., 'The origins of Pan-Islamism', *The American Historical Review*, XLVII (2): Jan. 1942, pp. 278–87.

Lemercier-Quelquejay, Chantal, 'Le monde musulman soviétique d'Asie Centrale après Alma-Ata (Décembre 1986)', *Cahiers du Monde Russe et Soviétique*, XXXII (1): 1991, pp. 117–22.

Lerch, W.G., 'Fur den Apfelvater sind schwere Zeiten angebrochen', *Frankfurter Allgemeine Zeitung*, 12 June 1993, p. 6.

——, 'Moskau ist an Ordnung und Berechenbarkeit interesiert', *Frankfurter Allgemeine Zeitung*, 22 July 1993, p. 3.

——, 'Pantürkismus oder Europa', *Frankfurter Allgemeine Zeitung*, 27 Apr. 1992, p. 14.

——, 'Schwerige Verhältnisse am Fusse des Tien Schan', *Frankfurter Allgemeine Zeitung*, 9 June 1993, p. 8.

——, 'Die Türkei als regionale Grossmacht', *Aus Politik und Zeitgeschichte*, 38–9: Sep. 1993, pp. 3–9.

——, 'Wirren in der "Stadt der Winde" ', *Frankfurter Allgemeine Zeitung*, 22 June 1993, p. 12.

Levine, Steve, 'Bartering for the riches of cash-starved Turkmenistan', *Financial Times*, 8 July 1992.

Lewis, Bernard, *The emergence of modern Turkey*. Oxford University Press, 1961; xv, 511 pp.

——, 'History-writing and national revival in Turkey', *MEA*, IV (6–7): June–July 1953, pp. 218–27.

——, 'The Ottoman Empire and its aftermath', *Journal of Contemporary History* (London), XV (1): Jan. 1980, pp. 27–36.

Luke, Harry, *The making of modern Turkey: from Byzantium to Angora*. London, Macmillan, 1936; viii, 246 pp.

Macartney, George, 'Bolshevism as I saw it in Tashkent in 1918', *Journal of the Central Asian Society* (London), VII: 1920, pp. 42–58.

Mackenzie, Kenneth, 'Azerbaijan and the neighbours', *The World Today* (London), XLVIII (1): Jan. 1992, pp. 1–2.

Maggs, W.W., 'Armenia and Azerbaijan: looking toward the Middle East', *Current History* CXII (570): Jan. 1993, pp. 6–11.

Malraux, André, *Les noyers de l'Altenburg*. N.p. [Paris], Gallimard, 1948; 299 pp.

Mango, Andrew, 'Azerbaijan as seen from Turkey', *Zeitschrift für Türkeistudien*, V (2): 1992, pp. 221–37.

Manisalı, Erol, 'Turkey and the new Turkic republics', *Turkish Review Quarterly Digest*, VI (29): Autumn 1992, pp. 57–9.

Marunov, Yu. V., 'Politika Mladoturok po natsional'nomu voprosu (1908–1912)', *Kratkiye Soobshchyeniya Instituta Vostokovyedyeniya* (Moscow), XXX, 1961, pp. 161–72.

——, 'Pantyurkizm i Panislamizm Mladoturok', *Kratkiye Soobshchyeniya Instituta Narodov Azii* (Moscow), XLV: 1961, pp. 38–56.

Masayuki, Yamauchi, *The green crescent under the red star: Enver Pasha in Soviet Russia 1919–1922.* Tokyo, Institute for the Study of Languages and Cultures of Asia and Africa, 1991; vi, 396 pp.

Massell, Gregory J., *The surrogate proletariat: Moslem women and revolutionary strategies in Soviet Central Asia, 1919–1929.* Princeton University Press, 1974; xxxviii, 448 pp.

Maurais, Jacques, 'Les Lois linguistiques soviétiques de 1989 et 1990', *Revista de Llengua I Dret* (Barcelona), 15: June 1991, pp. 75–90.

Mazov, Rahim and Farhad-Džumaev, 'Vers une fédération de l'Asie Centrale?', *Revue du Monde Musulman et de la Méditerranée* (Aix-en-Provence), LIX–LX (1–2): 1991, pp. 158–62.

Mende, Gerhard von, *Der nationale Kampf der Russlandtürken: ein Beitrag zur nationalen Frage in der Sovjetunion.* Berlin, 1936; v, 196 pp. (= *Monatsschrift des Seminars für Orientalischen Sprachen*, Beiband zum Jahrgang XXXIX).

Morgenthau, Henry, *Secrets of the Bosphorus: Constantinople, 1913–1916.* London, Hutchinson, n.d. [1919]; xii, 275 pp.

Motica, Raoul, 'Glasnost in der Sowjetrepublik Aserbaidschan am Beispiel der Zeitschrift *Azärbaycan*', *Orient* (Hamburg), XXXII (4): Dec. 1991, pp. 573–90.

Motyl, A.J. (ed.), *The Post-Soviet nations: perspectives on the demise of the USSR.* New York, Columbia University Press, 1992; xiii, 322 pp.

Moukhtar Pacha, M., *La Turquie, l'Allemagne et l'Europe depuis le traité de Berlin jusqu'à la guerre mondiale.* Paris and Nancy, Berger-Levrault, 1924; xix, 311 pp.

'Le mouvement Pantouranien', *L'Asie Française*, XVII (171): Oct.–Dec. 1917, pp. 174–82.

Mühlmann, Carl, *Deutschland und die Türkei, 1913–1914.* Berlin, Walther Rotschild, 1929; viii, 104 pp.

Müller-Vogg, Hugo, 'Kohl bringt Türken und Deutsche einander wieder nahe', *Frankfurter Allgemeine Zeitung*, 24 May 1993, p. 3.

Muhiddin, Ahmed, *Die Kulturbewegung im modernen Türkentum.* Leipzig, Gebhardt's Verlag, 1921; vii, 72 pp.

Munschi, Hilal, *Die Republik Aserbeidschan: Eine geschichtliche und politische Skizze.* Berlin, 1930; 64 pp.

Muçafir (pseudonym?), *Notes sur la Turquie.* Paris, Sirey, 1911; 93 pp.

Naval Staff—Intelligence Department, *A manual on the Turanians and Panturanianism.* (London), 1918; 256 pp. (= Publication no. I.D. 1199).

Niazi, Aziz, 'Tajikistan in transition', *Iranian Journal of International Affairs*, V (2): Summer 1992, pp. 364–8.

Nikitine, B., 'Le problème musulman selon les chefs de l'émigration russe', *RMM*, LII: Dec. 1922, pp. 1–53.

Nissman, David, 'Turkmenistan: searching for a national identity', in Ian

Bremmer and Ray Taras (eds), *Nation and politics in the Soviet successor states*. Cambridge University Press, 1993, pp. 384–97.

Nowikow, Nikolaj, 'Nationalitätenkonflikte im Kaukasus und in Mittelasien', *Aus Politik und Zeitgeschichte* (Bonn), 52–3: 20 Dec. 1991, pp. 24–34.

Oberhummer, Eugen, *Die Türken und das osmanische Reich*. Leipzig and Berlin, Teubner, 1917; iv, 115 pp.

Olcott, M.B., 'Central Asia's catapult to independence', *Foreign Affairs*, LXXI (3): Summer 1992, pp. 108–30.

——, 'Central Asia's post-empire politics', *Orbis: A Journal of World Affairs* (Philadelphia, PA), XXXV (2): Spring 1992, pp. 253–68.

——, *The Kazakhs*. Stanford, CA, Hoover Institution Press, 1987; xxvi, 341 pp.

——, 'Kazakhstan's global impact', *Iranian Journal of International Affairs*, IV (2): Summer 1992, pp. 369–82.

——, 'Perestroika in Kazakhstan', *Problems of Communism* (Washington, DC), XXXIX (4): July–Aug. 1990, pp. 65–77.

Okay, Kurt, *Enver Pascha der grosse Freund Deutschlands*. Berlin, Verlag für Kulturpolitik, 1935; 507 pp.

Ortaylı, İlber, 'Reports and considerations of İsmail Bey Gasprinskii in *Tercüman* on Central Asia', *Cahiers du Monde Russe et Soviétique*, XXII (1): 1991, pp. 43–6.

Önder, Zehra, 'Panturanismus in Geschichte und Gegenwart', *Österreichische Osthefte* (Vienna), XIX (2): May 1977, pp. 93–101.

——, *Die türkische Aussenpolitik im zweiten Weltkrieg*. Munich, R. Oldenbourg Verlag, 1977; 313 pp. (= Südosteuropäische Arbeiten, 73).

Pamir, Peri, 'Turkey, the Transcaucasus and Central Asia', *Security Dialogue* (Oslo), XXIV (1): Mar. 1993, pp. 49–54.

Park, A.G., *Bolshevism in Turkestan, 1917–1927*. New York, Columbia University Press, 1957; xvii, 428 pp. (= Studies of the Russian Institute of Columbia University).

Pears, Edwin, 'Turkey, Islam and Turanianism', *The Contemporary Review* (London), CXIV: Oct. 1918, pp. 371–9.

Pehnt, Wolfgang, 'Militär und Kaufmann', *Frankfurter Allgemeine Zeitung*, 7 July 1993, p. 10.

Pierce, R.A., *Russian Central Asia, 1867–1917: a study in colonial rule*. Berkeley and Los Angeles, University of California Press, 1960; viii, 359 pp.

Pinon, René, *L'Europe et la Jeune Turquie. Les aspects noveaux de la Question d'Orient*. Paris, Perrin, 1911; xvi, 500 pp.

——, 'L'offensive de l'Asie', *Revue des Deux Mondes* (Paris), XC: 15 Apr. 1920, pp. 799–815.

——, 'The Young Turk policy in Asia', *Current History* (New York), XI (2): Nov. 1919, pp. 331–6.

Pipes, Daniel and Patrick Clawson, 'Ambitious Iran, troubled neighbours', *Foreign Affairs*, LXXII (1): 1993, pp. 124–41.

Pipes, Richard, *The formation of the Soviet Union: communism and nationalism, 1917–1923.* 2nd edn, Cambridge, MA, Harvard University Press, 1964; xiv, 365 pp.

Pomianowski, Joseph, *Der Zusammenbruch des Ottomanischen Reiches: Erinnerungen an die Türkei aus der Zeit der Weltkrieges.* Zurich, Leipzig and Vienna, Amalthea Verlag, 1928; 455 pp.

Pope, Hugh, 'Bright horizon in the East beckons Ankara', *The Independent,* 1 June 1993.

——, 'Turkey weighs involvement in the conflict in Azerbaijan', *The Wall Street Journal,* 13–14 Mar. 1992.

'The racial propaganda in Turkey', *The Near East* (London), xii (308): 30 Mar. 1917, pp. 507–8.

Rafikov, A., 'Racist ravings in Turkey', *New Times* (Moscow), 37: 7 Sep. 1949, pp. 30–2.

Rahul, Ram, *Politics of Central Asia.* London, Curzon Press, 1974; ix, 185 pp.

Rakowska-Harmstone, Teresa, *Russia and nationalism in Central Asia: the case of Tadzhikistan.* Baltimore, MD, Johns Hopkins University Press, 1970; xiii, 326 pp.

Reddaway, Peter, 'The Crimean Tatar drive for repatriation: some comparisons with other movements', in E.A. Allworth (ed.), *Tatars of the Crimea: their struggle for survival.* Durham, NC, Duke University Press, 1988, pp. 194–201.

Resul-zade, M.E., *Das Problem Aserbeidschan.* Berlin-Charlottenburg, Verlag der Zeitschrift Kurtulusch, 1938; 64 pp.

Risal, P. (pseudonym of Moïse Cohen—Tekin Alp), 'Les Turcs à la recherche d'une âme nationale', *Mercure de France* (Paris), 16 Aug. 1912, pp. 673–707.

Ro'i, Yaacov, 'The development and Russian context of the development of nationalism in Soviet Central Asia', *Cahiers du Monde Russe et Soviétique,* xxxii (1): 1991, pp. 123–42.

——, 'The Islamic influence on nationalism in Soviet Central Asia, *Problems of Communism* (Washington, DC), xxxix (4): July–Aug. 1990, pp. 49–64.

Rondot, Pierre, 'L'expérience soviétique chez les peuples turcs de l'Asie Centrale', *L'Afrique et l'Asie* (Paris), 4: 1948, pp. 3–18.

Ronnenberger, Franz, 'Türkismus und Turanismus', *Volkstum in Südosten* (Vienna), Dec. 1942, pp. 197–203.

Rossi, Ettore, 'Dall'impero ottomano alla Repubblica di Turchia. Origine e sviluppi del nazionalismo turco sotto l'aspetto politico-culturale', *OM,* xxiii (9): Sep. 1943, pp. 359–88.

——, 'Publicazioni di Musulmani anti-bolscevichi dell'Azerbaigian Caucasico', *OM,* iv (6): 15 June 1924, pp. 395–408.

——, 'Uno scrittore turco contemporaneo: Ziya Gök Alp', *OM,* iv (9): 15 Sep. 1924, pp. 574–95.

Roy, Olivier, 'Ethnies et politique en Asia Centrale', *Revue de Monde Musulman et de la Méditerranée,* lix-lx (1–2): 1991, pp. 17–36.

Rumer, B.Z., 'The gathering storm in Central Asia', *Orbis*, XXXVII (1): Winter 1993, pp. 89–105.

Rustow, D.A., 'Enwer Pasha', *The Encyclopaedia of Islam* (Leiden), 2nd edn, II: 1965, pp. 698–702.

Rynd, F.F., 'Turkish racial theories', *Journal of the Royal Central Asian Society*, XLI (2–3): July–Oct. 1954, pp. 179–89.

Sadiq, Mohammad, 'The ideological legacy of the Young Turks', *International Studies* (New Delhi), XVIII (2): Apr.–June 1979, pp. 177–207.

Safvet, Réchid, *Les Türk-Odjaghis*. Ankara, 1930; 31 pp.

Saint-Hervé, 'Le Panturquisme sentimental et l'autre', *Le Temps* (Paris), 18 and 21–2 June 1942.

Saray, Mehmet, *The Turkmens in the age of imperialism: a study of the Turkmen people and their incorporation into the Russian empire*. Ankara, Turkish Historical Society, 1989; xiii, 281 pp.

Sarkisyan, Ye. K., *Ekspansionistkaya politika Osmanskoy Impyerii v Zakavkaz'ya*. Erevan, Academy of Sciences of Armenian S.S.R., 1962; 497 pp.

Sarrou, A., *La Jeune-Turquie et la révolution*. Paris and Nancy, Berger-Levrault, 1912; vii, 268 pp.

Schwidetzky, Ilse, *Turaniden-Studien*. Wiesbaden, Franz Steiner Verlag, 1950 (= Akademie der Wissenschaften und der Literatur in Mainz, *Abhandlungen der mathematisch-naturwissenschaftlichen Klasse*, 9: 1950, pp. 235–91).

Sezer, D.B., 'Turkey's grand strategy facing a dilemma', *International Spectator* (Rome), XXVII (1): Jan.–Mar. 1992, pp. 17–32.

Shahrani, M.N., 'Muslim Central Asia: Soviet development legacies and future challenges', *Iranian Journal of International Affairs*, IV (2): Summer 1992, pp. 331–42.

Shakibayev, Syerin, *Padyeniye 'Bol'shogo Tyurkyestana', povyest'-kronika*, transl. from Kazakh into Russian. Alma-Ata, Dzhashusi Press, 1972; 278 pp.

Shaw, S.J. and E.K. Shaw, *History of the Ottoman Empire and modern Turkey*. Vol. II, Cambridge University Press, 1977; xxv, 518 pp.

Shorish, M.M., 'Planning by decree: the Soviet language policy in Central Asia', *Language Problems and Language Planning* (Austin, Texas), VIII (1): Spring 1984, pp. 35–49.

Shukla, Ram Lakhan, 'The Pan-Islamic policy of the Young Turks and India, *Proceedings of the Indian History Congress, 32nd session, Jabalpur 1970* (New Delhi), part 2: 1970, pp. 302–7.

Skhinás, Konstantinos, 'Ee Tourkiki thieísthisi ston geopolitikó chóro tis Kentrikis Asías', *Tetrádia* (Athens), 29–30: Winter-Spring 1992, pp. 107–16.

Smith, Graham (ed.), *The nationalities question in the Soviet Union*. London, Longman, 1990; viii, 385 pp.

Stählin, Karl, *Russisch-Turkestan gestern und heute*. Königsberg, Ost-Europa Verlag, 1935; ii, 56 pp.

258   *Select Bibliography*

Steinbach, Udo, 'Kemalismus oder Fundamentalismus: die modell-politi-sche Konkurrenz zwischen der Türkei und dem Iran und die Zukunft der islamischen Welt', *Blätter für Deutsche und Internationale Politik* (Bonn), 7: July 1992, pp. 817–29.

———, 'Perspektiven der türkischen Aussen- und Sicherheits-politik, *Europa-Archiv*, XXIII (14): 1978, pp. 431–40.

Stoddard, T.L., 'Pan-Turanism', *American Political Science Review*, XI (1): Feb. 1917, pp. 12–23.

Stölting, Erhard, *Eine Weltmacht zerbricht: Nationalitäten und Religionen in der UdSSR*. Frankfurt a/M, Eichborn Verlag, 1990; 311 pp.

Stuermer, Harry, *Two war years in Constantinople: sketches of German and Young Turkish ethics and politics*. London, Hodder and Stoughton, 1917; 308 pp.

Sullivan, Charles D., 'Stamboul crossings: German diplomacy in Turkey, 1908–1914', unpublished Ph.D. thesis, Vanderbilt University, 1977; ii, 418 pp.

Swietochowski, Tadeusz, 'Islam and nationality in Tsarist Russia and the Soviet Union', in H.R. Huttenbach (ed.), *Soviet nationality policies: ruling ethnic groups in the USSR*. London, Mansell, 1990, pp. 221–34.

Şen, Faruk, 'Auf der Suche nach einem Entwicklungsmodell für Mittelasien', Essen, Zentrum für Türkeistudien, Oct. 1992; 7 pp. (= Working Paper, 9).

———, 'Die neue Rolle der Türkel und die europäische Sicherheit', Essen, Zentrum für Türkeistudien, May 1993; 14 pp.

———, 'Schwarzmeer—Wirtschaftskooperationsregion als eine mögliche Ergänzung für die Europäische Gemeinschaft?', Essen, Zentrum für Türkeistudien, 1992, 23 pp. (= Working Paper, 6).

Şimşir, B.N., 'Turkey's relations with Central Asian Turkic republics (1989–1992)', *Turkish Review Quarterly Digest*, VI (28): Summer 1992, pp. 11–15.

Tachau, Frank, 'The face of Turkish nationalism as reflected in the Cyprus dispute', *The Middle East Journal*, XIII (3): Summer 1959, pp. 262–72.

———, 'The search for national identity among the Turks', *Die Welt des Islams*, New Series, VIII (3): 1963, pp. 165–76.

Talaat, 'Posthumous memoirs of Talaat Pasha', *Current History* (New York), XV (2): Nov. 1921, pp. 287–95.

Taşhan, Seyfi, 'Black Sea cooperation: a framework for hope', *Turkish Review Quarterly Digest*, VI (28): Summer 1992, pp. 5–6.

———, 'Turkey from marginality to centrality', *Turkish Review Quarterly Digest*, VI (27): Spring 1992, pp. 47–56.

Tchokaieff, M.A., 'Fifteen years of Bolshevik rule in Turkestan', *Journal of the Royal Central Asian Society*, XX (3): 1933, pp. 351–9.

Thomas, David, 'Yusuf Akçura and the intellectual origins of "Üç tarz-ı siyaset" ', *Journal of Turkish Studies* (Cambridge, MA), ii: 1978, pp. 127–40.

Tibi, Bassam, 'The likelihood of an Islamic Central Asia', *German Comments* (Osnabrück), 30: Apr. 1993, pp. 72–8.
——, 'Pantürkismus als Menschenrecht?', *Frankfurter Allgemeine Zeitung*, 19 Mar. 1992, p. 14.
[Toynbee, A.J.], 'The militant Turk', *The Times* (London), 3, 5 and 7 Jan. 1918 (published anonymously).
——, *Report on the Pan-Turanian movement.* London, Intelligence Bureau—Department of Information, Oct. 1917, 26 pp. (signed A.J.T.).
——, *Turkey: a past and a future.* New York, George H. Doran, 1917; v, 85 pp.
Trumpener, Ulrich, *Germany and the Ottoman Empire, 1914–1918.* Princeton University Press, 1968; xv, 433 pp.
Türkkan, R.O., 'The Turkish press', *MEA*, I (5): May 1950, pp. 142–9.
' "Turanian" and Moslem: the Turkish apostasy', *The Near East*, XII (311): 20 Apr. 1917, pp. 567–8.
'Turkey, Russia and Islam', *The Round Table* (London), Dec. 1917, pp. 100–38.
Tvyeritinova, A.S., 'Mladotyurki i Pantyurkism', *Kratkiye Soobshchyeniya Instituta Vostokovyedyeniya*, XX: 1956, pp. 66–74.
Vambéry, A., 'The awakening of the Tatars', *The Nineteenth Century* (London), LVII: Feb. 1905, pp. 217–27.
——, 'Constitutional Tatars', *The Nineteenth Century*, LIX: June 1906, pp. 906–13.
Vambéry, H., 'Die Kulturbestrebungen der Tataren', *Deutsche Rundschau* (Berlin), XXXIII (10): July 1907, pp. 72–91.
Walker, C.J., *Armenia: the survival of a nation.* London, Croom-Helm, 1980, 446 pp.
Weber, Bernd, 'Das explosive Erbe der Sowjetunion', *Osteuropa* (Stuttgart), XLII (8): Aug. 1992, pp. 652–68.
Weiner, R.E., 'Languages equal and free?: minority languages in the Soviet Union', *Arizona Journal of International and Comparative Law* (Tucson, Arizona), VI: 1987, pp. 73–87.
Weisband, Edward, *Turkish foreign policy, 1943–1945: small state diplomacy and great power politics.* Princeton University Press, 1973; xiii, 377 pp.
Werner, Ernst, 'Pantürkismus und einige Tendenzen moderner türkischer Historiographie', *Zeitschrift für Geschichtswissenschaft* (Berlin), 8: 1965, pp. 1342–54.
Wheeler, G.E., 'Cultural developments in Soviet Central Asia', *Journal of the Royal Central Asian Society*, XLI: (3–4): July–Oct. 1954, pp. 179–89.
Winrow, G.M., 'Turkey and former Soviet Central Asia: national and ethnic identity', *Central Asian Survey*, XI (3): 1992, pp. 101–11.
Wipert, Karl, 'Der Turanismus', *Der Neue Orient* (Berlin), VI (4): Dec. 1922, pp. 202–10.
Wurm, Stefan, *Turkic peoples of the USSR: their historical background,*

their languages and the development of Soviet linguistic policy. Oxford, Central Asian Research Centre, 1954; ii, 51 pp.

X, 'Le Panislamisme et le Panturquisme', *RMM*, XXII: Mar. 1913, pp. 179–220.

Yérasimos, Stéphane, *Questions d'Orient: frontières et minorités des Balkans au Caucase.* Paris, Editions de la Découverte, 1993; 250 pp.

Yeryemyeyev, D. Ye., 'Kyemalizm i Panturkizm', *Narodi Azii i Afriki* (Moscow), 3: 1963, pp. 58–70.

Zagorski, Andrei, 'Die Gemeinschaft Unabhängiger Staaten: Entwicklungen und Perspektiven', *Berichte des Bundesinstituts für Ostwissenschaftliche und Internationale Studien*, 50: 1992, pp. 1–46.

Zarevand (pseudonym of Zaven and Vartouhie Nalbendian), *United and Independent Turania: aims and designs of the Turks.* Transl. from the Armenian by V.N. Dadrian. Leiden, Brill, 1971; xiii, 174 pp.

Zenkovsky, S.A., 'A century of Tatar revival', *The American Slavic and East European Review* (New York), XII: Oct. 1953, pp. 303–18.

——, 'Kulturkampf in pre-revolutionary Central Asia', *The American Slavic and East European Review*, XIV: Feb. 1955, pp. 15–41.

——, *Pan-Turkism and Islam in Russia.* Cambridge, MA, Harvard University Press, 1960; 345 pp.

——, 'Rossiya i Tyurki', *The New Review—Noviy Dzurnal* (New York), XLVI: 1956, pp. 172–98.

INDEX

Frequently-employed terms, like 'Ottoman Empire', 'Pan-Turkism', 'Turkey', or 'Turks', have not been incorporated into the index. The articles 'The', 'Le', 'Der', 'A' etc. have not been taken into consideration in the alphabetical sequence.

261

210, 215, 218; *see also* anti-Communism; Leftism
Conference of World Turkmens 199
Congress of the Muslim Anti-Bolshevik organisations 17
Congresses 11–12, 15–18, 43, 48–50, 82–3, 118, 121, 133–4, 149–52, 181–2, 189, 199, 205 ff, 209–13, 222–4
Constitutions 48, 77
Crimea 8, 9, 12, 14, 15, 19, 40, 45, 47, 53, 76, 111, 113–15, 121, 124, 129, 150, 155, 160, 162–5, 167
Crimean Turkish Committee 82
Crimeanism 165
Cultura Turcica 163
Cultural cooperation 4, 166, 183, 201, 204 ff, 208, 210 ff, 215–20, 222–4
Cumhuriyet 113
Cypriots 118, 195
Cyprus 21, 49, 75, 79, 121, 130, 135, 148, 153–4, 158–61, 163–5, 168, 190, 194–6, 213, 223

Çağatay, Tahir 121
Çağlayan 88, 126
Çakmak, Fevzi 114
Çanakkale 134
Çay, Abdülhalûk M. 165
Çelebi, Veled 39
Çetin, Hikmet 215, 219
Çil, Faruk 161, 167
Çınaraltı 92–3, 97, 113, 120, 128
Çokay, Mustafa 17, 82, 114, 121

Daghestanis 111, 114, 197
Danişmend, İsmail Hami 128, 158
Danube 90, 187
Darendelioğlu, İlhan Eğemen 128, 131
Dasht-i Kipchak 1
Debureaucratisation 208
Decentralisation 33, 208
Deliorman, Altan 131
Demirel, Süleyman 206, 216, 218–19, 222
Democrat Party (Turkey) 125, 129, 134
Demonstrations 116, 118, 122, 127–9, 131–3, 153–4, 161, 189, 195
Denktaş, Rauf 223
Depoliticisation 208
Derik 134

Detroit 150
Devlet 168
Diaspora ideologies and movements 182 ff, 187, 202 ff
Dictionaries 211–12, 218
Dilde, Fikirde, İşde Birlik 167
Dirāsāt Kurdiyya 221
Dış politikamız ve Kıbrıs 154
Dış Türkler see Outside Turks
Dış Türkler (book) 160
Dış Türkler ve Türkistan davası 121
Diyarbakir 37, 134
Dobruca ve Türkler 164
Dobruja 121
Dokuz ışık 154, 166
Dushanbe 200
Dülger, Bahadır 133
Duma 11–12, 15, 88, 95
Dutch 183
Dün, bugün, yarın 92
Dündar, Gülsün 158
Düsseldort 123, 150

East Asia 184
East Turkestan Emigrants' Society 118
East Turkic Review 123
Eastern Question Association 46
Eastern Turkestan's Refugees Association 150
Economic cooperation 4, 204 ff, 208 ff, 215 ff, 219–20, 222, 224
Economic Cooperation Organisation viii, 204–7, 221
Economics 152, 155, 160, 165–6, 184–5, 191, 197 ff, 208, 216–17, 223; *see also* Inflation
Edib (Adıvar), Halide 33, 41, 44, 51, 75, 123
Edirne 51, 83, 120
Education 9 ff, 13–15, 19, 35–6, 38, 42, 51, 77–8, 117, 163, 204, 208, 210–11, 213, 215–20, 223
Egypt 50, 160
Ekinci 14
Elbe 187
Elçibey, Abulfez 215
Elçin, Şükrü 158
Eldağ, Şükrü 203
Emel 114, 164–5
Emel Medjmuası 82, 164
Emrullah Efendi 39, 40